THE LABOUR PARTY'S
POLITICAL THOUGHT
A HISTORY

Geoffrey Foote

Second Edition

CROOM HELM
London • Sydney • Wolfeboro, New Hampshire

© 1985 Geoffrey Foote
Second Edition © 1986 Geoffrey Foote
Croom Helm Ltd, Provident House, Burrell Row,
Beckenham, Kent BR3 1AT

Croom Helm Australia Pty Ltd, Suite 4, 6th Floor,
64-76 Kippax Street, Surry Hills, NSW 2010, Australia

British Library Cataloguing in Publication Data

Foote, Geoffrey
    The Labour Party's political thought: a history.
    I. Title
    324.24107'09   JN1129.L32

    ISBN 0-7099-1097-5 (Pbk)

Croom Helm, 27 South Main Street
Wolfeboro, New Hampshire 03894-2069

Library of Congress Cataloging-in-Publication Data

Foote, Geoffrey.
    The Labour Party's political thought.

    Includes bibliographical references and index.
    1. Labour Party (Great Britain) – History.
2. Political science – Great Britain – History.
3. Socialism – Great Britain – History. 4. Great
Britain – Politics and government – 20th century.
I. Title.
JN1129.L32F64   1986   324.24107   86-11639
ISBN 0-7099-1097-5 (pbk.)

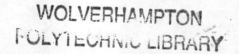
Printed and bound in Great Britain
by Billing & Sons Limited, Worcester.

CONTENTS

FOREWORD

An American poet called Delmore Schwartz once said that every point of view, like every experience, is limited and ignorant. He was unhappy, by all accounts, but it is hard not to agree with him. The fact that there is something very human behind the most abstract viewpoint must be one motive for anyone interested in political ideas. The process by which ideas are developed and related to one another is a relationship between people as well as a reflection of historical circumstance.

It is this process of ideas in the Labour Party that I have hoped to make accessible in one volume for people interested in socialism in Britain today. I have tried to avoid an approach which either over- or under-estimates the importance of ideas in the formation of policy and attitudes. I have also tried to take into account the historical context though in the final analysis the book remains a history of political ideas.

My hope is that this book will prove useful for the labour movement in a critical moment in its history. I am aware that my interpretation is contentious at various points — inevitably so, given the nature of the subject matter — but I would hope that its strength lies in that. There is no progress otherwise.

For Laurie
and my parents

ACKNOWLEDGEMENTS

The responsibility for this work is entirely mine. However, I am grateful to Jeffrey Weeks, Steve Howe, Bob Kant, and the students of my classes on British socialism for their helpful comments on this work; the staff of the British Library, the Marx Memorial Library, and the British Library of Political and Economic Science; for Sam, who knew not what he did, and Fiona, who did; Paul, Stuart and Gary for encouragement. Many thanks to Hilary Tomris and to my sister, Jennifer, for typing my horrible scrawl; also to Patsy Gallagher, who helped to type and edit the script under insufferable conditions. Finally, particular thanks are due to Jean and Bert, my parents, for looking after Laurie at a critical point in the writing of this book.

Geoff Foote

PART ONE

LABOURISM AND THE LABOUR PARTY

1 INTRODUCTION

In 1981 the Labour party underwent the most severe change to its power structure and constitution for sixty years. This change, giving the trade unions an even greater say in the party's affairs, took place amid an effervescence of ideas on the Left of the party, and a secession of several leading figures on its Right. It was followed, two years later, by a major electoral defeat, as large numbers of working class people refused to vote for a party which seemed paralysed by faction and incapable of overcoming the greatest social crisis Britain had faced since the war. This combination of events has led to a major reappraisal of the party's strategy and tactics as it seeks to recapture its traditional working class constituency which it needs in order to remain an electoral force.

In such a situation it becomes particularly important to understand the past, especially in terms of the diversity and limitations of its political thought. The previously accepted view that Labour is a non-ideological party, rejecting all forms of extra-parliamentary action, must be at least modified given the proliferation of books and tracts reasserting the importance of socialist ideas and policies, in particular the new Labour Left's demands for extra-parliamentary forms of democracy and political activity. Such changes need to be placed in the context of Labour's developing political thought.

However, no history of the Labour Party's political thought has appeared since G.D.H. Cole's *History of Socialist Thought*, itself dealing with world socialism. A mass of information is available on the political history of the Labour Party in the past eighty years; its achievements and failures in office and position; its policies and organisation; and individual biographies of its leaders and important figures. Anthologies of documents, speeches, manifesto commitments and policy statements have been assiduously collected, but a history of the Labour Party's political thought — its connections and development — has been missing for too many years.[1] Its absence is both surprising and deplorable, given the importance of Labour as a programmatic party and the contribution of thinkers like Tawney, Cole and Crosland to British political thought in this century.

3

Ideas and Political Power

The problems and difficulties of tracing such a history can be easily underestimated. The relationship between power and political thought is a complex one, and cannot be reduced to the simplicities of one determining the other. On the one hand, Labour is a party seeking political power, rather than a party attempting to put a preconceived philosophy into practice. On the other hand, it does not merely seek power for its own sake, but has ideals which inspire its policies to a certain extent. The general theories held about society and the state lead to definite prescriptions and attitudes for the Labour Party as much as for parties who are more inflexible and dogmatic in their ideas. John Maynard Keynes was well aware of this when he wrote that

> the ideas of economists and political philosophers, both when they are right and when they are wrong, are more powerful than is commonly understood. Indeed, the world is ruled by little else. Practical men, who believe themselves to be quite exempt from any intellectual influences, are usually the slave of some defunct economist.[2]

As an example, Labour's view of the state as an essentially neutral administration to be contested at election times leads to its attempt to win votes by appealing to the middle classes as well as the working class, and to an acceptance of the demands of loyalty and national unity at times of emergency.

The political thought of a party seeking power in a parliamentary democracy cannot be looked at in a vacuum. It is subject to social, economic and political circumstances outside any rational control. As a result, any history of Labour's political thought must show to the best of its ability how it has been shaped and formed by the history of the British working class and the Labour Party's own political experience. An individual philosopher's thought may evolve by obeying certain rules and canons of logic and internal consistency, but we are not dealing with an individual thinker, or a philosophical school here. Labour is a living political organism, always seeking new ways to adapt and develop older ideas, if only to gain and maintain political power.

As a result, the major difficulties in the way of tracing a history of Labour's political thought is the absence of any agreed ideological boundaries within which we can point to a specifically labourist ideology. This is in marked contrast to Marxism which, for all its diversities, can be referred back to one thinker's fairly rigorous social and economic analysis. The Labour Party is a particularly *British* institution, stressing specific policies to meet specific problems and only occasionally feeling the need to take its theorists seriously. Labour's leaders have never attempted to square their experience and practice in government with any worked out theory. This can be compared with the constant attempts by the Russian Communist leaders to justify their political practice with Marxist and Leninist theory.

It becomes a difficult and controversial task to trace a pattern of development in Labour's political thought in the light of this. The Labour Party is, as it constantly asserts, a 'broad church'. It has contained many minority strands in its history — Christian pacifists like Alfred Salter and George Lansbury, neo-Stalinists like D.N. Pritt and Konni Zilliacus, and various Trotskyist groups like the 'Militant' Tendency. However, none of them are remotely near the mainstream of Labour thinking, and it has been necessary to ignore them. Lansbury was actually leader of the party in the early 1930s but, as will be seen, this had nothing to do with his pacifist beliefs. An attempt to document every minority belief in the Labour Party would have the effect of reducing the narrative to incoherence. It would confuse rather than clarify the essential elements which sets Labour apart from its rivals on Right and Left in terms of ideology.

The existence of such minority groupings, and the apparently indistinct boundaries of Labour's political thought, have misled too many commentators in the past. As an example, H.M. Drucker regards the socialist doctrine of the Labour Party as insignificant compared with the ethos of loyalty to leaders and rigid adherence to the rulebook held by its dominant social group.[3] Labour's ideology is narrowed down to the doctrine of the mandate, as expressed in the election manifesto. In this interpretation, the specific commitments of the manifesto replace any general and divisive ideology.

The party manifesto is certainly used to rally all the main factions of the party, and is usually put in a sufficiently vague form of wording to satisfy Left and Right. However, it is a misunderstanding to say that the manifesto *replaces* ideology. The policy proposals, and the assumptions that underlie them, reflect the political thought of the dominant faction in the Labour Party at any one time — whether Morrisonian nationalisation in the 1940s, Gaitskellite revisionism in the 1950s, the Wilson technocrats in the 1960s or the Left today. It is vaguely written so that all sections of the party can rally round the dominant group at election times, but its vagueness does *not* indicate an absence of ideology.

It is therefore necessary to single out the fundamental similarity of ideas which has united the disparate groups of liberals, trade unionists, Christian radicals, and militant socialists in one political party since 1900. The diverse factions which have constituted the Labour Party since its birth have somehow been able to find a common factor to keep them together for all the fury and frustration of their debates, and this unifying force cannot simply be reduced to mere tactical alliances. Their debates have been carried on within specific ideological limits, so that they could all be described as 'labourist', distinct from the Liberal Party on their Right and from the various types of revolutionaries on their Left. Once this 'labourism' can be singled out and described, then it will be possible to document the changes which have developed and modified the fundamental tenets of the Labour Party's political thought.

Labour and the Unions

To disentangle the fundamental ideas of 'labourism' from the medley of political ideas proposed and fought over within the confines of the Labour Party, it is necessary to withdraw from the realm of ideas to look at the party's basic power structure. The relationship of the Labour Party to its trade union base provides the key to understanding the limits within which political debate has been held, and within which political theory has been evolved. If it can be discovered that this relationship has been expressed ideologically − as an elaborated and coherent set of ideas − then the 'labourist' boundaries of political thought in the Labour Party can be delineated.

The paradoxical relationship that Labour has with the trade unions has been most recently pointed out by Leo Panitch[4] (though Communist leaders like Lenin and Trotsky noted it many years earlier). The Labour Party was basically established by the trade unions as their political extension. As such, it was an expression of trade union politics − the protection of workers' living standards by political action. It is financially and politically dependent on the unions, and yet is often forced to attack them when in office. This paradox emerged at its clearest during the Wilson government of 1964-70, when a series of attempts to curb workers' living standards culminated in the White Paper, *In Place of Strife*, which sought to establish legal restrictions on union activities. The government was forced to back down in the face of open union and backbench revolt. On the one hand, its position as a 'national' party in office led the Labour government to attack the unions; on the other hand, its dependence on the unions meant that it was unable to push the White Paper on to the statute book.

Labour's reliance on the unions has *ultimately* proved more important than its commitment to 'national' policies time and again. The Labour Party was founded in 1900 to pursue the interest of the unions in the parliamentary sphere, and it cannot escape from this obligation without threatening its power base. Whenever the party has tried to pursue 'national' interests at the expense of the organised labour movement, as in the 1920s and 1960s, it has been rudely brought back into line – the General Council of the Trades Union Congress (TUC) was the real leadership of the party in the 1930s, and Wilson had enough political acumen to realise that a 'social contract' with the unions was necessary in the 1970s, whether he liked it or not.

This social and political relationship between the Labour Party and the trade unions is therefore crucial. It is what makes the Labour Party a *labour* party. It is also what makes it so difficult to pinpoint 'labourism' – trade union politics – as an elaborated ideology. Trade union aspirations within a capitalist society have been generally restricted to protecting and enhancing their members' living standards. Higher wages, shorter hours, and better working conditions do not lend themselves to a general philosophy of society. The clearest hint of such a 'labourist' ideology can be found in the aims adopted at the 1900 foundation conference of the Labour Representation Committee (LRC), as the Labour Party was originally called. The purpose of the new party was to work for

a distinct Labour group in Parliament, who shall have their own whips, and agree upon their policy, which must embrace a readiness to cooperate with any party which for the time being may be engaged in promoting legislation in the direct interest of labour, and be equally ready to associate themselves with any party in opposing measures having an opposite tendency.[5]

It can hardly be summed up as an ideology, but it reveals a set of assumptions which were to prove the bedrock onto which other political theories were to be grafted. To understand the fundamental ideological boundaries of the Labour Party's thought, it is necessary to look behind the socialist face worn by the party for much of its history to see this labourism, free of the clutter of any political doctrine other than pure and simple trade union politics.

The labourist assumptions on which the Labour Party was founded had, in fact, been expressed very clearly in ideological terms long before 1900. Indeed, to understand labourism as an ideology, it is necessary to look back much earlier than the conservative, mid-Victorian trade unions normally described as labourist to the very origins of the organised labour movement in the early nineteenth century. It was in 1825, the year after the Combination Laws repressing unions had been repealed, that labourism was presented as a theory free of the clutter of extraneous doctrines like Paineite radicalism, utilitarianism, or socialism.

Labourism

Thomas Hodgskin (1787-1869) was the first to present trade union politics as a consistent theory in his *Labour Defended Against the Claims of Capital* (1825). Now largely forgotten, Hodgskin was a former naval officer, dismissed for insubordination, whose interest in working class education led him to become a dominant figure in the labour movement in his heyday. His pamphlet, seen as the manifesto of the emerging labour movement, channelled the most advanced school of political economy into the defence of that movement. In doing so, Hodgskin presented labourism as a political theory with a clarity and lucidity which marked him out from his successors and followers. As an ideology, it was to be buried by the defeat of Chartism and the onset of a general period of prosperity in the middle of the century, but as a set of *assumptions* governing the political motivations of established trade union leaders it was to survive into the very different conditions of 1900 and beyond.

The first characteristic of the labourism elaborated by Hodgskin was to be a particular interpretation of the labour theory of value, then the dominant school of economic thought. This theory holding that the value of all commodities was determined by the amount of labour expended on them, had been used by David Ricardo to attack the landowners as a parasitic class, battening on the industrious classes. Hodgskin gave the theory a further twist by turning it against the capitalists. If labour created all wealth, he pointed out that labour received back only a part of that wealth. The surplus produce was being pocketed by the capitalists who were cheating the labourers of their rightful share, and a combination of workers in trade unions was necessary in order to fight for their rightful wages.

As an economic theory, it could not serve as a model of economic expansion, or of understanding how to cope with unemployment or under-investment. Marx sharpened the theory to give it a revolutionary dimension, but this was of little use to trade unionists seeking to ameliorate their members' living conditions. Nevertheless, as the basic economic philosophy expounded by Hodgskin, the theory has become a fundamental assumption in trade union attitudes, and indirectly in the policies of the Labour Left. The belief that labour is somehow prevented from getting its fair share of the national income provides a strong rationale for union organisers whose job it has been to bargain over the purchase and sale of their members' labour power. Other economic theories — the marginal utility arguments of the Fabians, the demand expansionism of the Keynesians — were to serve as the Labour Party's practical approach to overcoming the harsh cycle of boom and slump characterising capitalism, but the fundamental assumption that labour was denied its just share of the nation's wealth is ultimately derived from the arguments put forward by Hodgskin at the birth of the modern labour movement.

This leads to a second characteristic of labourism, which was the call to redistibute the wealth of the nation to those who create it. Hodgskin believed wealth to be badly distributed in favour of the capitalist. The employers had too much, while labour had too little, and the purpose of union activity was to cure this maldistribution by fighting for higher wages. Hosgskin argued that

> because those who have been masters, planners, contrivers, etc. . . . .
> have in general also been capitalists and have also had a command
> over the labour of those who have worked with their hands, their
> labour has been paid as much too high as common labour has been
> underpaid.[6]

In reducing the profits of the idle capitalists by increasing the wages of their members, unions have a major role to play in curing the maldistribution of wealth. This belief in redistribution was to provide a crucial point of labourism, where the trade union movement could shape the particular form British socialism was to take. The major difference was that, in the very different conditions of the twentieth century, the Labour Party was to see Parliament as a more important instrument of redistribution than the unions, whereas Hodgskin ignored Parliament altogether.

A third characteristic of labourism revealed in Hodgskin's thought was its attitude to the capitalists. While Hodgskin was in favour of redistribution of wealth, he did not question the social system by which wealth was produced. He was vigorously opposed to capitalists, but never to capital as a social and economic system. This point was noted by Marx, who held it to be a common characteristic of English socialists. Hodgskin constantly made a distinction between capitalists, who were bad, and employers, who were good. This was due to his identification of capitalism with usury and interest. As a result, he could argue that

> the wages of the master, employer, or contriver have been blended with the profit of the capitalist . . . Masters are labourers as much as their journeymen. In this character, their interest is precisely the same as their men.[7]

As capitalists, they idly reap profits at the expense of their workers, but as employers their labour deserves a reward as much as the labour of their employees. This mixture of hostility to capitalists and indifference to capital was to recur constantly in the Labour Party, where socialist language often sounded more militant than it actually was.

Hodgskin's ideas on this point were to be far reaching because they expressed the paradox of the trade union movement. Unless they were prepared to launch a profound social upheaval, the unions had to work both with and against the employers. Hodgskin's combination of hostility to capitalists and acceptance of a social system of bargaining between unions and employers expressed in theoretical terms the practical work of the trade union movement as it was to develop in Britain. His distinction between capitalists and employers was a fundamental characteristic of trade union politics, whose essential business was that of bargaining and negotiation over the system whereby labour power was bought and sold, not the abolition of that system.

The fourth characteristic of labourism flows from Hodgskin's hostility to capitalists. His version of the labour theory of value, geared as it was to the defence of the trade unions in their struggle against the capitalists, stressed the independence and self-reliance of workers as a class. Hodgskin's opposition to state intervention in trade union affairs has often been mistaken for a form of anarchism, but he never called for the abolition of the state. He argued only that its corrupt nature, whereby the capitalists used it against the unions, should be purged. If the state continued to support the capitalists, then the workers may turn their attention from 'combining for higher wages to amending the state'.[8] In the context of the times, with most workers denied the vote, Hodgskin's hint at independent political action had the air of a revolutionary threat. But with the later expansion of the suffrage to the working class, his rejection of the existing parties and his stress on the self-reliance of labour was to be echoed by trade unionists who sought to defend their interests in Parliament. Hodgskin's own political views were not totally synonymous with labourism later in the century – his belief that parliamentary action could not remedy social problems was alien to the labourist tradition – but his belief in labour's self-reliance was eventually to become an important characteristic of labourism as it turned to the parliamentary sphere.

The fifth and final characteristic of labourism was implicit in Hodgskin's theory. His call for the redistribution of wealth was always seen in a national context. In *Labour Defended*, Hodgskin protested that the Irish 'are imported here in crowds and beat down the wages of our labour'[9] giving nationalist expression to the trade union demand for the protection of living standards from the threat of cheap labour. As the system whereby labour power was bought and sold, whether dearly or cheaply, was not called into question, it was inevitable that labourism should demand that the workers of its own nation should be defended against the workers of other nations. Such a demand does not necessarily lead to racism or chauvinism, which have often been attacked by Labour and union leaders. However, the liberal internationalism which was to be so strong in the Labour Party was always based on adherence and loyal obedience to the nation state. Any ideology which denounced such obedience, as revolutionary Leninism was to do, could find no real home in a labourist party.

These characteristics of labourism – the theory that labour receives little of the wealth that it creates, redistributionism, hostility to capitalists and maintenance of capital, workers' self-reliance, and loyalty to the nation state – survived to become a set of assumptions in the labour movement. These assumptions were flexible enough to accommodate a large number of different political ideas – while distinct enough eventually to exclude the Liberal Party on the Right and various types of revolutionary on the Left.

The Limits of Labourism

The trade union politics expressed so clearly by Hodgskin and surviving as the assumptions of trade union practice constitute the fundamental labourist tenets of the Labour Party. They are flexible and loose enough to be capable of absorbing and modifying ideologies as diverse as militant syndicalism and moderate liberalism. Within its limits, different policies are fought for by different groups, and different political theories compete and evolve.

Whichever particular ideology is dominant at any one time is the result of a complex of factors ranging from the broad social and economic environment to the sordid mechanics of power politics (it was said at one union conference that the brothers were so confused that they were stabbing one another in the front — Labour politicians rarely need the excuse of confusion for such activity). If a group holding any of Labour's diverse ideologies fails to adapt it to the dominant trade union section of the party, it either cuts itself off from the mainstream of Labour thinking (like the Independent Labour Party on the Left in 1932 or the Social Democratic Party on the Right in 1981), or it is soon brought back into line (like the Wilson technocrats). If the ideological faction is to have any success, it must adapt itself to the labourism of the trade unions.

It follows that this 'labourist' ideology has limits, and excludes ideologies incompatible with it. As it involves a bargain over the sale of workers' labour-power, aiming to achieve a better position for wage-labourers against their employers, labourism tends to be more compatible with gradual and piecemeal solutions to problems than it is with radical and fundamental solutions. The socialist ideology which Labour had accepted since 1918 has generally been interpreted in a gradualist manner.

However, labourism does exclude political solutions which involve the overthrow of the state. Marxism was only acceptable to union leaders if it was shorn of any commitment to a workers' dictatorship — if its radical economic analysis was abstracted from its revolutionary political conclusions. Marxists who have refused to do this have been expelled, as happened to the Communists in 1925-7 and to the Trotskyists in the mid-1960s.

Moreover, while a liberal internationalism is strong in the Labour Party, the anti-British nationalism of many Marxists is unacceptable. The political structure accepted by labourism in which to conduct its social and economic struggle is the structure of the nation state. At times of national emergency when the country is under external threat, Labour rallies to the national flag. Pacifist dissent has been tolerated, but Lenin's policy of revolutionary defeatism would be unacceptable. In the late 1940s, the neutralist Keep Left group was (grudgingly) permitted to fight for its ideas, but the pro-Russian 'fellow-travellers' like Konni Zilliacus were expelled. Public association of the British Communist Party with the Soviet Union has been a major factor in dooming its persistent attempts to affiliate to the Labour Party despite its acceptance of parliamentary democracy since 1951.

If labourism is distinct from revolutionary and anti-nationalist ideologies on its Left, it is also distinct from the Liberal Party on its Right. This is due to its stress on self-reliance and independence against the employers. In the late nineteenth and early twentieth centuries, many unions did support the Liberals, sending a small collection of 'Lib-Lab' members to Westminster. The militant social liberalism of the Lloyd George variety could have adapted itself to the labourism of the trade unions, and for a time looked as though it would do so, but historical circumstances prevented the Liberals from ever agreeing to become a labourist party, and the growth of the corporate society of organised employers and unions favoured the formation of a new labour party. Many liberals have found a home in the Labour Party as the main radical alternative in British politics, but have had to pay the price of confirming to labourism. Individuals such as Woodrow Wyatt or Reg Prentice who became unable to do this have left the party. Recently the dominance of the Labour Left has become such that many leading members have broken away as an organsed block to form the SDP. They have not necessarily broken from labourism, as the attempts to win right-wing union leaders by some SDP leaders have demonstrated, but their organisational break with the trade union movement reinforces a strong tendency to break from labourism ideologically. The ideological limits of labourism, flexible as they are, have thus marked the Labour Party off from its rivals on Right and Left. Within these limits, the party is ideologically amorphous — a 'broad church' incorporating diverse ideas.

The Development of Labour's Thought

Labourism, or trade union politics, was more an assumption than an elaborated ideology when the Labour Party was formed in 1900. To pass beyond its vague assumptions to a clearly expressed theory it is necessary to turn to the birth of the trade union movement in the early nineteenth century. It was at this time, with no tradition of successful negotiation or tradition behind them, that working class theorists found it necessary to express clearly and unambiguously the political theory of trade unionism. The ideas of Thomas Hodgskin have been chosen as the sharpest and most popular expression of this theory. His analysis, buried with the defeat of Chartism, expressed both the flexibility and the limits of the assumptions with which the trade unions created the Labour Party.

This labourism has assumed a dynamic due to its ability to absorb or reject a series of challenges to its assumptions. The faults inherent in these challenges have been a factor in determining the shape in which the Labour Party's political thought has developed. The emergence of an ethical, peculiarly British, socialism in the late nineteenth and early twentieth centuries owes much to the weakness of the Marxist challenge to labourism. Marx's rigorous critique of capitalism was considerably diluted in its British form. The resulting theoretical weaknesses of British Marxism allowed its challenge to be contained by the Fabians and blunted by the ethical socialists of the ILP. Certain notions of both the Marxists and the Fabians had to be excluded, but in their different ways they gave a sharp focus to the blend of British socialism which eventually triumphed over 'pure and simple' trade union politics to be enshrined in Labour's 1918 Constitution.

In a similar way, the evolution of this British socialism into its corporate form was partly due to the weakness of the syndicalist challenge to labourism. The syndicalist theories were easily accommodated into the Labour Party's mainstream, unlike the challenge of revolutionary Leninsm after 1917. Shorn of its anarchist and revolutionary conclusions, syndicalism served as the basis of the guild socialism expounded by G.D.H. Cole, one of Labour's greatest political theorists. In this form it was adopted by the ILP and left-wing union leaders like A.J. Cook. It also became the foundation on which corporate socialism, with its stress on nationalisation and union participation in the 'welfare state', was able to evolve. The other foundation was supplied by the challenge of the liberal economist, Keynes, with his prescriptions of state intervention in a mixed economy. The blend of corporate socialism that emerged was accepted by both Left and Right of the Labour Party in its heyday of the 1940s, when it refashioned British society under Attlee, Morrison and Bevan.

Having fulfilled its main role, corporate socialism came increasingly to seem inadequate as an ideology for Labour. It has come under two successive challenges, from the revisionists on the Right and from the Bennites on the Left. Each challenge was conditioned by the evolution of the British economy and society after the traumas of the war and immediate post-war period. The prosperity of the 1950s and 1960s seemed to the revisionists to call for a fundamental redefinition of British socialism. Some even called for a break with labourism altogether, though this was generally dismissed as political suicide. The revisionist challenge culminated in the technocratic, class-neutral ideology of the Wilson era, but the strains this led to with the unions at a time of increasing economic recession resulted in the defeat of revisionism. As an ideology more suited to prosperity and full employment, revisionism seemed out of date and irrelevant to Labour in the new conditions of the 1970s. The result of this crisis of the revisionist Right was the evolution of a new ideology of social democracy, and the secession of several leading figures to form the SDP in 1981.

The disappointments of the Wilson era led to a new awakening of ideas on the Left. The seeds of this lie in the mid-1950s with the emergence of the New Left, disillusioned with Stalinism and dissatisfied with the ideological sterility of the Bevanite Left in the Labour Party. Burgeoning in the Campaign for Nuclear Disarmament, Vietnam Solidarity, and the Women's Movement, the New Left became very hostile to the Labour Party, which it saw as hopelessly lost to the British Establishment. Nevertheless, despite its hostility, the Bennite Left in the Labour Party had strong ideological roots in the protest movement, and by the early 1980s the Labour Left had successfully channelled much of it into the confines of labourism.

A clearer understanding of the *history* of the Labour Party's political thought as a process of development has now emerged. Labourism — its flexibility and limits — is the key to the variety of political ideas adopted by Labour in the last eighty years. The ability of new ideologies to fit into the labourist framework determines their chance of political success in the party.

The simplicities of reducing every new development to labourism must of course be avoided. However, the arguments of Gareth Stedman Jones and Raphael Samuel[10] seem to fall into the opposite simplicity. In denying 'labourism' as a useful model for understanding the Labour Party, they hope to see its history as a series of conjunctions which have no real continuity. This approach certainly has the advantage of recognising historical *development*, but in its view of the party as an empty shell which can be filled by currently contending political forces and aspirations it overestimates the flexibility of the party as an organisation. It ignores the *limits* of the party's ideology — of the factors which separate the party from both Right and Left — and consequently ignores the political *unity* of the party. Above all, it underestimates the extent to which the Labour Party is dependent on the trade union movement for its finances and its motivation. Many members of the party would prefer to weaken the links between Labour and the unions — from the early Fabians to the revisionists and beyond there has been a residual resentment of many in the party to the unions — but the very fact that such hopes have proved futile demonstrates the existence of continuity in the party despite the evident diversity of ideas and events over the past eighty years.

Notes

1. The two major books have been G.D.H. Cole, *History of Socialist Thought*, 5 volumes (Macmillan, 1953-60), and before him Max Beer, *History of British Socialism*, 2 volumes (London, 1929). Two useful anthologies are Frank Bealey, *The Social and Political Thought of the Labour Party* (Weidenfeld and Nicholson, 1970) and A. Wright, *British Socialism 1880-1964* (Longman, 1983).

2. J.M. Keynes, *The General Theory of Employment, Interest and Money* (Macmillan, 1974 ed.), p. 383.

3. H.M. Drucker, *Doctrine and Ethos in the Labour Party* (George Allen and Unwin, 1979).

4. Leo Panitch, *Social Democracy and Industrial Militancy. The Labour Party, The Trade Unions and Incomes Policy 1945-74* (Cambridge University Press, 1976).

5. *The Labour Party Foundation Conference and Annual Conference Reports, 1900-1905*. (London, 1967), p. 12.

6. Thomas Hodgskin, *Labour Defended Against the Claims of Capital*, (Labour Publishing Co., 1922), p. 89.

7. Ibid., pp. 89-90.

8. Ibid., p. 106.

9. Ibid., p. 26.

10. R. Samuel and G. Stedman Jones, 'The Labour Party and Social Democracy' in R. Samuel and G. Stedman Jones ed. *Culture, Ideology and Politics. Essays for Eric Hobsbawm* (Routledge and Kegan Paul, 1983).

The labourism thesis has been put forward by a number of New Left writers, notably Perry Anderson and Tom Nairn in 'The Nature of the Labour Party', *New Left Review* No. 27, September-October 1964 and No. 28, November-December 1964. However, it was never stated with precision as a set of *ideas*, its radical aspects wre ignored by a concentration on its conservative aspects, and its relationship with socialism was never adequately defined.

PART TWO

THE FORMATION OF BRITISH SOCIALISM

The Labour Party was created in 1900 as a federation of a number of trade unions with various socialist groups —the Marxists of the Social Democratic Federation (SDF), the gradualists of the Fabian Society, and the ethical socialists of the Independent Labour Party (ILP). Unlike many of the working class parties then emerging in Europe, the new party had no precise and worked out ideology to guide its actions. However, an ideology of sorts was emerging as a result of the ferment of socialist ideas which had been taking place since 1880. The ideology, acknowledged finally in the party's 1918 Constitution, was a distinctive brand of British socialism which has fed the party's basic ideals and ethics to the present day.

In his foreword to a 1948 book entitled *Socialism: The British Way*, Herbert Morrison wrote, 'I like the title of this book. The British Socialists, and our Labour government, have a distinctive approach to the problems of democracy, of economics, of Socialism'.[1] British socialism had an ethic and a political outlook of its own, stamped with peculiarly British characteristics and separate from the socialist parties elsewhere in Europe. In other countries a dogmatic form of Marxism prevailed, as in Germany; or socialist parties were divorced from the trade union movement, marked by fractious dissent and revolutionary tendencies, as in France, Italy or Russia. The debates which consumed European socialism appeared in Britain, too, but on the margins of working class politics. The main form of socialism in Britain was intimately woven into the labourism of the trade union movement, and connected in countless ways to the social, political and intellectual environment in which that movement grew.

To understand the nature of the new ideology of British socialism, it is necessary to separate its different strands. The ideas of Labour Marxism, Fabianism, and ethical socialism held by the constituent organisations and individuals supporting the Labour Party had been formed in the last two decades of the nineteenth century, and were still evolving in the early years of the new party. Keir Hardie, the first

17

Labour leader, was to bring the strands together and to seal the conjunction with a labourism which would attract the unions. The new ideology, developed in different directions by prominent Labour politicians such as Ramsay Macdonald and H.N. Brailsford, was to be severely tested by war and slump after 1914, but in its heyday it served to keep divergent political groups in a party still unsure whether it had a future.

Notes

1. E. Durbin ed., *Socialism: The British Way* (London, 1948), p. 1.

2 MARXISTS, FABIANS AND ETHICAL SOCIALISTS – THE TRADITIONS OF BRITISH SOCIALISM

It was in the turmoil of the 1880s that the different and conflicting views which were to make up the ideas of British socialism were formed and fought over. At a time of a major crisis of profitability in world capitalism with riots by the unemployed and strikes by unskilled workers, the educated and critical sections of the middle and working classes began to challenge seriously the traditional assumptions of *laissez-faire* liberalism. In their different ways, they began to call for the regulation of an economy which was no longer satisfying the aspirations and needs of the population.

The Labour Marxists

The Marxism of the SDF appealed to many young workers who sought an explanation of the poverty and unemployment around them. Major political and union leaders of the future – Tom Mann, George Lansbury, Ramsay Macdonald, and Herbert Morrison among them – served their political apprenticeship in its ranks, and its interpretation of Karl Marx was to play a major role in the Labour Party's politics.

The political and economic ideas elaborated by Marx were, however, fundamentally opposed to the labourism of the British trade union movement. In his major work, *Capital*, written while in exile in Britain, Marx had sharpened the labour theory of value into a revolutionary understanding of the dynamics of capitalist society. He attempted to demonstrate that capitalism was trapped in a fatal mechanism in which it would eventually fall into increasingly severe crises, transforming the many capitalist firms into a few monopolies and trusts. This crisis was not the result of the greed of the usurers, as Hodgskin believed, but was inherent in the very system whereby labour-power was bought and sold.

The very fact that the working class, which created all value, was divorced from the means of production and had a surplus value extorted from it, led not merely to class conflict, but to the drive to accumulate capital. If any capitalist failed to accumulate, another would take his place:

> Accumulate, accumulate! That is Moses and the prophets! . . .
> Accumulation for accumulation's sake, production for production's
> sake; by this formula classical economy expressed the historical
> mission of the bourgeoisie, and did not for a single instant deceive
> itself over the birth-throes of wealth.[1]

As capital accumulated, the amount of surplus value would become
smaller and smaller against the total capital needed for production,
and crisis would set in as the rate of profit[2] fell. There were many
factors which could delay this event — such as increasing the exploitation of the working class, colonial acquisition, or export of capital —
but *eventually* the rate of profit would fall, and crisis ensue. The class
war inherent in capitalism would then turn into the overthrow of the
system by the working class.

Marx and Labourism

Marx's revolutionary analysis of capitalism was incompatible with the
labourism of the British trade union movement in a number of ways.
He never regarded unions as ends in themselves, as Hodgskin did. To
Marx, they were centres of resistance to capitalist rule, but could only
be partially effective at best. Where the unions negotiated over the sale
of their members' labour-power, Marx called for the abolition of the
system of wage labour altogether. The destruction of the employing
class, not simply better wages and working conditions, was the conclusion of Marx's theory of value, and it flew in the face of the
labourism of the union leaders of that time.

It also flew in the face of the ideas of redistribution of wealth so
popular among English socialists, then and since. Marx derided those
French and English radicals like Proudhon and Hodgskin who did not
connect the glaring inequalities of wealth and poverty to the system
of wage labour which underlay them. The consequences of such a
partial understanding would be to turn socialism into a question of
ameliorating the effects of capitalism rather than digging out the root
cause of inequality. They were attacking the symptoms rather than the
disease.

This was directly connected to Marx's attack on the labourist belief
that it was capitalists, not capital as a social system, who were the
enemy. Marx criticised Hodgskin for such a view,[3] and asserted that the
behaviour of the capitalists was determined by the harsh rhythms of
capital acccumulation. Where Hodgskin (and most labourists since) saw
the employer as just another worker who happened to control the

purse-strings of wage-labour, Marx saw the employer as a representative of a class which had to be destroyed. Where Hodgskin and labourism saw greed, Marx saw wage-labour as the disease to be cured.

However, the greatest challenge to labourism lay in Marx's attack on loyalty to the nation-state. His call for a proletarian dictatorship seemed a foreign expression of tyranny to the majority of British workers, especially after they gained the vote. Labourism could easily have accepted that the state was controlled by the employers, and needed to be captured by a workers' party during elections, but this was not Marx's prescription. In *The Civil War in France* (1871), Marx specifically asserted that the state was to be smashed and replaced by a totally different state machine to protect the workers' interests. This view of the state as an instrument of class violence, to be destroyed by violence, was inimical to the labourist tradition. Labour disputes could be occasionally violent, but to admit that violence was inherent in all sections of society, underlying power relationships from the factory to the state, would lead to intolerable conclusions for the majority of trade union leaders. When Marx called on English workers to side with the Irish Fenians against their own state,[4] a call for virtual treason against that state, he placed himself outside the pale of the labourist tradition.

On one point, Marx did agree with labourism, and that was the issue of class independence and self-reliance. Marx constantly argued that the liberation of the working class was the task of the working class itself, acting in its own interests and thereby in the interests of humanity as a whole. As a result, he argued that 'the working class cannot act, as a class, except by constituting itself into a political party, distinct from, and opposed to, all old parties formed by the propertied classes'.[5] His belief in an independent working class party, acting in its own interests against the interests of the employers, generally fell on deaf ears until the formation of the SDF in 1881.

Labour Marxism

However, the Marxism of the SDF was dominated by the autocratic rule of H.M. Hyndman, an amateur cricketer who became a Marxist after reading *Capital* in French during an American cruise. Hyndman's Marxist terminology concealed a crude national chauvinism and a belief that socialism could be achieved by the existing state.[6] Marx found him personally and politically abhorrent, while Engels eventually derided the SDF as 'purely a sect. It has ossified Marxism into a dogma and, by rejecting *every* labour movement which is not orthodox

Marxism . . . it renders itself incapable of ever becoming anything else but a sect'.[7]

Hydnman's sectarian rejection of trade unions[8] as simply reactionary doomed him from playing any major part in the labour movement, and the SDF was to withdraw from the Labour Party only a year after its creation in pique at their failure to force an acceptance of class war on the new party. However, his state socialism was to play a major part among those Labour Marxists who rejected the SDF and sought to win the Labour Party to a policy of class warfare and to a view of socialism as synonymous with simple nationalisation of industry.

Many of the individuals who were forced out of the SDF because of their opposition to Hyndman — people like William Morris, Eleanor Marx, John Burns, and Tom Mann, a list of individuals whose loss was enough to guarantee failure for the parent group — took an active part in the militant labour movement then emerging in Britain. They sought to build a more genuine Marxist party with roots in the British working class, and many were to see the Labour Party as the organisation which had to be won over to Marxism. Their political ideas were generally ill-formulated, but they looked for guidance to Marx's collaborator and friend, Friedrich Engels.

Engels (1821-95) inherited Marx's belief in an independent working class party in Britain, opposed to both Conservatives and Liberals. In contrast to the SDF, he believed that such a party must be based on the unions if it was to have any chance of success, and argued that the erosion of the privileges of the old 'aristocracy of labour' which had dominated the unions was creating the possibility of a party of the entire working class. Even before the growth of New Unionism among the unskilled, Engels considered it 'an immediate question of forming an English Labour Party with an independent class programme'.[9]

In doing so, Engels modified, if he did not push aside, Marx's revolutionary view of the state. In an Introduction to Marx's *Class Struggles in France*, Engels called for socialist parties to place their emphasis on the gradual and patient work of winning the working class to the socialist standard by means of electoral struggle. He continued to maintain the right of revolution if Parliament tried to prevent socialists from attaining their goal by constitutional means, but he argued that the rise of universal suffrage, together with the developments in military technology which made the barricade and the insurrection outmoded forms of struggle, called for a major change in political tactics.

Marx himself had not been dogmatic in his political views, and had

admitted that in the special conditions of Britain a peaceful transition
to socialism was possible. He saw as a possibility that a working-class
majority in Parliament could transform traditional political institutions
into expressions of working-class rule, but he was much more cautious
than Engels in his attitude to the bourgeois state. His hope that violence
could be avoided in a country like Britain was always tentative, and he
never modified his views on the need for a different *type* of state
institution than bourgeois parliaments. However, Engels was able to
throw his considerable authority behind a constitutionalist socialist
movement, and in doing so helped the Labour Marxists to dilute considerably Marx's revolutionary view of the state. The far left of labourism
was to accept Marx's theory of class war, and to warn of the possible
contempt for the constitution by the ruling class, but the need raised
by Marx for a new type of state was forgotten. This had the indirect
effect of removing a major barrier preventing Marxism from becoming
assimilated to labourism.

The role of the Labour Marxists in the beginnings of the Labour
Party was to serve as a channel for ideas formulated by Marx and Engels
rather than as a directly innovatory force. With the exception of
William Morris, their theoretical contribution was a poor affair, partly
because of their reaction to the abstract propaganda of the SDF. Moreover, Morris himself cannot be said to have made any real contribution
to *Labour* Marxism — his contempt for Parliament and his denuncia-
tions of the capitalist state machine remove him from consideration as
a Labour theorist — and his main influence was to be felt through the
ethical socialists.

Tom Mann (1856-1941) was the most famous of the SDF dissidents. He was born the son of a colliery clerk, and was working in the
mines at the age of ten. He eventually became an apprentice in the
engineering trade. As a member of the Amalgamated Society of
Engineers (ASE), he remained committed to the trade union movement throughout his life, a commitment which eventually led him out
of the SDF and into the leadership of the 1889 Dockers' Strike. He
became a symbol of the New Unionism, disregarding old craft distinctions in its emphasis on class unity.

Mann based himself on the trade unions, attacking the old union
leaders for their class collaboration, and calling on the union rank and
file to stress their own interests against those of the employers. Once
their independence was recognised by workers through their trade
union struggles, then political organisation would follow. It was a view
which was to lead him into the ILP, where he stressed the need for both

political and industrial mobilisation —

> as a collectivist and a member of the ILP, I know for a certainty that
> the greatest hindrance to the democratic movement of the present
> time is the lack of effective industrial organisation, backed up by
> equally effective political organisation, for purposes of industrial
> change.[10]

His recognition of the importance of the industrial organisation of his
class was eventually to blossom into syndicalism.

The Labour Marxists were instrumental in making Marxism a force
in the British labour movement, and in the Labour Party. Although it
was never to be acceptable to more than a small section of the labour
movement, that section was to be influential beyond its numbers.
Indeed, while the original Labour Marxists were to move on to greener
pastures — Mann and Champion emigrated to Australia, while John
Burns left labour politics altogether to become a Liberal cabinet
minister — their stress on class war lives on in the Labour Party of
today, as seen by individuals such as Eric Heffer and Arthur Scargill.

Marxism has served as a constant point of reference, fascinating and
repelling Labour theorists. The strength and coherence of Marx's
analysis has forced them continually to relate themselves to, or distin-
guish themselves from, him in a way they never needed to do with
Robert Owen or John Ruskin. The criticisms of labourism inherent in
his theories were to make Marxism an uncomfortable ideology in the
Labour Party, however, constantly opening it to attack from their
political opponents on the Right and just as constantly serving as a
critical force from within.

The Fabians

The social foundations on which British politics rested proved too solid
to be shaken by the Marxist challenge. Marx's prophecy that sections
of the middle class and the intelligentsia would break away from bourgeois domination may have proved to be correct on the Continent, but
in Britain their pragmatic and reformist traditions proved impervious to
revolutionary politics, particularly in the dogmatic manner in which
they were presented by the SDF. However, a number of intellectuals
in the Fabian Society did feel the need to formulate a British version of
the socialist ideas beginning to make headway in Europe.

The Fabian Society, formed in 1884 by a group of disillusioned mystics and bohemians, soon attracted a serious following. George Bernard Shaw (1856-1950), an Irish playwright then struggling against poverty and English class snobbery, attempted to convert them to Marxism. However, a series of discussions at the home of Mrs Charlotte Wilson led to Shaw's Marxist views being criticised and rejected in favour of the more orthodox economic viewpoint of W.S. Jevons, who emphasised the needs of the consumer in the market place rather than the relations of production in the factory. Shaw eventually admitted defeat, writing,

My last word for the present is — Read Jevons and the rest for your economics; and read Marx for the history of their working in the past, and the conditions of their application in the present.[11]

In rejecting Marx, the Fabians were mainly influenced by Sidney Webb (1859-1947), a regular contributor to Mrs Wilson's economic tea parties. Born into a lower middle class family, Webb became a junior clerk at the age of 15. His high results in Civil Service examinations led him to the top Administrative Grade within eight years, and to a study of law at London University. Webb joined the Fabians in May 1885 and rapidly stamped his intellectual dominance on its politics. Fascinated by the prevailing doctrines of Positivism, with its belief in a gradual evolution of harmonious and well-ordered society guided by an educated elite, Webb's Civil Service background reinforced his collectivist belief that individuals must subordinate themselves to the common good. In a letter, he wrote that his theory of life was 'to feel at every moment that I am acting as a member of a committee . . . I aspire never to act alone or for myself'.[12] His intellectual grasp of sociology and economics set him apart in the eyes of the young Fabians.

However, his dominance was never exercised in the same way as Hyndman's control over the SDF. Both Webb and Shaw were matched by other individual Fabians. Graham Wallas (1858-1932) brought his intellectual abilities to bear on questions of morality and political theory, though he was never happy with the anti-liberal elitism of most of his colleagues. Annie Besant (1847-1933), a free-thinking Radical, was probably the most prominent woman in British politics when she joined the Fabians. Sidney Olivier (1859-1943), another Civil Servant, believed that the virtues of socialism lay in its moral superiority over 'the evils of the Capitalist system which, if moralised, I am not sure is not economically superior'.[13] Hubert Bland (1856-1914), an ex-Tory journalist, was much more sympathetic to the ideas of the Labour Marxists than the other Fabians.

It was such a varied and individualistic collection of writers and journalists as these that put the Fabian Society on the map with their *Fabian Essays in Socialism* in 1889. In stark contrast to the didactic Marxism of the SDF, Shaw claimed in his Preface that 'there are at present no authoritative teachers of Socialism. The essayists make no claim to be more than communicative learners'.[14] They sought to make socialism perfectly compatible with the traditions of British liberalism and tolerance.

Such differences should not, however, disguise the fact that the Fabians were united by a certain conception of politics, economics and society. Moreover, a definite informal leadership emerged as a constant factor in the society's writings and discussions. It was the agreement among a few leading Fabians which set the distinctive seal on Fabian thinking, despite the disagreements over the importance of the Labour Party and the nature of imperialism. After Olivier left for British Honduras in 1890, and as Wallas became increasingly disillusioned with Fabian socialism, the dominant figures were Shaw, Webb, and his wife Beatrice.

Beatrice Potter (1858-1943) was the daughter of a pottery manufacturer who, after the failure of a passionate romance with Joseph Chamberlain, had sought solace in studies of poverty and labour in London. Her work led her to become a socialist, and she eventually married Webb in August 1892. It was initially a rather sad marriage — Sidney was not the most handsome of men and repelled Beatrice at first before she finally agreed to 'an act of renunciation of self and not of indulgence of self'[15] — but it soon turned into a remarkably successful intellectual partnership. After 1892, the informal Fabian leadership of Shaw and the Webbs was definitely finalised.

Fabian Economics

In their economic thinking, the Fabians initially found themselves in an impasse after rejecting Marx's labour theory of value. If Jevons was correct in concentrating on market price and the consumer, then any notion of surplus value was invalid. This had important implications for socialist politics, which rested on the protest against social privilege in the midst of poverty. If Marx was incorrect in his argument that the worker was exploited by the employer, as the Fabians believed him to be, then a new notion of how one class enjoyed the surplus produced by another was needed. The Fabians attempted to construct such a notion in their analysis of rent. They believed that the wages of the workers were determined by the demand for their different skills. Any wages above a basic subsistence level were seen by the Fabians as a form of rent for ability — just as economic rent was a reward for the advantages of a particular site and rent of opportunity (or profits) a reward for speculation. However, in capitalist society a large proportion of the workers' rent was directed into the pockets of the private owners and preserved for the children of the capitalists. In this way, skilled workers were robbed of the full fruit of their skills through the sale of their abilities to the capitalists.

Thus, the Fabians believed that they had discovered the real nature of the class war. It lay not between workers and employers, but between the idle rich and the industrious masses. 'The material interests of the small nation pledged to exact rent from its monopolies, and the great nation, thereby driven to receive only the remnant of the product, are permanently opposed'.[16] They drew a distinction which was very similar to that drawn by Hodgskin between the leisured classes and the talented leaders of society — tradesmen, managers, supervisors, writers — who worked hard for their living. These latter are in fact workers who 'render inestimable services to the community and receive rewards relative to the scarcity of their abilities',[17] among which Webb pointed explicitly to profits and salaries.

The Fabian notion of rent was intrinsic to their politics.[18] Where Marx attacked the capitalists as a class of employers, the Fabians attacked them as a class of parasites. It was not the hard-working employers, but the 'leisured class' which aroused their anger. As a result, the evils of society could be overcome by taxation of the capitalists' unearned income rather than by the expropriation of the capitalists. The economic thinking of the Fabians was a necessary premise for their political thinking.

Fabian Politics

In contrast to the revolutionary politics of Marx and the wild insurrectionism of the SDF, the Fabians sought to show that socialism was perfectly compatible with British political institutions and modes of behaviour. They were strict constitutionalists who looked on Parliament and the Civil Service as an adequate means of achieving socialism, especially after their limited constitutional demands for the extension of the franchise, payment of MPs, and reform of the House of Lords had been granted.

Where Marx had called for the existing state machinery to be replaced by a very different type of state, the Fabians identified socialism with the extension of the existing British state — with its monarch, Parliament, courts and military. As Shaw pointed out, 'The Socialism advocated by the Fabian Society is State Socialism exclusively'.[19] While Fabians may accept that the State was at the moment controlled by the leisured classes, it could be captured by the industrious classes through their socialist representatives by means of elections. This was the reason for the rejection of violence and unconstitional action as being totally inappropriate for the British political scene. In Fabian eyes the State was *fundamentally* neutral, despite the class nature of some of its actions. It could be used to hinder progress, or it could be used to further the evolution of humanity toward its collectivist goal. There was nothing inherent in the State which dictated its class nature. The problem was merely one of which class was in control of its function, and therefore of which class controlled the House of Commons. The state machine of army, police and law courts 'will continue to be used against the people by the classes until it is used by the people against the classes with equal ability and equal resolution'.[20]

A socialist majority at Westminster was therefore the goal of the Fabians. This could be done by persuasion, local exercises in municipal socialism, and working towards a parliamentary majority. As Sidney Webb argued in 1923,

> For the Labour Party, it must be plain. Socialism is rooted in political democracy; which necessarily compels us to recognise that every step towards our goal is dependent on gaining the assent and support of at least a numerical majority of the whole people.[21]

The future arguments by the Labour Right that Labour must appeal to middle-class interests as well as those of the working class if it wished to obtain parliamentary power can be found in Fabian political thought.

This faith in parliamentary democracy as the best means of moving towards socialism was reinforced by the Fabian belief that they were acting in accordance with the gradual and irreversible evolution of history — 'the inevitability of gradualism', as Sidney Webb told the 1923 Labour Party conference. The rapid progress of collectivism, as seen by the spread of municipal socialism and increasing state regulation of factories, was a result of social laws by which humanity was being led into a realm of reason and order. Nobody could stop this progress, or accelerate it beyond its natural rhythm, and the task of socialists was to point to the inevitability of the development so that it could take place in a totally rational manner.[22] This faith in the inevitability of progress was an optimistic belief which ignored the demands of capital accumulation, and it has come into much disrepute after the horrors of the present century, but its importance for Labour could be seen in the assumption until recently that the welfare gains of Labour governments were irreversible.

The Fabian acceptance of parliamentary representative democracy did rule out, however, any alternative view of democracy as direct participation by the producers. The participation of the working class was ruled out by the Fabian leadership as impractical —

> the utmost function that can be allotted to a mass meeting in the machinery of democracy is the ratification or rejection of a policy already prepared for it, and the publication of decisions to those concerned.[23]

Direct democracy would merely ensure that orators would be elected, rather than responsible representatives; even the referendum and initiative were ruled out as inefficient, impeding the decisions of the expert.

In Fabian eyes, the civil servant was to be the real governor of a socialist Britain, with representative democracy acting as a mere check on the administrators. To Webb,

> a body of expert representatives is the only form capable of coping with expert administrators. The only way to choose expert representatives is popular election, but that is just the worst way to obtain expert administrators.[24]

Officials should be chosen by a select committee from a short list drawn up after competitive examinations. The class background and interests of these administrators, and the possibility that they might attempt to hamper a socialist government, were ignored by Webb as irrelevant.

The élitism which came so naturally to the Fabian leaders combined naturally with a commitment to a Socialist Empire. This became clear in a series of articles entitled 'What is Socialism?', in the *New Statesman*, in 1913. At home, guided by an elite army of expert administrators, the British people were to be guided towards adulthood; abroad, the British élite would govern the non-adult races in a co-operative empire free of the selfish competitive spirit of private owners. Such an empire could prove the basis of international co-operation — 'In the Socialist view, the guardianship of the non-Adult races of the world must be undertaken as a corporate duty by the Eight great Powers, either jointly or separately'.[25]

At home, the Fabian leaders supported the campaign for national efficiency launched by Unionists and Liberal Imperialists after the Boer War had revealed the poor physical conditions of working-class recruits. They dabbled in eugenics, with Shaw proposing in his play *Man and Superman* (1903) that national suicide could be averted only by scientific breeding. In a Minority Poor Law Report in 1909, the Webbs called for labour training camps, or 'human sorting houses', in which paupers were to be given a course of rigorous physical training to prevent national waste. The more recalcitrant and rebellious would be packed off to semi-penal detention colonies.

Abroad, they were led by their political adherence to the nation state to support the government in the Boer War of 1899-1902, when Britain annexed two small Afrikaans republics which happened to corner much of the world's gold supply. This policy alienated many of the society like Ramsey Macdonald and Graham Wallas who held to a liberal internationalist viewpoint, but the leadership justified their support in *Fabianism and the Empire*, edited by Shaw in 1900. They argued that as the world was going to be partitioned by the great powers anyway, Britain must ensure that it would not be relegated to the status of an unimportant and uninfluential island.

However, the Fabian leaders insisted that Britain should be a *beneficial* world power, underpinning its imperialism with socialism. 'The British Empire, wisely governed, is invincible. The British Empire, handled as we handled Ireland and the American colonies . . . will fall to pieces without the firing of a foreign shot'.[26] Such wise policies would include self-government and democracy within the Empire for the white dominions, and benevolent bureaucracy for the lower breeds who were unfit for parliamentary democracy — 'the democratic institutions that mean freedom in Australasia and Canada would mean slavery in India and Soudan'.[27] In this way, the early Fabian leaders linked their demand for benevolent socialism at home with their support for imperialism abroad.

Fabianism and Labour

The early Fabians made little attempt to adapt their socialism to the labourist assumptions of the trade union leaders, if only because of their contempt for the working class. Where other middle-class socialists often took a romanticised view of the labour movement, Beatrice Webb was horrified at the immorality and mental dullness of the lower orders. At the turn of the century she noted, 'To us, public affairs seem gloomy; the middle classes are materialistic, and the working classes stupid, and in large sections sottish, with no interest except in racing odds.'[28]

The Fabian leaders were constantly exasperated by the narrow-minded prejudice of the class which suffered most from the existing system, and looked instead to enlightened members of the two main parties, rejecting the idea of an independent workers' party. Some Fabians, like Hubert Bland, were more sympathetic to a workers' party than others, but the general attitude of the Fabian leadership was to permeate the Liberal and Conservative parties, municipally and nationally.

Their conception of permeation was reinforced by their extremely narrow conception of trade unionism as a limited *economic* instrument. In *Industrial Democracy* (1897), the Webbs defined the fundamental object of trade unions as 'the deliberate regulation of the conditions of employment in such a way as to ward off from the manual working producers the evil effects of industrial competition'.[29] This was perfectly compatible with capitalist or socialist government, but it ruled out any extra-parliamentary action concerning questions of national politics. Their belief that unions were legitimately concerned with the protection of their trade, not the overall class of workers, led the Webbs to argue that unions could not become political bodies dealing with questions wider than their trade. Their legal needs did force the unions 'to secure a permanent influence in the House of Commons',[30] but this could be fufilled by either the Conservatives or the Liberals.

This attitude dictated a general indifference by the Fabians to the new Labour Party from its foundation. They had a member, Edward Pease, on the new party's executive, but continued their interest in permeation. It was only the rejection of their Minority Poor Law Report in 1909 that pushed the early Fabian leaders into the Labour Party. The conversion was initially lukewarm, with Beatrice noting privately as late as February, 1914, that socialists were 'by their adhesion to the present parliamentary party bolstering up a fraud . . . [But] to go back on the creation of a Labour Party would be to admit failure'.[31] Only Sidney Webb was enthusiastic for the new party. Wallas moved away from Fabian socialism to concentrate on political psychology in *Human Nature in Politics* (1908). Shaw eventually became disillusioned with parliament, and was to praise the national efficiency inculcated by Stalin and Mussolini. The Webbs still had a contribution to make to the Labour Party, but in the 1930s they were to desert Labour and praise Stalin's Russia as a fulfillment of their dream of a well-ordered and harmonious society run by a benevolent élite.

Nevertheless, these early Fabians gave to the Labour Party an intellectual framework to fit its labourist structure. They made a major contribution to the emerging ideology of British socialism with their doctrines of gradual progress towards a collectivised economy, the necessity of constitutional action, and a new theory of the economic surplus which could counter the Marxists. Not all their views were acceptable to British Socialism – their pro-imperialism offended the liberal strain in most socialists – but they succeeded in giving socialism a distinctive British form, distancing it from its subversive European trappings. They gave the Labour Party an intellectual credibility which was to *supplement*, not *replace*, its labourism. To make British socialism a popular force, however, more than theoretical coherence was needed, and this the ethical socialists were to provide.

The Ethical Socialists

The Fabians appeared too cold-blooded and abstract to fire the imaginations of a class whose collective emotions had been formed by radical Christian and libertarian traditions stretching back to the seventeenth century and beyond. The ethical socialists emerged to fill the emotional gap left by the Fabians. They espoused the consequences of the Fabian theory of rent and commitment to constitutional action, and in some cases they combined this with an acceptance of the Labour Marxists' motions of class war and an independent workers' party. However, in their Utopian vision of a New Jerusalem, they contributed a religious fervour to the early Labour Party. The ILP, formed in Bradford in 1893, served as their political centre. It was committed to a socialist objective – the collective ownership of the means of production, distribution and exchange – interpreted in the light of Christian nonconformity rather than Marxism or Fabian élitism. The intellectual abstractions and logical nostrums of socialist theory were regarded, at least initially, as distinctly inferior to the genuine and honest feelings of nobility and dignity offered by a socialist morality. They looked to the co-operative notions of Robert Owen and the mediaevalist values of John Ruskin for their ideas, and saw in the utopian fantasies of William Morris — particularly *John Ball's Dream* (1887) and *News from Nowhere* (1891) — a vision of a new socialist world. It was a vision of dignity and craftsmanship, in which beauty and a community spirit replaced the grubby and self-seeking search for poverty which characterised the ugly, dehumanised values of competitive capitalism. This vision inspired Edward Carpenter and, through him, the Glasiers and Robert Blatchford, to impart to the Labour Party a highly emotional, near-religious passion.

Carpenter

Edward Carpenter (1844-1929) was born into a wealthy middle-class family, but renounced a career in the Church after a major crisis of identity. His poetic dream of an alternative society where social hypocrisy would be replaced by a natural camaraderie led him to the democratic and agrarian values of American radicals like Thoreau and Whitman, and to a farm which an inheritance allowed him to buy. His acceptance of his own homosexuality, combined with an ecstatic feeling of relief at his mother's death, led him to write *Towards Democracy* (1882). This book was Carpenter's central statement about the unhappiness he saw around him, and its gradual replacement by a new age of liberation and natural relationships. It went through several editions, each one becoming more infused with Carpenter's personal vision of socialism.

However, his attacks were on modern civilisation rather than capitalism as a social and economic system of exploitation. He bitterly pointed to capitalist *ethics* in which money is accumulated and worshipped, and in which all human values were sacrificed for material gain. He saw private property as the institution by which the spiritual beauty and dignity of man was stained by the disease of artificial manners and culture. He portrayed the nightmare of competing and aggressive 'individuals' which destroyed the simplicity of honest and warm human relations.

However, Carpenter's ethical criticisms applied to the sentiments and values of capitalism rather than its institutions. The close analysis of Marx or the Fabians were irrelevant to his vision. Carpenter's enemy was neither the capitalist class nor the parasitic leisured class, but the indifference and artificiality of civilised manners and culture. The fact that these were entangled in a system of private property was almost accidental. Since the problem was one of a sentiment, to be replaced by a better sentiment, there was no fundamental need to change formal capitalist institutions. In a speech at a by-election in Chesterfield in 1908, Carpenter acknowledged as such —

> We should be able to say to private owners of industries that if they managed their own concerns in the public interest, with fair consideration for the health and welfare of their employees, the day for taking over those industries might be indefinitely postponed.[32]

It was not capital, but the selfish behaviour of capitalists, which was Carpenter's concern.

Carpenter's influence was felt directly by the propagandists of the early Labour Party, particularly the Glasiers and Blatchford, who gave his vision a more substantial political form.

The Glasiers

John Bruce Glasier (1859-1920) was the illegitimate son of a radical Scots farmer. His stern Calvinist faith was carried into his political activities, and he became a leading member of the ILP, serving as Chairman and allying himself with Keir Hardie and Ramsay Macdonald in establishing it as a major political force.

The apocalyptic strain in his thought was reinforced by his wife, Katharine St John Conway (1867-1950), the daughter of a well-to-do preacher who became a socialist after seeing bedraggled strikers invading one of the rich Bristol churches in which she worshipped. To Katharine, the ILP was 'a child of the spirit of liberty. Life, love, liberty and labour make liquid music. The Labour Party is in league with life, and works for liberty that man may live'.[33] It was in this spirit that she married Glasier, and it was this spirit which inspired their writings from *The Religion of Socialism* (1890) to *The Meaning of Socialism* (1919).

They saw socialism as a religion free of supernatural beliefs and expressing the highest ideals of human life. In his Chairman's Address to the 1903 ILP Conference, Glasier talked of 'the sacrament of Socialism' which the rich were welcome to receive as much as the poor. A belief in the co-operative commonwealth was the faith that fired the martyrs of the socialist religion; men and women who fought and died 'in the hope of making a heaven for you and me and all mankind upon earth'.[34]

Their vision was anchored, however, by a more down-to-earth view of the State as the agency by which the New Jerusalem was to be achieved and organised. Far from being an instrument of class violence, the State was 'the expression, however imperfect or erroneous, of the communal or national body politic'.[35] It had swept away the rack and the thumbscrew to guarantee political and religious freedom. It was not the State which had forced children to work long hours, but the capitalists – the State, true to its selfless nature, had restricted harsh labour conditions. It was not the State which broke up pacifist protest meetings during the Great War, but vigilante mobs – the State had granted exemption to conscientious objectors. However, the State praised by Glasier also sent millions to fight in the trenches of Flanders; deported and harassed militant socialists and shop stewards; and detained pacifist and Marxist conscientious objectors in conditions which killed 73 of them and made 31 mad. Glasier did admit that the State had been somewhat tyrannical during the war, but this was due to the prevailing political conditions – 'it would be most unfair . . . to judge the State, or indeed nations, by their comportment during the anarchical condition of war'.[36] However, the violent reaction of the peacetime State to nationalist resistance in Ireland and India, the increasingly sophisticated weaponry being created and used for the defence of the nation, and the plans being forged to suppress major strikes within Britain itself were indications ignored by Glasier of the State's merciless capacity to crush any threat to its supremacy. Glasier's stress on the welfare aspect of State activity had led him to belittle or ignore its violent and coercive ability to protect the existing power structure in any society.

Blatchford

Robert Blatchford (1851-1943) was the most important propagandist of the early Labour movement. Born into a working class family in Halifax, he eventually became a popular journalist with the Manchester *Sunday Chronicle*. He set up a socialist journal, *The Clarion*, in 1891, combining radical politics with entertaining populist articles on sport and other working-class hobbies, and encouraged social activities through the Glee Clubs and Clarion Cycling Clubs. Above all, he gave Carpenter's evangelical vision a popular form in *Merrie England* (1894), a bluff and no-nonsense appeal to a mythical working man, John Smith, which won an enormous readership.

It was the dehumanising and loveless nature of the city slums which appalled Blatchford. In a didactic and rhetorical style, he drew a picture of destitution and filth where vice and hooliganism flourished. In the midst of enormous riches, the people were plagued by misery, poverty and ill health. Patriotism, to Blatchford the noblest of virtues, had been turned into a mockery and disgrace in a country peopled with caricatures of human beings trapped in a selfish and cruel society.

In its place, Blatchford pointed to a utopian vision of socialism as the earthly realisation of the New Jerusalem. In his direct style, he argued that this was the only solution to the social evils blighting Britain —

> John Smith, do you know what Socialism is? You have heard it denounced many times, and it is said that you do not believe in it, but do you know what it is? Good or bad, wise or foolish, it is all I have to offer as a remedy.[37]

However, such a practical style was not matched by a similar grasp of practical realities. Blatchford's revulsion from the hideous factory system led him to a Luddite dream of ridding the country of industry. He believed that Britain should turn the clock back to a de-industrialised society where pure air and fine food produced the sturdy breed of English yeomen who had first made the nation great. Britain could then feed itself, existing in isolation from world trade by the application of scientific agriculture.

At the same time, he put forward the vision of a beautifully planned community free of the filth and squalor of the slums. He foresaw 'wide streets with detached houses, with gardens and fountains and avenues of trees . . . I would institute public dining halls, public baths, public wash-houses on the best plans.'[38] These sentiments echoed a real need in the workers' movement, and worked themselves into the ethos of that movement. The concept of town and country planning, together with the creation of new towns, owed much to this ethos.

However, it was an ethos resting on a narrowly insular basis. Blatchford's faith was in the *British* working class, exploited by the unpatriotic monopolists. He described the process of State ownership as nationalisation, not socialisation. He even opposed the manufacture of British goods for sale abroad, holding to a 'little England' ideal of a self-sufficient community free from foreign influences. To Blatchford, 'We want Britain for the British. We want the fruits of labour for those who produce them'.[39] The nation and the working class were identical for him, so that the working class of other nations were always potential enemies. It was an ugly side to labourism, and unfortunately left its legacy in the labour movement.

Conclusion

It would be too easy to mock the naivete of ethical socialism. This naivete was important, because it was to reverberate in the hopes and aspirations of the labour movement. Its conception of a society of healthy and happy families living in a New Jerusalem was to be echoed by Labour politicians throughout the first half of the twentieth century. Its moralistic critique of the corruption and degradation of a competitive society was to be at the heart of British socialism. It may have verged on self-righteousness but this was perfectly in keeping with the traditions of the chapel and the God-fearing, upright workman who was to be the backbone of the early Labour Party. It may have been unrealistic, but in that lay its appeal. Like religion, it was a cry from the heart — a vision that there was an alternative to the mean and stunted life of an ugly industrialised society, and an affirmation that an unselfish and caring community would one day replace an indifferent and cruel social order.

However, the appealing and attractive qualities of the ethical socialist vision should not blind us to the basic fact that it was ingenuous and ultimately inconsequential. It was incapable of delivering what it promised. Horrified by the ugliness and ruthless brutality of capitalism, the political thought of the ethical socialists was utopian in the worst sense of the word. It was basically a withdrawal from the world and, as such, it was impossible to translate into the practical politics of government. It had no answer to the problem of budget deficits, mass unemployment, or the conflict between national and class loyalties which would be forced on the labour movement by war. Even in its grander notions of transforming a selfish society, it had no answer to the real world of armies and police, of the scheming political manoeuvres and cynical contempt for human life which has characterised this century's politics. When those problems were brought out by the sharp tests of war and slump, British socialism would be found wanting as a result.

Notes

1. Karl Marx, *Capital* Volume 1 (Lawrence and Wishart, 1974), p. 558.
2. Marx defined the rate of profit as the ratio of surplus value to the total capital in society, differentiating it from the rate of surplus value of labour power. Hodgskin confused the rate of profit with the rate of surplus value, and did not recognise the importance of the falling rate of profit. To Marx, this fall

was 'in every respect the most important law of modern political economy, and the most essential for understanding the most difficult of relations' (*Grundrisse*, trans. M. Nicolaus, Penguin, 1973, p. 748).

3. Marx, *Theories of Surplus Value* Part III (Laurence and Wishart, 1972), especially p. 296.

4. See, for example, Marx's letters on Ireland in Marx, *The First International and After*, D.Fernbach ed. (Penguin, 1974).

5. Quoted in Marx, ibid., p. 270.

6. See, for example, H.M. Hyndman, *England for All* (London, 1881), p. 6.

7. Marx and Engels, *On Britain* (Lawrence and Wishart, 1968), p. 574.

8. See, for example, Hyndman, *The Historical Basis of Socialism in England* (London, 1883), p. 287

9. Engels to Sorge, 4 May 1887, in Marx and Engels, *Selected Correspondence* (Progress, 1975).

10. Tom Mann, *What Is The ILP Driving At?* (Manchester, 1894), p. 11.

11. G.B. Shaw, *Bernard Shaw and Karl Marx: A Symposium* (Random House, N.Y., 1930), pp. 170-1. This contains the early debates on Marx's theory of values in the Fabian Society.

12. Webb to Davison, 12-13 December 1888, quoted in W. Wolfe, *From Radicalism to Socialism* (Yale, 1975), p. 276.

13. Quoted in P. Clarke, *Liberals and Social Democrats* (Cambridge University Press, 1978), p. 28.

14. G.B. Shaw, Preface to *Fabian Essays in Socialism* (London, 1932 ed.), p. XIV.

15. Quoted in N. and J. McKenzie, *The First Fabians* (Weidenfeld and Nicholson, 1977), p. 153.

16. Sidney Webb, *Facts for Socialists* (Fabian Tract 5, London, 1887 ed.), p. 5.

17. Ibid., p. 8.

18. For another view, holding the Fabians' economic theory to be irrelevant, see A.M. MacBriar, *Fabian Socialism and English Politics 1884-1918* (Cambridge University Press, 1962), p. 47.

19. Shaw, *Report on Fabian Policy* (Fabian Tract 70, London, 1896): p. 5.

20. Shaw, *The Impossibilities of Anarchism* (Fabian Tract 45, London, 1893), p. 27.

21. Labour Party, *Annual Conference Report*, 1923, p. 178.

22. See, for example, Sidney Webb, *Towards Social Democracy* (Fabian Tract 15, London, 1890).

23. *Fabian News*, November, 1896, p. 35.

24. *Fabian News*, January, 1897, p. 43.

25. *New Statesman*, 2 August, 1913, p. 525.

26. Shaw, *Fabianism and Empire* (London, 1900), p. 15.

27. Ibid.

28. Beatrice Webb, *Our Partnership* (London, 1948), p. 195. See also Shaw, 'Illusions of Socialism', in Edward Carpenter ed., *Forecasts of the Coming Century* (London, 1896).

29. S. and B. Webb, *Industrial Democracy* (London, 1926 ed.), p. 807.

30. Ibid., p. 539.

31. B. Webb, *Diaries 1912-24* (London, 1952), p. 19.

32. Quoted in C. Tsuzuki, *Edward Carpenter 1844-1929*, (Cambridge University Press, 1980), p. 117.

33. Quoted in L. Thompson, *The Enthusiasts: A Biography of John and Katharine Bruce Glasier* (Victor Gollancz, 1971), p. 66.

34. J.B. Glasier and K. St John Conway, *The Religion of Socialism* (London, 1890), p. 16.

35. J.B. Glasier, *The Meaning of Socialism* (Manchester, 1919), p. 182.
36. Ibid., p. 185.
37. Robert Blatchford, *Merrie England* (London, n.d.), p. 119.
38. Ibid., pp. 47-8.
39. R. Blatchford, *Britain for the British*, (London, 1902), p. 151.

3 THE EMERGENCE OF BRITISH SOCIALISM

The debates and discussions around the different options facing the socialist movement in Britain took place against a background of change in capitalism. Capital accumulation was resumed on an extended scale, yet in a very different form than in earlier periods. The real nature of the crisis in Britain — a crisis of gradually declining profitability — was both disguised and offset by a massive export of capital overseas by British finance houses. Capital investment was expanding rapidly, but it was expanding outside Britain. The massive profits reaped by the financial houses increased divisions between financial and industrial capital, with important consequences for British politics, but from the point of view of capital as a whole, accumulation was able to take place on a far wider scale than ever before.

In Britain itself, despite a decline in real wages through most of the period, the prospect of economic collapse receded after 1890. As a result, the dogmatic Marxism of the SDF became increasingly irrelevant as social revolution appeared less important. Class struggle within capitalism over the share of national income was certainly seen as an essential need by an increasing number of workers, and the number of industrial workers organised in trade unions rose from 8 per cent in 1890 to 27 per cent in 1914. However, the moral considerations of the ethical socialists made far more appeal to political workers than the economic considerations of the variants of Marxism then on offer, while the bulk of the organised working class remained committed to the Liberal Party. The socialist movement's attempt to relate to the labourism of the trade union movement thus inevitably expressed itself as an ideological relationship to Liberalism.

The debates between different sections of the socialist movement was in the final analysis meaningless if socialism could not gain the support of the labour movement. The ILP did not really have this support — all 28 ILP candidates were defeated in the 1895 election, while the trade union movement remained committed to the Liberal Party. After a great deal of ILP maneouvring, a resolution calling for more labour representatives in Westminster was passed at the 1899 TUC, and a few unions formed the Labour Representation Committee (LRC) with the socialist factions in February 1900. However, the bulk of the unions continued to support the Liberals, and only two LRC MPs were returned at the 1900 election, fought amidst a wave of chauvinism after victories in the Boer War. It was the Taff Vale judgement of 1901, threatening the financial status of trade unions, which gave the LRC more of a basis in the labour movement, with unions like the ASE and the Textile Workers affiliating. Even so, a major union like the Mine-workers remained faithful to the Liberals until 1909. Even the LRC victory in the 1906 election, when 29 MPs were returned, was totally due to an electoral pact worked out with the Liberal Party by the LRC secretary, Ramsay Macdonald, three years earlier.

The new Labour Party's relationship with the Liberals was crucial, and not merely in organisational terms. In terms of ideas, the Labour Party became the battleground in which British socialism had to work out its precise relationship with the labourist assumptions of trade unions that remained essentially Liberal in politics. The Labour Party did not have any sort of socialist programme (one of the reasons for the SDF withdrawal in 1901), and any attempt to force one on the unions would destroy the new grouping. Moreover, the ideological sterility of Gladstonian Liberalism was being replaced in the new century by the social liberalism of Haldane and Lloyd George. Their rejection of the old individualist formulae of *laissez-faire* in favour of an active role in welfare and redistribution by the State posed a major ideological problem and political challenge to the British socialists.

The new party had already been distinguished from the Left by the Fabians and ethical socialists, in their rejection of the Marxist theory of value and the revolutionary overthrow of the State. It was in this period that the leaders of the Labour party distinguished it ideologic-ally from the Right. This distinction did not lie in an acceptance of nationalisation of basic industry (at least not until 1918). It lay in developing the contradictions, both logical and political, between labourism and the Liberal party. It was a fine distinction, and was indeed seen by the ILP Left as a practically negligible distinction in the period between 1906 and the Great War. Nevertheless, the principles separating Labour from the Liberals, delineated in these formative years by Labour leaders like Hardie, were labourist rather than socialist. It was the socialist movement's absorption of labourism which com-pleted the formation of a specific British socialism.

Keir Hardie

James Keir Hardie (1856-1915) was a particularly apt figure in the evolution of British socialism. His political views were not formed as a result of disillusionment with his class background, as with Hyndman or Carpenter, or as a result of any visit to the poverty stricken, as with Beatrice Webb or Blatchford. Still less did he bring to bear the analytical subtlety and insights of Marx. Hardie's politics were formed as a result of a lifetime's experience in the trade union movement and in Parliament.

His main influences lay in his poor background, particularly in the democratic tradition of the Scottish working class. Hardie had been born the illegitimate son of a farm servant in Lanarkshire. He was raised in a grim and restrictive poverty, constantly on the brink of desti- tution; he worked as an errand boy at the age of eight, and down the mines from the age of ten. This experience of misery and recurrent economic worries nourished the Christian egalitarian instincts which remained the lifeblood of his political thinking. He combined temper- ance reform work with labour activity, helping to form the Ayrshire Miners Union. His trade union background made him particularly representative of the new type of labourism growing in the 1880s, critical as it was of the Gladstonian Liberalism espoused by the Lib- Lab MPs. At the 1887 TUC, he launched a stinging attack on Henry Broadhurst, the General Secretary, for supporting Liberal candidates who were bad employers. Hardie wanted the Liberals to adopt the eight-hour day in its platform, and was incensed at Liberal indifference to the trade union movement. When in 1888 the Liberals rejected his candidacy at the Mid-Lanark by-election, preferring a London barrister, he stood as an independent labour candidate. He came bottom of the poll, but the support given him by Labour Marxists like Champion and Mann was indicative of the political direction in which he was now travelling. Under their influence, together with socialists in the Scottish Land and Labour League, Hardie formed the Scottish Labour Party in August 1888. The crucial organisational break with the Liberal Party had been taken.

Socialism and Labourism

Hardie had rejected the Liberals, but he did not accept the tenets of the Labour Marxists. In 'An Indictment of the Class War', written for the ILP paper, the *Labour Leader*, Hardie made clear his opposition to the unemotional and dry nature of Marxism, deriding the *Communist Manifesto* as devoid of feeling. To Hardie, the Marxist notion of class war reduced socialism from the level of a crusade against materialism and selfishness to that of a faction fight. The antagonism which existed between capital and labour would be intensified by Marxism, whereas Hardie wished to remove that antagonism — 'Socialism makes war upon a system, not upon a class'.[1] It was hardly a rigorous critique of Marxism — after all, Marxists also called for war against the system — but it was not intended to be.

It was the Liberal Party, not Marxism, which presented itself to Hardie as the chief enemy. In an early editorial in the *Labour Leader* arguing against an alliance with the Liberals, Hardie declared, 'I take it that the aim of the Labour Party is to wean the workers from their allegiance to Liberalism and Toryism, and to unite them under a standard of their own raising'.[2] Unlike the SDF, Hardie saw the need to look to the workers organised in the trade unions if labour was to have any chance of political success. They had the numbers, the organisation, the money and, most importantly, they were the only force capable of emancipating themselves. To emancipate the working class from above, as sought by the middle-class Fabians, would be dictatorial and self-defeating. To Hardie, as a democrat, the workers must stand on their own feet without the help of intellectuals or benefactors.

This belief was the basis of Hardie's socialism. It was a labourist basis, in that he appealed to the almost instinctive assumptions of a trade union movement which found itself in a fundamental conflict with capitalist employers. Indeed, this labourism was essential if he was to be successful in creating a trade union political party. If the union leaders could not be won to a socialist party, as was clear after the ILP electoral defeat in 1895, then for Hardie his socialism would take a secondary place to his labourism. At the LRC foundation conference in 1900, he willingly accepted a power structure in which the unions had an institutionalised predominance over the socialist groups. He willingly acquiesced in the rejection of socialism as an aim of the new party, in favour of the defence of trade union principles and organisation by political means.

His conception of socialism was particularly fitted for these concessions to labourism. The traditions of radical Christianity and egalitarian democracy in Hardie's upbringing gave him a sense of socialism as a religious creed rather than as a political or economic system. It was a new conception of society based upon Christian teaching, rejecting the evil selfishness of drunkenness and competition in favour of the selfless co-operation of a people who would care for one another. Hardie wrote that 'Socialism, like every other problem of life, is at bottom a question of ethics or morals. It has mainly to do with the relationships which should exist between a man and his fellows'.[3] As such, it was an extension of the teachings of the Christian fathers, in particular the Sermon on the Mount, with its message of hope for the poor and forgotten. Christianity had been a creed of the poor for hundreds of years before being taken over cynically by the rich. Hardie saw the task of socialism as being the recovery of the original Christian teachings, attacking the inequalities of wealth and banishing unhealthy competition. It was 'a handmaiden of religion, and as such entitled to the support of all who pray for the coming of Christ's Kingdom upon earth'.[4]

This Christian ethic was very vague — not many people would wish to resist kindliness in favour of selfish cruelty, at least not explicitly — but in that lay its strength and appeal. In being vague, it was malleable, capable of being applied to the semi-anarchist Utopia of Edward Carpenter or the welfare state socialism of the ILP. Hardie applied it to the native democratic traditions of his class to call for labour to capture the institutions of the State in order to emancipate itself from industrial serfdom. These institutions, which had protected the dominant class in society throughout history, could now be used by the working class as the new dominant force. In protecting its interests, the working class would be forced to nationalise the property which was owned by a small and undemocratic group — 'The fundamental fact which the working class is now beginning to recognise is that property, or at least its possession, is power. This is an axiom which admits of no contradiction'.[5] Since the possession of property was power, it followed that a real democracy must 'democratise' property. The democracy won by male workers in the narrow political sphere must be extended to the wider industrial sphere.

This socialist element in Hardie's political thought certainly differentiated labour's interests from any possible Liberal conception, and the ILP's adoption of a programme calling for the collective ownership of the means of production, distribution and exchange was a recognition of this. However, as it became clear that the unions were not falling over themselves to endorse a socialist party, the vagueness of Hardie's conception allowed him to drop the demand for a New Jerusalem to a more politically expedient time. It was not socialism, but labourism which was to be the line separating the new Labour Party from the Liberals on their Right.

As the bulk of the working class supported the Liberal Party, and could not be weaned away by the call for a new socialist society, then Hardie was forced to stress the contradiction existing between labourism and liberalism. Hardie argued that the trade union movement, in its industrial conflict with the employers, was hamstrung by its political support for the employers' party in Parliament. He sought to bring out the logic of the independent industrial organisation of the workers by calling for its extension to the political arena. Only by resurrecting this crucial aspect of independence, elaborated by Hodgskin and all but buried since the defeat of Chartism, could Hardie succeed in winning the unions to a new party. The other aspects of labourism — its demand for redistribution of wealth, for example — were not logically incompatible with the Liberal Party. The Liberals generally ignored social questions, but this did not mean that hard work and argument could not force the Liberals to adopt a radical stand on social inequality. Indeed, the emergence of the New Liberalism around Lloyd George and Haldane augured well for any advocate who might argue that labour should work inside the Liberal Party. However, the fundamental antagonism which set employers and unions against one another in industry could not be resolved by their political co-operation in the same party. This industrial conflict demanded political expression, and Hardie's political instinct led him to a recognition of this.

Unless the unions realised the need to organise politically as well as industrially, Hardie argued that they would never fulfil their aim of protecting labour. Trade unions could regulate wages and protect living standards, but this could only go so far. The miner, for example, would be paid the minimum wage for the number of days he is given work, as negotiated by his union, but he may only be employed half the week —

> Neither he nor his union had any hand in shaping the circumstances which led to his being fully employed . . . He feels himself to be under the sway of forces which work quite without his ken, and which have the power to make him the victim of their caprice.[6]

The working class may have attained a measure of political democracy, but in industry they were mere serfs, totally at the mercy of their masters, the employers. The unions were of little use against unemployment and hunger, and were powerless against the closely-knit and omnipotent industrial autocracies which were increasingly replacing the small employers. The only answer left was for the unions to organise politically to defend their interests in Parliament. Hardie was confident that the worker 'will use the political freedom which his fathers won for him to win industrial freedom for his children . . . the real inward meaning of the rise of the Labour Party'.[7]

As a result, Hardie's main attacks were on labour collaboration with the Liberal Party, the party of their employers. He pointed to the inactivity and careerism of the Lib-Lab MPs as an example of the results of the trade unions' political subservience —

> Irksome as it is to endure the apathy of the [Liberal] government, it is tenfold more so to look on at the inaction of these men. They are supposed in a special degree to represent labour, and so long as they are silent the Government can, with some show of justification, plead not guilty to the charge of neglect. If men who have been sent to Parliament holding a special brief for labour have nothing to say, why should a Cabinet drawn exclusively from the wealthy classes begin to make a fuss?[8]

Only a genuine, independent labour party could take up the cudgels on behalf of organised labour. Through political independence, the self-respect and manhood of the workers could be developed, forcing the major parties to take labour questions seriously. Without it, the worker would be forced into political submission, scrounging for charity from the high and mighty. As Hardie put it in 1903,

> I aim at a party which, on labour questions, shall lead Liberalism and the nation, and which shall not be content to play the part of a political Lazarus sitting at the gate of a rich man's party humbly begging crumbs from his table.[9]

Once a Labour Party had been established, the difference between labourism and liberalism appeared harder to define. With the Liberal government after 1906 pursuing a policy of social reform, the precise role of the Labour Party appeared highly problematic. Indeed, its very electoral success had been due to a secret pact worked out with the Liberals by Hardie and Macdonald. It appeared to many on the Left after 1906 that Hardie's stress on labourism had been incorrect, as the difference between the social Liberalism of Lloyd George and a non-socialist labourism seemed inconsequential. This left-wing discontent, manifesting itself with Victor Grayson's by-election victory in the Colne Valley in 1907 as a 'Labour and Socialist' candidate was a threat to the ILP leadership's established strategy. In 1908, Ben Tillett attacked the non-socialist labourism of the Labour Party in his pamphlet, *Is the Parliamentary Party a Failure?*, where he described Labour MPs as hypocrites corrupted by a superficial careerism, repaying 'with gross betrayal the class that willingly supports them'.

Hardie agreed with the principles of the ILP Left, but he disagreed with their tactics. The organisational independence of the Labour Party was all-important, and only after its consolidation could the socialist goal be asserted. As he wrote in a rejoinder to the Left in 1909,

> the friction does not lie between old-fashioned Trade Unionists who want to improve the condition of the worker and Socialists who want to change the industrial order. The friction lies between people, all of whom are Socialists, who want Socialism, who put Socialism before anything else.[10]

It was a question of *how* the Labour Party was to be won to socialism, not *whether* it could be.

Hardie may have been secretly chafing at the unimaginative way in which the Labour leaders were going about this task, but he was convinced that it was a gradual process which must not be disrupted by impatience. For Hardie, a socialist movement was useless unless it was connected to the labour movement, based on the trade union and co-operative organisations of the working class. This was the strength of the new party — 'the outstanding value of the Labour Party is that it is what its name implies, an uprising of the working class, overseered and guided by that class, painfully and slowly working out its own emancipation'.[11] Only with the support of the Labour Party could socialists be elected to Westminster, and only through the Labour Party could socialists appeal to workers as part and parcel of their own movement, rather than as outside missionaries. Hardie was only recognising political realities when he wrote, 'It is not so much Socialism, nor the absence of it, which wins elections, as the fact that the candidate is representing a party which the average man, who does not indulge overmuch in theories, understands and approves'.[12]

There was no fundamental change to his labourist version of socialism, merely a different response to a different situation. His main aim was to instill a sense of political independence into the ranks of the labour movement. Only socialism could do this properly, but his labourist interpretation made sure that the dividing line between Labour and the Liberals was not the question of collective ownership but that of trade union independence. This was Hardie's fundamental contribution to the Labour Party's political thought.

Its political consequences were never really thought through by Hardie. His opposition to dogmatism was also an aversion to theory as such, which he saw as abstract and divisive compared with the living emotions of the democratic sentiment of socialism. This sentiment would be enough for Hardie — 'Abstract theories with them count for very little . . . Socialism supplies the vision and a united working class satisfies the senses as a practical method of attaining its realisation'.[13] He had an intuitive grasp of the needs and understanding of his class, and he sought to embody its traditions and hopes through his actions, as when he was driven to Parliament in 1892 on a two-horse carriage, dressed in a cloth cap and tweed jacket. He was aware of the import-ance of symbol, much to the chagrin of other Labour MPs who were annoyed by his showmanship. He knew how to win an audience by his clear and simple style of speaking, expressing the hopes of a new society in Sunday School style. In one speech, typical of many in which he described socialism, Hardie assured his listeners that

> the ugliness and squalor which now meets you at every turn in some of the most beautiful valleys in the world would disappear, the rivers would run pure and clear as they did of yore . . . and in the winter the log would glow on the fire the while that the youths and maidens made glad the heart with mirth and song, and there would be beauty and joy everywhere.[14]

It may be churlish to ask how this state of affairs was to be brought about — after all, the sentiment was a major motivating factor in the lives of thousands of socialists — but, given subsequent events, perhaps more people should have raised objections. Hardie was lulling himself and his audience into a state of vague elevation while concealing unre-solved political problems in his conception which would have profound consequences for the movement he sought to serve. He was aware of the economic and social problems of poverty, unemployment, ignorance and bad health, yet he had no real policies to overcome these problems beyond the vague panacea of State regulation and co-operation. It was capitalism which was the cause of all suffering, but the real nature of this capitalism was left out of his analysis. Capitalism was often just another word for selfishness, and socialism another word for democratic Christianity, so that the speed and urgency of replacing capitalism was determined by the education of people in basic goodness. Where capit-alism was identified as an economic system of private ownership, the nature of its workings and the manner of its replacement was never analysed seriously. The potential resistance to change by the capit-alist class was never measured, and plans to counter this resistance were never countenanced. Instead, Hardie's socialism remained labourist and radical democratic, rather than collectivist. The limitations of this approach can be seen in his reactions to women's suffrage and imperialism.

Feminism and Imperialism

Unlike other Labour leaders, such as Macdonald and Snowden, who were opposed to all extra-parliamentary activity, Hardie fully supported the struggle of the Suffragettes for the vote. He did so as a result of his democratic conviction that all of humanity, men *and* women, were equal. It was a sentiment which stretched to Tom Paine and beyond, but it ran into a deep prejudice in the labour movement. Bruce Glasier was only the tip of the iceberg in his rejection of women's suffrage, so that Hardie was forced to take up the demand of socialist feminists for equality of work and regard. In 1909, he called attention to the opposition to women's equality in the socialist movement, arguing that 'our work will be handicapped and our movement lopsided until women take their place with men as comrades and political equals in our great world-wide agitation for industrial and economic freedom'.[15]

In this, he was taking up the call of an increasing number of women in the ILP who were attempting to link the feminist demand for the vote with the socialist demand for the emancipation of labour. Isabella Ford, an ILP feminist from Leeds, was much more aware of the oppression of working-class women than were many of the middle-class Suffragette leaders, yet she was involved in a constant fight against male prejudice in the ILP and Labour Party. In her pamphlet, *Women and Socialism* (1904), she attacked both the Labour Party and the Suffragette movement for failing to recognise the economic basis of women's oppression in their total dependence on men for a living. The ruling parties were hostile to State protection of women by maternity benefits and other social measures, which could only be granted by the pressure of the labour movement. She called for both Labour and the suffrage movement to recognise that working-class women are particularly oppressed through low wages and miserable working conditions. These were examples of

> moral evils which are eating at the heart of the nation, pressing the most heavily, as do all such evils, on the lives of the very poorest and most helpless women, and long experience has shown that they will never be remedied till women have full political power, and can themselves deal with them.[16]

She argued that only the vote would give women the political protection which the trade union movement was incapable of providing.

Hardie echoed such sentiments in his writings and speeches, attempting to show the labourist nature of women's oppression — 'the sex problem is, at bottom, the Labour problem'.[17] Women were economically dependent on men in all classes, with the daughters of the middle class groomed for a 'successful' marriage. However, working-class women were particularly oppressed at home and work, and Hardie called on the trade union movement and the Labour Party to recognise that without equality between the sexes, social progress was impossible. This call was couched in terms of his romantic view of socialism, however, rather than any thorough analysis of why women are *necessarily* oppressed by capitalism (though women to the Left of the Labour Party, such as Lily Gair Wilkinson and Dora Montefiore, were attempting such an analysis on a Marxist basis). To Hardie, women's emancipation in a socialist society seemed to mean that women would mate with men for other than economic reasons —

the strong, good-looking male attracts the best of the females, and thus the best qualities on both sides get transmitted to offspring and are by them passed on to succeeding generations until they become permanently incorporated.[18]

Apart from Hardie's own contribution to the current debate on eugenics, his conception of women's emancipation was as vague as that of labour emancipation. There was no reason, given the understanding of Hardie or Ford, why women could not throw off their chains in a capitalist society. Indeed, their demands for the vote and State welfare measures have all to a greater or lesser extent been obtained from governments of all parties. The freedom of women to choose good-looking males is too controversial a subject to be touched upon here, but in Hardie's analysis the economic subjection of working-class women was due more to the selfishness of individual capitalists, than to capital as a system. It was to be overcome by trade union action and State regulation rather than by the ending of a particular society.

Hardie's opposition to imperialism was more confused as it was very difficult to apply his labourism outside Britain. As a result, he fell back on the democratic traditions of nineteenth century Liberalism, with its opposition to the oppression of small nations. Unlike the Fabians, Hardie belonged to the vociferous anti-war movement during the Boer War of 1899-1902. He denounced it as a war fought for the benefit of capitalists, grinding down the poor and independent Afrikaaner, but in this he did not differ from the main Liberal opposition to the war. The Liberals also argued that the selfish gains of a few capitalists was no justification for the oppression of a small nation. Thus, Hardie could mourn Queen Victoria's death as an example of the war's most tragic victim,[19] while warning that the war was harming the interests of the Empire. In one article castigating the war as a capitalist conflict, Hardie wrote that

> there is not a single British interest at stake . . . Russia wants to see us out of India, France out of Egypt, Germany out of Africa. With the entire British army locked up, and our last gun with it, it only needs these three powers to agree and the Empire goes to pieces like a house of cards. By ending the war, this becomes at once impossible, the Empire would be saved, and the national honour redeemed.[20]

The fact that class interests and national interests may not coincide was obviously not clear to Hardie because labourism was an insufficient basis for an analysis of imperialism.

This was demonstrated in Hardie's call for reform rather than the destruction of the British Empire. His visit to India in 1908 convinced him that reforms were desperately needed, as British rule there resembled a military despotism tempered by a civilian bureaucracy. He called for Home Rule, not independence, to prevent the Congress Party becoming seditious. Only an effective self-government could preserve both the Empire and the liberties of the native peoples. Hardie's essential loyalty to British institutions at home was thus reflected in his loyalty to their extension abroad. This was why Hardie could argue for reform of the imperial institutions as essential 'if India is to be pacified and kept loyal to the British Raj'.[21] He was not opposed to imperialism, merely to its militarist and undemocratic form.

Hardie's democratic radicalism and his evident sympathy with the sufferings of his class gave him a special place in the affections of the Labour Party. He made no original contribution to the party's political thought – echoing an eclectic mixture of ethical socialism, Labour Marxism and Fabianism – and was often deliberately obscure and contradictory in his statements. As a politician he had to demonstrate a necessary flexibility in order to build the Labour Party, but in his belief in the necessity to build that party he never wavered. As a politician, the formation of an independent political force of the working class assures his place and importance in Labour's history. As a political thinker, Hardie's major significance lay, not in his socialism, but in his resurrection of Hodgskin's view of labourism as independent of the employers. With Hardie, the contours of the Labour Party's political thought were formed, separating it from the Liberals on the Right by this labourism.

Snowden and Macdonald

If Hardie marked out the contours of British socialism, separating it from the Liberal Party by his demands for Labour's political independence, he did so from a position on the Left of the new party. His past experience of suffering and trade union struggle gave him a conception of class struggle which was similar in substance to that of Labour Marxists like Tom Mann. However, the flexibility of the new party's political thinking was shown by two other Labour leaders of the time, Philip Snowden and Ramsay Macdonald, who occupied a position on the Right of the Labour Party while claiming to be socialists. Each made his specific contribution to Labour Party thinking in this formative Edwardian era and each was to follow through the logic of his conceptions when faced with the realities of government office in a later decade.

Snowden

Philip Snowden (1864-1937) was born in Yorkshire's West Riding, the son of a poor weaver. He was steeped from an early age in Liberal politics and Methodist religion, and worked in a local tax office at the lowest Civil Service grade until an illness paralysed his legs. His interest in temperance and the evangelical nature of his religion quickly won him to the ethical socialism being preached in the West Riding by Blatchford's *Clarion*, and he joined the ILP in the mid-1890s. His evangelical and blood-curdling speeches, in which the present system was seen as a moral hell and socialism as the earthly paradise, went down well with his audience, and Snowden's pamphlet, *The Christ That Is To Be* (1903), established him as a popular figure. After his election as a Labour MP in 1906, Snowden was chosen as the party's spokesman on finance, and his gaunt, crippled figure seemed to symbolise the puritanical inflexibility of his socialism. He was described as the new Robespierre, the symbol of an incorruptible refusal to compromise with the capitalist face of mammon.

In fact, Snowden's political conceptions were much less intractably hostile to capitalism than appeared on the surface. The economic policies with which he became associated were very close in some important respects to the Gladstonian doctrines of the most orthodox Liberal, and the differences separating Labour from the Liberals were paradoxically blurred by someone who regarded himself as belonging to the socialist wing of the new party. This should not be misunderstood, however. When Snowden became Chancellor of the Exchequer in the Labour governments of the 1920s, the economic orthodoxy of his thinking was indicated by Churchill's biting prose —

We must imagine with what joy Mr. Snowden was welcomed at the Treasury by the permanent officials . . . Here was the High Priest entering the Sanctuary. The Treasury mind and the Snowden mind embraced each other with the fervour of two long-separated lizards .[22]

This image was not really accurate because Snowden's economic orthodoxy, unlike that of the Treasury, laid claim to a socialist basis. Snowden was particularly firm in his belief that capitalism was an immoral system based on privilege and injustice, and that political economy was merely a justification for such a system. In *The Christ That Is To Be*, he wrote, 'We care not a rap about your political economy. It is enough for us to know that the many who toil hard and long are in poverty, and the few never work at all'.[23] The paradox cannot be explained away merely by political expediency, or a sense of awe at the Treasury mandarins. Other Ministers have been tough enough to overcome the resistance of their civil servants, and Snowden was not one to waver when faced with resistance to his views.

It was the very nature of his socialist outlook which lent itself to the orthodox economics of the Treasury. Snowden conceived his socialism in moral rather than economic terms. He was profoundly opposed to the individualist basis of Liberal economics, as presented by nineteenth century free traders like Richard Cobden and John Bright. Politics and economics, for Snowden, were not separate from religion and ethics, but an expression of moral truths. Indeed, a healthy religious life was impossible under a corrupt political or a selfish economic system. Individualist competition was particularly immoral — 'it is not in harmony with the essential conditions of a healthy social life. Unhealthy industrial and social conditions spring from the want of harmony and co-operation between things which are essentially and vitally connected'.[24] Such a system had bred the idle rich, a leisured and parasitic class who took no part in creating the wealth which they enjoyed. The anarchical system of competition on which they fed had placed the community at the mercy of cartels and combines, and the unearned rent of this class of usurers was merely the other side of a coin which contained overcrowding, slums, drunkenness and pauperism.

However, Snowden believed that a moral economic system of co-operation was growing within the old society. Production had grown so interdependent that there would no longer be an individual operation for individual use in factory and commercial life, but a social operation for the use of all. This growing co-operative system was making nonsense of the structure of distribution in capitalist society, exposing for all to see the antagonism between the industrious classes and the usurers who lived off unearned rent. Snowden made it clear that it was the usurer, not the private employer, who was the parasitic enemy. Like the Fabians (and Hodgskin) he distinguished between the earned and the unearned elements in the capitalist's income. While the capitalist was wrong to take unearned income in his role as a usurer, he was an essential aspect of production in his role as a manager – 'Many landlords and many capitalists act as the directors of agriculture or commerce, and in so far as this work is useful, the remuneration they take is not rent or profit, but salary'.[25]

It was a highly muted form of opposition to capitalism which was proposed by Snowden. The transfer of ownership from the rentier class to the State was a purely nominal change in his conception, leaving the basic structure and organsiation or production intact. Indeed, Snowden was explicit in leaving a role for capitalists who happened to have technical knowledge and managerial ability. Such efficient capitalists would be allowed to continue their firms as long as they recognised and maintained decent living standards for their employees. Snowden's acceptance of a mixed rather than a socialised economy was evident from his argument that

> it would be unwise on the part of the community to deprive private enterprise of the opportunity of proving its superiority over nationalisation. But private enterprise could not be permitted to exist unless it conformed to the standard of wages, hours, and conditions prevailing under public employment.[26]

It was not the capitalist nature of production, but its results of low wages and exploitative working conditions, which was criticised by Snowden. Along with the Fabians, Snowden accepted the system of production as natural and eternal.

It was the system of distribution which was at fault, and Snowden sought to correct this through a policy of taxation of unearned wealth. He rejected the Gladstonian Liberal idea of taxation as an evil burden on the individual to be reduced to a bare minimum. On the contrary, taxation had a special usefulness in helping to secure some of the wealth accrued by the monopolist in order to use it for the community. The decadent gains of such usurers could be disgorged by the State through a strict fiscal policy, redistributing the wealth from the parasites to the industrious classes via a State committed to social reform. Such a redistribution would revitalise the economy, overcoming the deficient demand of the workforce and leading to more production through the increased consumption of the people.

Such political and economic thinking had little in common with orthodox Gladstonian political economy, owing much more to the Fabian outlook than any concept of *laissez-faire*. Snowden's conception of socialism led him to oppose strikes as an example of the immoral competitive spirit. Since the system of distribution was governed by competition, then obviously there was an inevitable conflict between capital and labour over the share of industry's product. However, this industrial strife was an example of the worst kind of warfare – civil war – in which there were no victors, merely the vanquished. This was fatal to industrial progress, keeping alive a sectional outlook which blinded the employer and the worker to their common interests in industrial progress. In pamphlets like *The Living Wage* (1912) and *Socialism and Syndicalism* (1913), Snowden opposed the current strike movement as an expression of a competitive spirit alien to socialism.

It was a belief which continued to be held by Snowden in the post-war period, dictating his policies as Chancellor. He called for the labour movement to be more far-sighted in its methods, making the existing system more efficient and productive, and devising plans by which the worker could get a just reward for his work. He argued for Wages Boards and Industrial Courts to establish a rational and regular system of wage regulation (as was consistent with his acceptance of the existing system of production), and as Chancellor claimed in his 1924 Budget speech that his mildly expansionary measures were 'vindictive against no class and no interest'.[27] His policies, far from springing from the economic orthodoxy of the Treasury, sprang from his own view of socialism as the co-operative aspect of the present society. In Snowden's view, the gradual redistribution of wealth, regulated by the popular support for a socialist government, would extend the spirit of co-operation. This spirit

> will permeate everybody from the most responsible manager to the humblest worker, and each will feel that in doing his best he is not only contributing to the common good, but is promoting his own personal interests.[28]

In this way, Showden's conception of socialism converged with the orthodox Liberal view in the collaboration of capital and labour in the national economic interest. His socialism really had very little to do with the labourism of Keir Hardie.

The lack of a parliamentary majority, forcing Labour to rely on the Liberals, was to prevent Snowden from carrying out his belief in even a mild redistribution of wealth. The monetarist orthodoxy of his economic policies, with devastating consequences for working-class living standards, should not lead to misunderstandings about his political and economic thought. They were a right-wing interpretation of British socialism, not at all akin with Gladstonian Liberalism. He merely lacked any immediate programme to counter the cyclical effects of capitalist slump, forcing him to carry out the policies dictated by the logic of an economic system in crisis. Socialism was postponed until the capitalist crisis had sorted itself out. As he told the Commons in February 1931,

> I have been in active political life for forty years, and my only object has been to improve the lot of the toiling millions. That is still my aim and object, and, if I ask for some temporary suspensions, some temporary sacrifices, it is because that is necessary to make future progress possible.[29]

The failure of his policies was a failure of his right-wing interpretation of British socialism as much as one of orthodox political economy.

Macdonald

It was Ramsay Macdonald who amplified the right-wing interpretation of British socialism in Labour's *political* thinking, as Snowden had done in its *economic* approach. Macdonald was a leading member of the ILP, and then the Labour Party, because of his socialist ideas rather than any sympathy for trade unionism. Where Hardie's socialism had a strong ground in the labourism of the trade union movement, Macdonald attempted to link his socialism to the more advanced strands of Liberal thinking at the turn of the century. His charismatic personality and administrative ability pushed him to the foremost place in British politics, becoming the country's first Labour Prime Minister. However, his agreement to form a coalition with the Conservatives and Liberals in 1931 led to his expulsion from Labour's ranks, and he was to become a pariah for the party he helped to create, a prime example of class collaboration and treachery. The reasons for his success, and his ultimate infidelity, can be traced to the political conception of socialism which Macdonald brought to bear on the problems of the day.

James Ramsay Macdonald (1866-1937) was, like Hardie, an illegitimate child, born to a Scottish fisherwoman in Lossiemouth. He educated himself to a competent standard and, driven by the type of burning ambition often felt by people whose youth had been spent in poverty, he moved to Bristol at the age of 19. After a brief flirtation with the SDF — a flirtation from which he emerged with a feeling of revulsion against their dogmatic Marxism — Macdonald became a private secretary to a Liberal MP, joining the Fabians shortly afterwards. He was ambivalent on the Fabian notion of 'permeating' the Liberal Party, but after being rejected by the local Liberal Party as their candidate at Southampton, he became convinced that the Liberals were dissociating themselves from the advancing socialist and Labour movement. He joined the ILP in July 1894, declaring that

the decision of the Southampton Liberal Council was but part of a national policy which is compelling what was once the advanced wing of Liberalism to sever itself from an old alliance and form itself into an independent Labour party.[30]

His marriage to the wealthy Margaret Gladstone in 1896 enabled him to work as a journalist while maintaining a comfortable financial position, and he threw all his energies into the ILP, moving onto its National Council in 1898.

When the LRC was set up in 1900, Macdonald took the crucial post of secretary. In this position, he established himself as the leading administrator of the party, consuming his great energy in the wearing work of building a new party. His Liberal predilections, which had never left him, and the political realities of the new party's weakness, pushed him to making a secret electoral pact with the Liberal Chief

Whip, Herbert Gladstone, in 1903. This pact, known only to Hardie and himself, created the conditions for the return of 29 Labour MPs in 1906. Only five of the new MPs were returned against Liberal opposition, and Macdonald himself entered the Commons in tandem with a Liberal at Leicester. He rapidly became associated with the moderate image presented by Labour which came under increasing attack from the ILP Left, an image intensified after he became chairman of the parliamentary party in 1911. With Macdonald as leader, Labour seemed barely distinguishable from the Liberals, and soon began to lose electoral popularity. Nevertheless, Macdonald's opposition to the Great War in 1914, leading to his resignation as parliamentary chairman and subjection to a campaign of personal slurs, revived his image as a man of the Left. It was an image only too wide of the mark.

Unlike Hardie, whose stress on the independence of labour made him aware of the Liberals as a party of the employers, Macdonald had a much closer intellectual and political relationship with the Liberals. (Shortly after joining the ILP, he worked with Liberal collectivists such as Herbert Samuel and J.A. Hobson in the Rainbow Circle.) He went much further than most of his ILP colleagues in associating socialism with Liberalism, and in advocating friendship with the Liberals who would bring respectability and intellect to a party sorely lacking in both qualities — a far cry from Hardie's faith in the working class.

The clarity with which Macdonald expressed his theory of society gives us an insight into his political conceptions. He had much more respect for theory than Hardie, and often bewailed the philistinism of the British labour movement. The replacement of reason by blind party loyalty in Parliament, and the failure of government to recognise social problems, was an expression of the British distrust of theory. In books like *Socialism and Society* (1905), *Socialism* (1907), and *Socialism and Government* (1909) he attempted to express the relationshp between socialism and Liberalism in terms of a scientific analysis.

Evolution and Society. Marx had, of course, seen his own analysis as 'scientific', counterposing it to the utopians who merely wished to bring about socialism. However, Macdonald lumped Marx together with the utopians as trapped in a pre-Darwinian conception of society. Marx was critical and destructive in his dialectical method, whereas the new biological views stressed an evolutionary and constructive approach to society. This could be applied to society in a much more accurate manner than the revolutionary method. The class war had not destroyed

capital, but had created constructive trade unions; the working classes
had not become pauperised, but had become citizens with a stake in
society. Marx had taken the superficial clash of social forces at its face
value, whereas Macdonald pointed to the underlying progress being
achieved *within* society.

Only biology could do this, as it studied changes in physical
organisms. The organic form was not merely a physical shape, as in
plants or animals, but could be seen in social terms. Society, too, had
an organic form, in which the different relations between the organs
were co-ordinated to make a living whole which was greater than its
constituent parts. These social organs were 'connected by a living tissue
of law, of habit and custom, of economic inter-dependence of public
opinion, of political unity'[31] to create a general stability. These laws
and customs were evidence of a keen *social* self-consciousness, standing
above the thought of the individuals and classes which were the organs
constituting the social whole. To Macdonald,

> society belongs to the biological type of existence because it is no
> mere collection of separate individuals . . . but a unified and organ-
> ised system of relationshps, in which certain people and classes
> perform certain functions and others perform other functions.[32]

However, the competitive nature of capitalist society totally disrupted
the organic character of the community. Instead of the different organs
— capital, land, labour, for example — co-operating in the interests of
the whole, they preyed on one another to the detriment of the whole.
The wealth of the nation was controlled by private interests, with the
result that two civilisations were growing side by side — 'the civilisation
of the idle or uselessly employed rich, and the civilisation of the industrial poor'.[33] The physical and moral conditions of the poor degenerated under the impact of periodic unemployment and chronic
insecurity, while the capitalist suffered as the intense competition and
threat of business failure led him to spending his life in business rather
than leisure. Conflict, rather than co-operation, between the different
social organs, or functions, became the norm.

Macdonald counterposed the organic community of socialism to the
present state of affairs, a community where the different functions
would be co-ordinated and regulated in the interests of the whole. In
such a community, true social individuality would flourish as each
person would be happily integrated in the advanced whole and would
work for the whole. Just as in biology the individual cell has both a

function *and* an individual existence through the totality, so in society the different classes and people would have a social function *and* an individual part to play in the whole. In the gradual process of social evolution by which the new organic phase was developing, conflicts between different functions like capital and labour did occur. However, 'the predominant or vital fact is not that conflict, but rather the steady subordination of all functional and sectional interests to the living needs of the whole community'.[34] The conflicts and contests would gradually die out as the *cause* of the conflicts — the selfish and sectional nature of the different functions — were removed by the co-ordination of the State.

It was the establishment of political democracy which provided the foundations for the new phase of social evolution, according to Macdonald. With the extension of the franchise and the increasing power of the House of Commons, the State could no longer be taken as an authority external to the community, imposing its laws on unwilling subjects. It had become a part of the community, expressing the will of the social organism and demanding the obedience of its constituent parts.

> The democratic State is an organisation of the people, democratic government is self-government, democratic law is an expression of the will of the people who have to obey the law — not perhaps the will of every individual, but the communal will voicing the need of all classes in their relation to the community.[35]

As such, the State was an instrument capable of responding to the public will in the form of Parliament. It was an extension of his biological analogy — 'Parliament is a laboratory; its legislative experiments must be undertaken in precisely the same scientific frame of mind as those of the chemist or the physicist'.[36]

Labour and Liberalism. His conception of society as an organism composed of different social classes performing different functions gave him a very different outlook to the labour movement, and to labourism, than that held by Keir Hardie. To Macdonald, labour constituted merely one element in a social whole. It was a functional part which was important only in terms of the whole community, headed by the State. Therefore, capital was as important as labour, and the consumer was just as much a part of the community as the producer. In capitalism, labour had to look out for itself, so that its strikes were not to be condemned outside their context of a society in which each function and group preyed on the other. A socialistic party, to Macdonald, must therefore base itself and its appeals to the *community*, rather than to the working class as a class. Its practical policy must be based,

> not on functions [like labour], but on the complete civic unity to which functions are only contributory, and upon the citizen, of whom the worker is only a differentiated and specialised aspect . . . The community idea must be the dominant note: the thought must be of the co-operation of citizens, not of workmen nor of consumers .[37]

It was a conception which placed Macdonald on the right wing of the Labour Party, more akin to the Liberals than to labourists like Hardie. The working class suffered materially at the hands of the capitalists, but material suffering was not all. The capitalists also suffered, developing a selfish and unsentimental attitude to life. Macdonald's socialism was more to do with a sense of social community rather than class unity — 'Socialism marks the growth of society, not the growth of a class. The consciousness which it seeks to quicken is not one of economic class solidarity, but one of . . . growth towards organic wholeness'.[38]

It was a conception which led him to reject the partisan labour theory of value, held to by Hodgskin and Marx in their different ways. For Macdonald, the quashing of the dogmas of this working class theory would not hurt socialism at all. Of course, the worker's service in capitalism carried an inadequate payment — 'poverty rather than property is the reward of labour today'.[39] The labourer's whole life was spent in servitude to capitalists, who absorbed and used up his energies before casting him on the scrapheap of retirement. However, this was due to the competitive nature of a de-regulated society, rather than to class exploitation, as held by a labour theory of value. It would be ended by bringing capital and labour together in a moral partnership. Thus, it was perfectly logical for Macdonald to argue that 'capital creates values too . . . Therefore, labour's quarrel with capitalism is not in the sphere of production, but in that of distribution'.[40] Capital and labour were antagonists in the distribution of wealth, but in producing wealth they were necessary partners. In Macdonald's conception of socialism, their partnership would be affirmed as their different functions were co-ordinated.

Macdonald's belief that 'there must be co-operation and not conflict between labour and capital',[41] led to his hostility to the strike and
other manifestations of class conflict. Unlike Snowden, Macdonald
did not reject strikes out of hand; he held them to be a rational action
of the trade unions in their defence of living standards. However,
unlike Hardie, Macdonald was unsympathetic to strikes. They expressed
an instinctive, rather than a rational, aspect of the labour movement,
encouraging resentment towards good employers as well as bad. Labour
had to look to Parliament, not to its own resources, if it was to achieve
its aims. He argued that the trade union conflict should be turned into
a movement towards organic regulation and co-ordination — 'the field
upon which it [the union conflict] has to be fought out is the State,
not the workshop; the weapon is to be the ballot box and the Act of
Parliament, not collective bargaining'.[42]

Macdonald saw the Labour Party in socialist terms, then, but it was
a socialism which was much more loosely connected with the labour
movement than that held by Hardie and other Labour politicians.
Labour representation was the awakening of the submerged elements
of society, but its intention was to raise the worker to be a full citizen
just as Macdonald himself had fought his way out of poverty to become
a respected member of the community. In an important article in the
New Liberal Review in September 1903, he expressed his distinctive
attitude to his party —

> If the new Labour movement were simply an attempt of Trade
> Unionists to use their political power for purely sectional ends . . .
> it would be a menace to all the qualities that mark public life with
> distinction and honour . . . Trade Unionism in politics must identify
> itself with something higher and wider than Trade Union industrial
> demands. It must set those demands into a system of national well-
> being; the wage earner must become the citizen; the Union must
> become the guardian of economic justice.[43]

Labour politics was a national, not a class, question. That Labour's
interests should ever clash with the interests of the nation was incomprehensible to Macdonald.

His understanding of Labour's needs led Macdonald to a much more
conciliatory attitude to the Liberal Party than that of Hardie and the
ILP Left. He believed that the Liberals had exhausted their role in the
scheme of social evolution, with the battle for universal suffrage and
political democracy being virtually won. They had disrupted the

organic relationships of feudal society without replacing them with new organic relationships. Their life was not coming to an end, just as life came to an end in the vegetable and animal kingdoms. However, 'like the cell which is about to divide and create a new organism', new ideas were growing in the Liberal Party, more akin to socialism than to Gladstonian Liberalism. A new epoch was being born in the remnants of the old — 'Socialism, the stage which follows Liberalism, retains everything of permanent value that was in Liberalism, by virtue of its being the hereditary heir of Liberalism'.[44] Thus, vital principles of Liberalism such as free trade and national self-determination were taken up much more resolutely by the Labour Party, while the Liberal party faltered.

Macdonald's conception of socialism was *internally* coherent. His evolutionary method, based on current conceptions of biology, was in logical terms as sound as the revolutionary method of Marx, and it had a far greater rigour than the loose formulations of Keir Hardie. However, its ability to fit the external reality of British politics was far more questionable. In one sense, it had a clear grasp of the solidity of British political and social institutions. Macdonald's belief that socialists should work within these institutions rather than against them had far more political future than the hostility demonstrated by the SDF and other left-wing groups of the time. These institutions — Parliament, the trade unions, the family — commanded the support and obedience of all social classes in the country, and to go against them would isolate the socialist movement to a sectarian impotence.

However, in another sense, the support given to these institutions ran into political dilemmas which were to prove fatal to Macdonald's aspirations. He saw no contradiction between the national interest and the interests of the working class, a notion which logically led to the view that the workers' movement should bear the burdens of national crisis as well as share in the wealth of national prosperity. Such a view ran counter to the aspirations of the labour movement, which had set up a party to *protect* its interests, even if those interests were, in Macdonald's terms, merely sectional. As his own view of socialism was not a class but a *national* conception, he was led into constant attempts to collaborate with other parties representing other sections of the national organism. In the debate on the Address in 1929, when he headed a minority Labour government, he asked the opposing parties to join Labour to 'consider ourselves more as a Council of State and less as arrayed regiments facing each other in battle'.[45] When he dumped the Labour government in 1931, he was genuinely hurt when other

Labour politicians responded to his view of the national interest in a hostile 'sectional' manner. As his biographer has noted, 'later Labour suggestions that he was glad to break with the party and no longer cared what it thought of him do not fit the facts'.[46]

Macdonald's fatal dilemma was to hold a classless view of socialism in a class society. The Labour Party fundamentally represented one class in that society (though it continually sought to appeal to the middle classes to join it), and Macdonald could not accept the consequences of this. His socialism had much more in common with the advanced strains of Liberalism than it had with the labourism of other leaders such as Keir Hardie and Arthur Henderson. It was the absence of labourism in Macdonald's political thinking which blurred the distinctions between Labour and the Liberals, and which eventually led to his decision to break with the party he had nurtured and led to national respectability.

The Test of War

The export of capital, which characterised British capitalism in these years, tied Britain more closely into the world economy, and into the division of the world between a few capitalist nations which had taken place by the turn of the century. The agrarian economies of Africa, Asia, and Latin America were subordinated economically to the major industrial powers. On the basis of this economic division of the world between the major capitalist powers, a system of political and military alliances developed from which Britain initially held aloof before naval and colonial rivalry with Germany forced her into the *entente* with France. The capitalist world was being impelled into a major war by a dynamic which seemed to evade the conscious control of its politicians. War, and imperialism, were becoming major questions confronting the British labour movement, forcing it to clarify its conceptions of class and national loyalties.

Upon the outbreak of war in Europe in August 1914, the Second International collapsed under the pressure of calls for national unity. The most evident symptom of this collapse was the support given by the German Social Democrats, the strongest party of the International, to the Kaiser's demand for war credits. Throughout Europe, the Socialist and Labour parties were each rushing to sanction their own national governments, leaving numerous pacifist and revolutionary minorities dazed by the ruin of their illusions in workers' internationalism.

The war intensified the divisions between the trade unionist and the socialist wings of the Labour Party. The parliamentary party and the unions, together with the Fabians, generally supported the government, while the bulk of the ILP opposed the war. However, despite the strains on the labour alliance, the Labour Party avoided the deep divisions which split the European socialist movement apart. Indeed, Labour's survival as a united party through the tribulations of war was eloquent testimony to the essential unity of British socialism as an ideology covering Right and Left.

This unity of British socialism was not initially apparent. The war divided the Labour Party between those who were more interested in national defence and those who were more interested in national change. On the Right, parliamentary and union leaders of the labour movement went on the recruiting platform, urging workers to serve the national and imperial interest, whether in the charnel-house of the Western Front or in the streets of Dublin. At home, these Labour and union leaders agreed to the suspension of trade union rights, including strike action, for the duration of the war.

On the Left, the ILP took a diametrically opposed approach, issuing a Manifesto on International Socialism a week after the war's outbreak, declaring its faith in international socialism. The Labour Marxists in the ILP, like James Maxton, refused to fight for capitalism; ethical socialists and Christian pacifists, like Alfred Salter, rejected violence as immoral; while ILP leaders like Ramsay Macdonald and Philip Snowden saw the war as an example of militarism and secret diplomacy.

However, the differences between Right and Left proved ultimately less important than their similarities. These similarities were indicated by Keir Hardie. Hardie, who had led mass anti-war rallies in the days leading up to the outbreak of war, was a broken man when he realised the depth of pro-war sentiment in the British labour movement. He refused to support the war, but he refused to oppose it, too. His sympathies remained with the *British* working class, even if this meant ignoring the interests of the international workers' movement. In an article in the *Merthyr Pioneer* in August 1914, he wrote,

A nation at war must be united, especially when its existence is at stake. With the boom of the enemy's guns within earshot, the lads who have gone forth to fight their country's battles must not be disheartened by any discordant notes at home .[47]

Hardie's sentiments indicate the factors unifying Left and Right in the British labour movement even though they were not in harmony with the ILP's opposition to the war.

The lynchpin of British socialism and of labourism was the acceptance of a national framework within which the labour movement would work. Both Left and Right in the Labour Party held steadfast to the belief that the British state, parliamentary and representative, could be used to change British society. The class nature of British society was admitted by all, as was the need to change the balance of class power towards the working class. The class tensions in British society were to be resolved by a peaceful and gradual change which would respect British institutions while emptying them of their class nature. However, national change went hand-in-hand with national defence. The fact that changing a class society and defending a capitalist nation-state may be contradictory did not really occur to the founders of British socialism.

As a result British socialism did not disintegrate. The tensions between the Labour majority and the ILP never reached breaking point because both sides were too wary of the dangers of a split. From the point of view of the Left the ILP felt that its chances of winning support for the anti-war movement could only lie in the Labour Party as the political representative of the working class, and it was very careful in its propaganda and activities as a result. It concentrated its activities on issues of civil liberties through the No-Conscription Fellowship and a defence of trade union rights and conditions in wartime.

In maintaining the Labour alliance, the ILP was prevented from breaking with British socialism. Its criticisms of the war remained within an ethical and a radical democratic form. Clifford Allen, a later Chairman of the ILP, spoke at the 1915 Conference in the nostalgic terms of ethical socialism —

> We as Socialists are concerned primarily with the sanctity of human life. When we are concerned about improved wages and better facilities for education, it is not merely the material things with which we are concerned, but the spiritual things. Our object is to make life expensive and valuable; war makes it cheap and of no account. As Socialists we must apply to foreign and international affairs the same philosophy as guides us in our social legislation.[48]

On the Right, the pro-war majority still recognised the need for labour to organise, politically and industrially, independently of the employers; they merely saw the co-operation of Labour in the war effort, including participation in the Coalition government, as a temporary suspension of independence. It was rather like the tactics of a trade union, which had to recognise both co-operation and conflict with the employer in collective bargaining. This was put succinctly by G.J. Wardle, the Chairman of the 1917 Labour Party conference: Labour

> has fought where instinct and reason taught it fighting was essential; it has bargained where it saw a reasonable chance of success; it has entered into partnership where political sagacity and national safety seemed alike to call for that method. It still remains a separate party. Partnerships can be dissolved, arguments can be revived, fighting can be resumed, each in its proper place and each at its proper time.[49]

Indeed, the Labour Party emerged from the war finally agreed on the platform of British socialism for which Hardie and the ILP had been assiduously working for over 20 years. This platform included the foreign policy demands of the one significant theoretical contribution to British socialism made during the war. These demands for a democratic peace and a League of Nations found their theoretical grounding in the anti-war writings of H.N. Brailsford, but they were gradually accepted by Right and Left.

Brailsford

H.N. Brailsford (1873-1958) had been born into a middle-class family of Yorkshire Methodists. After a university education at Glasgow, his youthful rebellion against the Methodism and Liberalism of his parents had led him to the ILP, which he joined in 1907. Influenced by the anti-imperialist writings of J.A. Hobson, he wrote articles on foreign and imperial affairs for various journals. His *War of Steel and Gold* (1914) became a textbook for many on the Left, influencing Macdonald, Snowden (and President Wilson) in their attempts to formulate a new foreign policy.

Brailsford argued that the insecurities and strategic shufflings for power and influence in pre-war Europe were merely symptoms of a much deeper economic malaise. The growing crisis was not really over the personal vanity of the Kaiser or national feelings of inferiority, but the growing power of financial capitalists. The panics and fears

are the psychological irrelevancies of the process. The tangible realities at stake are measurable, and they turn out to be nothing but
certain opportunities for expansion valued by the restless finance of
one power or another.[50]

The magnates of high finance, pursuing their selfish goals of profit
through usury, were the real reason why workers were being mobilised
to fight one another. Diplomacy was no longer in the hands of the old
ruling order, but had become the means whereby these magnates fought
over the share-out of the world. Brailsford drew a picture of

the vast aggregations of modern capital in oil trusts, steel trusts,
and money trusts . . . Wherever rival combinations of capital are
competing, as British and American oil companies compete in
Central America, the reaction will be felt in the relations of their
governments. The struggle for a balance of power is in effect a
struggle to map out these exclusive areas of financial penetration.[51]

It was a picture very similar to the one drawn by Lenin in his *Imperialism* (1916). Like Lenin, Brailsford pointed to the economic nature of
the war, specifically the new power of finance capital. Moreover Brailsford, like Lenin, pointed to the cause of the new imperialism in the
export of capital as a means of escaping a crisis of falling profitability
and overproduction. Brailsford argued that 'the fundamental fact is
the rapid accumulation of surplus capital. It grows in the hands of trust
magnates, bankers and ground landlords more rapidly than the demand
for it at home'.[52] The resulting slump had been avoided by imperialism,
but the dangers of war had been intensified.

However, unlike Lenin, Brailsford did not call for the defeat of his
own imperialist government. Instead, he joined the Union for Democratic
Control, arguing that only an end to secret diplomacy and a democratic
control of foreign policy could avoid such wars. To Brailsford, the problem for men who have reached a humane vision of international relations
is to bring about some organic change in the machinery which governs the
action of the Powers abroad. A system of free trade, and a European
League to carry on foreign policy openly and pacifically, were Brailsford's
prescriptions for an international outlook suitable to British socialism.
His arguments became the basis for a foreign policy agreed to by Left
and Right, as demonstrated by their adoption in a joint Labour-TUC
statement of war aims in December 1917, drafted by Macdonald. This
statement was almost indistinguishable from the programme which the

UDC had been preaching since the beginning of the war. It was a foreign policy well suited to the ethical aspects of British socialism.

The divergence of political conclusions between Brailsford and Lenin indicates the reason why Right and Left in the Labour Party maintained their precarious unity. It is a signal of the profound differences separating the Left of British socialism from revolutionary Marxism in their economic analysis.

For Lenin, imperialism was not a policy carried on by individual capitalists, to be overcome by a different policy of regulating these capitalists. It was a particular phase of capital accumulation, whereby the crisis of profitability temporarily resolved by the export of capital reasserted itself in a struggle over the world's resources and territory. This struggle was inevitable because it was due to capital rather than merely capitalists. Brailsford, however, held that imperialism was a militarist policy carried on for the benefit of armaments manufacturers and other capitalists. There was nothing inevitable about it, and it could be cured by the existing State — this underlined 'the importance of securing first of all that diplomacy shall control finance, and secondly that public opinion shall control diplomacy'.[53]

Where Lenin saw war as the only means whereby capital's tensions could ultimately express themselves, Brailsford took up the cry of Hobson that crisis and war could be avoided by redistribution of wealth —

Had a little more of the profits of a trade 'boom' gone to labour, and a little less to capital, it is manifest that labour would have had more money to spend, and the new surplus capital . . . might have been employed in meeting this new demand.[54]

The belief that capitalists, rather than capital, were to blame for the fighting, entailing as it did the call for redistribution of wealth and a new morality in foreign policy, helped to cement the new consensus which emerged between Right and Left at the end of the war.

The war had transformed British society, forcing the State to organise the country on the lines of a wartime collectivism which had delighted the Fabians. The disintegration of the Liberal Party between the supporters of Asquith and of Lloyd George, together with the entry of Labour ministers into a coalition government, had pushed the Labour Party into the forefront of British politics. Its status as a small pre-war pressure group had been transformed by the end of the war into the dizzy position of a potential government. To meet its changed role, the Labour Party adopted a new constitution in February 1918, by which it became a centralised party with individual membership through constituency parties. A socialist philosophy was accepted as the aim of the party, while the unions were given even greater power over the National Executive Committee.

Together with *Labour and the New Social Order* the 1918 Constitution linked labourism and British socialism as complementary and interdependent sets of ideas. It was fitting that it should mainly be the work of the Fabian leader, Sidney Webb, leading Miliband to describe the policy proposals as 'a Fabian blueprint for a more advanced, more regulated form of capitalism'.[55] It expressed the advance of wartime collectivism, which was lauded by the Fabians as a major advance towards State socialism. Labour's calls in 1918 for a capital levy on the idle rich, an extended role for public ownership, and a democratic peace without annexations appealed to the Left as much as to the Right.

In 1918, the ideas of British socialism — emerging for over three decades in the forms of Labour Marxism, Fabianism and ethical socialism — were finally cohered into an integral whole. They were a *supplement*, not a replacement, for the labourism of the trade union movement, whose dominance was now assured in its control of the Conference and the NEC.

Notes

1. *Labour Leader*, 19 September 1904.
2. *Labour Leader* April 1893.
3. Keir Hardie, *From Serfdom to Socialism* (London, 1907), p. 35.
4. Ibid., p. 44.
5. Ibid., p. 24.
6. Ibid., p. 79.
7. Ibid., p. 77-8.
8. *Labour Leader*, January 1894.
9. Hardie, *Labour Politics* (London, 1903), p. 8.
10. Hardie, *My Confession of Faith in the Labour Alliance* (London, 1909), p. 5.
11. Ibid., p. 6.
12. Ibid., p. 12.
13. Quoted in Frank Johnson, *Keir Hardie's Socialism* (London, 1922), p. 9.
14. Quoted in Ibid., p. 11.
15. Hardie, *My Confession*, p. 3.
16. Isabella Ford, *Women and Socialism* (London, 1904), p. 8.
17. Hardie, *From Serfdom to Socialism*, p. 63.
18. Ibid., pp. 68-9.

19. *Labour Leader*, 26 January 1901.

20. *Labour Leader* 27 January 1900.

21. Hardie, *India: Impressions and Suggestions* (London, 1909), pp. 78-9.

22. Winston Churchill, *Great Contemporaries* (London, 1937), p. 293.

23. Philip Snowden, *The Christ That Is To Be* (London, 1903), p. 10.

24. Snowden, *The Economic Case for Socialism* (London, 1921), p. 11.

25. Snowden, *Labour and the New World* (London, 1921), p. 10.

26. Ibid., p. 112.

27. *Hansard* (1924), vol. 172, col. 1610.

28. Snowden, *The Way to Industrial Peace* (London, 1927), p. 13.

29. *Hansard* (1930-1), vol. 248, col. 448.

30. Macdonald to Crisp, 16 July 1894, quoted in David Marquand, *Ramsay Macdonald* (Jonathan Cape, 1977), p. 36.

31. Macdonald, *Socialism and Society* (London, 1905), p. 29

32. Ibid., p. 31.

33. Ibid., p. 2.

34. Ibid., p. 61.

35. Ibid., p. 70.

36. Ibid., p. xx.

37. Macdonald, *Parliament and Democracy* (London, 1920), pp. 35, 71.

38. Macdonald, *Socialism and Society*, p. 127.

39. Macdonald, *Socialism* (London, 1907), p. 12.

40. Ibid., p. 55.

41. Macdonald, *Socialism: Critical and Constructive* (London, 1921), p. 175.

42. Macdonald, *The Social Unrest: Its Cause and Solution* (London, 1913), p. 104.

43. Quoted in Marquand, *Ramsay Macdonald*, pp. 83-4.

44. Macdonald, *Socialism and Society*, pp. 159, 164.

45. *Hansard* (1929-30), vol. 229, col. 65.

46. Marquand, *Ramsay Macdonald*, p. 641.

47. Quoted in Carl F. Brand, *British Labour's Rise to Power* (California, 1941), p. 69.

48. I.L.P., *Annual Conference Report* 1915, pp. 109-10.

49. Labour Party, *Annual Conference Report* 1917, p. 82.

50. H.N. Brailsford, *The War of Steel and Gold* (London, 1915 ed.), p. 62.

51. Ibid., p. 63.

52. Ibid., p. 80.

53. Ibid., p. 231.

54. Ibid., p. 80.

55. Ralph Miliband, *Parliamentary Socialism* (Merlin, 1972 ed.), p. 62.

4   R.H. TAWNEY AND THE PHILOSOPHY OF BRITISH SOCIALISM

With the adoption of a new constitution in 1918, the Labour Party had an official ideology as well as a new organisational structure. The ideology may have been extremely vague — a commitment to common ownership was meant to mean all things to all people — but in the final analysis the old ILP strategy had proved successful. The Labour Party was now committed to socialism.

The formation of British socialism had been a long process, beginning before the Labour Party was itself born. The Labour Marxists had asserted the need of the trade union movement to break politically from the class enemy; the Fabians had provided an intellectual answer to the revolutionary implications of Marx's thinking, asserting the possibility of peaceful transformation; and the ethical socialists had provided a libertarian, semi-Christian morality as a guiding light for the new faith. British socialism had finally emerged in the first decades of the present century, hammered into shape in politics and organisation by Hardie, Snowden and Macdonald, its contours bounded by the labourist assumptions of a trade union movement which was the new party's financial lifeblood.

It was to be R.H. Tawney who was to provide a *philosophy* for British socialism, providing its various strands with a rational and coherent vision of society. His contribution stamped him as one of the major British political thinkers of our century. It was powerful enough for both Shirley Williams and Tony Benn to claim Tawney as their intellectual ancestor. It is little wonder that the exact nature of his contribution to British socialism should be so controversial.[1] His political stance shifted radically over time — from an endorsement of Guild socialism in 1921 through his authorship of the gradualist *Labour and the Nation* (1928) and his attack on gradualism in the 1930s to his endorsement of revisionism in the 1950s[2] — so that he cannot be easily categorised into any one political stream.

However, these different political stances were in a fundamental sense superficial. Tawney's importance lies in his ability to propose a coherent socialist philosophy which transcends any particular political situation. In this sense, his mature political thought never *really* changed. His attack on gradualism in the 1930s was always radically

distinct from the near-Marxism of Laski and Cripps[3] — a mere change
of tactics to bring his socialist philosophy of fellowship into practice
much more effectively — and could be dropped as easily as his earlier
advocacy of Guild socialism and gradualism. As Tawney himself wrote,
in relation to the British labour movement, 'the essence of a movement
is not to be understood merely by an analysis of its constitution and
programme . . . [but] of what, for lack of a better phrase, I will call its
social philosophy'.[4] It was to be this philosophy for which British
socialism was to owe Tawney such a debt.

Tawney

R.H. Tawney (1880-1962) was born into an upper middle-class family in
imperial India, and was educated at Rugby and Oxford. Influenced by
the social Christianity of William Booth, he went to Toynbee Hall after
his graduation in 1903, where he worked among the poor of East
London. His sense of outrage at the poverty and homelessness around
him turned him from orthodox evangelicalism to socialism, and he soon
joined the Fabians and the ILP. He became particularly identified with
the Workers Educational Association (WEA), committing himself to
teaching those who had been long rejected and forgotten by the British
educational system. He sought to give the WEA a more political tinge,
and came to see education as being the essential element in bringing
about a socialist society.

On the outbreak of war in 1914, Tawney enlisted in the army, consciously rejecting both pacifism and jingoism. He fought because he
identified Prussia with tyranny, and Britain — even the socially blighted
and divided Britain which he had come to recognise — with democracy.
His experience of the full horrors of the battle of the Somme, in which
he was wounded, was to be brilliantly described in his essay 'The
Attack',[5] but did not shake his commitment to his nation. He was
one of those who wrote an appeal to strikers at home not to damage
the national cause as symbolised by the fighting soldier in the trenches,
and constantly stressed the need of all classes to subordinate their old
prejudices in the interests of the war effort.

After the war, Tawney was one of Labour's representatives on the
Sankey Commission on the mines in 1919, where he made an unheeded
call for nationalisation as the solution to the troubles of the coal industry. Thereafter, despite a deep interest in the agrarian situation in
China and his continued commitment to the cause of working-class

education, Tawney's main work was academic. As an economic historian, he wrote the much praised *Religion and the Rise of Capitalism* (1926), where he bemoaned the division between commerce and social morality brought about under the Reformation, leading as it did to the subordination of Christian teaching to the pursuit of material wealth. To Tawney, 'compromise is as impossible between the Church of Christ and the idolatry of wealth, which is the practical religion of capitalist societies, as it was between the Church and State idolatry of the Roman Empire'.[6]

It was a moral philosophy which he had painfully evolved just before the Great War, in his diaries.[7] Here, he expressed his horror at the vulgar materialism and insensitivity towards humanity which characterised capitalist society. He rejected the crude belief that the abolition of poverty would make men any happier, and focused on moral justice rather than the mere amount of wealth as the aim of socialism. To Tawney, socialism was merely the social expression of a Christian morality. He wrote that

in order to believe in human equality, it is necessary to believe in God. It is only when one contemplates the infinitely great that human differences appear so infinitely small as to be negligeable [sic] . . . What is wrong with the modern world is that having ceased to believe in the greatness of God, and therefore the infinite smallness (or greatness − the same thing!) of *man*, it has to invent or emphasise distinctions between men .[8]

It is not that Tawney was unaware of the terrors of the material world and the deprivation caused by the absence of wealth − far from it − but he was convinced that such terrors were made by men who had forgotten God.

It was this moral philosophy which received full expression in his widely acclaimed book, *The Acquisitive Society* (1921). Tawney was particularly influenced by Guild socialism at this point, but this was merely a convenient form in which the substance of his moral philosophy could be expressed. He saw poverty as a mere symptom and consequence of the much more profound disorder in our social values.

Tawney traced this disorder to the formation of capitalism, when there was an emphasis on individual rights without any reference to the function played in society by the individual. This emphasis on rights, abstracted from any social purpose, was aided by the decline of organised religion. The ritual of the Church was retained, but what was familiar, and human, and lovable — what was Christian in Christianity had largely disappeared. God had been thrust into the frigid attitudes of infinite space. There was a limited monarchy in Heaven, as well as upon earth.[9]

The very keystone of society had vanished, with the consequence that the eighteenth century liberals brought about a new set of material privileges, hidden behind their abstract categories of property and individual rights. They created a conflict between individual rights and social functions which was becoming open for all to see as private and public interests began to clash.

In capitalism, argued Tawney, the primary motive and criterion of industry was not the service of the community, but individual gain and self-interest. 'Such societies may be called Acquisitive Societies because their whole tendency and interest and preoccupation is to promote the acquisition of wealth'.[10] They invite people to use their skill and energy without any regard to fundamental principles or morality. To the strong, they give unrestrained freedom to use others as mere instruments of self-advancement; to the weak, they give the hope that one day they may be as ruthless and powerful as the strong. Moral principles and love of humanity dissolve into expedient attempts at material gain.

Under the impulse of such ideas men do not become religious or wise or artistic; for religion and wisdom and art imply the acceptance of limitations. But they become powerful and rich. They inherit the earth and change the face of nature, if they do not possess their own souls.[11]

This powerful criticism of capitalist morality becomes the philosophical basis for Tawney's acceptance of Fabian economics. The divorce of gains from service, or rewards from functions, leads to a class division between usurers who contribute nothing and the industrious who contribute all. The usurers have persuaded people that they are to be admired and applauded, as though they were the source of wealth; the labourers are regarded with contempt because their function is seen as unimportant. Wealth is the basis of esteem, and work of contempt. In this way, social life is turned from an organic community to an arena of social antagonisms.

Tawney calls instead for a 'functional' society, based on the performance of duties rather than the maintenance of rights. In giving social purpose precedence over individual gain, society must above all

rearrange its values to preach a social Christianity of duties and obligations to society, rather than a stress on rights against society. Such a
society would be based on union and co-operation, not division and
mutual antagonism. Dignity and esteem would be given to labour,
whose purpose would be to provide the material foundations for the
good, social life, while usury would be abolished.

This emphasis on dignity and Christian values, central to Tawney
long before he became a Guild socialist, remained after his Guild ideas
had fallen away. A social Christianity is the core of his social philosophy,
in whatever political guise it presented itself. It enabled him to expand
the horizons of British socialist thought, as is most spectacularly seen in
his most impressive book on political thought, *Equality* (1931).

This is a ferocious attack on the caste system in British society. The
upper classes continually denounce class struggles as damaging to
national unity and prosperity, yet they practise it all the time. They see
it as quite natural that their children are beginning a serious education,
and that employers are able to control the lives of thousands of families
by their right to dismiss workers without appeal. The enormous
inequalities in society — of incomes, security, culture, and health — are
seen as just and inevitable, not as grotesque and barbarous.

However, Tawney did not believe that equality would come about
merely through a redistribution of material wealth. He saw equality in
very different terms than those normally seen by the labour movement. He pointed out that equality did not merely mean similarity of
character or intelligence — a view Tawney regarded as obviously untenable — but also an equality of esteem and dignity based on a common
humanity. He saw a spiritual question at stake in this second, crucial
definition of equality —

> men are men, social institutions — property rights, and the organ-
> isation of industry, and the system of public health and education
> — should be planned . . . to emphasize and strengthen, not the
> class differences which divide, but the common humanity which
> unites them.[12]

Equality is not the same as identity, because differences in education,
health and background should not mean superiority or inferiority of
consideration by society.

While natural endowments differ considerably, therefore, society
must eliminate inequalities which have their source in its own organisation rather than individual differences. A society which values

equality would give a high degree of significance to such natural individual talents and qualities as exist, but it would give a low degree of significance to economic and social differences between different groups. Only a socialist society could have any sense of civilisation, because only such a society could be based on dignity. 'Where the treasure is, there will the heart be also and, if men are to respect each other for what they are, they must cease to respect each other for what they own'.[13]

When capitalism sought to strip individuals of any human dignity they possess, Tawney saw the working class as an embodiment of solidarity and social justice. He was not romantic enough to ignore the narrow concerns of material wealth which often preoccupied the labour movement, but the moral faith in a society which cares for people lay behind the questions of poverty and unemployment taken up by Labour. As a result, Tawney stressed the inequality of power in industry itself. Power was not merely political power, nor could politics be seen in isolation from the economy. In industrial societies, economic power was particularly important because of the concentration of ownership and rights in one class. Tawney called for that power to be made more equal by breaking down the rigid divisions between labour and management. The employer must recognise that

> the wage-earner is as much entitled as the property-owner to claim equitable consideration for his established expectations . . . and that workmen have precisely the same right to be satisfied that organisation is efficient, and management up to date, as management has that workmen are earning their wages.[14]

However, it was the inequality of education and health which particularly concerned Tawney. In the sphere of social services, if nowhere else, it should be possible to ignore the vulgarities of social inequality existing in all other areas of our society. To educate and care for people, we must regard them as human beings, not as employers or workers, masters or servants, rich or poor.

However, inequality was at its most criminally evident in this sphere. Ill-health, incapacity and high infant mortality rates were concentrated in working-class areas, while education suffered from the hereditary curse of the privileged public school system. Children were taught from an early age of their class background, both at home and at school, in the shape of overcrowded classes, lack of facilities, restricted housing space, and impoverished medical care. An obsolete social tradition pampered a few children and deprived the rest. Indeed, to Tawney, the grotesque and vicious system of educational privilege and segregation 'does more than any other single cause, except capitalism itself, to perpetuate the division of the nation into classes of which one is almost unintelligible to the other'.[15]

The remedy, he argued, lay in greater collective action to end the social divisions in health and education. A state hospital service, greater care for the expectant mother, increased hospital facilities and the free medical treatment of children were among a series of social reforms proposed by Tawney as immediate measures to improve the health of the nation. In terms of educational reform, he called for open-air nursery schools, a proper staffing and equipment for primary schools, a more nutritious system of school meals, and more state control of the public schools to ensure that they are more socially representative.

Tawney's social ideas fed his conception of the political relationship between liberty and equality. He admitted that if liberty was to be defined as individual freedom from restraint, then it was incompatible with equality, but argued that this was a very limited definition. Under such a restricted interpretation, freedom was restricted to only a few people, while the majority were condemned to unfreedom. To Tawney, liberty was the freedom to act positively for the community, as well as to resist its more tyrannical demands. In this sense, freedom for *all* meant the acceptance of certain social rules to prevent the abuse of power.

As economic power had become concentrated in monopolies and oligopolies, the lack of freedom for the many was obvious to all. The working class — the majority of the nation — was forced to work for these firms, or to starve. As a result of this servitude, with one person's livelihood placed at the mercy of another, any material wealth earned by the worker is at the expense of his freedom. To Tawney,

> society is divided, in its economic and social relations, into classes which are ends and classes which are instruments. Like property, with which in the past it has been closely connected, liberty becomes the privilege of a class, not the possession of a nation.[16]

He always saw freedom in relation to social power, and consequently argued that liberty must be seen in an economic as well as a political sense. In this way, with the freedom of the economically weak taken into account, there is no incompatibility between liberty and equality.

The Limits of British Socialism

Tawney's philosophical elaboration of British socialism provided a morality which was to remain constant as an ideal in the Labour Party's political thought. It is, indeed, difficult for any socialist to disagree with his revulsion at the acquisitive motive which governs our social life, dividing people from one another and stunting the creative initiative of the working class. His view of the dignity and respect that must be accorded to the individual (couched though it often was in terms of his Christian faith) cannot fail to strike a chord in anyone who feels disgust at the obsession with creating material wealth which is the basis of our society.

However, Tawney's moral philosophy failed to advance beyond the fundamental weakness of British socialism — its lack of any practical proposals to create realistically the social basis of co-operation on which any social advances could be *permanently* based. The economic crisis which destroyed the Labour government in 1931 was to brutally illustrate this, making a mockery as it did of the proposals for social reform written by Tawney for that government. In the final analysis, the economic prosperity on which those reforms depended disintegrated, and Tawney had no practical proposals to take the teeth out of that crisis. His calls for love and dignity were mere empty words in the face of the mass unemployment and social misery which engulfed Britain and Europe in the thirties.

Tawney's inability to recognise the economic dynamics of accumulation and crisis which lay behind the acquisitive morality of our society profoundly affected his analysis. Along with the Fabians and ethical socialists, he identified the usurer as the enemy, rather than the wage-relationship identified by Marx. It was not private property which was wrong, but the functionless property of the capitalist usurer. Thus, he called on socialists to discriminate between the different kinds of property and employer. He argued that

functionless property is the greatest enemy of legitimate property itself. It is the parasite which kills the organism that produced it . . . When property for acquisition or power and property for service or for use jostle each other freely in the market . . . the latter tends normally to be absorbed by the former, because it has less resisting power.[17]

To Tawney, property could be morally healthy, but only when it was used for the community rather than the privileged class of idlers and parasites.

This Fabian view (congruous as it was with labourism) gave Tawney's ideas on industrial democracy a very narrow interpretation. He called merely for greater consultation between employers and their employees on all matters concerning the workers' welfare, from discipline to the introduction of new processes. The existence of a fundamental conflict between employers and workers was just not acknowledged, so that the fundamental question of which class has the final power of decision is not raised in any fundamental manner. Instead, there is merely a repetition of the calls for a *genuine* partnership between capital and labour. Tawney expressed a crucial aspect of British socialism in calling upon employers to realise 'that they cannot at one moment talk eloquently of the partnership between labour and capital, and refuse labour the ordinary rights of a partner at the next.'[18] It was a similar conception of the relations of labour and capital to that put forward by Snowden and Macdonald with such disastrous consequences.

It was, then, a mixed economy which was envisaged by Tawney. Private ownership was to be subject to regulation by a variety of state agencies to ensure that it worked in the public interest, and there was to be a major extension of state ownership, but in the final analysis a fully socialised economy was not part of Tawney's vision. His view of morality was divorced from the wage-relationship which underlies capitalist society, and tied to a critique of 'functionless' property. The actual process of capitalist production was accepted by Tawney. The English economy was a 'system which at every turn involves mutual understanding and continuous co-operation',[19] so that the lack of a common culture between the classes became the main target for Tawney's ire. It was as though capitalism could be moral but, in the absence of state restraint, it had instead opted to be unpleasant. All that was needed was the removal of its unacceptable face by state action.

Tawney's importance in the realm of political thought, and in his contribution to the Labour Party, cannot be overestimated. His calls for specific reform in health and education were important in laying the basis of the Labour Party's plans for a welfare state, while his criticisms of the aquisitive morality were an important intellectual and emotional basis for many future politicians who were committed to social reform. However, the reforms in the social services which were eventually to be put into effect by a Labour government took place in the confines of the acquisitive society condemned by Tawney. The social advances made by the Labour Party were not based on the social basis of a co-operative society and economy necessary for them to be *permanent*, and they were eventually to be seriously eroded by a new economic crisis. The absence of any realistic measures to create the social basis of a dignified society were eventually to prove decisive to Tawney's hopes, and to the hopes of British socialism.

Notes

1. For the varied nature of interpretations of Tawney, see Ross Terrill, *R.H Tawney and His Times* (Andre Deutsch, 1974), who sees him as a Fabian and ethical socialist; and J.M. Winter, *Socialism and the Challenge of War* (Routledge and Kegan Paul, 1974), who points to the impact of Christianity and guild socialism on Tawney's beliefs.

2. For which see his article, 'British Socialism Today', published in *The Radical Tradition* (George Allen and Unwin, 1964), edited by Rita Hinden.

3. For which see chapter 8 of this book.

4. R.H. Tawney, *The British Labour Movement* (Yale, 1925), pp. 144-5.

5. Published as *The Attack and Other Papers* (George Allen and Unwin, 1953).

6. R.H. Tawney, *Religion and the Rise of Capitalism* (Pelican Books, 1938), pp. 253.

7. See *R.H. Tawney's Common Place Book* ed. J.M. Winter and D.M. Joslin (Cambridge University Press, 1972).

8. Ibid., p. 54 (diary entry for 6 March 1913).

9. R.H. Tawney, *The Acquisitive Society* (London, 1921), p. 13.

10. Ibid., p. 32.

11. Ibid., p. 34.

12. R.H. Tawney, *Equality* (George Allen and Unwin, 1952 ed.), p. 38.

13. Ibid., pp. 86-7.

14. Ibid., pp. 198-9.

15. Ibid., p. 158.

16. Ibid., p. 185.

17. Tawney, *The Acquisitive Society*, pp. 93-4.

18. Tawney, *Equality*, p. 198.

19. Ibid., p. 24.

PART THREE

THE FORMATION OF CORPORATE SOCIALISM

The political ideas of British socialism, accepted by the Labour Party in its 1918 Constitution, served as an adequate ethic to unite the overwhelming majority of the organised labour movement. This was particularly important at a time when the example of triumphant Bolshevism in Russia was disrupting European socialism, dividing it into reformist and revolutionary strands. In Britain, it had little impact, failing to detach the ILP or the majority of the shop stewards' movement from their commitment to the Labour Party. Under leaders like Ramsay Macdonald and the stolid trade unionist, Arthur Henderson, the Labour Party emerged from the Great War as a mass party with a large degree of working-class support. In the 1920s it became the official opposition, forming two minority governments under Macdonald.

However, as the new opportunities forced Labour to see itself as a party of government, it was to become increasingly clear that the ethic of British socialism was totally unsuited to the demands of a complex economy beset by slump and heavy unemployment. The practical tasks of changing society in accordance with their socialist ethic proved too much for Labour, which was overwhelmed by the world economic crisis in 1931. By the 1930s it had become obvious to the Labour leadership that British socialism had to be supplemented by a more relevant political theory if it was to reshape society in the interests of the labour movement.

The relationship between ideas and government become particularly difficult to grasp at this point. Capitalism as an efficient method of production, even in its imperialist phase, was manifestly a failure after the onset of world depression at the beginning of the 1930s. It desperately needed a drastic reorganisation if it was to escape the vicious circle of low productivity and general unemployment in which it found itself. In the circumstances, the state stood as the only force capable of intervening to restructure capital and overcome the crisis of profitability which beset it. This was done in very different ways in different countries, but a common factor in the major capitalist powers was the cor-

porate form into which the State moulded society. However unequal
they might be in terms of prestige and social power, organised business
and organised labour were brought into the discussions and decisions
taken on political and economic issues. In Germany and Italy, corporatism was ruthlessly imposed by Fascism, so that labour's participation in industry and society was a hollow formality; in the United
States, labour was encouraged to organise by a Democratic administration which had only loose connections with the unions; but in Britain
it was to be the Labour Party, the party of a well-organised and independent trade union movement, which was to champion the corporate
solution to the crisis of capitalism.

The formation of corporate socialism, like that of British socialism,
was an intellectual dynamic related to social and political events
between the wars. Its origins lay in two challenges to labourism from
the Left and the Right. The revolutionary challenge of syndicalism
was incorporated into labourism by the Guild socialist ideas of G.D.H.
Cole, which were then translated into corporate terms. This stood in
sharp contrast to the fate of syndicalism in Italy, serving as it did there
as the ideological source of a Fascist corporatism. At the same time,
the Liberal Party challenged labourism from the right, in its espousal of
state intervention and welfare expressed by Keynes and Beveridge. This
challenge was incorporated into labourism by Labour Keynesians like
Ernest Bevin and Hugh Dalton. The final result, emerging in a series of
debates in the 1930s, was a corporate socialism which gave a more
precise form to the vague ethic of British socialism. This new form of
socialist political thought, eventually accepted by both Left and Right
in the Labour Party, was to refashion British society in the 1940s.

5 THE SYNDICALIST CHALLENGE

The mass strike movement which shook Britain in the period immediately preceding the Great War alerted many on the British Left to the new ideas of syndicalism which had been recently formulated on the Continent and in the United States. At a time when the Labour Party seemed hopelessly compromised by parliamentary politics, and when the trade union leaders were safely shielded from their members' concerns by a comfortable bureaucracy, a new Left began to look to the direct action and spontaneous democracy of the working class at the point of production, the factory. In doing so, they presented the greatest challenge to labourism since Marx.

The social and economic circumstances of Britain at that time favoured the importation of a foreign ideology like syndicalism onto British soil. The export of capital which characterised the economic nature of British imperialism had averted a crisis of profitability by the turn of the century, but the low yields on capital invested in British industry at home and the accompanying stagnant productivity led to a fall in real wages under the impact of inflation. There was still an aristocracy of skilled labour, where the skilled worker's earnings might be three times the amount of the unskilled worker, but his status and relative privileges were increasingly threatened by mechanisation and new technology at the turn of the century. These developments undermined the traditional distinctions between the craft unions of skilled artisans and the general unions of the unskilled which had been so marked in the British labour movement up to that time. The new trends were intensified by the powerful new employers' organisations, made possible by the emergence of cartels and oligopolies in certain sectors of British industry. The new, centralised power of the employers meant that the old craft forms of workers' organisations were becoming obsolete and vulnerable, and seemed to call for unity and centralisation on the workers' side.

At the same time, the long delays in wage settlements caused by the increasingly professional negotiations, carried on behind closed doors, led to a disillusionment with centralised, national bargaining and a sense of alienation from the union leaders. The more militant workers looked to their own localised power as a far more effective deterrent to the demands of the employer than their national union. The comparatively low levels of unemployment throughout the Edwardian era placed workers in a powerful position to obtain concessions from the employers if they were willing to fight for them, strengthening the militant belief in direct action at the local level. The demands for a more powerful and united workers' movement on the one hand, and the distrust of a union bureaucracy on the other, were answered by the syndicalist calls for industrial unionism and direct democracy.

It was not any theoretical challenge which alarmed the rulers of Britain in the Edwardian era, but the violent forms of industrial action in which syndicalists played a leading role. A fierce strike in the Cambrian Combine coalfields of South Wales in the autumn of 1910 led to rioting and the use of troops as the state, threatened by what it regarded as potential insurrection, rallied to the side of the employers. A mass strike wave in 1911 swept the country's docks and halted its railway system, leading to a widespread deployment of troops and police against mass picketing, to fierce rioting, and to the deaths of strikers in Liverpool and Llanelly. The intense resentment felt by the strikers against both the State and the employers, together with the breakdown of official union leadership, increased the popularity of syndicalist militants like Tom Mann. The failure of a national strike of miners in early 1912 and the defeat of the London Transport workers' strike later that summer was a temporary setback, but by 1914, when a Triple Alliance of rail, coalminers, and dockers unions was formed, trade union membership had nearly doubled from two and a half million four years earlier to over four million.

However, it was the theoretical challenge posed by syndicalism which was to be more important in the long run for the Labour Party. As such, it has often presented a problem of interpretation, leading one historian to write that 'despite the "ism" which lends it so theoretical an air, it was originally the name given to a movement rather than a theory'.[1] There was definitely a *theory* of syndicalism, but it often seemed more like a militant practice of class war than a conception of a new society. Moreover, its inchoate nature meant that syndicalism could take a variety of political forms. Anarchist theoreticians like Fernand Pelloutier and Arturo Labriola elaborated anarcho-syndicalism, and anarchists even temporarily won conrol of the French union federation, the CGT;[2] Industrial Unionists like 'Big Bill' Haywood, of the American IWW saw industrial action by one big union as perfectly compatible with membership of the moderate Socialist Party of America;[3] and some syndicalists in France and Italy saw nothing wrong with collaboration with ultra-nationalist movements like the Italian nationalists or *Action Francaise*.[4] Syndicalism was nothing if not versatile.

However, the fact that syndicalism was capable of adapting itself to a range of political ideas from anarchism to Fascism should not disguise its nature as a positive view of a new society. The anarchist, Pelloutier, first put forward the idea that the unions were not merely instruments of class struggle, but were also the nuclei of a collectivist, stateless society. In doing so, he pointed to the fundamentally anti-parliamentary nature of syndicalism, which saw the political world as a hollow form which disguised the real decisions taken in the world of the factory.

Daniel De Leon (1852-1914) had been converted to socialism by the American Utopian, Edward Bellamy. Shortly after joining the American Socialist Labour Party (SLP) in 1890, he became its leader, ruling it with a stern and autocratic discipline. His views were based on an uncompromising rejection of reformism in all its manifestations. The non-socialist trade union leaders were denounced as 'labour fakers' and 'the labour lieutenants of capital' while the political leaders of the working class, who sought to emancipate it from above, would inevit-ably be compromised by the parliamentary machine.

The reformist work of parliamentarian and union leaders must, according to De Leon, be replaced by the direct action of unions based on industry rather than craft. These industrial unions, transcending obsolete craft divisions, would eventually call a general lockout of the capitalists, peacefully taking over their industries and thereby abolishing wage labour. In the new Socialist Republic, the bourgeois institutions of representative democracy would be replaced by prole-tarian institutions of direct democracy. Instead of geographical constit-uencies, illogical in that they did not express economic realities, there would be the more meaningful industrial constituencies of a workers' democracy. This did not, however, rule out political action since he believed that a strong and disciplined party was essential as an agency of propaganda (a belief which caused a major schism in the IWW).

The ideas of De Leon were directly imported into Great Britain by the Irish revolutionary, James Connolly, together with some of his Scottish allies on the Left of the British SDF. Connolly (1868-1916) had been born in Edinburgh to Irish parents who had been forced by economic necessities to emigrate. He educated himself in conditions of extreme poverty and, after a few years in the army, became active in the early 1890s in the Scottish Socialist Federation (then the Scottish variant of the SDF). The impossibility of providing for his wife and children forced him to move between Britain, Ireland and the United States, where he was able to keep in touch with the most advanced socialist ideas. Shortly after establishing the Irish Socialist Republican Party in 1896, Connolly seized on De Leon's pamphlets as an uncompromising attack on reformism. His advocacy of De Leonism among his friends in Scotland, dissatisfied as they were with the SDF's opportunism and Hyndman's anti-semitism, led in 1903 to the establishment of the Socialist Labour Party in Britain. The SLP was to be the main exponent of De Leon's ideas and Connolly wrote a series of articles for their paper, *The Socialist*, in which he expounded the theory of Industrial Unionism. In terms of political activity, Connolly was in the USA in 1903-10, working as an organiser for the IWW and the American SLP, and on his return to Ireland was instrumental in organising the Irish Citizens Army, the first Red Army according to Lenin. His execution by the British after the abortive Easter Rising in Dublin in 1916 made him a martyr to the Irish Republican and socialist cause.

Connolly's own interpretation of Industrial Unionism, propagated in Britain by the SLP, was the forerunner of an attempt to create a syndicalist movement in Britain after 1910. This movement, centred in groups like the Industrial Syndicalist Education League, and expressed in the Labour paper, the *Daily Herald*, was as divided as its European and American counterparts, with both anarchist and apolitical wings, but it looked to Tom Mann as its principal spokesman. Mann, as may be recalled, had been one of the Labour Marxists in the ILP before he left for Australia in 1901. While he had accepted parliamentary activity, his main interest had been in organising the unskilled into militant unions. This favourably disposed him to the syndicalist ideas of Industrial Unionism growing in Australia, where an IWW was set up in emulation of the Americans. When Mann returned to Britain in 1910, he brought the fame and experience needed to put syndicalism on the map of the British Left. Influenced by the French CGT, Connolly and E.J. Allen (who wrote *Revolutionary Unionism* in 1909, denouncing all political activity), Mann was instrumental in organising the ISEL in 1910. He took a leading part in the strike wave that followed, sitting on the unofficial committee which ran the 1911 dockers' strike in Liverpool, and was arrested during the 1912 miners' strike for calling on soldiers not to shoot on their fellow workers. His tireless advocacy of Industrial Unionism, through mass meetings and through his paper, *The Industrial Syndicalist*, made him the foremost exponent of syndicalism in Britain.

The Nature of Syndicalism

Marx's challenge to labourism had been considerably watered down by his British exponents until, diluted of its revolutionary nature, it had become a respected strand on the Left of the Labour Party's thought. In the case of De Leon and the syndicalists, their British disciples had no need to water down the militancy of the doctrines to suit the conditions of the trade union movement. Indeed, while syndicalism never won over the majority of British trade unionists, it fitted the realities of an Edwardian Britain in which the violence of industrial strife increased distrust of a respectable Labour leadership.

Syndicalism thus presented a real challenge to labourism in Britain. Indeed, in its destructive aspects — its prescriptions for combating the strength of the employing class — it was generally incompatible with labourism as it had developed during the previous century. This was due to its clear demands for the expropriation of capital and the abolition of the system of wage-labour. As the British SLP put it in their manifesto in 1906,

> We call upon the workers to organise themselves, not in trade unions based upon the capitalist principles and trade sectionalism, but in industrial unions recognising the unity and solidarity of the working class and the establishment of socialism as their avowed aim.[5]

As such, the Labour Party was attacked as a political Babel, with no clear aim except the protection of the salaries of those union bureaucrats who supported them.

This uncompromising stance lay behind the rejection by all syndicalists of the 'Servile State', as the modern state was described by Hilaire Belloc. Their militant opposition to the state socialism of the Labour Party lay in the syndicalist belief that the mass of the working class must directly and actively participate in its own emancipation. Against this revolutionary conception of direct democracy, the state socialism of Labour implied a body of representatives in Parliament who could not be controlled by the workers. Tom Mann pointed out that this political elitism would be extended to the industrial sphere, perpetuating the autocratic despotism of the employer — '*The Industrial Syndicalist* declares that to run industry through Parliament, i.e. by State machinery, would be even more mischievous to the working class than the existing method, for it would assuredly mean that the capitalist class would, through Government departments, exercise over the natural forces, and over the workers, a domination even more rigid than is the case today.'[6]

It was not so much a protest against private ownership of the means of production as a libertarian rejection of industrial autocracy. The syndicalists inferred that political democracy was a hypocritical sham which concealed the social dictatorship exercised by capital in the industrial life of capitalist countries. Where the Fabians saw the growth of state intervention in the economy as a sign of the capitalists being forced to bow to the necessity of socialism, the syndicalists argued that state intervention was merely another sign that the capitalists needed the coercive power of the state to support them in their struggle with the workers.

Where British socialism concentrated on political means to effect social change, the syndicalists argued that the mere right to vote was of no protection to workers unless they developed a strong economic organisation behind them. It was the economic struggle over wages and working conditions in which the real decisions would be taken, because it was in the factories that power lay. To Mann, the Labour Party's reliance on Parliament ignored this basic fact of class society. Parliament was historically a bourgeois institution − it

> was not brought into existence to enable the working class to obtain ownership and mastery over the means of production. Parliament was brought into existence by the ruling class to have more effective means of dominating and subjugating the working class.[7]

As a result, any parliamentary action was subsidiary to the real struggle, industrial in its nature. Until the workers awoke to this fact of their economic oppression, then any political changes would affect only the shadow of reality, not its substance. To Mann and the other syndicalists,

> there is no possibility of achieving economic freedom unless the workers themselves are conscious that what they suffer from, as a class, is economic subjugation. Workers must organise at the point of production − 'The strong right arm of the labor movement is direct economic organisation'.[8]

This faith in the primarily industrial nature of class struggles was closely linked in syndicalist eyes with an all-out attack upon a major institution of labourism − the trade union bureaucracy. If it was true that the industrial vote, the decision on whether or not to take strike action against the employer, was far more important for the worker than any political vote could be, then the democratic nature of the worker's industrial organisation became fundamental. The tendency of the union leaders to attempt to substitute negotiation for conflict was an indication to the syndicalists of their class treachery, and was to be explained by the comfortable bureaucratic niche which they had made for themselves in the union. They were seen as the worst sort of parasite, who had risen on the backs of their fellow-workers only to turn on the very people who had placed their trust in them. To the syndicalists, the unions belonged to the rank and file, whose direct involvement in class war purged the tendencies to corruption present in the union leadership. The spontaneous and direct democracy of the unions was therefore essential — 'The engines of war to fight the workers' battles to overthrow the capitalist class, and to raise the general standard of life while so doing, must be of the workers' own making. The unions are the workers' own',[9] as Mann put it.

This theme was taken up by a group of South Wales miners, organised in the Unofficial Reform Committee of their union, whose *The Miners' Next Step* was published November 1911. Prominent in this group was Noah Abblett (1883-1935) who had been converted to Marxism at Ruskin College after suffering a pit accident. Abblett had then organised educational classes in which he taught the new ideas of Industrial Unionism, and successfully fought the moderate leadership of the South Wales miners' union (interestingly enough, he saw no contradiction between such views and his membership of the ILP). In *The Miners' Next Step*, Abblett and his fellow authors skilfully pointed to the plenary powers over the rank and file which gave the union leaders special privileges among their class. These privileges gave the leader 'an interest — a vested interest — in stopping progress. They have therefore in some things an antagonism of interests with the rank and file'.[10] Their very jobs as leaders of *trade* unions, representing particular crafts, were at stake when faced with the demands of *industrial* unionism.

Of course, Abblett recognised that leadership had its beneficial qualities, especially efficiency and order, but in the end it implied power, and power held by a leader, no matter how representative, would lead inevitably to corruption. The workers would be as corrupted as the leadership —

this power of initiative, this sense of responsibility, the self-respect which comes from convinced manhood, is taken from the men and consolidated in the leader. The sum of *their* initiative, *their* responsibility, *their* self-respect, becomes his.[11]

Against this, the Unofficial Reform Committee proposed a new democratic constitution for their union to place their leaders under the direct control of the rank and file, and to end the sectional character of the workforce in the mining industry.

This attack on the union leadership was not necessarily incompatible with labourism, or even with electoral success in the labour movement (as evidenced by Abblett's election to the Executive of the South Wales Miners Federation), but many syndicalists took the anti-bureaucratic stance to the point of breaking with the existing union structure and setting up new, revolutionary unions. The SLP put this clearly when, greeting the formation of the *IWW*, it called for the emulation of such 'dual unionism' in Britain.

> When we take up the positive work of organising the workers in the economic field in a clean revolutionary union, those workers upon whom our exposure of and attack on pure-and-simpledom convince, will pass over from their [the established unions] ranks to ours.[12]

In pursuit of this, the *SLP* totally isolated themselves from the labour movement (outside a small base in Glasgow). It was the recognition of this result that led Tom Mann to reject 'dual unionism' as totally irrelevant to the conditions of the British labour movement, which had struggled for over a century to build up the unions. Though the issue broke up the *ISEL* in 1913, Mann called for the reform, not the destruction, of the unions in order to win them to a policy of class war.

Syndicalism and Government

It is in the context of this general atack on labourism and state socialism that the syndicalists put forward the constructive aspect of their doctrines. The formation of industrial unions would eventually lead to such intensive class conflict with the capitalists and their State that the working class could then seize control of the factories. They would do this through the industrial unions, the institutions that they had created for their defence. The unions' organisation, thoroughly democratised, would thus be 'the embryo of a working-class republic. Our national unions, local unions, and other bodies will be the administrative machinery of an Industrial Commonwealth'[13] as it was put by E.J. Allen in *The Industrial Syndicalist*. In this way, the schema of historical materialism put forward by Marx appeared to approach completion. Just as the bourgeoisie had created the basis of their new society within the confines of the old feudal order, so the proletariat was creating the basis of *their* new society within the confines of the capitalist order. Whereas the bourgeois revolution had taken a political, parliamentary form, the proletarian revolution would take an economic, industrial form.

The strategy was put at its clearest by James Connolly. The relationship between the formation of industrial unions and the eventual constitutions of a socialist republic was seen in pure De Leonite terms —

In the light of this principle of industrial unionism, every fresh shop or factory organised under its banner is a fort wrenched from the control of the capitalist class and manned with soldiers of the revolution to be held by them for the workers. On the day that the political and economic forces of labour finally break with capitalist society and proclaim the Workers' Republic, these shops and factories so manned by industrial unionists will be taken charge of by the workers there employed. . . Then and thus the new society will spring into existence ready equipped to perform all the useful functions of its predecessor.[14]

It was a logically impeccable scenario, but the logic disguised its unrealistic nature. The revolutionary response of the working class was seen as an automatic reaction to the development of capitalism to a monopoly form, which was much too mechanical a conception to grasp the nature of social reality. The armed power of the state which could resist what would be an industrial insurrection was almost totally disregarded,[15] while political parties and government were naively seen as shallow reflections of the real industrial struggle.

Nevertheless, it was this conception of Industrial Unionism which underlay the 'functionalist' ideas of the structure of a socialist society put forward by the syndicalists. Marx had rejected the idea of a detailed blueprint for a new society, but the syndicalists felt that they had grasped the outline of the future. The geographical constituencies that made up a representative democracy were no longer natural ones. They were a survival from earlier times, when the parish and the local community actually constituted the centre of popular life. In the modern industrial society created by capitalism, democracy should be based upon the factory and the workshop which had become the new focal point of the lives of most people. The unions, based on industry, would democratically control the life of the workshops and would regulate the routine of labour as determined by the needs of industry and society. Such a system would be *more* efficient than the present division between political democracy and industrial despotism. While any capitalist government which took over an industry would be forced to turn to professional experts for advice on technical questions, the industrial government of socialism would have the full expert knowledge born of experience.

This 'functional' view of government was *not* a corporate conception, however. This was because the syndicalist distrust of union bureaucracy led to their advocacy of direct spontaneous democracy, based on the workshop. Connolly succinctly expressed the difference between the two differing conceptions of democracy in pointing out that 'Social Democracy must proceed from the bottom upward, whereas capitalist political society is organised from above downward'.[16] The rank and file union member would elect representatives to the various departments of industry, which themselves would elect representatives to the industrial administration. This administration would take over the tasks allocated by capitalism to a political government. As the life of each workshop would be regulated and governed by the workshop itself, the bureaucratic tendencies of centralised government would be either avoided or placed under strict democratic accountability. In this way, the political state would be replaced by the social republic. Political activity was rejected by only a few 'pure' syndicalists like E.J. Allen, but it was seen by all syndicalists as a subsidiary activity of agitation and propaganda for the more important industrial work — 'the workers will be industrially organised on the economic field and, until that organisation is perfected . . . the Socialist Party will carry on an independent campaign of education and attack upon the political field'.[17]

Syndicalism and Labourism

In its destructive aspects — its opposition to state socialism, union bureaucracy and representative democracy — syndicalism was a direct challenge to the labourist ideology underlying the Labour Party's political thought. It was generally incompatible with British socialism, and as such had nothing to offer the Labour Party as it sought a doctrine flexible enough to unite its various strands. In its *constructive* aspects, however, syndicalism was to prove very fruitful for labour, though its revolutionary trappings would have to be removed first. The syndicalist proposition that the major unions should have a direct role to perform in governing an industrial economy was, of course, intimately connected to their proposition that neither the State nor the capitalist corporations should have any role whatsoever in such government. As such, it was inimical to everything that the Labour Party stood for. However, if such revolutionary encumbrances could be disentangled, then an extension of labourism rather than its destruction could be envisaged.

The possibility of this lay in certain weaknesses inherent in the critique of labourism by the syndicalists. Indeed, in many important respects, syndicalism had much in common with the Labour Party and the trade union movement. Its commitment to the independence of the working class from the bourgeoisie was expressed in much more militant terms than most prominent Labour politicians were prepared to support. At a special conference of the national mineworkers' union in January 1911, Noah Abblett pointed to the growing unrest in the minefields and called for militant strike action against the capitalists — 'There is nothing else. There is no other way by which it is possible to beat the employers who are arrogant and insolent in regard to our demands for the minimum wage.'[18] The authors of *The Miners' Next Step* placed as their first policy recommendation for their union that 'the old policy of identity of interest between employers and ourselves be abolished, and a policy of open hostility installed'.[19] However, this militancy was by no means incompatible with labourism. The demand for independence from the employers had been a touchstone of Hodgskin's ideas, and had been made a primary element in the Labour Party's thought by the Labour Marxists and Keir Hardie. Noah Abblett's syndicalism did not prevent him from working within the ILP for his ideas, while a group of his syndicalist followers (including Nye Bevan) were to be active in Labour Party politics.

Apart from this fundamental similarity, the narrow concentration on trade union activity opened up syndicalism to its eventual absorption into the labourism of the Labour Party. Syndicalism was always marked by a dual nature. While it proclaimed its *eventual* goal as the emancipation of the proletariat through a general strike, it had as its *immediate* task the defence of the workers' living standards by militant strike action. Some theorists, particularly in France, attempted to construct a scenario by which strikes over wages would inevitably become embroiled in a general revolution, but this had more to do with fantasy than with realistic preparations for an industrial insurrection. In practice, such strikes over wages were nothing more than that, ending in either wage-gains or in grim defeats. The syndicalists' doctrine, however revolutionary its rhetoric might be, essentially emphasised the organisation of mass strikes for higher wages. As such, it was a mirror of the ideas of parliamentary socialists in the Labour Party (and the Second International) who saw a collectivist society as a maximum goal to be achieved in the mythical future while they concentrated on the immediate tasks of social reform through parliamentary action. When Tom Mann called on British workers to emulate the French CGT, he pointed out that 'while working for the revolution, they do not neglect to do all possible to secure general betterment'.[20] Shorn of the revolutionary rhetoric, such ideas were no more than a militant extension of labourism, perfectly acceptable to the Labour Left and to trade unionists like Ernest Bevin, then seeking the amalgamation of unions into powerful corporate bodies to defend workers against the capitalists. The formation of the Transport and General Workers Union (TGWU) in 1920, the future bulwark of the Labour Party, was no more than a reformist application of syndicalist principles of Industrial Unionism.

Moreover, the syndicalists' narrow concentration on the point of production not merely overlooked production outside the factory (the most glaring example being the domestic labour carried on by women in the family), but also ignored the non-industrial areas of life. The political state was totally underestimated, with the result that syndicalism was much more ambiguous than at first appeared. Of course, revolutionaries like Connolly and the SLP were absolutely opposed to reformist political action, but this was not a *necessary* tenet of syndicalism. Many syndicalists, while regarding political action as definitely secondary to industrial action, remained open to the parliamentary help which political action could receive. Tom Mann expressed this ambiguity towards politics in *The Industrial Syndicalist* —

Let the politicians do as much as they can, and the chances are that, once there is an an economic fighting force in the country, ready to back them up by action, they will actually be able to do what now would be hopeless for them to attempt to do.[21]

This was not so much an attack on the Labour Party as a reminder that the party represented a powerful force *outside* Parliament. This was acknowledged as much by Keir Hardie, who declared in a speech to the Commons in May 1912, that

> syndicalism is the direct outcome of the apathy and indifference of this House towards working class questions, and I rejoice at the growth of syndicalism. The more syndicalism we have outside, the quicker will be the pace at which this Chamber will move. [22]

The labourist potentialities of syndicalism were seen in a dramatic fashion at the outbreak of the Great War in 1914. The hopes of the revolutionaries throughout Europe that a general strike would greet the declarations of war crumbled in face of the millions of enthusiastic working-class recruits to the various armies. The diverse tendencies in syndicalism tended to splinter on the question of national defence. The very nature of syndicalism, with its narrow concentration on wage struggles, meant that it had no consistent attitude to imperialism or war. It was possible for syndicalists (such as Gustave Hervé in France) to become fiery patriots, while others (like Connolly) saw imperialism as the main enemy. However, it was 'Big Bill' Haywood of the American IWW who summed up the syndicalist attitude of neutrality when he declared that

> the fight of the IWW is one of the economic field and it is not for me, a man who could not be drafted for war, to tell others that they should go to war, or tell them that they should not go to war.[23]

In Britain, the syndicalist stress on local militancy was continued in the Shop Stewards' Movement, many of whose members belonged to the SLP. They continued to advocate industrial unionism and were, after some initial confusion, hostile to the war effort. However, it was the economic struggle over wages which they regarded as the primary struggle, and they generally remained silent on the war. The syndicalist nature of the shop stewards' movement was pointed to by a leading SLP militant of the time. J.T. Murphy, when he wrote that

> none of the strikes that took place during the course of the war were anti-war strikes. They were frequently led by men such as myself who wanted to stop the war, but that was not the actual motive. Had the question of stopping the war been put to any

strikers meeting it would have been overwhelmingly defeated. The stoppages had a different origin and a different motive,[24]

economic rather than political. When the group around John Maclean, an anti-war Marxist, tried to raise the question of the war at the Clyde Workers Committee, he was excluded from the discussions. As James Hinton noted, 'whatever its members might say as individuals the Committee itself was neither for nor against the war'.[25]

In thus ignoring the patriotic sense of national loyalty, the syndicalists failed to confront the force which had crippled their hopes of an industrial insurrection. The State which conducted war outside its boundaries would demand peace within, and the syndicalists were by their nature a threat to this internal peace. In refusing to court unpopularity by opposing the war, they ensured that their disruption of the internal peace would be limited from the beginning. They also indicated that their differences with labourism, which similarly accepted the national boundaries between the working class, were much less substantial than appeared on the surface. The syndicalist challenge to labourism would, as a result, be integrated into the Labour Party with a startling ease.

The Reaction of the Labour Party

This challenge was not at first recognised by the Labour leaders, who reacted to the syndicalist threat by holding fast to the accepted ethic of British socialism. Keir Hardie, while welcoming the trade union unrest which went under the name of syndicalism, expressed contempt for syndicalist theory. Snowden, in his *Socialism and Syndicalism* (1912), rejected syndicalism as hostile to authority and political action. Their militant preaching of class war appalled his sense of socialism as social peace and order. Macdonald, though marginally less hostile to the union unrest than Snowden, was similarly horrified at the syndicalist rejection of traditional political action as defined by Victorian Liberalism.

However, the more alert representatives of British socialism saw the need to adapt their ideas to take account of the syndicalist challenge. This was particularly true of the Webbs, the arch exponents of elitism and representative democracy. Their hostility to the revolutionary aspects of syndicalism was absolute, but it was the constructive proposals of control by the producers which caught their eye. Up to the advent of syndicalism, the Webbs had seen the trade unions merely as bodies which would negotiate wages with the employers, but the strike wave of 1910-12 forced them to attempt to give the unions a more positive role.

In a series of articles in the *New Statesman* in 1913, the Webbs argued that democracy, or more specifically representative democracy on the parliamentary model, should be extended from the political to the industrial sphere. The citizen was not just a consumer, but a producer as well and, as such, needed to be represented in all spheres of economic life. In industry this was to be done by workers' *participation*, by which the Webbs meant the use of the real and vivid knowledge of industry built up in the experience of the unions. 'There is no reason why the fully recognised Trade Unions should not, we do not say merely acquiesce in scientific management, but actually promote the new science.'[26] The unions, an expression of grass roots democracy, would thus advance from their restrictive role to take their place in the rational movement of historical evolution.

However, to the Webbs the syndicalist emphasis on producer control to the exclusion of the consumer and the State was totally unbalanced. They were demanding that power be concentrated in a minority of the community, thereby increasing the likelihood that unions would become conspiracies against the public interest. The Webbs argued that 'to base any governmental organisation on Associations of Producers is to negative democracy';[27] and proposed a society based on voluntary associations of consumers as well. Such consumer groups as the Co-operative retail societies were, in fact, superior as an instrument of democracy because, unlike trade unions, they had no vested interest to protect and no tendency to restrict membership. The State, based upon these associations, would be an extended co-operative society, supplying national services such as posts, museums, and libraries. In this way, 'the Socialist State, far from being a centralised and coercive bureaucracy, presents itself to us as a highly diversified and extremely numerous set of social groupings'.[28]

These proposals, elaborated in a modified form in the Webbs' *A Constitution for the Socialist Commonwealth of Great Britain* (1920),[29] are a striking foretaste of the corporate socialism that was eventually to emerge as the political thought of the Labour Party. They are also an indication that syndicalism contained within it strands which could be taken out of their revolutionary context to fit a capitalist society in which political organisation needed to be supplemented by social organisation. However, it was not the Webbs who were to absorb the syndicalist challenge into the Labour Party's thinking. They remained too committed to an elitist Fabianism to adapt themselves to the working-class appeal of the syndicalists. It was to be a close sympathiser with the class war belief of the syndicalists, G.D.H. Cole, who was to blunt their revolutionary challenge and demonstrate their similarities with, and political contribution to, the Labour Party.

Notes

1. F.F. Ridley, *Revolutionary Syndicalism in France: The Direct Action of its Time* (Cambridge University Press, 1970), p. 1.

2. Ridley, *Revolutionary Syndicalism*; see also G.D.H. Cole *History of Socialist Thought* vol. III, chapter 8; George Woodcock *Anarchism* (Penguin, 1970), pp. 298-304.

3. See Patrick Renshaw, *The Wobblies: The Story of Syndicalism in the United States* (Doubleday, 1967).

4. See Paul Mazgaj, *Action Francaise and Revolutionary Syndicalism* (University of North Carolina, 1979); David D. Roberts, *The Syndicalist Tradition and Italian Fascism* (University of North Carolina, 1979).

5. *The Socialist*, January 1906, p. 1.

6. *The Industrial Syndicalist*, vol. 1, no. 10, April 1911 (Spokesman Books, 1974), pp. 327-8.

7. *Industrial Syndicalist*, vol. 1, no. 7, January 1911, p. 221.

8. Ibid., vol. 1, no. 3, September 1910, p. 80.

9. Ibid., vol. 1, no. 1, July 1910, p. 45.

10. The Unofficial Reform Committee, *The Miners' Next Step— Being A Suggested Scheme For The Reorganisation Of The Federation* (Pluto Press, 1973 ed.), p. 15.

11. Ibid., p. 19.

12. *The Socialist*, August 1905, p. 4.

13. *Industrial Syndicalist*, vol. 1, no. 5, November 1910, p. 145.

14. James Connolly, *Selected Political Writings*, edited by Owen Dudley Edwards and Bernard Ransom (Jonathan Cape, 1973), p. 322.

15. Connolly never ceased to hold to the ideas of Industrial Unionism, collaborating with Irish nationalists like Pearce in an armed rising in 1916 on the grounds that it was an exceptional situation.

16. Connolly, p. 273.

17. Ibid., p. 281. |

18. Quoted in R. Page Arnot, *South Wales Miners: A History of the South Wales Miners' Federation 1898-1914* (George Allen and Unwin, 1967), p. 244.

19. *Miners' Next Step*, p. 29.

20. *Industrial Syndicalist*, vol. 1, no. 1, July 1910, p. 47.

21. Ibid., pp. 49-50.

22. *Hansard* (1912), vol. 38, col. 520.

23. Quoted Renshaw, , p. 277.

24. J.T. Murphy, *New Horizons* (London, 1934), p. 44.

25. James Hinton, *The First Shop Stewards' Movement* (Routledge and Kegan Paul, 1973), p. 131.

26. *New Statesman*, 7 June 1913.

27. Ibid.,, 24 May 1913, p. 204.

28. Ibid., 21 June 1913, p. 334.

29. In this book, the Webbs argued for a social parliament, separate from a political parliament, though having equal powers. The foreign, military and coercive powers would lie with the political parliament; the social parliament would oversee industrial administration.

6 G.D.H. COLE AND THE GUILD SOCIALIST RESPONSE

The response of many on the Labour Left to the new syndicalist doctrines was much more sympathetic than that of Macdonald or the Fabians. Indeed, through their adaptation of syndicalist ideas to British socialism, they were to play a major part in the evolution of the Labour Party's political thought. This particular inheritance of syndicalist theory has often been underestimated by later commentators who recognise only the revolutionary aspects of syndicalism.

The development of British syndicalism in the direction of Communism, via the shop stewards movement, would certainly explain the recent concentration on these aspects. The Industrial Unionism preached by the SLP was given its most complete radical exposition in William Paul's *The State: Its Origins and Functions* (1917), where the libertarian analysis of the State as rooted in class society resembled the analysis put forward in Lenin's *State and Revolution*, published in the same year. Indeed, the similarities of the syndicalist stress on industrial self-government with the actuality of working-class rule through the Soviets (or workers' councils) in Russia after 1917 won many syndicalists throughout Europe to the support of Bolshevik rule there. They saw Lenin as healing the old split between the Marxist orthodoxy of the Second International and the revolutionary spirit of syndicalism and anarchism. The destruction of the substance of Soviet democracy under the impact of civil war and economic collapse did not quench their belief that Bolshevism was the natural heir to syndicalist ideas, and SLP militants were an important element in the early politics of the Communist Party of Great Britain, founded in 1920-21.[1] Indeed, at the second congress of the Third International in 1920, Industrial Unionists like Jack Tanner and William Gallacher clashed with Lenin on the question of affiliation to the Labour Party,[2] though they later accepted Lenin's belief that Communists should work inside the Labour Party in order to win over Labour's mass working-class support (a policy marked by eventual failure).

However, it has been noted, syndicalism had other aspects which were to be much more important in Labour's thinking. Its revolutionary form contained within syndicalism an implicit corporatist strain. This was seen most clearly in Italy, where syndicalists constituted the radical wing of Mussolini's Fascist movement. Many Italian syndicalists, rejecting the stultifying effects of parliamentary democracy as an expression of a timid and materialistic bourgeoisie, found it easy to transfer their allegiance from the working class to the nation as an agent of social change. Mussolini himself was relatively uninterested in ideology, but his radical followers like Sergio Pannunzio and Filippo Corradini saw Fascism as a logical consequence of their syndicalist beliefs. The rule of a narrowly based Parliament, representing only the bourgeoisie, would be replaced by the rule of economic bodies based on the realities of the social nation. To Pannunzio in 1922, 'syndicalism . . . is the negation of the old political conception, the negation of the parties, the affirmation of the classes and of their organisation in the corporations or syndicates'.[3] There was an intense struggle between these syndicalists and the more conservative supporters of Fascism after Mussolini came to power, but by 1925 the syndicalists had been victorious. Italy was ready, as Pannunzio put it, 'to be the first to give Europe a real living example of a national state, based on syndicates, which is the ultimate and the primary and essential spirit of fascism'.[4] The syndical laws which established the corporate state in Italy, organising employers and unions into different economic groups, was hailed as the culmination and fulfilment of the Italian syndicalist tradition.

In Britain, this corporatist strain in syndicalism was not to take a Fascist form. For all its rhetoric on the equality of classes within the nation, Fascist corporativism was a fundamentally anti-union movement. Their destruction of the freedom of the trade unions to collectively bargain with the employers made the corporate state an empty form, covering a basic social inequality between employer and worker. As such, it was *absolutely* incompatible with any strain of socialism which was likely to be accepted by the Labour Party, even if its hostility to parliamentary democracy could be set on one side. However, this corporatist aspect of syndicalism was to take a peculiarly British form through the evolution of a new type of socialist thinking in the Labour Party. The manner of this evolution was determined by one of the most subtle and complex of Labour's theorists, G.D.H. Cole.

Cole was deeply moved by the labour unrest which swept Britain before the Great War, and he explained the popularity of syndicalist theory as an indication that Fabian collectivism had had its day. The new claim for freedom from a bureaucratic state was taking form as a demand for a greater degree of self-government than could be granted by the narrow political democracy of the ballot-box. However, Cole argued that syndicalism was too one-sided to be a suitable doctrine to fit English conditions. It was too rooted in the small, localised trade unions which flourished in France (the US influence was always under-played by Cole). In Britain, syndicalism would have to adapt itself by evolving into a new theory based on national and centralised unions. In an article in *New Age* in February 1914, Cole argued that

> syndicalism can only stand by its power to adjust itself to the new situation, and to develop . . . a new theory grounded on the accept-ance of the National Union as the necessary unit of industrial action and organisation.[5]

To point syndicalism in the direction required, Cole drew on the theories of the English guild socialists and, in doing so, provided an important stepping stone in the evolution of revolutionary socialism to the corporate socialism eventually accepted by the Labour Party.

The Guild Socialists

The theory of guild socialism was originally born as the intellectual fantasy of Arthur J. Penty. Penty (1875-1937) had become an architect after working in his father's office at the age of thirteen. As such, he was appalled by the ugly utilitarianism of industrial capitalism and became a disciple of the medievalist ideas of John Ruskin and William Morris. He felt that mankind had become trapped in an industrial system which had corrupted morality and had replaced craftsmanship and imagination by the machine and repetitive drudgery. He was init-ially a member of the Fabian Society, but by the turn of the century he became convinced that the state socialism of the Fabians and the ILP was merely a new expression of the basic evil of industrialism.

Penty advocated another solution in *The Restoration of the Gild System* (1906). He argued that it was necessary to transfer the control of industry from the hands of the financer into those of the craftsmen organised in guilds. There would be a return to the organic society of the Middle Ages, as a closed economy of handicrafts and agriculture would supersede the evil leviathan of factory production. As in the days of yore, craftsmen would serve a local market under the direction of their guilds, which would regulate the hours worked, the prices of the products, and the myriad other decisions made on grounds of profit-ability in a capitalist society. Competition between the guilds would take the form of quality rather than price, while politics would be transformed as the guilds became the upper house of Parliament. The thorough rejection of existing society was fully recognised by Penty, who pointed out that 'the nature of the reforms is such as to place the centre of gravity of the reform movement outside the sphere of politics'.[6]

These quaint ideas could well have passed by as a pleasant, but inconsequential, whimsy if Penty had not been in close touch with A.P. Orage (1873-1934), a member of the ILP whose fascination with the irrationalist philosophy of Nietszche inclined him to consider ideas of a new morality for new men. After first meeting Penty at the Leeds Theosophical Society, Orage came under the influence of his ideas and turned the popular weekly, *New Age* (which he bought in 1907) into a political platform for guild socialism. Moreover, the arcadian setting of Penty's theories was removed by the most prominent of the guild theorists to be identified with the journal, S.G. Hobson.

Hobson (1870-1940) born to a Quaker background in Ulster had written a series of articles in *New Age* between 1912 and 1914 and collected in book form as *National Guilds: An Inquiry into the Wage System and the Way Out* (1914). Hobson attempted to draw out the revolutionary nature of guild socialism. He rejected Penty's medievalism, arguing that it was capitalism rather than industrialism which was the enemy of human fulfilment. Under the wage system, labour was a mere commodity, valued at a price, hired and fired according to the needs of profit, and excluded from the management of industry. In the face of this, the narrowly political concerns of the Labour Party and the ILP with capturing state power were laughable – 'political emancipation leaves the worker quite as much at the final disposition of the employer as was the Greek helot'.[7] State socialism was to Hobson merely another name for state capitalism, as labour would be exploited by the State.

It was the wages system which was the cause of labour's troubles, and it would be through the abolition of the wages system that labour would find its real emancipation. This would be done by the trade unions, who must move from their present basis of negotiating wages to the control of industry. This could be done by monopolising the supply of labour to the employer, forcing him thereby to pay labour's wages to the union, which would itself divide them among the workers. In this way, the unions would be in a position to take control of industry in co-operation with the state. The unions would thus become national guilds, based on industry rather than handicrafts, and closely co-operating with other guilds to satisfy the needs of the people. The State would be the final arbiter of conflicts, as it represented the community, but generally Hobson believed that the State should totally disentangle itself from economics, restricting itself to the narrowly political concerns of foreign policy, defence, and law.

It was obvious that this critique of state socialism (which bore marked similarities to the syndicalist critique) would lead some guild socialists to a total rejection of the Labour Party. Hobson was particularly hostile, seeing the failure of the ILP to attack the wage system as a cause of its opportunist degeneration. Indeed, according to Hobson, even if the Labour Party accepted guild socialism, it should be rejected as an agency of change. It was a *political* party, operating in the narrowly political sphere, and thus incapable of effecting the *economic* changes that were required. Hobson, echoing the syndicalists, argued that 'the lesson would have been learnt in due season that the Socialist conquests of the industrial system is an economic and not a political operation; that economic power must precede political power'.[8]

It is understandable, then, that many commentators should see guild socialism as incompatible with the Labour Party's political thought. As one recent writer has put it,

> Guild Socialists well understood the nature of the British political system and were willing to argue against participation from within on the grounds that such participation must always involve the falsi-ification of ideals and aspirations. For them the political labour movement was wrong at its core simply because it had chosen to work within the system.[9]

If guild socialism as a theory was restricted to the works of Penty and Hobson, this would certainly be the case. However in taking up guild socialism as an English answer to syndicalism, a group of young Fabians around G.D.H. Cole turned it from an interesting theory into a major political force to be reckoned with. In doing so, they demonstrated the malleability of the Labour Party's political thought, and made an invaluable contribution to its development.

Cole and Guild Socialism

G.D.H. Cole (1889-1959) was the son of an estate agent, and was educated at Balliol College, Oxford, where he developed an interest in modern poetry and in Rousseau. He was also converted to socialism by the literary writings of William Morris, and joined the Fabian Society. The labour unrest of the pre-war years excited the romantic in Cole, who saw militant class conflict as giving the worker a sense of dignity and vitality of which he had been robbed by capitalism. He attempted to accommodate the syndicalist theories which were then becoming popular into the mainstream of English politics by drawing on the guild socialism of *New Age*. In *The World of Labour* (1913), Cole elaborated his own ideas of socialism, expanding and modifying them in books like *Self-Government in Industry* (1917) and *Guild Socialism Restated* (1920). In this task, he was aided by William Mellor (1888-1942), with whom he worked closely throughout the decade. Their frustration in the Fabian Society led them to form the National Guilds League (NGL) in 1915. They found ready ears on the Labour Left, and were to have a major impact in the next few years, influencing R.H. Tawney and Clement Attlee[10] among others.

Cole's ideas were, with some exception, close to Hobson's own modernist conception of a guild society. However, he gave the ideas a formidable intellectual weight and pragmatic quality which identified him as *the* theorist of guild socialism. Cole's grasp of political theory enabled him to link *New Age* with the participatory democracy of Rousseau and with the pluralist beliefs of J.N. Figgis, whose *Churches in the Modern State* (1913) asserted the importance of social groups in relation to the State. Cole's own fascination with the ideas of the dignity of craftsmanship put forward by William Morris and John Ruskin enabled him to link syndicalist theory with the ethical socialist strain in the Labour Party's thinking. His intellectual grasp and ability thus placed Cole in an important confluence of political theory, merging several different currents into one formidable political force.

The Syndicalist Influence

Rousseau and Figgis had their intellectual attractions for Cole, but it was the syndicalist assertion of workers' management of industry which held his attention. It seemed to be an urgent and concrete expression of the demand of the working class for freedom as well as bread, clearly demonstrating the inadequacies of the Fabian call for the abolition of poverty. The collectivists were attacking the symptom rather than the cause, as the tyranny of the wage system lay behind the poverty of the working class.

> What, I want to ask, is the fundamental evil in our modern society
> which we should set out to abolish? There are two possible answers
> to that question, and I am sure that very many well-meaning people
> would make the wrong one. They would answer POVERTY, when
> they ought to answer SLAVERY.[11]

It was the slavery of the wages system which destroyed freedom and
individuality in the worker, reduced men to the status of a machine,
and treated human beings as a mere means to producing wealth.

Cole saw the labour unrest as a reaction against such a system, and
fully supported the syndicalist calls for a class war in society. The
strike weapon was not merely a bargaining weapon, but an assertion of
Labour's free will, without which the worker would cease to be a
human being — 'the finest thing that can be accomplished by Labour
Unrest is a heightening sense of being alive, an awakening that will lead
men from mere discontent to the positive striving for a better life'.[12]
This occasional exultation in militancy was not merely a youthful
display of aggression, however, as Cole recognised the realities of a class
society which made class conflict necessary. Unlike Ramsay Macdonald
whose organic conception of society excluded class conflict, Cole did
not see strike action as selfish. He merely pointed to the actuality of
class struggle, and took his stand on the belief that he could not be
neutral in it. The two classes were not the same as one another in terms
of justice or liberty, because the capitalist class exploited and the
working class was exploited through the wage system. Thus, Cole called
for militant working-class action

> not on the grounds that it is desirable, but on the grounds that it is
> a monstrous and irrefutable fact. The class structure is established
> in our social institutions, and it is only by means of the class struggle
> that we can escape from it.[13]

This view, as can be imagined, did not gain a sympathetic ear from the
more traditional Fabians.

However, Cole was in revolt againsg the State socialist and collectivist traditions of the Fabian Society. He believed that the failures of
collectivism were bearing fruit in the labour unrest. Collectivism,
according to Cole, had carried the anti-capitalist arguments to their
logical conclusion in their call for nationalisation, but in doing so had

forgotten that socialism was a human proposition as well as a business one. As a result, they had identified the ideal socialist state with the State of the present, falling into the illusion that a mere extension of the existing powers of the State's sphere of action would bring socialism. They saw nationalisation as the panacea for the problems of anarchical competition, and had failed to notice that capitalism itself had eliminated competition by means of creating an even deadlier enemy in the monopoly. By accepting the logic of collectivist socialism, capitalism had entrenched itself more firmly than ever.

The reason for the failure of collectivism, to Cole, lay in its nature as a theory of the distribution of wealth. The relations of *production* were left untouched, so that there was a mere transfer of ownership from the capitalist to the State. In asserting redistribution, the collectivists denied the humanity of the working class, reflecting the narrow materialism of capitalist society.

> They believe that working class ideals begin and end with higher wages, with the securing of a slightly better standard of material comfort. They do not realise that the foundation of inefficiency in industry lies in the divorce of the mass of the workers from power and responsibility.[14]

To Cole, the transfer of ownership to the State was of secondary importance compared with the question of who controlled industry. His antipathy to State socialism seemed to be a return to Marx's critique of labourism as a theory of distribution which sought to maintain capital while getting rid of capitalists.

In contrast to collectivism, syndicalism raised once again the point of view of the producers, but in a very one-sided manner. Where the collectivist totally disregarded the producer, the syndicalist totally disregarded everything but the producer. In doing so, it not merely ignored the interests of the consumer, but restricted humanity to a mere economic function. As a purely economic theory, it totally disregarded morality, culture and nationality as important elements in life. Syndicalism thus presented itself to Cole as a vague assertion of producers' power which had never been sufficiently thought through.

> In affirming the value of industrial action and of the workers' natural organisation it lays down the true principle of a philosophy of labour; but in taking this doctrine to imply the denial of the State, it goes too far, and is led into extravagance and perversity.[15]

Cole attempted to extract the constructive aspects of syndicalism from the narrow economism with which the theory had been presented. 'Syndicalism is strong in what it asserts and weak in what it denies.'[16] The weakness of syndicalism lay in its economism and its denial of political democracy. However, its strength lay not only in its assertion of class war but in its positive proposals for *social* democracy. It recognised that representative democracy was meaningless if it was restricted to the narrow sphere of politics while leaving the everyday social life of people untouched.

Political and Functional Democracy

Cole accepted that 'the bare ballot-box democracy of the great State'[17] disguised social inequality and injustice, making it a parody of real democracy. The power of the press, dependent as it was for finance on the advertisements of rich capitalists, moulded public opinion into a mood hostile to the radical socialist changes needed in society. The unequal education system, by which the few were trained to rule while the many were trained to obey, extended from the industrial to the political sphere. Working people had neither the confidence, leisure-time, nor wealth to understand the society around them, making the democratic forms of government an empty structure without substance. Moreover, the voters in a parliamentary democracy have no control over their representative on issues that arise in the House of Commons, can change their representative only at infrequent intervals, and have only a limited choice of candidates from which to select. In these circumstances, representative government was in reality misrepresentative since social inequality had the effect of 'perverting and annihilating in practice the theoretical democracy of modern politics'.[18]

Cole wished to supplement political democracy with 'functional' democracy. The totality of a person cannot be represented by any other person, since each of us has many different aspects — at work, in the family, as a consumer, as a citizen — which demand different representatives. If they are to be truly represented, people must be represented through their different functional aspects so that democracy would really require each person to have not one but many votes. Only in this way could society, as a complex of associations, find a full democratic expression — 'all true and democratic representation is therefore *functional* representation'.[19]

Of the many functions in society, however, Cole was particularly interested in the economic function of labour. It was in the factory, by means of the wage system, that despotism was most evident, and the guild socialist ideas of Penty and Hobson were to Cole the best machinery by which the producer could be represented. It was also the means by which Cole could link up the syndicalist nature of the labour unrest with the traditions of ethical socialism so important to the Labour Party's outlook. Guild socialism always exercised its fascination over Cole because of its demand for the more harmonious, organic society called for by Ruskin, Morris and Carpenter.

He always used the term 'guild' rather than 'syndicate', because of its medieval associations (though he was adamant that there could be no return to a pre-industrial order). To Cole, the guild idea was essentially a demand for 'pleasure, joy, interest, expression in the works of a man's hand, taken from the worker by Capitalistic Production and the Industrial Revolution'.[20] Years later, after guild socialism had collapsed as a political movement, Cole was to pessimistically write that

> men will rightly work far better if their task is made as light as possible, and if they are clearly conscious that it is worth performing. This was the truth behind Guild Socialism, the valuable truth which has outlived its cant.[21]

Guilds and Unions

Cole did not want to restore the medieval guilds by returning to the material conditions of the Middle Ages. He saw the factory as the natural unit of guild life, internally self-governing and the basis of the wider functional democracy. The factory was the smallest and, therefore, to Cole as a disciple of Rousseau, the most intimate centre of an individual producer's working life. Consequently, the principle of factory representation had to be the foundation of the regional and national organs of guild representation. Unless the worker was a positive and active member of a community, the communal spirit which was the motive of the socialist society envisaged by Cole would be absent. Guilds, unlike the modern capitalist factories, were not 'a mere prison of boredom and useless toil, but a centre of free service and associative enterprise'.[22] Therefore, while the regional and national guilds would regulate and co-ordinate the activities of the local guilds, representing them in their external associations with other economic corporations, the factory would remain the fundamental unit of a guild democracy, appointing technical experts through their elected representatives, and developing its own sense of discipline and efficiency.

These guilds were to be the trade unions in the modern conditions of industrial society, rather than the closed and privileged corporations of the Middle Ages. This meant that the unions had to develop much further than their present defensive functions in capitalism, but the structure of the future guilds could already be discerned in the present unions. Their first duty, to Cole, was to fight the employers, beside which all other activities were secondary and comparatively unimportant.[23] This duty determined the democratic structure of the unions. While the initiative in taking and organising strikers was necessarily local, the finances for strike activity had to be centralised in order to help the wider class struggle. This contrast between local democracy and centralised co-ordination was a perfect reflection of the future guild system. The democratic structure was, however, constrained by the negative approach forced on the unions by their exclusion from th actual conduct of industry. As a result, 'viewed from the standpoint of any theoretical system, the British trade union movement is merely an appalling chaos of contending atoms'.[24]

However, the very fact that unions were the rudimentary defence of the worker against total wage-slavery was reason for hope. At the moment, they imposed negative restrictions on the capitalist, restricting the production of wealth on the grounds of the safety and living standards of the worker. The labour unrest, caused according to Cole by a loss of faith in capitalism, provided the opportunity for this negative power to be turned into the positive power of executive and legislative control.

> Regarded merely as the instruments of collective wage bargaining, the Unions are the most powerful weapons in the hands of labour; if they are in addition the germs of the future organisation of indusgry as a whole, their importance becomes at once immeasurably greater.[25]

When seen in this light, the unions' functions and structure became as central to the guild socialists as they were to the syndicalists.

In analysing this structure, Cole echoed the criticisms of union bureaucracy by many syndicalists, particularly by the authors of *The Miners' Next Step*. He argued that union leaders were, by the nature of their job, efficient clerks rather than people of initiative and originality. They would make good officials if they were the servants of the rank and file, but their increasing respectability divorced them from the viewpoint of workers on the shopfloor, making them a burden on the workers' movement. Consequently, there was a growing breach between the leaders and the workforce, as the leaders forgot their origins and initial sympathies. While the capitalists organised, the unions squabbled amongst themselves in the selfish and sectional approach of fighting one another rather than the real class enemy. The union leaders were interest-bound in maintaining this emotional approach, based as it was on the outmoded craft structure of their unions.

Against this, Cole called for rank and file action to overcome the conservatism of the leadership (though he left the actual organisational structure of rank and file control to the unions themselves). This would create what Cole called the Greater Unionism[26] of co-operation between industrial unions, overcoming demarcation disputes and other differences within the working class, and increasing the co-operation of that class. In this Greater Unionism, the unions would be organised industrially as a preparation for their guild role — 'the basis of organisation would be neither the craft to which a man belonged, nor the employer under whom he worked, but the service on which he was engaged.'[27] The new, reorganised unions would become the guilds which ran industry. Like the medieval guilds, they would enjoy a statutory and recognised position in society; exercise a monopoly over the market; be an association of masters, because all would be masters; and would stand for the lost morality of pride in craftsmanship.

Guilds and Corporatism

It was the corporatist strain in syndicalism which had been drawn out by Cole. The guilds, or unions, were to be 'self-governing independent corporations with the widest powers'[28] to run their affairs. These corporations were to be fully democratic, electing their own officials and managers, and free to administer themselves within their own sphere. While ownership was vested in the community, represented by the State, control would normally be in the hands of the unions, or guilds. The character and amount of production would be determined by the State, but the methods and processes of production would be entirely in the hands of the guilds. Each national guild would elect an executive committee, and each year there would be a Guild Congress (similar to the TUC) composed of representatives from each guild and working in co-operation with the government. This was seen by Cole to be as practical as the government's relationship to the armed forces – with total independence being respected within the limits of the state as ultimate authority.

If the guilds were to take executive and legislative control of industrial affairs, this did not mean that they could forget the limits of their sphere of interest. One of Cole's major disagreements with the syndicalists lay in his rejection of their narrow, one-sided economism. The power of the unions might be absolute within its rightful realm, but outside that realm other functions needed to be represented. 'The control of industry may be the future existing destiny of the trade unions; the direct control of the whole national life is most emphatically not for them.'[29] The consumers needed representation, too, as the guild idea was a denial of the sovereignty of the consumers. Cole changed his mind on how consumers should be represented – in *The World of Labour*, he nominated the State as representative of the community, while by *Guild Socialism Restated* he proposed consumer associations – but he was adamant about the balance needed between producers and consumers, so that one fraction of society did not obtain undue power over others. 'The solution must surely lie in a rational division of functions , allowing both producer and consumer a say in the control of what is, after all, supremely important to both'.[30]

If the citizen needed representation as both producer and consumer, then representation as a citizen of a country was particularly needed. Cole was aggressive in asserting his nationalism, though it had a decidedly left-wing stance. As far as he was concerned, national ties remained of enormous importance in social, moral and political terms. It was 'still the strongest bond which can join men together'.[31] uniting them in a common inheritance of history and culture and transcending class divisions. In 1913, he prophetically wrote that while a general strike against war looked very well on paper, in practice 'there is nothing so certain as that, at the breath of a war scare, all the peaceable professions of the workers will be forgotten, and jingoism will sweep like a scourge over the country'.[32] This was because Britain was a nation based on natural differences, tied together by a common descent which went far deeper than bonds of neighbourhood or class. It was true that the working class were exploited throughout the world, facing the same capitalist enemy, so that the citizen as a worker was cosmopolitan. The difficulty was that the citizen was not merely a worker, but a member of a nation shaped by two thousand years of history. Thus, while throughout the world parliamentary democracy was an illusion as a result of industrial autocracy, 'it does not follow from this, as some Syndicalists would have us believe, that the worker must abjure patriotism, and become a citizen of the world of labour, pure and simple'.[33]

In the light of his rejection of the one-sided economism of syndicalist theory, and his assertive nationalism, Cole was led to a pluralist view of politics. As the representative of the geographical group known as the nation, the political State could claim sovereignty, but it was a strictly limited sovereignty. Parliament, representing the citizen, would be elected on a territorial basis, while the guilds, representing the producer, would be elected on an industrial basis. On the inevitable question of whether Parliament or the guilds (or any other association) was supreme, Cole took a libertarian stance. While the State was sovereign in regard to national matters such as defence and foreign affairs, it had no right to interfere with areas such as industry or religion which were *not* common to its citizens. As soon as this pluralist nature of society was recognised, then the role of the democratic state as the first among equals would become clear. As Cole put it,

> the demand for functional devolution is not a demand for the recognition of associations by the State, but a demand that the State itself should be regarded only as an association − elder brother, if you will, but certainly in no sense father of the rest.[34]

While it retained ultimate power, the State had to recognise the restricted limits within which it could operate.

Guild Socialism and War

The outbreak of war in 1914 made Cole's peculiar mix of elements such as his aggressive nationalism, his assertion of class war, and his libertarian rejection of the strong State untenable. However, Cole continued to act as though his theoretical system could easily take the strain. He was certainly aware of the contradiction forced into his system by the grim reality of war. If he was to call for the continuation of class war, it would be a denial of nationalism; if he was to acquiesce in the wave of jingo sentiment which swept the country, it would be a denial of the injustice of a class system. Cole believed that, when national security was threatened, socialists must rally to the aid of their country − 'they cannot logically take advantage of the economic situation for an attack on capitalism, if in so doing they hamper the country in the conduct of the war'.[35] However, he also understood that in such conditions the

State would act on behalf of the capitalists by attacking trade union rights.

In these circumstances Cole called on the worker both to serve the nation and to maintain the strength of the unions. He sought to justify this stand by making a distinction between the State and the nation. The former was corrupt and to be resisted; the latter was a fundamental bond which demanded obedience. Thus, Cole argued,

> the class struggle is suspended, or largely suspended, in times of external strife, not because the State is greater than the Trade Union, but because the individuals in such times transcend the groups through which they ordinarily act.[36]

If the corrupt State were to take advantage of such patriotism, it was to be fiercely resisted. In particular, the State's sovereignty even in times of war was limited by the individual conscience of the dissenter.[37] Nevertheless, when the nation was in danger, the worker must serve even as corrupt an institution as the State.

It was a solution which had more theoretical appeal than common sense. If the nation was in danger, then a class state was duty bound to curb the rights of any group (such as the unions) which threatened national unity. In such a situation (which did exist in Britain as a result of the 1915 Treasury Agreement), any socialist would be forced to *choose* between nation and class. The State and the nation could not be separated in practice, so that Cole was forced into a metaphysical defence of the right of the existing class state to mobilise its citizens in its defence. He held that 'the State, as it exists today, is a mere parody of the true expression of the national unity; Labour, in giving it allegiance, is offering it service in virtue of what it might be'.[38] His system was saved at the expense of reality. As a result, Cole's political activity in the NGL throughout the war was marked by the refusal, common to many syndicalists, to recognise the existence of war. Politically, Cole was not neutral as much as neutralised.

Cole and Labourism

Cole had performed a remarkable juggling act in constructing his system of ideas known as guild socialism. He had balanced syndicalism and state socialism, Rousseau and Figgis, industrial and political democracy. However, Cole's belief in the renewing power of the trade union movement inevitably forced him to relate his ideas to its labourism and to its political party.

Cole's attitude to the Labour Party in its pre-socialist period can easily be misunderstood. On the surface he seemed to regard it as at best an irrelevancy, and at worst as reactionary. He saw the party as incapable of obtaining a parliamentary majority, and incapable of knowing what to do if it ever did obtain one. Its narrow reformism could be compared only with the narrowest view of a trade union as a body concerned with obtaining higher wages. As a result the Labour Party could be of no concern to those interested in socialist transformation. Cole regarded it with contempt, as 'that sad failure of Socialism, endeavouring, by a trick, to seem stronger than it really is'.[39] It had ceased to fulfil the real needs of the wider labour movement, forcing the working class to turn back to the trade unions as agents of social reconstruction.

Unlike the Labour Party in Parliament, the trade unions could deliver material gains to their members. Their social and economic power stood in marked contrast to the weakness of the parliamentary representatives. The political arena was a mere debating society in comparison with the economic arena, where the real decisions would be fought out. Consequently, the Labour Party could not advance beyond the limits set for it by trade union power. It was a reflection of union struggles rather than a major force in its own right —

> in politics democracy can nibble, but it may not bite; and it will not be able to bite until the balance of economic power has been so changed as to threaten the economic dominance of capital.[40]

However, despite his initial contempt for the Labour Party, Cole was never an anti-Labour politician. The subsidiary role played by the political party in relation to the trade union did not mean that it played no role. On the contrary, he argued that the failure of the Marxists (both the SDF and the SLP) to gain any working-class support demonstrated the importance of the Labour Party for socialists. Indeed, if Labour could be purged of its non-socialist element it would become the key element in the transformation of society through its political position as a party seeking state power. As the unions rose in dominance through their militant success in strike action, so would the Labour Party become more important in its wake, capturing electoral success as a result of trade union success. Industrial action is thus put in its context as industrial, not political, in its influence. In stark contrast to the syndicalists, Cole argued that 'even if strikes can succeed in raising real wages and in bettering conditions, it does not follow that they can ever by themselves bring about the expropriation of the capitalist'.[41] It would not be right if they could, because of the necessarily sectional nature of the unions. Only the state, as the representative of the community, had the right to bring capitalist ownership to an end.

This raised the question of nationalisation. Cole's attitude to state socialism *as a tactic* changed over time, from an early neutrality on the question of state ownership to a position of advocacy by 1917.[42] However, his opposition to the *principle* of state socialism was absolute. It was a denial of self-government and, as such, a denial of the essential freedom of the worker. The State, as representative of the community, must *own* industry, but *control* of industry must lie with the guilds. As a result, state ownership would be a necessary stage in the transition to guild control. State socialism would certainly be a major advance compared with the system of state capitalism, or state intervention to protect the capitalist class, that had evolved during the Great War. To Cole,

> under either system, the power of the State is arrayed on the side of the wage system; but the chance of developing the Guild idea and the Guild demand among the workers seems to me very much greater under national ownership then under State capitalism.[43]

As the political party capable of legally endorsing the transfer of capital to the workers, the Labour Party was inevitably seen by Cole as a critical area for guild socialists to capture for their ideas. Cole became much more active in the Labour Party during and after the war, helping to draft the guild socialist constitution accepted by the ILP in 1922. However, his theoretical position on the Labour Party and the place of political action remained fundamentally the same as that proposed in *The World of Labour*.[44] He welcomed Labour's 1918 Constitution as a bridge for co-operation between the political and economic wings of the Labour movement, but maintained that constitutional action by itself would achieve little. There was never any chance, given the realities of public opinion in a capitalist society, that the working class would vote as a block for a socialist society, while the power of the middle classes meant that counter-revolution could be easily provoked. Therefore, political action, while necessary, was secondary to economic action. The industrial order was the vulnerable point of the existing system, and it was there that the Labour movement could be mobilised with a strength which it could not exercise in any other direction. Cole succinctly expressed the relation between industrial and political action, between the unions and the Labour Party, in 1918 – 'In the Commonwealth today, power in the economic field is the key which alone can unlock the gates of real political power'.[45]

Cole's acceptance of the Labour Party did not mean that guild socialism fell easily into the framework of labourist ideology. Indeed, Cole continued the syndicalist attack on labourism in several ways. As has been noted, he rejected Labour's politics of merely redistributing wealth, pointing to the need to change the capitalist relations of *production* through the abolition of the wage system. In doing so, he resurrected Marx's challenge to labourism, in that he identified capital (as a social relationship), rather than individual capitalists, as the enemy of the working class. Moreover, Cole's rejection of simple parliamentary representation and his views on functional representation, seem to put him outside the boundaries of mainstream political thought in the Labour Party. His rejection of the existing state as deserving loyalty, compared with the ideal socialist state, seem at first sight to place him on the revolutionary side of the workers' movement.

However, Cole's critique of parliamentary democracy was not as radical as it appeared. Where the syndicalists wished to destroy the political state, replacing it with a social republic, Cole wished to maintain the state. The syndicalists, like Lenin, regarded parliamentary democracy as a sham, disguising the realities of class dictatorship. If that dictatorship should ever be threatened, it would react savagely. If the socialists ever came close to capturing parliamentary power, they would find that Parliament would have power taken away from it by capital. This was why their ideas could never be reconciled with the Labour Party's political thought. In contrast, Cole never thought in such revolutionary terms, despite his awareness of the close relationship between class and power. Parliamentary democracy was not so much a sham as an outpost of popular rule which needed to be reinforced by the social democracy of economic associations. The rule of the capitalist through the wage system was seen as an autocracy, but never anything so beyond recovery as a dictatorship. To acknowledge such an extreme view would propel Cole to a revolutionary standpoint which he never wanted to reach. He would go so far, but no further. He would point to the despotism of capitalist rule in the factory –

in politics we do not call democratic a system in which the proletariat has the right to organise and exercise what pressure it can on an irresponsible body of rulers; we call it modified aristocracy; and the same name adequately describes a similar industrial structure.[46]

However, Cole's solution to this was industrial democracy; not the revolutionary general strike preached by the syndicalists ('a fool's idea of how to run a revolution'),[47] and certainly not the revolutionary party called for by the Leninists.

This was a result of Cole's conception of the State, which was rooted firmly in Fabian thought as much as Rousseau. He profoundly disagreed with the syndicalist idea of the State as a fundamental instrument of class rule. Cole often criticised the state socialists as identifying the present State with the ideal State, but he ultimately agreed with Shaw's view (in *The Impossibilities of Anarchism*) that the State, no matter how badly used by the capitalists, was capable of being used well if the working class could capture its citadel. Thus, he could point out in 1917 that 'in the Society of today, the State is a coercive power, existing for the protection of private property, and merely reflecting, in its subservience to Capitalism, the economic class structure of the modern world'.[48] He could even go so far as to argue, as he did throughout his ten years as an active guild socialist that

it is of no use for the workers to look to the State for salvation: the State responds only to economic pressure, and the salvation that will be got from it will be strictly in proportion to the economic pressure applied.[49]

However, even in his most enthusiastic celebrations of class war, Cole never forgot the power of the State, and its ability to crush the trade union movement in any direct constitutional clash in the sense envisaged by the revolutionary syndicalists. The State was far stronger than any single employer, and the unions must co-operate with it, not destroy it. His view of class war was restricted solely to the economic struggle at the point of production; in politics, he believed that the State stood above class struggles between employers and workers, and could be pressured into supporting the union cause. To Cole, 'it is in warring with Capitalism that they (the unions) will learn to do without Capitalism; but they must realise their freedom in partnership with, and not in opposition to, the State'.[50]

In rejecting the revolutionary implications of syndicalism, Cole was able to extricate its corporatist strain which he regarded as its constructive and positive element. He believed that 'syndicalism is strong in what it asserts and weak in what it denies',[51] and that its strongest point lay in recognising that social life in the economic sphere was totally unregulated by the democratic mechanism that governed the political sphere. In this way, Cole made the 'constructive', or corporatist, aspects of syndicalism more palatable to British socialism.

Moreover, Cole's acceptance of political, parliamentary action to achieve political ends made his anti-capitalist ideas into a utopian blueprint, acceptable only to the Labour Left at a certain time. He realised that the State was too powerful to be overthrown by the economic action of a general strike, as advocated by the syndicalists, and hoped that the combination of parliamentary action and union power would bring about a social revolution. In practical terms, it was a forlorn hope, as the growing strength of the unions was emasculated by the economic depression of the 1920s. However, it was a forlorn hope even in Cole's terms of the powerful, repressive state. If the strength of the Labour Party *was* so dependent on the strength of the unions, then there would be no reason for the State to allow a social revolution quietly to gather strength without striking out against it. Any such attack on the unions might, or might not, be successful, but it would certainly involve the sort of extra parliamentary action envisaged by the syndicalists and deplored by Cole. In this context, Cole's ideas were an intellectual fantasy, with no practical answer to the problem of transition to a guild society. Cole's old friend, William Mellor, recognised as much when he (temporarily) joined the Communist Party. In an article criticising his old belief in guild socialism, Mellor argued that 'it hovers in a state of uneasy equilibrium between the mediaevalist and the revolutionary',[52] explaining its contradictions in Cole's own personality.

This criticism is underlined by the startling inaccuracy of Cole's own theory. He elaborated his ideas at a time when the unions were growing in strength, and he simply assumed that this would continue. However, the onset of economic depression in the early 1920s led to a severe weakening of trade union power, though this weakening was certainly not reflected in Labour's political success during the decade. Cole's failure to develop an economic theory of *the present*, as opposed to an economic blueprint for the future, was to impress itself upon him only after the slump had destroyed the National Building Guild, and with it guild socialism, in 1922.

However, this is to overlook the importance of guild socialism for the politics of the Labour Party. In the short term, it served as an intellectual rallying point for the Labour Left in the immediate post-war period. Until 1918, the ILP had seen itself as the socialist agency inside the Labour Party, whose task it was to push the trade unions in a socialist direction. With the 1918 Constitution, this task was accomplished, while the creation of individual party membership threatened the ILP's organisational existence. The party's search for a *raison d'etre* was intensified by the appeal of Leninism and the ideas of Soviet democracy to its own left wing, some of whom helped to form the Communist Party in 1920-21. In these circumstances, Clifford Allen, a leading member of the No-Conscription Fellowship, who identified the guild idea with the nobler aspects of Soviet Communism,[53] fought successfully for a guild socialist constitution for the ILP. Written partly by Cole, the constitution as adopted in 1922 called for the achievement of both political and economic democracy, with the internal management of each industry in the hands of its workers and co-operating with the representatives of the consumers. The new constitution accepted that

> the best way of effecting a peaceful change to Socialism is by the organisation of the workers politically to capture the power of the State, and industrially to take over the control and management of the industrial machine.[54]

It was ironic that this constitution was adopted in the very year that guild socialism collapsed as a political force. The distinctive voice for which the ILP was searching in the 1920s would come from another direction.

In the long term, guild socialism left a much more important legacy for the politics of the Labour Party. In eliminating the revolutionary aspects of syndicalism, Cole had made its corporatist strain acceptable to Labour thought. Previously, British socialism had regarded the unions as purely defensive instruments of the working class in a capitalist society, with the Labour Party alone concerned with the problem of government. Cole had widened the scope of Labour theory, demonstrating the possibility of economic associations such as the unions taking part in the government of the country's economic affairs. The old panacea of nationalisation, contributed to British socialism by the Labour Marxists, had been found wanting by the Left, and a call for the economy to be run by extra-governmental organisations raised.

This should not be taken to mean that guild socialism was an early version of the corporate socialism which came to be accepted by Labour in the 1940s. There were many crucial differences, as will be seen. Cole's ideas were too democratic and anti-capitalist to be acceptable to anybody but the Labour Left. However, in raising the question of functional as well as representative democracy, guild socialism was an essential transitional stage in the evolution of corporate socialism. Cole himself was well aware that guild socialism was an eventual ideal, and that a series of stages would be required before it could be attained. State socialism was acceptable to him as such a stage, but so, if necessary, was joint control of industrial affairs by the unions with the State and the capitalists. He was privately ambiguous on the Whitley Council ideas of joint control, while in 1917 he argued that

> the workers must be prepared, if necessary to assume, through their trade Unions, a half share in the ownership of capital, as a step in the direction of National Guilds. They must not, however, accept any joint responsibility with capitalism in return for less than a half-share in ownership.[55]

John Parker even recalled Cole's 'initial sympathy with Mussolini's corporate state. . . He saw it as a development of Sorel possibly leading to a form of socialist syndicalism'[56] though he soon recoiled from the Fascist suppression of free trade unions.

These statements demonstrate the extreme flexibility of Cole's use of corporate ideas. He remained a guild socialist for the rest of his life, though after 1922 he ceased to regard it as a practical alternative for the immediate future. For the Labour Party, guild socialism had a passing effect in the short term, but in the end its corporatist stance was to be resurrected in a new form, with Cole playing an important part in its evolution. However, before this could take place, Labour faced a new intellectual challenge from the Liberal Party on its Right.

Notes

1. See J. Klugmann, *History of the Communist Party of Great Britain*, vol. I, chapter I (Laurence and Wishart, 1968).

2. See *The Second Congress of the Communist International*, volume II, pp. 178-88.

3. See David D. Roberts, *The Syndicalist Tradition and Italian Fascism* (University of North Carolina, 1979), quoted p. 255.

4. Ibid., quoted p. 233.

5. G.D.H. Cole, 'The Genesis of French Syndicalism – and Some Unspoken Morals' in *New Age* 12 February 1914, vol. XIV, p. 458.

6. Arthur Penty, *Restoration of the Gild System* (London 1906), p. 57.

7. S.G. Hobson, *National Guilds: An Inquiry into the Wage System and The Way Out*, ed. A.R. Orage, (London, 1914), p. 3.

8. Ibid., p. 16.

9. Frank Matthews, 'The Ladder of Becoming: A.R. Orage, A.J. Penty, and the

Origins of Guild Socialism in England' in David E. Martin and David Rubinstein, *Ideology and the Labour Movement, Essays Presented to John Saville* (Croom Helm, 1979), p. 147.

10. See W. Golant, 'The Early Political Thought of C.J. Attlee' in *Political Quarterly*, July-September 1969.

11. G.D.H. Cole, *Self-Government in Industry*, (London, 1917), p. 110.

12. G.D.H. Cole, *The World of Labour – A Discussion of the Present and Future of Trade Unionism* (London, 1928 edition), p. 319.

13. Ibid., p. 21.

14. Cole, *Self-Government*, p. 30.

15. Cole, *World of Labour*, p. 126.

16. Ibid., p. 25.

17. Ibid., p. 17.

18. Cole, *Guild Socialism Restated* (London, 1920), p. 14.

19. Ibid., p. 33.

20. Cole, *World of Labour*, p. 9.

21. Cole, *The Next Ten Years in British Social and Economic Policy* London, 1930 ed.), p. 17.

22. Cole, *Guild Socialism Restated*, p. 58.

23. See, for example, *Cole, World of Labour*, p. 259.

24. Cole, 'Recent Developments in the British Labour Movement' in *The American Economic Review*, vol. VIII, no. 3, September 1918, p. 490.

25. Cole, *World of Labour*, p. 11.

26. See, for example, Cole and William Mellor, *The Greater Unionism* (London, 1913).

27. Cole, *World of Labour*, p. 213.

28. Ibid., p. 363. See also p. 369.

29. Ibid., p. 26.

30. Ibid., p. 352.

31. Ibid., p. 27.

32. Ibid., p. 196.

33. Ibid., p. 45.

34. Cole, 'Conflicting Obligations' in *Proceedings of the Aristotelian Society 1914-15*, vol. XV, London 1915, p. 157.

35. Cole, *Labour in Wartime* (London, 1915), p. 18.

36. Cole, *Labour in the Commonwealth* (London, 1919), p. 50.

37. See Cole, with Bertrand Russell and C. DeLisle Burns, 'Symposium: The Nature of the State' in *Proceedings of the Aristotelian Society 1915-16*, vol. XVI, London,1916.

38. Cole, *Labour in Wartime*, p. 19.

39. Cole, *World of Labour*, pp. 242-3.

40. Cole, *Self-Government*, p. 76.

41. Cole, *World of Labour*, pp. 405-06.

42. See Cole, *Self-Government*, Appendix B.

43. Cole, ibid., p. 326.

44. Here, I must disagree with J.M. Winter who overestimates the impact of war on Cole's political thought. See Winter, *Socialism and the Challenge of War: Ideas and Politics in Britain 1912-18* (Routledge and Kegan Paul, 1974), chapter 5.

45. Cole, *Labour in the Commonwealth*, pp. 104-05. See also Cole's *Guild Socialism Restated*, p. 180.

46. Cole, *Guild Socialism Restated*, p. 358.

47. Cole, ibid., p. 358.

48. Cole, *Self-Government*, p. 104.

49. Cole, ibid., p. 16.

50. Cole, *World of Labour*, p. 392.

51. Cole, ibid., p. 25.

52. William Mellor, 'A Critique of Guild Socialism' in *Labour Monthly*, vol. I, no. 5, November 1921, p. 402.

53. See Allen's memo on his visit to Soviet Russia in Arthur Marwick, *Clifford Allen: The Open Conspirator* (Oliver and Boyd, 1964), pp. 62-4. See also H.N. Brailsford, *Parliament or Soviets?* (London, 1919).

54. See Report of *ILP Conference 1922*, pp. 92-3.

55. Cole, *Self-Government*, p. 163.

56. A.W. Wright, *G.D.H. Cole and Socialist Democracy* (Clarendon Press, Oxford, 1979), Letter from John Parker, MP, quoted p. 109, n. 13.

7 THE ILP AND THE KEYNESIAN CHALLENGE

Outwardly, the 1920s was a decade of political progress for the Labour Party. With the enfranchisement of working-class men and (after 1928) women, its future electoral success seemed assured. It replaced the fractured Liberal Party as the official Opposition in 1922, and quickly advanced to form minority governments in 1924 and 1929. The belief in the inevitability of gradualism — the slow evolution of capitalism into socialism propagated by the Fabians and Macdonald — was being borne out.

However, a different story could be discerned in the economic reality which lay behind the political realm. After an initial post-war boom, an economic depression set in after 1920 which overshadowed all other issues in British society. The decline of British manufacturing in the world market, together with the savagely deflationary measures of a cost-conscious government, led to a fall in industrial production by a quarter in 1920-1. Unemployment rose from 2 per cent of the labour force to more than 18 per cent within a year, while money wages fell by 38 per cent in the four years after 1920. When the economy gradually recovered after the mid-1920s, unemployment remained obstinately high, rarely sinking below 10 per cent for the rest of the decade. The export of capital abroad, which had been the mainstay of British prosperity in the pre-war period, was ceasing to be sufficient to prevent a crisis in the accumulation of capital in the 1920s.

In these circumstances of mass unemployment and shrinking export markets, the trade union foundations of the Labour Party's political power were badly battered. The defeat of the miners and the collapse of the Triple Alliance in April 1921, followed by the defeat of the engineers in the 1922 lockout, effectively ended the first Shop Stewards Movement. This destruction of the power of the union rank and file strengthened the hold of the union leadership and prepared the way for the defeat of the General Strike in 1926, when the TUC General Council quickly capitulated to the government and the employers as the constitutional implications of the strike became clear to them. The government followed up their victory with a vindictive Trades Disputes Act in 1927, which banned sympathy strikes and made trade union financial support for the Labour Party more difficult. The success of the employers in these disputes, together with the fear of unemployment, led to a drastic decline in union membership, which fell from over eight million in 1920 to under five million by the decade's end. Any realistic hope that progress could be made in the industrial as well as the parliamentary arena was ended for all but a few militants on the Left. Instead, the concern of union leaders like Ernest Bevin of the Transport Workers was with the immediate question of overcoming unemployment within a capitalist society.

However, it was precisely in the question of unemployment that the bankruptcy of British socialism was revealed. It was able to postulate a morally superior system of co-operation to replace a class-divided society, but it was unable to put forward realistic schemes for the regulation of a trade cycle which was entering into a vicious circle of unemployment and falling productivity. Macdonald seemed more concerned with the minutiae of parliamentary behaviour and court manners than with developing his earlier political ideas.[1]

In response to an ILP campaign, the Labour leadership did adopt a new programme (drafted by Tawney), *Labour and the Nation* (1928), but this contained little more than the old platitudes of British socialism. A variety of palliatives from higher direct taxes to enlarged powers for the Food Council were proposed, but there was no new political strategy underlying them. A belief in 'the familiar commonplace that "morality is the nature of things" and that men are all, in truth, members of one another'[2] was very uplifting, but hardly met the requirements of the time. It was as if nothing had changed since the days of Carpenter and Blatchford.

It was believed on both Labour's Right and Left that unemployment and poverty would disappear when capitalism had finally ended, a belief which fed the ILP demand that Labour should refuse to govern the country until it had a parliamentary majority to introduce socialist measures. In realistic terms, though, Labour was unable to achieve such a majority in the conditions of the 1920s, and the ILP refused to entertain the idea, equally impractical at the time, of a workers' dictatorship. The real weakness which underlay Labour's electoral progress in the decade was its bankruptcy of economic solutions to overcome the immediate crisis. It was all very well to dream of healthy young boys and girls dancing around campfires in the socialist commonwealth, but in the meantime the rent had to be paid and the diseases of malnutrition cured.

An ILP committee around Brailsford and Hobson did produce a set of proposals, *The Living Wage*, in 1926, while Oswald Mosley put forward his solution of protectionism and credit expansion in his

'Birmingham Proposals' in 1925, but both groups were unable to change Labour thinking in the short term. The *Living Wage* proposals were soon submerged in a militant campaign for *Socialism in our Time*, and suffered from theoretical shortcomings. Mosley's proposals gained popularity in certain sections of the Left under the second Labour government, but were obscured for a time by his own personal ambitions which led him to leave the Labour Party. Moreover, they had more in common with the advanced Liberalism of Keynes than they had with any socialist programme.

It was, indeed, from Keynes and the Liberal Party with their programme for reviving a capitalist economy that the main theoretical challenge to British socialism rose in the decade. Keynes was particularly prominent in this challenge. His subversion of Neo-classical economic theory in the early 1930s, known as the Keynesian Revolution, had its foundations in his double challenge to *laissez-faire* and to British socialism in the previous decade. It was, however, an ambiguous challenge since Keynes was led, at first implicitly, to identify the lack of effective demand as the main economic problem facing capitalist society. As such, he came to agree partially with the principal Labour economist of the twenties, J.A. Hobson. The ambiguity of the Keynesian challenge to British socialism, and the ultimate Labour response to that challenge, must be found in Keynes' criticisms of the Labour economists of the twenties.

The Labour Economists

The causes of, and remedies for, unemployment in the Labour Party of the 1920s tended to revolve around the ideas of J.A. Hobson, described by Brailsford as 'the most respected intellectual influence in the Labour Movement'.[3] This may seem at first sight paradoxical, as most of his ideas had been formulated while he was an active Liberal.

Hobson

John A. Hobson (1858-1940) was born to a middle-class family in Derby, educated at Oxford, and quickly developed a disregard for intellectual orthodoxies, particularly in political economy. Together with a like-minded businessman, A.F. Mummery, he wrote *The Physiology of Industry* (1889) in which Say's law that supply and demand would always balance was challenged. Mummery, who was apparently the more original of the two, died shortly afterwards, but Hobson developed their 'under-consumptionist' ideas in a long series of books for the rest of his life. As a Liberal Radical, his bitter opposition to the Boer War led him to write *Imperialism* (1902), in which the vaguely anti-capitalist ideas of the Liberal and Labour parties were given a coherent theoretical form. The book had a major effect on Brailsford's analysis of the Great War, as has already been noted, as well as being a model for Lenin to develop its anti-capitalist ideas in a revolutionary direction. As an anti-war Liberal in the UDC, Hobson decided to join the Labour Party after the Great War, though he regarded the ILP as too extreme.[4] By this time his writings on poverty and unemployment had won him recognition in the labour movement, where both Macdonald and Snowden were adherents of his economic heresies.

Hobson was a radical critic of orthodox political economy, which he regarded as a sophisticated attempt to justify the necessity and finality of an unjust economic system. Their conservatism had prevented economists from developing marginalist theories to cover a consistently human theory of wealth. Instead, they had concerned themselves merely with the determination of prices, failing to lift their horizons above the mean limits of the business world. Hobson pointed to the class nature of political economy, arguing that

> its immanent conservatism recommends it, not only to timid academic minds, but to the general body of the possessing classes who, though they may be quite incapable of following its subtleties of reasoning, have sufficient intelligence to value its general conclusions.[5]

In its place, he attempted to revive Ruskin's conceptions of a humanist political economy which would cover the economics of welfare as well as profit. Like Ruskin, Hobson was aware that economics had a human and social, as well as a commercial, importance, and that the principles of justice and health should be the foundations of political economy, rather than the subjective valuations of 'consumers'. Against those Liberals who held to *laissez-faire* and free trade, Hobson pointed out that the growth of cartels and monopolies had severely restricted free competition in industry, leading to much greater profits than were due to entrepreneurs. These profits had totally upset the 'natural' balance of spending and saving, leading to a situation where too much was being saved and not enough spent. This 'surplus' of saving was becoming unearned income, idly accumulated by the rich, rather than flowing along the healthy channels necessary for economic growth. The constant tendency towards gluts and overproduction in capitalist society, unexplained by the orthodox economists, could only find a satisfactory solution in recognising the surplus of unearned and excessive incomes incapable of consuming the increased production of industrial society.

The limited consumption of the working class was the other side of the coin of the 'surplus' incomes. As a result of their under-consumption, the working class provided only a limited market for the goods they produced, so that every increase in output would *not* eventually find its outlet in consumption, as orthodox economists claimed. Consequently, the limited market, which had led to the export of capital characteristic of capitalist imperialism, was identified by Hobson as bringing about overproduction, leading directly to deflation and unemployment. The war had made the depression deeper and longer than previous depressions, but it was not the real *cause* of the depression. 'The general shrinkage of effective demand which constitutes a cyclical depression implies a failure of consumption to keep pace with production in the industrial world taken as a whole'.[6] This normal tendency of production to outrun consumption, experienced by businessmen as a difficulty in selling their produce, was to be ended by increasing consumption through the reduction of the surplus of unearned income. A policy of redistributive taxation and increased wages would raise the consuming power of the working class, who would then provide the expanded markets needed to absorb the increased output.

Hobson's analysis fitted in neatly with the labourist traditions of the British trade union movement. He regarded it as one of his aims to establish 'an intelligible and consistent theory alike of the harmony and the antagonism of capital and labour'.[7] In doing so, he removed the ambiguities in the labour theory of value as propagated by Hodgskin. This theory, that all value was created by labour, had disappeared from non-Marxist economic thought, which excluded the capitalist relations of production from its sphere of concern. Hobson, too, excluded production relations from his analysis. He rejected Marxist economics because it confused

> the economics of a hypothetical society in which the state, owning all the instruments of industry, need no longer take into account the categories of rent, interest, and profit, with the economic analysis of current industry.[8]

This was not really true,[9] but Hobson rejected the labour theory of value along with Marx. He believed that *all* factors of production, capital and land as well as labour, contributed to social wealth, and that there was consequently an underlying harmony of the interests of capital and labour in the sphere of production.

In a society of free competition, 'a law of natural harmony of interests among the owners of the factors of production determines the distribution'[10] of wealth. If there was no surplus, or if the surplus was fairly distributed between capital and labour, there would be industrial peace. However, the surplus was *not* fairly distributed. Instead, the brute laws of force determined the distribution of wealth among the different social classes, with some obtaining excessive and unearned portions of the surplus. The harmonious relations of production were disrupted by the unequal relations of distribution. Hobson was clear as to the real villains of the piece – 'Among entrepreneurs, the financier or manipulator of fluid capital and of credit is at present in a position of such vantage that his share of the surplus is out of all proportion to his services'.[11] It was the financier, the parasitic *rentier*, who mulcted the wealth created by honest employers and workmen, and who was consequently an enemy of industrial progress and justice. The bankers were the unpatriotic rascals who diverted wealth abroad while leaving British industry starved of capital,[12] and together with the idle plutocrats accumulated their unused surplus.[13]

The trade unions emerged for Hobson as the major force in industrial society working for progress. As economic crisis was caused by underconsumption, then trade union action to raise wages was socially beneficial, enhancing rather than harming the efficiency of the economy. Trade union struggles, through their raising of the level of consumption, were a counterforce to the plutocrats who disrupted the essential harmony of the social classes – 'if capital or ability takes too much, and labour not enough, industrial progress continues to lag, for the healthy march of industry requires a proportionate advance of all the factors'.[14] Therefore, where labour was able to eat into the surplus of unearned income, industrial harmony and prosperity would result. It followed that social reform, whether carried out by Liberal or Labour, should be aimed at strengthening the power of the unions in collective bargaining.

Hobson's economics may well have fitted in with the labourist tradition, but there was nothing particularly socialist about them. Indeed, he was an active Liberal for a large part of his life, collaborating with Macdonald and other moderate socialists in the Rainbow Circle and the UDC. His decision to join the Labour Party after the Great War was more a mark of his recognition of political realities than of any conversion to socialism. Hobson later wrote,

> Though. . . my sympathies have been with the Labour Party, I have
> never felt quite at home in a body governed by trade union members
> and their finance, and intellectually led by full-blown Socialists. For
> neither section of this Labour Party avowedly accepts that middle
> course which seems to me essential to a progressive and constructive
> economic government in this country.[15]

He saw his economic theories as seeking a reconciliation between socialism and individualism, which would avoid the disastrous wastes and perils of class conflict and international strife that proceeded from unregulated capitalism.

Hobson believed in a mixed economy because he believed that the acquisitive motive, selfish and immoral though it might be, was the only incentive which could make industry work. It was necessary to modify, rather than destroy, the egoistic motive by directing it into socially useful projects. It was a regulated capitalism to which he directed his energies — 'the industrial system thus envisaged consists, partly of nationalised industries, operated by representative government, partly of private industries working either by automatic competition or by some scheme of profit-sharing'.[16] Hobson thus remained a Liberal, in economics as in politics, yet his analysis was taken up by the ILP, the far Left of the Labour Party in the twenties.

The Living Wage and the ILP

Hobson's economics found early favour in the labour movement, profoundly influencing Macdonald, Snowden and Brailsford. In particular, they fulfilled a need of the ILP in the 1920s to act as a distinct left-wing body within the labour movement.

As has been noted, the ILP's *raison d'être* had been threatened by the 1918 Labour Party constitution, which had accepted socialism as its eventual aim and had created local Labour Parties to accommodate individuals hitherto able to join Labour only through the ILP or the Fabian Society. The ILP needed a coherent ideology to attract people who would otherwise turn to a local Labour Party or to the Communist Party. Guild socialism had served as a distinctive and attractive brand of socialism, but by the time it was adopted by the ILP in 1922, the collapse of the Building Guild and the NGL had robbed it of any practical relevance. The moderation of the first Labour government, with its emphasis on respectability, appalled the militant Clydeside group in the ILP, and seemed to demonstrate that Labour's acceptance of socialism had been at best lukewarm. As a result, the ILP felt that they must still convince the trade unions of the necessity of socialism and in doing so appointed an economic committee – Hobson,[17] Brailsford, Frank Wise, and Arthur Creech Jones – to formulate immediate proposals to overcome the crisis of unemployment.

The Living Wage document, published in September 1926, was the result. The demand for a living wage – a minimum wage for all workers – had become generally accepted in the Labour movement,[18] but the novelty of this latest appeal lay in the terms in which the ILP economists couched their demand. In this document, profound in its consequences for Labour's political thought, they pointed to the lack of effective demand in capitalism rather than private ownership as the key problem awaiting Labour's immediate solution –

All of us realise that the low purchasing power of so many millions of wage earners is among the most potent causes of the widespread unemployment which has cursed our country during the last six years.[19]

The ethical argument for a living wage – that the mental and physical growth of most of the population was stunted by poverty and low wages – was pointed out, but the main weight of the argument was based on Hobson's economic theory that low wages limited the home market. The power of the masses to consume failed to keep pace with the power of industry to produce, so that the benefits of mass production were withheld and unrealised. 'We produce less wealth than our technical resources would enable us to create because the mass of the wage-earners lack "effective demand". The owning class has misused the advantage of its position.'[20]

The immoral selfishness of the 'owning class' was arraigned, but it was the lack of effective demand rather than capitalist relations of production which was singled out as the real obstacle to prosperity. It followed, and these ILP economists recognised the logic, that nationalisation was no real solution to the crisis of demand. The state ownership of declining industries in itself would neither avert unemployment nor prevent wage reductions. While nationalisation, as a measure of reorganisation, might be suited to certain key industries – those governing the pace and direction of economic growth, such as credit, coalmining, and transport — it was unsuitable for depressed trades such as engineering, textiles, and agriculture. The ILP economists argued that 'it would be folly to suggest nationalisation as the appropriate method for reorganizing these weaker trades',[21] and proposed in its stead an Industrial Commission which could take under its survey all industries which were not capable of paying the living wage. This Commission would have the power to suggest and ultimately enforce amalgamation of companies within each industry in order to strengthen them by realising the economies of mass production.

As the lack of effective demand was the key problem, it was agreed that the solution to economic crisis and unemployment lay in a general and simultaneous increase of the purchasing power of the masses through the policy of the living wage, particularly in introducing family allowances to help working-class women faced with the heartbreaking task of raising children in poverty. This could be done without inflation through the control of credit. At the first signs of a slump, the banks would be forced to expand credit and reduce interest rates, while restrictive measures could regulate a boom. In the slump conditions of the twenties, it was necessary to increase credit even at the expense of inflation, which was regarded as 'a slight evil in comparison with the increase in production and employment which will be brought about.'[22] However, the expansion of credit with such disregard for price rises was to be seen as an emergency measure, rather than the norm. This policy of credit control, with the object of maintaining steady prices and employment, could only be effective if the independent powers of the Bank of England were taken away by nationalisation. If the state owned the Bank, then nationalisation of the joint stock banks was unnecessary in the short term as they could be controlled quite easily by the central Bank.

Once the problem of inflation was mastered through credit control, the policy of a living wage — based on need and deliberately estimated as higher than the present level of industrial efficiency — would be able to stimulate economic growth. In an early formulation of the multiplier, the ILP economists argued that the new stream of purchasing power generated by the raising of wages would create new employment, as the engineer, for example, would be able to buy boots from the hitherto unemployed bootmaker, who would then be able to provide new employment from his sale and so on in a ripple effect. In this way, the unemployed would be absorbed into the labour force and trade stimulated. The trade unions, which would maintain their freedom to bargain with the employers, were thus given an economic as well as a moral justification for negotiating higher wages.

This document was a remarkable portent for Labour's new economic ideas, but suffered from a number of defects. The problem of how to reconcile continually rising wages with stable prices was ignored as inapplicable to a situation of mass unemployment, but the role of the trade unions could not be so easily shunted aside. The freedom of the unions to negotiate higher wages was affirmed, but the ILP economists argued that the unions were incapable of obtaining a general living wage. Their bargaining power was closely tied to the trade cycle, and the slump of the twenties had demonstrated their current weakness. Moreover, even in times of prosperity, the lowest-paid workers who most needed a living wage found combination in a union very difficult to achieve without being dismissed. As a result, it would be through political rather than trade union action that the living wage would be achieved, though the authors made an almost ritual obeisance to the idea that, 'in the last resort, it is on the organised refusal of men to work for less than a living wage that our hope of securing it lies',[23] a point nowhere explored. In effect, it was being argued that the negotiation of higher wages should be taken from the industrial into the political arena. It would be government representatives, not trade unionists, who were to dictate collective bargaining. This attitude aroused widespread hostility among the trade union leaders, with Ernest Bevin warning the ILP leaders not to interfere with the proper role of the unions by dragging wages into a political programme.[24]

A further problem arose over the *socialist* nature of the programme. Oswald Mosley had already asked the 1926 ILP Conference,

> Could a wage giving a civilised standard be paid until reorganisation had taken place or a credit policy on Socialist lines be operated? How could we win the Socialist Commonwealth by operating the capitalist system of finance? [25]

Mosley had his own interpretation of a socialist credit policy, as will be seen, but his question touched a raw nerve among delegates. Brailsford had to reassure them that

> their task was to guide the country in this period of difficulty into Socialism. They must have their clear-cut plan. Every wondering, every irrelevance, meant a waste of effort. . . Their purpose should be not to administer the capitalist system, but to transform it.[26]

It was hard to see how such conclusions followed from *The Living Wage* document, however. It was argued there that, 'by all these conquests, the transition to the further socialisation of industry would be immensely eased',[27] but it was difficult to see how such a conclusion could emerge from the arguments presented. It was acknowledged that nationalisation was *not* a cure for declining industries, and that prosperity could be achieved through an upward movement in wages instead. Once these industries were rising in prosperity, then it would be easier to nationalise them. However, if a well regulated capitalism could ensure prosperity, then there seemed little *reason* to nationalise industry. The whole question of ownership would become irrelevant from an economic standpoint, though the moral issue of the evil nature of competition and the tyranny of employers remained of some validity.

The reformist implications of the document were quickly buried by the militant campaign of the ILP Left, led by James Maxton and John Wheatley, around the campaign document, *Socialism in our Time* adopted at the 1926 ILP Conference. In this document, the demands for a living wage and family allowances were seen as part of a resolute socialist policy to carry labour quite quickly into a new society. Fenner Brockway linked the demand to the guild socialist ideas of the ILP by arguing that capitalism was incapable of providing such reforms. The campaign for a living wage could, therefore, never be successful under capitalism, serving merely as a propaganda point to win the workers to the recognition that only a fully socialist society could help them. In this way, the living wage demand

> would have the effect of exerting the fullest pressure of the trade union movement for such concessions as Capitalism can provide and of revealing in all its bareness the inability of the existing system of society to do justice to the workers.[28]

This campaign was carried a stage further in 1928, when James Maxton and the militant miners' leader, A.J. Cook, issued a manifesto against the increasing trend of the Labour Party and the unions toward a corporate solution to the problems of capitalism. *Our Case for a Socialist Revival* was a full-blooded exposition of Labour Marxism stressing that socialism could only arrive as a result of class struggle. They rejected the programme of the Labour leaders as an enlightened Liberal programme and argued that the new policy of collaboration with the employing class was merely an invitation to the unions to participate in their own exploitation. Such 'progressive' attitudes would merely lead to an increase in slave-driving as employers used the unions to increase their profits. As for the Labour programme 'if every measure. . . was carried, then we would not have socialism but rationalised capitalism, in which the main industries of the country remained in the hands of the exploiting capitalist class'.[29] In its stead, Cook and Maxton called for a full-blooded socialist programme, including the abolition of the monarchy and the nationalisation of all manufacturing industry under workers' control.

As a result of this identification with the ILP Left, the *Living Wage* proposals were rejected by the majority of the Labour leadership, which saw them as a mere ploy to challenge their evolutionary socialist policies. Hobson, aware of this, virtually dissociated himself from the ILP campaign in order to save the substance of his proposals. He wrote to Ramsay MacDonald,

> I was asked as an economist, not as a politician, to join the small Committee which drew it up, and am not concerned about the use which may be made of it in the Labour Party or the country. . . In the Committee, at an early stage, I found some disposition to utilise the minimum wage in a way that seemed to me dangerous. Its present form is not I think at all open to such criticisms.[30]

Hobson's attempt failed as Macdonald and the Labour Right rejected the programme outright in face of the ILP threat, turning instead to the comfortable if vague nostrums of British socialism in *Labour and the Nation*. It was Keynes, an opponent of the Labour Party, who was paradoxically to retrieve Hobson's ideas for eventual absorption into the Labour Party's thought.

Keynes and the Liberal Challenge

The Liberal Party, which had achieved a fragile reunification of its Asquith and Lloyd George wings in 1923, was in desperate straits during the twenties, squeezed between Conservatives and Labour. They elected only 40 MPs in the 1924 election, while the shaky coalition of *laissez-faire* free traders and radical interventionists was constantly threatening to tear itself apart, as demonstrated by the bitter acrimony in the 1926 General Strike when Lloyd George refused to condemn the TUC without equally condemning the government. It was this desperate situation which forced the Liberal leadership to undertake a major overhaul of its ideas, and in so doing to put its finger on the weakness of British socialism as an immediate remedy for the economic crisis.

It was Lloyd George who began the great Liberal debate with an article in *The Nation* in April 1924, when he pointed to the need for a great rethinking on the use of national economic resources. It was to be a totally fresh approach, since it was independent of the interests of employers and unions, and of their two parties, Conservative and Labour — 'Capital and labour are alike strangled by vested prejudices and traditions. Both are capable of producing infinitely more wealth for the benefit of the community than they are doing'.[31] A reply was immediately forthcoming from the Liberal economist, Keynes, who called on Liberals to turn their back on *laissez-faire* and to endorse state intervention to guide the economy back to prosperity.[32] Lloyd George then used the immense personal funds that he had accumulated during the years to launch a series of Liberal committees and summer schools which, by the late twenties, had produced several reports, notably on land and industry. It was the Yellow Book, *Britain's Industrial Future* (1928), which was the foundation of the challenge to *laissez-faire* and British socialism, and it was Keynes who was mainly responsible for it.

John Maynard Keynes (1883-1946) was born into a Victorian academic background, and was educated at Eton and Cambridge, where he became a member of the élite 'Apostles' (an unofficial academic group which included Bertrand Russell and Lytton Strachey). As a Fellow at Cambridge after 1908, his initial work was philosophical, concerning the logical foundations of probability. However, he first made his mark with the public as a result of his *Economic Consequences of the Peace* (1919), a trenchant critique of the Versailles Treaty which ended the Great War. He followed this in the twenties with a series of books on current monetary policy in which he called for a state-managed currency level and public works to stimulate trade and employment. It was in the following decade, with his *General Theory of Employment, Interest and Money* (1936), that he made his main claim to fame.

This was a major attack on the orthodoxy of the neo-classical economics of Marshall, Jevons and Pigou in which Keynes (and the early Fabians) had been raised. Influenced by a new generation of economists — Joan Robinson, Piero Sraffa, and Richard Kuhn in particular — Keynes was impelled by the mass unemployment of the Great Depression of the early thirties to question the normal economic law that the trade cycle was of short duration so that long-term unemployment was voluntary. The general slump conditions of the early thirties were a glaring disproof of such a theory, and Keynes was led in his attempt to solve the problem to join the economic heretics, whose ideas 'only live on furtively, below the surface, in the underworlds of Karl Marx, Silvio Gesell, or Major Douglas'.[33] He came to agree with Hobson and the Labour economists that the problem was one of ineffective demand. The orthodox ideas of the neo-classical economists were held to be true for the special case where capital and labour were fully employed; they were totally unable to grasp the general case of involuntary unemployment due to a vicious circle of falling productivity and prices. To explain this situation, Keynes turned to 'the brave army of heretics . . . Mandeville, Malthus, Gesell and Hobson, who, following their intuitions, have preferred to see the truth obscurely and imperfectly rather than to maintain error'.[34] The 'Keynesian Revolution' was launched.

However, this revolution in academic thought in the thirties, with all its consequences for political economy, had been prepared in Keynes' double challenge to *laissez-faire* capitalism and British socialism in the previous decade. In terms of his theoretical presumptions, Keynes was firmly trapped in the orthodox economics of Marshall in the twenties,[35] but his concern with immediate practical problems led him to stretch the orthodox theories to their limits. To all intents and purposes the radical solutions to particular economic problems put forward by Keynes, culminating in his writings for the Liberal Party, were solutions to a situation of underconsumption, or lack of effective demand.

This was due to his recognition that capitalism had developed well beyond its golden age of free competition between small entrepreneurs. In such circumstances as the development of cartels and oligopolies, *laissez-faire* had ceased to be a libertarian concept and had become a disguise for allowing the worst aspects of capitalism to come to the fore. However, this was precisely the course taken by the free-trade Liberals, fighting on the outmoded battlegrounds of political democracy, individual liberty and free competition. They did not realise that cut-throat competition was devastating in its effects on prosperity and industrial efficiency, or that the day of the small business unit had passed forever. Combination in the business world, as much as in the labour world, was the order of the day, and the Liberal task was to take advantage of it, to regulate it, to turn it into the right channels. All the mistakes of government economic policy, according to Keynes, were the result of continuing 'to apply the principles of an economics, which was worked out on the hypotheses of *laissez-faire* and free competition, to a society which is rapidly abandoning these hypotheses'.[36] Keynes may have couched his ideas in the terms of Marshall, but he was already in 1925 aware of the inadequacy of traditional economic nostrums.

However, Keynes was a critic of British socialism as well as of *laissez-faire*. He was frank in his criticisms of the Labour Party, which was fundamentally too democratic for his tastes. One of his main objections to Marxism had been his refusal to accept 'a creed which, preferring the mud to the fish, exalts the boorish proletariat above the bourgeois and the intelligentsia who, with whatever faults, are the quality in life'.[37] The Labour Party was a party where the mud had ensnared the fish — where the intellectuals who should lead were dominated by the illiterate trade unionists — and as a result was not the party for Keynes. Labour

> is a class party, and the class is not my class. If I am going to pursue sectional interests at all, I shall pursue my own . . . I can be influenced by what seems to me to be justice and good sense, but the class war will find me on the side of the educated bourgeoisie [38]

He did not believe that Labour allowed the educated bourgeois to lead the uneducated masses, who had no clue as to the way forward. Instead, it was the ignorant trade unionists — 'once the oppressed, now the tyrants, whose selfish and sectional pretensions need to be bravely opposed'[39] — who led the intellectuals behind their banner.

Keynes was to modify his views on the unions, partly as a result of his work with Bevin, but he constantly pointed to the strength of the Left, the party of catastrophe who hated the existing order, as the most dangerous aspect of Labour's class base. The Left's strength compelled the Labour leaders continually to protect their flank by appealing to the more base instincts of the working class. Instead of working out realistic solutions to the immediate problems of falling productivity and rising unemployment, the Labour Party remained trapped in the passions of jealousy and resentment of their betters. They were their own worst enemies, since the only ones to suffer from their class war rhetoric were themselves. To Keynes,

> the Labour Party has got tied up with all sorts of encumbering and old-fashioned luggage. They respond to anti-Communist rubbish with anti-capitalist rubbish. The consequence of all this is that, whether in or out of office, the business of orderly evolution seems

likely to remain in Liberal hands.[40]

Such blatantly anti-working class sentiments may at first sight appear to bar any possibility of the Labour Party being able to absorb Keynesian thinking in any way, but this would be to ignore the novelty of Keynes' ideas. The anti-union prejudice which appeared to cut him off forever from Labour thinking, was superficial, as he entertained high hopes of the Labour Party as an agent for his ideas if channelled by Liberal strength. He recognised even in the mid-twenties that 'great changes will not be carried out except with the active aid of Labour. But they will not be sound or enduring unless they have first satisfied the criticism and precaution of Liberals'.[41] It was up to the Liberals to become more progressive and more far-sighted than Labour if they were to mould the future in a beneficial manner. The strength of Liberal ideas would, for Keynes, far outweigh the great party machines of Conservative and Labour.

Moreover, many of Keynes' ideas made a particular appeal to discontented Labour intellectuals. The aristocratic temperament which led him to reject the working-class mud in favour of the educated fish also led him to a contempt for the vulgar and greedy materialism of the idle plutocrat and the timid businessman. These were aspects of the more objectionable features of capitalism which Keynes felt could be gradually removed. His later calls for 'the euthanasia of the rentier and, consequently, the euthanasia of the cumulative oppressive power of the capitalist to exploit the scarcity value of capital'[42] could be found in his writings of the twenties, where he called for the State regulation of such vested interests as the Bank and the Usurers. It was not capitalism, but a few capitalists who were to blame for the crisis. It was a small group of conservative and unimaginative men who withheld investment from the economy in case their profits were endangered, causing mass unemployment and criminal waste of human and economic resources. To Keynes, 'the powers of uninterrupted usury are too great. If the accretions of vested interests were to grow without mitigation for many generations, half the population would be no better than slaves to the other half'.[43] Only the State, as the representative of the whole community, could curb their power and guide the economy in a socially useful direction.

In his reply to Lloyd George's call for a great Liberal debate on the economy, Keynes wrote that

we are brought to my heresy — if it is a heresy. I bring in the State.

I abandon *laissez-faire* — not enthusiastically, not from contempt of that good old doctrine, but because, whether we like it or not, the conditions for its success have disappeared.[44]

In turning to the State as an agency of economic direction, Keynes was thus aware of the novelty of his ideas for Liberal thought. The New Liberalism at the turn of the century had accepted the State as an instrument of social reform, but had retained the traditional Liberal belief in *laissez-faire* and free trade. Keynes was calling on Liberals to recognise the reality that such a system had turned into a wasteful economic juggernaut of finance houses and monopolies which crushed human hopes and social justice.[45] The State would need to be used to stop such injustice, not merely in the realm of social welfare, but also in the economic bedrock of production on which welfare rested. In calling for a system of public works to create employment, and in demanding that the fluctuations of the currency should not be based on gold, Keynes turned in the statist direction which would be confirmed in the *General Theory*.

He also presented a dramatic alternative to British socialism. The belief of the Fabians, reflected in the ideas of the Labour leadership of the twenties, was that the State as representative of the community would inevitably supersede the private interests of an unregulated capitalism. In his call for State direction of a capitalist economy Keynes was putting forward a formidable challenge to a Labour intelligentsia who abhorred the cut-throat competition of private enterprise while having no realistic solution to the problems of the trade cycle and general unemployment. Keynes agreed with their fears of capitalism while providing an immediate strategy for the pressing problems of the British economy.

However, Keynes was clear that capitalism was to remain. The greater economic role of the State was not to be at the expense of the merits of *laissez-faire*. To Keynes and his fellow Liberal authors of the Yellow Book, private enterprise was an unrivalled method for a decentralised management in touch with local needs, an excellent means of testing efficiency and innovation, and the only practical way in which the various goods and services could be evaluated. These merits should be retained, while state intervention was necessary where privately owned industries failed. This was particularly the case in areas such as slum clearance, canal and dock development, and similar social enterprises —

it is not a question of choosing between private and public enter prise in these matters. The choice has been already made. In many directions, . . . it is a question of the State putting its hand to the job or of its not being done at all.[46]

In this way, State activity could develop and equip the country to meet the challenges of world competition through the existing economic system leaving the old debates between individualism and socialism behind.

The corporatist nature of the Liberal proposals on the management of public enterprise and the mixed economy was a natural supplement to their rejection of *laissez-faire* capitalism. They rejected syndicalist and guild socialist demands for workers' management in favour of a system of profit-sharing and diffused ownership to restore to the worker a sense of dignity. The attempt to create a popular capitalism did not resolve the problem of management of public industry, which must be firmly geared to economic efficiency (in the commercial, rather than the social, sense). To Keynes and the authors of the Yellow Book,

> our object must be to work out, more consciously than hitherto, the best type of organisation for the great body of public services which have already crept half-unnoticed out of private hands, and to recruit a class of officials for running them as capable as the General Managers of great industrial companies.[47]

This should be done by means of a public corporation, such as the British Broadcasting Corporation which would have an autonomy of decision-making within the limits of final accountabilty to the government or the local council — 'but only in the sense in which a company is responsible to its shareholders'.[48] These ideas of a public *enterprise*, run on capitalist lines, were to have an important future for the Labour Party.

The acceptance of corporate industry was extended to the national direction of the economy. The old division of responsibility whereby the State looked after politics while industry looked after the economy was to be transcended by a partnership of the State, organised capital, and organised labour. Trade Boards and Joint Industrial Councils would be responsible for making recommendations on productivity, wages and economic goals for individual industries and trades. A Council of Industry should be established which would be responsible for sanctioning these recommendations, and ready to give authoritative advice to an Industry Minister, whose decisions would be final. This overall Council 'should be so constituted as to represent, and to commend the confidence of, the industrial world',[49] and would be supplemented by a series of other Boards and Councils to guide Britain rationally in the direction of economic revival. Such corporatist agencies were crucial for a capitalist economy in which the State was to play a major role in restoring economic efficiency and profitability.

Keynes and Hobson

The onset of world depression in the early 1930s led Keynes finally to break from his orthodox background in Marshall and Jevons, with their belief that the normal condition of a market economy was a balance between saving and spending. Recognising that this was a special rather than a general case, Keynes pointed to the lack of effective demand as the cause of economic crisis. He was thus forced to come to terms with the economic heresy of Hobson, and, in doing so, to sharpen his critique of the Labour economists.

In a series of letters to Hobson in the early thirties, Keynes admitted an increasing interest in the under-consumptionist argument, but never fully accepted it.[50] He recognised that consumption lagged behind production, and vigorously criticised the belief of the Treasury and the Bank that a policy of thrift and cutting consumption would lead to recovery by way of a balanced budget. On the contrary, such measures would worsen the crisis, hastening the collapse of private investment by taking wealth out of the economy. To Keynes, as to Hobson, 'what we need now is not to button up our waistcoats tight, but to be in a mood of expansion, of activity — to do things, to buy things, to make things'.[51] If such a policy of expansion, particularly in the form of increasing government spending, were carried through, then consumption would revive, and with it would revive investment.

However, it was investment, not consumption, which was the key to economic recovery according to Keynes. This was the essence of his disagreement with the Labour economists. He recognised that production in any economy was the key to increasing consumption, and that in a capitalist economy production could take place only if entrepreneurs could be persuaded to stop saving their capital and start spending it. If the whole of increased investment were absorbed in consumption, employers would not make a profit and would therefore refuse to invest. There must be a certain amount of investment to cover unsold stocks — 'unless there is this amount of investment, the receipts of the entrepreneurs will be less than is required to induce them to offer the given amount of employment'.[52] It was under-investment of capital, not under-consumption, which was the real problem to be tackled, according to Keynes.

Consequently, he rejected the demands of the Labour economists for a rise in wages to overcome the crisis of unemployment, as he did their calls for a redistribution of wealth. He believed that wage-bargaining did not really affect unemployment, pointing to the coincidence of high unemployment and a docile labour force, and called for the reduction of real wages through a monetary policy which would drive prices higher than money-wages.[53] As for redistribution of wealth, Keynes regarded such a policy as unnecessary and harmful to initiative. While the disparities of wealth between rich and poor may be too high, 'for my own part, I believe that there is social and psychological justification for significant inequalities of incomes and wealth'[54] as the money motive was highly valuable for many human activities. To Keynes, an expansion of wealth, rather than its redistribution, should be the aim of any community.

The trouble was that in choosing to overcome the vagaries of the trade cycle by State intervention, Keynes still remained trapped in the shortcomings of orthodox economics. He believed that 'consumption — to repeat the obvious — is the sole end and object of all economic activity',[55] and that for all its shortcomings a market economy was the best regulator of such activity. His economics began and ended with market relations of purchase and sale, and as a result could only indirectly touch on the process of producing wealth which lay behind the market. For Keynes, the problem arose from a gradually declining demand for consumer goods, itself causing a reduction in demand for capital goods. The failure of capitalists to invest was attributed to *psychological* causes of consumer demand. Marx's argument that the real object of *capitalist* economic activity was the pursuit of surplus value, and his insights into the *social* causes of crises arising ultimately from the subjection of labour to capital through the wages system was lost, as it was to be lost for the bulk of the Labour Party.

The Keynesian challenge to British socialism was, then, highly ambiguous in its analysis and conclusions. It was no accident that he remained a Liberal throughout his life,[56] as he was totally opposed to State socialism as a tyrannical system which stifled both freedom and efficiency. He disliked the working-class base of the Labour Party (though he respected individual trade unionists such as Ernest Bevin, with whom he worked on the Macmillan Committee in 1930), and his support of social inequality flew in the face of the important ethical element in British socialism. However, his criticism of *laissez-faire* and his call for State intervention in a mixed economy through the stimulation of investment, touched a vital weakness in the Labour Party's political and economic thought. A need for an immediate economic programme to overcome the crisis of unemployment was glaring in the Labour Party of the twenties and early thirties, leading the Labour economists around Hobson to propose the living wage. Keynes' critique of Hobson's underconsumptionism, together with his calls for a corporate organisation of public enterprise in a mixed economy, were to sharply divide Labour's Right and Left in the thirties. Thus, while he never joined the Labour Party, Keynes' ideas were to have a major effect on its thought.

Notes

1. See, for example, J. Ramsay Macdonald, *Why Socialism Must Come* (London, 1924).
2. The Labour Party, *Labour and the Nation* (London, 1928), p. 6.
3. H.N. Brailsford, *The Life Work of J.A. Hobson* (OUP, 1948), p. 13.
4. *The Dictionary of Labour Biography*, vol. I (Macmillan, 1972), states that Hobson joined the ILP, but according to Brailsford he was never a member. Presumably, Brailsford should know, and Hobson's view of socialism was certainly at odds with his ILP colleagues over the living wage. For Hobson's autobiography, see *Confessions of an Economic Heretic*, (Harvester, 1976).
5. J.A. Hobson 'Neo-Classical Economics in Britain', *Political Science Quarterly*, vol. XL, no. 3, September 1925, p. 352.
6. J.A. Hobson, *Economics of Unemployment* (London, 1922), p. 30.
7. J.A. Hobson, *The Industrial System: An Inquiry into Earned and Unearned Income* (London, 1927 ed.), p. 210.
8. Hobson, ibid., p. 227.
9. See K. Marx, *Capital*, vol. III, especially Part VII, where Marx deals with these categories, relating them to his theory of value.
10. J.A. Hobson, *Industrial System*, p. 79. See also p. 210.
11. Ibid., p. 142.
12. See J.A. Hobson, *Imperialism: A Study* (London, 1902). Such thinking became a hallmark of the Labour Left.
13. 'The "overflow" stream of savings is of course fed not exclusively from the surplus income of the "rich"; the professional and industrial middle classes and to some slight extent the workers contribute. But the "Hoarding" is distinctly due to the automatic saving of the surplus income of rich men' (Hobson, *Imperialism*; p. 90).
14. J.A. Hobson, *Industrial System*, p. 215.
15. Hobson, *Confessions*, p. 126.
16. J.A. Hobson, *Incentives in the New Industrial Order* (London, 1922), p. 145.

17. Hobson was not a member of the ILP. See note 4.

18. See, for example, Philip Snowden, *The Living Wage* (London, 1912).

19. H.N. Brailsford, J.A. Hobson, E.F. Wise, A. Creech Jones, *The Living Wage* (London, 1926), p. 2.

20. Ibid., p. 8.

21. Ibid., p. 37.

22. Ibid., p. 15.

23. Ibid., p. 7.

24. Alan Bullock, *The Life and Times of Ernest Bevin*; vol. I *Trade Union Leader 1881-1940* (Heinemann, 1960), p. 390.

25. ILP Conference Report (1926), p. 83.

26. Ibid., p. 78.

27. Brailsford *et al., Living Wage*, p. 53.

28. A. Fenner Brockway, *Make the Workers Free: The Industrial Policy of the ILP* (London, 1925), p. 13.

29. J. Maxton and A.J. Cook, *Our Case for a Socialist Revival* (London, 1928), p. 17.

30. Hobson to Ramsay Macdonald, 7 October 1926, quoted D. Marquand, *Ramsay Macdonald*, p. 455.

31. D. Lloyd George, 'The Stateman's Task' in *The Nation and the Athenaeum*, vol. XXXV, no. 2, 12 April 1924, p. 40.

32. See *The Nation*, vol. XXXV, nos. 8 and 10, 24 May, 7 June 1924.

33. J.M. Keynes, *The General Theory of Employment, Interest and Money*, vol. VII of his *Collected Writings* (Macmillan, 1973), p. 32.

34. Ibid., p. 371.

35. See, for example, his *Tract on Monetary Reform* (1923), *Collected Works*, vol. IV, p. 85.

36. J.M. Keynes, *The Economic Consequences of Mr. Churchill* (1925), in *Collected Writings*, vol. IX, p. 224.

37. J.M. Keynes, *Essays in Persuasion: Collected Writings*, vol. IX, p. 258.

38. Ibid., p. 297.

39. Ibid., p. 309.

40. J.M. Keynes, 'Liberalism and Industry', in H.L. Nathan and H.H. Williams ed., *Liberal Points of View* (London, 1927), p. 208.

41. J.M. Keynes, *Essays in Persuasion*, p. 311.

42. J.M. Keynes, *General Theory*, p. 376.

43. J.M. Keynes, *Tract on Monetary Reform*, p. 56.

44. J.M. Keynes, 'A Drastic Remedy for Unemployment – A Reply to Critics', in *The Nation*, vol. XXXV, no. 10, 7 June 1924, p. 312.

45. 'On grounds of social justice no case can be made out for reducing the wages of the miners. They are the victims of the economic juggernaut. They represent in the flesh the "fundamental adjustments" engineered by the Treasury and the Bank of England to satisfy the impatience of the City Fathers' (Keynes, *Economic Consequences of Mr. Churchill*, p. 223).

46. J.M. Keynes, *Essays in Persuasion*, p. 113.

47. Liberal Industrial Inquiry, *Britain's Industrial Future* (London, 1928), p. 81.

48. Ibid., p. 77.

49. Ibid., p. 222.

50. See Hobson-Keynes correspondence in Keynes, *Collected Writings*, vol. XIII, p. 330-6.

51. J.M. Keynes, *Essays in Persuasion*, p. 138.

52. J.M. Keynes, *General Theory*, p. 27.

53. See, for example, ibid., chapter 19.

54. Ibid., p. 374.

55. Ibid., p. 104.

56. Keynes sat on the Liberal benches when he entered the House of Lords in 1942, and expressed great alarm at the prospect of a Labour victory in 1945 — see R.F. Harrod, *The Life of John Maynard Keynes* (Macmillan, 1951), p. 331.

8   THE EMERGENCE OF CORPORATE SOCIALISM

Britain had suffered mass unemployment for a decade when she was struck by the ravages of the world depression which began with the Wall Street Crash of October 1929. For forty years, the export of capital had served to cushion capitalist societies from major crises, but the 'Great Slump' of the 1930s seemed proof of the Marxist belief that capitalism was doomed to end in collapse. Lenin's assertion that imperialism was the final phase of capitalism inspired or terrified many as Europe plunged into protectionist trade wars and social crisis.

In Britain, already suffering from the slump conditions of the previous decade, industrial production fell by a further 17 per cent, while unemployment soared to three million by 1932. The economic crisis and the rising level of unemployment made a mockery of the ethical demands of British socialism, demonstrating to supporters and opponents alike that the Labour government had no economic theory with which to tackle the crisis. Instead, it fell back on orthodox policies of retrenchment and was eventually swept aside in the financial crisis of August 1931, unable to put through the anti-working class measures demanded by the bankers and unwilling to fight those bankers. After Ramsay Macdonald deserted the second Labour government to head a National government of Conservatives and Liberals, the country settled into a relative political stability compared with that of its rivals. The decimation of the Labour Party after the 1931 elections, when it sank to 46 MPs; the weakening of trade union organisation by unemployment and the industrial defeats of the previous decade; the minuscule size of the British Communist Party; and the dominance of National, mainly Conservative, governments with large parliamentary majorities throughout the decade, all served to underline the stability of the State, making the need for a Fascist movement superfluous for most of the patriotic and Right-thinking men and women drawn to the far Right elsewhere in Europe.

However, political stability did not bring about any substantial economic recovery. It is true that the Midlands and south-east England enjoyed a minor burst of prosperity with the development of new, light industries,[1] but the conditions of slump and poverty persisted in Scotland, northern England and South Wales while, in general terms, the recovery of the economy after the mid-thirties was insufficient to pull

149

these depressed areas into prosperity. The onset of a minor downturn in the trade cycle in 1937-38 was a reminder of the precarious situation of British capitalism in the decade.[2] In this situation, the National government drifted indecisively after taking Britain off the Gold Standard and ending free trade in 1931-2. Its political cunning was matched by an inability to bring forward any imaginative economic measures.

In other countries, whether dictatorships as in Germany or democracies as in the United States, the State actively intervened to stimulate production and create employment. A major turning point was being reached, as the State now took over the role of staving off capitalist crisis played earlier by the export of capital (though this still continued to play a major part in the determination of investment decisions). The practical policies of State intervention carried out by Roosevelt and Hitler were reflected in the development of Keynesian economic theory, which now argued that a market economy was incapable of sustaining itself without crisis, and needed the State to supplement its activities. As Marx had once put it,

> As long as capital is weak, it still itself relies on the crutches of past modes of production, or of those which will pass with its rise. As soon as it feels strong, it throws away the crutches, and moves in accordance with its own laws. As soon as it begins to serve itself and become conscious of itself as a barrier to development, it seeks refuge in forms which, by restricting free competition, seem to make the rule of capital more perfect, but are at the same time the herald of its dissolution.[3]

Just as the State aided capital at its birth, so now it was required to step in as its nurse and saviour.

The Labour Party, politically immobilised throughout the decade now came into its own in the realm of ideas. On the surface, Labour at tempted to rid itself of the taint of Macdonald, regarded as a heinous traitor who had deserted the class and party which had placed him in such high position. The Left were in full cry, as their mixture of traditional radicalism and Marxian rhetoric appeared increasingly justified by social misery at home and the growth of Fascism abroad. Their call for an urgent policy of class militancy and alliance with the Communists led to fierce debate and the temporary expulsion of several left-wing leaders from the Party. However, behind the more spectacular splits and polemics within the Labour Party during the thirties, a solid foundation of unity was being built around a new ideology of corporate socialism

Labour was now able to solve the problem of ideas bequeathed by the British socialism of the party's founders. It was able to provide an economic theory for the present to supplement the ethical ideas which had served the Party during its infancy. The needs of capitalist society, and of the organised working class within that society, were met as the Labour Party incorporated the syndicalist and Keynesian challenges into the general framework of its traditional ideas. In doing so, Right and Left were united on the fundamentals of a minimum programme of social and economic reform which would reshape British capitalism in the 1940s.

The Left and the State

The ILP and Socialist League. The failure of the Labour Government of 1929-31 appeared to the Labour Left as the fullest justification of all their criticisms of Fabian gradualism and elitism. The attacks of the Communists on Labour's acceptance of a parliamentary democracy which was nothing more than a cover for a bourgeois dictatorship appeared very close to the mark in the light of the 1931 crisis, when a Labour Government was easily pushed out of power by a bankers' cabal. A drastic reappraisal of tactics and ideas was needed if Labour was to recover its credibility among working-class socialists and an increasingly Marxist intelligentsia.

In this reappraisal, the Labour Left suffered a major reverse with the decision of the ILP to disaffiliate from the Labour Party in July 1932. In formal terms, the ILP secession was concerned with party discipline, but in practice the leadership around James Maxton and Fenner Brockway had become convinced that the time was ripe to build a separate Labour Marxist party based on the class war and unadulterated socialism. Brockway, in *The Coming Revolution* (1932), argued that in the new circumstances of the thirties even the method of *Socialism In Our Time* had become inadequate. The ILP was not prepared to wait for an election in five years time, during which the misery and deprivation of the working class promised to be intolerable. Brockway called on workers to break with the gradualism of the Labour Party, and with the trade union bureaucracy which had vested interests in that gradualism, in order to step up extra-parliamentary activity.

The language was revolutionary, but it was mere rhetoric. Brockway's view of extra-parliamentary action had more in common with pressure-group activity (on the lines of tactics already demonstrated as futile during the General Strike) than it had with a threat to the State His pacifist views led him to ask the ILP 'to contribute to the revolu tion a technique in which the main method will be, not armed conflict but action by the working class to take control over industry in their disciplined strength'.[4] It was certainly a view too extreme ever to gain a majority against Labour's entrenched interests of the union leaders but it was not incompatible with Labour Party membership. The ILP' belief that it could strike out on its own was the factor dividing it from the Labour Left, not its ideas. It was a false belief; ILP membership dropped from 17,000 in 1932 to 4,500 by 1935, and it ceased to have political significance, a chilling reminder to the Labour Left of Keir Hardie's belief that socialists must subordinate their socialism to their labourism if they were to survive.

Under E.F. Wise the ILP dissidents who remained within the Labour Party joined with dissident Fabians in 1932 to form the Socialist League in order to continue the grand ILP tradition of converting Labour to socialism. It was this body which served as the fount of left-wing initia tives for a reappraisal of tactics and ideas on Labour's part. Its opposi tion to the Labour leadership — expressed in its *Programme for Action* (1933), where there was a call for an Emergency Powers Act and increased public ownership — was largely ineffective, since the League inherited from the ILP a lack of trade union support, but its attack on the gradualism of Macdonald had wide echoes in the movement after 1931.

R.H. Tawney, who had drafted *Labour and the Nation*, now called upon Labour to rediscover the reasons for its existence. Labour's hesi tancy under Macdonald could not be remedied by a reorganisation or new programmatic proposals. It was a weakness of political philosophy — an indecisive conception of what type of society Labour wanted Tawney's conception was one of radical rather than mild reform; it was 'to abolish all advantages and disabilities which have their source not in differences of personal quality, but in disparities of wealth opportunity, social position and economic power'.[5] This was certainly radical, but hardly revolutionary, and Tawney maintained his rejection of class hatred in favour of sentiments more suitable to a socialist com monwealth. Nevertheless, the 1931 crisis had convinced even Tawney that devious counter-attacks could be expected from the plutocracy which could be more effective than Labour had hitherto anticipated and he, too, called for emergency powers to attack the citadels of private wealth as a priority above the immediate relief of economic distress. He now argued that 'onions can be eaten leaf by leaf, but you cannot skin a live tiger paw by paw; vivisection is its trade and it does the skinning first'.[6] It was a view of capitalism which came uncomfortably close to that of the Labour Marxists.

Cripps. Stafford Cripps, who succeeded Wise as Chairman of the Socialist League on the latter's death in 1933, came to be seen as the embodiment of the Labour Left's attack on moderation. Cripps (1889-1952) was the nephew of Beatrice Webb, and after the usual upper-class education at Winchester and Oxford made his name as a constitutional lawyer with a knack for mastering very complicated documents and evidence. A firm Christian and political moderate, he was induced to join the Labour Party by Herbert Morrison, and was almost immediately appointed Solicitor General in 1930. His class background and political moderation led Macdonald to ask him to join the National government in 1931; Cripps not merely declined, however, but performed an astonishing political somersault to become one of the most militant spokesmen of the Left.

His logical mind had led Cripps to grasp the implications of the 1931 crisis quickly. In a letter to William Graham immediately after the formation of the National government, he argued that

it seems absolutely necessary to throw off once and for all the attitude of compromise which was impressed upon us by reason of the minority position in which the Labour Government found itself . . . We must, I feel, completely divorce ourselves from the past.[7]

This he proceeded to do in his analysis of the undemocratic nature of the British ruling class, in a Marxist style which concealed his Christian socialist outlook. He believed that the 1931 crisis — 'the clearest demonstration of the power of capitalism to overthrow a popularly elected Government by extra-parliamentary means'[8] — was proof that the capitalists and plutocrats would go to any lengths to defeat Parliament.

If there was to be any hope of the peaceful parliamentary change called for by Labour, then the dangerous power of the capitalist enemy had to be recognised and defeated quickly. A Labour government, democratically elected, must proceed to take power away from capital, in the lifetime of a single Parliament. This could only be done if an Emergency Powers Bill to control capital was passed on the first day of office to give Ministers extraordinary powers, similar to those granted in 1914. If the House of Lords rejected the Bill, the government would ask the Crown to create enough peers at immediate notice to ensure eventual passage; if the Crown refused, the government would either resign or rule unconstitutionally, disregarding the Lords entirely. If the armed forces intervened, then the government must be prepared to become a temporary dictatorship. There must be no time allowed for the anti-democratic forces of capitalism to gather and to exercise their subtle influences on the legislature before the strong points of private wealth had been transferred to the State.

With these arguments, Cripps rapidly became the *bête noir* of the British establishment, especially when he darkly hinted at possible opposition from Buckingham Palace. He made it clear that he was referring to Court circles rather than the Crown itself, but it was not enough to prevent a storm of abuse descending on his head, including censure from a Labour leadership terrified of being seen as anti-royalist and unconstitutional. In fact, Cripps merely envisaged action to protect parliamentary democracy against any illegal moves from the ruling class. He was, given his belief that the National government was introducing Fascism into Britain,[9] excessively constitutional, willing to wait on an eventual Labour majority which he believed to be inevitable. He did envisage trade union action to protect Labour against any armed attempt to unseat it, but this was hardly unconstitutional given the right of any government to protect itself against undemocratic action.

Laski. The attack on gradualism had major implications for Labour's conception of the nature of the State. Ever since the early Fabians, Labour had regarded the State as an essentially neutral instrument which happened to be in the hands of capitalist parties but which could be wrested from them by the workers' party through democratic elections. The 1931 crisis had led many of Labour's radicals to doubt whether this was in fact the case and Harold Laski, the political theorist who sat on Labour's National Executive during the decade, set about reformulating the theory of the State. In doing so, he demonstrated the limits of the radicalism to which the Labour Left could go without becoming Leninist. Laski flirted with the Leninist theory of the state in order to frighten the British ruling class, but ultimately he refused to grasp the revolutionary implications of his flirtation.

Harold Laski (1893-1950) had been born into an orthodox Jewish

family in Manchester and educated at Oxford, but had rejected his background to write for the *Daily Herald* during the syndicalist unrest.
After a period teaching at Harvard University (1916-20), he returned to
an active role in the Labour Party as well as an academic job in political
science at the London School of Economics. During the 1920s he had
adopted a federalist approach to society, based on the pluralism of
J.N. Figgis, and elaborated his theories in *A Grammar of Politics*
(1925). However, in the aftermath of the 1931 crisis, he quickly recognised the grave constitutional implications of the formation of the
National government. A party which had been elected by the people,
with a larger number of seats than any other at Westminster, was unable
to carry its principles into practice because it was frightened of how
the investing public might act. The refusal of international bankers to
grant a loan to the Labour government was 'an announcement that
finance-capital will not permit the ordinary assumption of the constitution to work if these operate to its disadvantage'.[10] In other words,
grave doubts had arisen as to whether a socialist society could come
about by constitutional means. In these circumstances, Laski felt that
the Left should go beyond the constitutional measures sought by
Cripps to make a radical reappraisal of the nature of the State which
would ascertain whether the Labour Party, born and nurtured within
the framework of the British constitution, was capable of transforming
society.

In doing so, Laski moved considerably away from the pluralist
ideas put forward in his *Grammar of Politics* (1925). In a new preface
to that book, he made it clear that he had not rejected the libertarian
principles first laid down there — indeed, time had reinforced their
truth — but that he had underestimated the ease with which such a
society could emerge. He now realised that only Marxism could explain
the naked force which had come to the fore in Nazi rule in Germany
and which lay implicit in the democratic state in capitalist Britain. In
the face of this, his pluralism was not discarded as much as submerged
in Marxism — 'I now recognise . . . that the pluralist attitude to the
State and law was a stage on the road to an acceptance of the Marxist
attitude to them'.[11] In doing so, he reduced the importance of all the
ethical and philosophical grounds on which the State demanded the
allegiance of its citizens to concentrate on the ugly, but unavoidable,
realities of power and violence. Lenin's theory that the State was
nothing but armed bodies of men existing to protect the ruling class
was now accepted by Laski, who then proceeded to test it against the
traditional liberal theory of the State.

This liberal conception was a philosophical one in the worst sense of the word, existing in ideas only without any relation to reality. It saw the State as an expression of reason, existing to promote the good life of its citizens by curbing the excesses of individualism. Obedience was based on the recognition of self-interest, as argued by Hobbes, while the right of rebellion was allowed whenever the State threatened this self-interest. The liberal tradition, as a result of the right of rebellion was a perpetual challenge to tyranny and repression, but it could not be divorced from the men who created and exploited it. It could be traced to a decisive shift in economic power from the monarch to the middle-class property-owners in the seventeenth century, when the ideas of liberty were put forward by John Locke to defend a bourgeois Parliament from Royal encroachments. The rights of property were the reality behind the empty and legalistic notions of liberty and equality In the real world the formal doctrine of equality before the law was confounded by the social inequality between rich and poor, who had very different access to court protection because of the costs of legal action. If the poor sought to end their exploitation, they would find the forces of the State arrayed against them to protect the legally entrenched interests of the rich exploiters.

To Laski, it was 'the first duty of a political philosophy to examine the character of the State in its actuality rather than in its idea.'[12] It was in what the State did in practice, and not in its claims, that its real nature lay. In practice, the State existed in a society distorted by class relations, and would do everything in its power to protect the ruling class. This was not merely a question of the personnel of administration, law and the military being drawn from the upper classes; it was the belief of the ruling class that they were the natural and justifiable rulers of a social hierarchy which would lead them to identify any threat to property as an evil conspiracy to subvert a traditional and law abiding community. Their long rule had blinded them to the class nature of their society, just as the liberal theory of the State concealed the central nature of the property system which lay behind it. This economic factor was the bedrock on which social and political institutions were built, as demonstrated whenever a threat arose to property. Racial and religious antagonisms might alter or determine the personnel of the State, but did not threaten its unity in the same way that class antagonisms did. When a socialist movement threatened the ruling class, then it subtly deflected the threat, as in Britain, or turned to Fascism, as in Italy and Germany, to protect itself. Thus Laski, like Marx and Lenin saw the state as 'an instrument not of the community as a whole — that is an abstract entity devoid of intellectual expression – but of the class which owns the instruments of economic power'.[13]

With this view of the State as an instrument of the ruling class, Laski attempted to investigate parliamentary democracy in Britain to ascertain the possibility of a peaceful transition to a socialist society. The success of representative government in Britain had been due to particular historical causes – a unified nation free from invasion; a sense of popular liberty after the seventeenth-century revolutions; economic, military and imperial success; and above all a sense of security. If the economic system of capitalism on which parliamentary government rested could provide security for the vast majority of the people, then the State could command allegiance from its citizens, no matter how grudging. In its phase of expansion, capitalism could afford to be tolerant; to grant suffrage to the property-less, women and ethnic minorities; and to offer a better standard of life to all its citizens. However, the class nature of British society remained through all these liberal reforms. The justice and wisdom of reform was determined by its effect on the existing order.

As capitalism plunged into economic crisis and was suddenly confronted by a socialist threat, all the gifts of political and social reform were called into question. Indeed, when two parties differing on the rights of property and class power confronted one another, the Constitution itself was placed in jeopardy. To Laski, 'Constitutional principles and forms do not operate in a vacuum of abstract reason',[14] and the manifest failure of the economic system to provide security for a growing number of its citizens placed representative government itself in the dock. The performance of the second Labour government had made it clear that socialist measures might not be compatible with a generally accepted democratic government. The fall of that government had been an admission that, whatever the will of the electoral majority, the owners of economic power were the permanent masters of the Constitution – 'the State is their State; and its supreme coercive power can only be directed to those objects of which they are willing to approve'.[15] Should the Left take power it would force a loss of confidence on the Right. There would be economic strains, a flight of capital, and a halt to investment. This withdrawal of confidence would shatter the consensus on which the unity of the State rested, so that representative government lost its meaning in the British Constitution. This would present a challenge to any government, forcing it either to retreat or to attack the power of capital in a much more fundamental and urgent manner than had been envisaged by Fabian gradualism.

To Laski, 'the British Constitution. . . is the expression of a politically democratic government; it is not the expression of a democratic society'.[16] In politics, universal suffrage and the party system ensured frequent elections and peaceful changes of government. In society, a good education was generally reserved for the rich, while access to the civil service, the legal profession and the military establishment was denied the working class. For men and women who had the misfortune to be born into the working class, their lot was a poor education, toil tempered by mindless entertainment, and the misery of a tiny pension at the end of a life spent working for capital. The schools, the press, and the Church were geared to teaching obedience and acceptance of a proper station in life, while those socialists and trade unionists who did not bow to capitalist rule were denounced as unpatriotic agitators. The whole social system in Britain was based on the fear and hatred of the ruling classes for their inferiors, disguised as a patronising liberalism which could easily turn into a ferocious repression if threatened.

It was the possibility of repression which profoundly disturbed Laski. The British Constitution was so vague and shifting — 'a matter of understandings and ideas and sentiments that are always half-articulate rather than explicitly expressed'[17] — that repression and suspension of democratic rights could take place without abuse of the law. When capitalism enjoyed prosperity and the political climate was calm, a generous interpretation of the Constitution could be allowed. At a time of economic and political crisis, the interpretation was likely to be strict and authoritarian. The House of Commons was procedurally slow; the Lords could hamstring legislation for two years; while the Crown, the reserve power of the Constitution, could always add legitimacy to any suspension of democratic government and legal rights.[18]

Despite this pessimistic analysis of parliamentary democracy in the capitalist State, Laski rejected Communist revolution as a futile appeal to the irrational in human nature.[19] Violent resistance to a dictatorship might be morally justifiable, but the slightest possibility of peaceful change must be exploited to the full to avoid violence and a leftist dictatorship. In a capitalist democracy, Laski had no doubt that the scales were weighed against socialist change, but 'I believe that it is the duty of the citizen to exhaust the means placed at his disposal by the constitution of the State before resorting to revolution'.[20] The development of military technology and the efficiency of the modern State made successful revolution, rather than a fearful blood-bath, extremely difficult, if not impossible. As a result, Laski advocated constitutional change through the Labour Party, He pointed out that Britain could escape violence as a result of its historical tradition and its capacity for tolerance, but his pessimism and grave doubts as to the democratic convictions of the ruling class make his constitutionalism appear as a forlorn grasping at straws. In looking at the profound differences between the parties on the question of property, Laski believed that 'the prospect of solving them in terms of reason, instead of terms of power, becomes a matter of extraordinary difficulty'.[21]

This raises the question of the nature of Laski's Marxism. In one sense, it came close to the revolutionary theory of the State held by Lenin. Laski attempted to denigrate the liberal theory of politics as an exercise in logic rather than life, and pointed to the violence and power relationships which stood behind the ethical and philosophical defence of State power. Like Lenin, he saw the State as a coercive instrument of class rule, ready to turn to armed force as the capitalist economy went into crisis. His concentration on *realpolitik* rather than philosophical justification thus marked a major evolution of Laski's thought from the previous decade.

However, its resemblance to Marxism was more superficial than real. Unlike Marx and Lenin, he continued to see the State in fundamentally moral terms. He accepted that it was an instrument of coercion, but held that it did have a purpose and a justification − to satisfy the demands of its subjects. Indeed, 'the fulfilment of the state-purpose can only be accomplished when the incidence of its actions is unbiased'.[22] The state in capitalist society was biased, but the state in a socialist society would be unbiased. It was a utilitarian theory, not a Marxist one. Where Marxism sought finally to abolish the State, Laski was attempting to rescue the liberal theory of the State from its capitalist trappings.

The dabbling with Lenin practised by Cripps, Laski, and a large section of the Labour Left aroused strong opposition in the rest of the party. In 1933, Labour's National Joint Council issued a manifesto, *Dictatorship versus Democracy*, in which Communism and Fascism were equated as sinister evils threatening the democratic state. Clement Attlee (who became leader of the party in 1935) rejected the belief that capitalism was inevitably anti-democratic and ready to reject the Constitution. He acknowledged that Britain's rulers had become more callous and ruthless than they had been in his youth, but believed that the long tradition of personal and political freedom, together with universal suffrage, would safeguard the democratic process. Attlee argued that there is nothing more misleading than to try to apply to all countries a cast-iron theory of historical necessity and to argue that Britain must go the Moscow road unless she follows the example of Berlin or Rome. The theorists at the end of the eighteenth century might equally well have argued that Britain must go the way of France unless she was prepared to align herself with Austria and Prussia.[23]

Whether or not Britain *should* have gone the way of France or Moscow, Attlee was undoubtedly right in his arguments against the dogmatism of many on the Left, but he was himself too sanguine on the resistance of the ruling class and the extreme flexibility of the British Constitution which could be used against any real threat to their power. He held that, while Labour's acceptance of the Constitution relied on its opponents' similar acceptance, 'as long as the workers have it in their power to achieve their ends by the use of the ballot-box, they have no right to seek to obtain them by other means'.[24] In the particular conditions of the 1940s, this resistance did not materialise, but then again there was no real threat to the capitalists as a whole by the structural and social reforms of that decade.

Foreign Policy and the State

The deepening international crisis in the thirties brought to the fore the confusion felt by the Labour Left about the class nature of the British State in a much sharper form than that posed in the Great War. In the earlier crisis, the ILP had refused its support to the war effort on anti-capitalist and pacifist grounds, but refused to go as far as Lenin in denying the authority of the State by a policy of revolutionary defeatism. In the thirties, the Left's dilemma was sharpened by the fact that the German threat was also Fascist, with a record and a promise of anti-working class measures much more vicious and far-reaching than those of the Kaiser.

It was George Lansbury (1859-1940) who gave the old pacifist answer to the crisis. Lansbury had become leader of the party after the 1931 election. He was chosen because he was the most senior figure to survive the electoral rout, but he was also a Christian pacifist whose views became increasingly embarrassing to the other party leaders as the problem of national defence came to the fore. At the 1935 Party Conference, Lansbury opposed sanctions by the League of Nations to prevent Italy invading Abysinnia on the grounds that it might lead to war, and in doing so presented a coherent connection between the party's domestic and foreign policy. Despite the dire poverty and distress among the working-class people to whom he had devoted his life, he had rejected the militant doctrines of class war as a solution to their plight. He declared,

> I have no right to preach pacifism to starving people in this country and preach something else in relation to people elsewhere. And that has been a fundamental state, it has not been something of an expediency. It has been a belief that we should sooner or later in the world win our way with waiting.[25]

This sentimental pacifism was not seen as very realistic against the armed might of ruthless Fascists. The party as a whole swept Lansbury aside at this conference, while the Left realised that the new situation required very different answers than those given twenty years earlier. Cripps and the Socialist League called for a distinct policy which was as fundamentally opposed to the National government in foreign affairs as it was in home affairs. On the grounds that workers should have nothing to do with wars caused by capitalism, the Left opposed rearmament for a Tory government, which might well use its weapons against Soviet Russia rather than Germany. As Cripps told the 1935 Conference, 'To me, the central factor in our decision must turn not so much upon what we as a country should or should not do, but upon who is in control of our actions'.[26] The League of Nations was rejected as a viable instrument for world peace on the grounds that it was warped and neutralised by the conflicting interests of the imperialist powers. Indeed, Cripps went far towards a denial of the authority of the nation-state in declaring that

> it is impossible for us to serve two masters — our own selfish interests as British imperialists and our desire for peace as world citizens. The interests of the British Empire and the world are not identical.[27]

The distinct foreign policy presented by the Left called for an alliance of a socialist Britain with other socialist powers, including the Soviet Union, in a quarantine of the Fascist powers,[28] though the exact policy to be followed if war broke out *before* Britain became socialist was not investigated. Instead, the immediate policy of the Left was a domestic alliance of progressive forces against Fascism as a preparation for government. This demand for a United Front of Labour, the ILP and the Communist Party was later extended to a call for a Popular Front of all progressives, including Liberals and anti-appeasement Conservatives. It was reinforced by the electoral success of the Popular Front in France while the Spanish Civil War, in which the Spanish Popular Front was attacked by reactionary generals, became an example for the Left of the defence of democracy against Fascism. All talk of specifically working-class defence against *capitalism* was dropped, along with any demands smacking of socialism, in the interest of unity between all classes in the nation against the Fascist threat.[29] The Popular Front policy sealed the fate of the Left; the Socialist League was disaffiliated from the Party in 1937, while Cripps and two of his lieutenants were expelled in 1939 (to be readmitted during the war).

Their policy of fundamental opposition to the government on foreign policy never really stood any chance of being adopted by a constitutional party with the political traditions which lay behind Labour. In rejecting both Lansbury and the Left, Labour reaffirmed that the needs of national defence stood as a priority above the class divisions in British society. Clement Attlee (1883-1967), who succeeded Lansbury as leader in 1935 and was eventually to become Prime Minister, rejected the Cripps policy as breaking up this national unity.

> If a Capitalist Government is in power, the workers must resist everything that the Government does. If a Socialist Government is in power, the Capitalists will do the same. The result is that the country ceases to count as a factor in word affairs. It is immobilised until the class struggle is resolved.[30]

When Cripps turned to the Popular Front, the Labour leadership was even able to expel him on the grounds that he was resurrecting the Macdonald policy of collaboration with middle-class Liberals.

Despite the differences over foreign policy and the Popular Front, the Left and Right of the party ultimately remained united in the thirties as they had in the Great War. Just as the ILP was unable to take up Lenin's call for revolutionary defeatism, so the Socialist League was unable to echo the call of Trotsky (taken up momentarily by Orwell as a result of his experience fighting with the Spanish Anarchists)[31] that the 'progressive' elements of the middle class were just as much enemies of the workers as the Fascist elements. It was too uncompromising a position in its logic, and to have taken it up would have involved a total denial of loyalty to a class-divided nation-state. On the other hand, the Left were unwilling to accept the bi-partisan policies of the Labour leadership, implying as it did a fundamental trust in the ruling class. As a result, they fell between two stools, seeking to deny their government the means to arm itself against a foreign threat while unable to take this denial to its logical conclusion. They were neither revolutionaries nor patriots, finding themselves instead in a position of moral righteousness which became increasingly untenable and finally impossible as war approached. The outbreak of war saw the Left's 'independent' foreign policy collapse, as they rushed to support their government. Ultimately, for the Left as much as the Right, the forces which divided Britain were less important than the forces which united her.

The Labour Keynesians

Until the Great Depression of the thirties, Labour economic thinking had been based on the underconsumptionism of J.A. Hobson. It was believed, on both Right and Left, that trade union successes in obtaining higher wages and a policy of redistributive taxation would increase both working-class and national prosperity. The ILP, in its living wage policy, sought to use Hobson's economic ideas to force the pace in the transition to socialism, but Macdonald and Snowden were no less committed to the underconsumptionist 'heresy'.

However, the economic policy pursued by Snowden in government in 1929-31 was marked by a respect for orthodoxy expected of a Tory Chancellor. His acceptance of Hobson was combined with a belief in the Quantity Theory of Money — the theory that any increase in purchasing power without any corresponding rise in productivity would cause inflation. That prospect was terrifying for any Chancellor for whom the recent hyper-inflation suffered by Germany in 1923 was a dark reminder of dabbling in wild experiments. Snowden had this in mind when he rejected radical economic ideas in an address to the 1929 Labour Conference —

> in the control of credit and currency, the administration of the control must be kept free from political influences . . . I have seen and I know something of the danger of the control of credit and the means of starting an inflation policy, and it might be highly dangerous in the hands of a Government that wanted to use this means.[32]

In other words, the incorruptible socialist, Snowden, was forced into

upholding the market and the bankers as the forces determining finan
cial policy. The result was financial crisis and the desertion of Labou
by Snowden and Macdonald.

Alternative policies were already being presented as the Keynesia
challenge to British socialism was making itself felt. Keynes did no
fully work out his theories, particularly his modification of th
Quantity Theory of Money through the multiplier, until the earl
thirties. However, his calls for state management of credit and curr
ency markets had been quickly absorbed into the labour tradition b
the agile mind of Sir Oswald Mosley.

Mosley

Mosley (1896-1980), born into a baronetcy, became a Unionist MP i
1918 after experience as an officer in the trenches had imbued in hin
a sense of comradeship and heroism which he took into politics. H
became an Independent in 1920 in protest at the unheroic terrorism o
the 'Black and Tans' against the Irish, and gradually moved to th
Labour Party, attracted by the guild socialist ideas of the ILP. By th
mid-twenties he had grasped the implications of Keynes' criticisms o
Treasury policy to develop an economic policy distinct from the livin
wage proposals of the Left. He later wote that 'the background of my
economic thinking was first developed by a study of Keynes — more i
conversation with him than in reading his early writings'.[33] As a result
he elaborated his new policies in a pamphlet, *Revolution by Reason*
in 1925.

Arguing that the economic crisis made evolutionary socialism out o
date, Mosley called for an emergency policy of credit expansio
through nationalisation of the banking system. The state banks would
through their bold and vigorous use of monetary policy, reverse th
crisis of a lack of demand in the home market. They would ensure tha
the new credit would go into the hands of the working class, so that th
purchase of necessities rather than luxury goods would lead to a revers
of the decline of the staple industries of Britain. Social justice an
economic sense would go hand in hand in reviving the nationa
economy.

In calling for an expansion of credit, Mosley remained committe
to the orthodoxies of the Quantity Theory of Money, but was muc
more imaginative about it than the timid Labour leadership. The evil
of inflation were recognised, but Mosley argued that they could b
overcome by a vigorous adoption of State planning — 'Here ou
Socialist planning must enter in. We must see that more goods are forth

coming to meet the new demand'.[34] This point was elaborated after he became Chancellor of the Duchy of Lancaster in the 1929 Government. He called for a bold programme of public works to create enough goods to accommodate an expansionary credit policy. Dissatisfied with the lack of response to his proposals, and calling for a strong central direction of unemployment policy, he resigned from the government in May 1930, and then left Labour to form the New Party in February 1931. His subsequent career as a Fascist obscured his importance for introducing Keynesian ideas into the Labour movement, demonstrating as he did that as a short-term remedy for unemployment they were far from incompatible with State planning of the economy. His support among the Left (Arthur Cook, the militant Miners' leader, and Aneurin Bevan were among the signatories of the Mosley Manifesto) indicated the forthcoming unity in the party on economic issues.

Durbin

However, the Left's commitment to the underconsumptionism of J.A. Hobson led to a great reluctance on their part to accept the Keynesian challenge. It was a Labour moderate, Evan Durbin (1906-48), who grasped the significance of Keynes' differences with Hobson. In his book, *Purchasing Power and Trade Depressions* (1933) (with which Hugh Gaitskell collaborated), Durbin set about a criticism of underconsumptionist theories of the economy from a Keynesian point of view. He put his finger on the fundamental difference with Hobson when he worte, 'I share Mr. Keynes' view that all the existing theories of underconsumption have failed to take account of the importance of the activity of investment in the solution of the problems of monetary income'.[35]

Durbin attacked Hobson's theories directly by pointing out that an excess of saving as a result of low consumption was not necessarily disastrous. On the contrary, the growth of industrial capitalism in the nineteenth century was direct proof that a restriction of consumption promoted the accumulation of capital for investment in new industry. While saving could check industrial expansion if it was in the form of a hoard, it could positively promote growth of the economy if it was in the form of investment. An increase in investment, through its power to increase physical productivity, would increase consumption in its wake. Thus, 'the investment of the savings has brought into existence new capital of a type which enables costs to be reduced on the average'.[36] The need to reduce incomes could in this way be removed by new investment, which would allow general wealth to grow rather than redistributing the existing wealth. It was not an attack on the ruling class that was needed, but a concerted policy to increase the general wealth.

If Durbin rejected the traditional radicalism of the Labour Left, he also made it clear that the market system was not able to increase social wealth. The failure of a planless economy to respond to a rise in savings by converting those savings to investment would cause a general depression, since the hoarding of capital would lead to a contraction of consumption goods and, therefore, capital goods (which Durbin believed to be totally dependent on the market for consumption goods). This would bring about a general contraction of the economic system, leading to unemployment and social insecurity. Only a planned socialist economy − where government, banking, industrial and trade union action was centrally co-ordinated − would be able to overcome the trade cycle of boom and slump which had come to characterise capitalism.

However, Durbin rejected the Mosley policy of relying on a bold policy of credit expansion as much as he did the Labour Left demands for a raising of incomes. Both policies would lead to inflation, according to Durbin, because price stabilisation was not possible in a market economy, or even in the necessary transition to a planned economy, as it was impossible to control fully the effect of credit expansion. There was no real certainty in such a situation that any saving of capital would not be hoarded rather than invested. In a socialist economy, the State could control the direction as well as the size of the new credit flow, but practical difficulties meant that such an economy could only be established gradually.

As a result, Durbin argued for a mildly expansionary monetary policy through the use of low interest rates, a discriminatory tax policy to encourage private capital investment, and a firm commitment to check inflation by imposing higher taxes. His main hope in preventing the inflationary consequences of cheaper money lay in an agreement by the unions to maintain stable incomes, avoiding what would later be called 'cost-push' inflation. Only in this way could unemployment be gradually reduced in what was bound to remain a semi-planned economy for a prolonged period. Durbin believed that Labour's economic policy

must be based upon the necessity of making a large quantity of *private* industry expand its demand for labour, at the existing level of wages, and upon the demand of the Trade Unions for the maintenance of money wage rates [37] [Durbin's italics].

In this way, as incomes for all consumers remained constant, more of the fall in prices would go to capital for investment and the economy would gradually move towards a stable prosperity.

Dalton

Durbin's adoption of Keynesian policies was echoed by other prominent Labour figures, particularly Dalton and Bevin. Hugh Dalton (1887-1962), was born to an upper-class family — his father was Canon of St George's Chapel and tutor to the Royal Family — and was educated in economics at Cambridge by Keynes. He joined the Fabian Society at university, and entered politics in 1922 after an academic career at the London School of Economics. He was a leading moderate on Labour's National Executive during the thirties, where he was instrumental in securing eventual Labour acceptance that only the Bank of England, not the joint stock banks, should be taken into state ownership. In doing so, he was closely advised by the XYZ Club, a group of Labour sympathisers from the City. The participation of Durbin and Gaitskell in this club ensured the conversion of Dalton to the new Keynesian economics, as seen in his *Unbalanced Budgets* (1934) and *Practical Socialism for Britain* (1935).

Dalton argued that the world crisis had arisen purely and simply as a result of the conservative policies of bankers. In Britain, the 1931 crisis was a 'bankers' ramp', after a small group of plutocrats had taken the decisions to deflate the economy without public discussion or parliamentary sanction. As unemployment and the faltering in private investment had unbalanced budgets throughout Europe — by reducing the number of companies and individuals from whom revenue could be taken by the State in taxes — the bankers had totally sacrificed the need to fight social inequality and a better distribution of wealth in favour of the sacred task of balancing the budget. In the face of the conservative economic policies successfully imposed by these financiers, Dalton concluded that 'the world-wide crash in the price level since 1929, with all its disastrous consequences, is a bankers' achievement'.[38]

To remedy this situation and pull the nation out of slump, Dalton advocated the control of the financial institutions through a nationalised Bank of England, enforcing public direction of economic policy, which would be given a purpose of benefitting the community rather than a few profit-making individuals. Monetary policy would thus be determined by the State, rather than the anarchical forces of the market or the rigidities of the Gold Standard. It would be used to move gradually towards a prosperous, planned economy by means of a controlled expansion of credit, avoiding the twin evils of inflation and deflation. Such a policy must, however, ensure that the new wealth generated in what would be at first a mixed economy would accrue to the working class as well as forming a reserve for new investment. As he put it to Labour's 1932 Conference, 'in a period when productive power is increasing you must be increasing purchasing power equally with productive capacity, and therefore. . . more purchasing power is distributed to our people.[39] This concern that the plan should be for the benefit of the working class differentiated the Labour Keynesians from Keynes himself, who, while not averse to reducing unfair inequalities of wealth, maintained a patrician and disinterested attitude to the labour movement.

Dalton himself distanced his own ideas from those of Keynes by arguing that an expansionary fiscal and monetary policy could not take place in a capitalist economy, which was geared to private pursuit of profit rather than the public good. He argued that the capitalist system was unsuited to large changes in the value of money and, while admitting his technical agreement with the Keynesians, believed that

> their policy, in order to be effective, needs to be pushed a good deal further than most of them seem willing to push it. I believe that freedom from the plague of recurrent boom and slumps can only be found in a planned economy .[40]

Therefore, to control the capital markets which could thwart Keynesian policies, Dalton advocated a National Investment Board, which would be able to licence and direct new investment in industries, mobilising financial resources in a rational and co-ordinated manner. He saw the creation of such a Board as a major step towards socialist financial institutions, able to deal with both the immediate problem of unemployment and the longer-term need for a planned development of industry and the economy.[41]

Bevin

The position of Ernest Bevin in the labour movement during the thirties made him a particularly influential figure in pushing the labour movement towards Keynesian economics. Bevin (1881-1951) had been an illegitimate child, born in a Somerset village and orphaned at eight. After working as a farm boy, he took a series of unskilled jobs in Bristol before becoming an official in the Dockers' Union in 1910. The industrial unrest of those years strengthened his labourist politics, and he was never to escape the dualism of a profound hostility to employers and a recognition of the value of negotiation with them. As the first leader of the powerful Transport and General Workers' Union from 1922, Bevin played a major part in trade union politics, and was a dominant influence in the General Council of the TUC, and thereby in the Labour Party, which was very much under union control in its weakened parliamentary condition of the thirties.

As a member of the Macmillan Committee on Finance and Industry in 1930, Bevin worked closely with Keynes, learning the new economics quickly as the Treasury and Bank officials were subjected to close and critical questioning, and becoming one of the few union leaders to earn Keynes' respect. He had none of Snowden's awe for the guardians of financial orthodoxy, and asked Montague Norman, the Bank's Governor, whether it was not possible

> to have some direction through public bodies, municipalities, of the whole operation of credit, and therefore while you restrict one form of credit you maintain the volume of home credit, to prevent the blow falling upon the workpeople .[42]

He believed that if incomes had to be so reduced, the burden should not fall on the working class to the exclusion of the wealthier sections of society. However, Keynes was demonstrating that a resolution of the crisis need not be at the expense of his members and, having grasped this, Bevin went on to attack the financial orthodoxy which upheld the Gold Standard and respected the private nature of the Bank of England.

In a series of pamphlets, Bevin called for an end to the reign of the financial autocrats, with their belief in balanced budgets and their infliction of misery on the labour movement. Instead, there should be a recognition that people are the only genuine subjects of economic concern —

> We are being congratulated on a balanced Budget and the possibility of a surplus, but if we approach the question of balance correctly we must not do so in terms of money only, but in terms of life, health and opportunity.[43]

A budget surplus was not to be valued if it was achieved at the expense of a deficit in health.

Against orthodox economic policies, Bevin called for state inter-vention in the world of high finance, so that increased investment through the creation of credit would lead Britain away from the vicious circle of low investment and high unemployment. As a minimum pro-gramme of reform within capitalism, he argued that 'we must socialise the Bank of England, as most other countries have socialised their Central Banks, in order to be free to pursue an expansionist monetary policy on the basis of a managed currency'.[44] However, like the other Labour Keynesians, Bevin believed that the only real solution to the crisis lay in the public control of industry. Only in a planned, socialist economy could Keynesian techniques work.

However, this planned economy was to take place in a national con-text. Bevin, steeped in the labourist traditions of the British working class, saw the protection of the workers of his own nation as taking a priority over the workers of other nations, just as he saw the interests of workers in his own union as taking precedence over those of workers in other unions. Under his influence, the TUC Economic Committee rejected free trade in favour of trade within the economic bloc of the British Empire, rich as it was in resources and geared by its imperial tradition to supplying Britain itself. This labourist trait of Bevin was strikingly demonstrated at the 1930 TUC —

> What I say is this, and I am not afraid of saying it. I sit on a Colonial Development Committee under an Act passed by the Labour Government, and I see the expenditure of millions of pounds going on for the development of areas where native races have not yet begun to be industrialised. You talk about the coal trade. Ought there not to be some control against the possible development of coal in Tanganyika and in East Africa, which might come into competition with your coal here at a time when the world does not want it ?[45]

At a time when trade wars were about to begin, it was a recipe which neatly combined a commitment to his own workers with a commit-ment to the British State and its Empire.

It was this belief in a planned economy of publicly controlled finance and industry which provided a bridge to the Labour Left for the Keynesians. The Left were at first suspicious of Keynes. They were not just objecting to reforms of a capitalist economy, since their support of the living wage proposals and the Mosley manifesto demon-

strated their awareness that immediate measures to relieve distress had
to be taken. Their objection was more fundamental, as they felt that
the Labour Keynesians, in identifying capitalism with the free market
and socialism with planning, were ignoring the whole question of class
power. If Keynes was correct, there would be no need to redistribute
wealth from the rich; in contrast, Hobson's economic theories of the
surplus and underconsumption had the maldistribution of wealth
between social classes at their very centre.

Cole

It was G.D.H. Cole who attempted to reconcile the Left to Keynes. He
remained a guild socialist, but the collapse of the Building Guild and
the militant trade union movement in the twenties had left him politically impotent and theoretically isolated. As a result, he abandoned the
abstract heights of socialist theory to engage in a series of concrete
studies of practical social and economic policies. He took Hobson as
his guide in these matters at first,[46] and attempted to counter the
Keynesian Liberal proposals of the late twenties with his *The Next Ten
Years* (1929). Here, he accepted the Liberal assertion that capitalism
had, through abandoning *laissez-faire*, succeeded in increasing production, but argued that its class nature prevented it from solving the problem of distribution of the wealth produced. As a result, the market
was unable to buy all the new goods, leading to a crisis of overproduction and resulting in mass unemployment.

A different method was needed, if the market was to be expanded
to buy these new goods. He adopted the Liberal plan for a National
Investment Board, but hoped to use it to replace capitalism eventually.
To Cole, the Liberal proposals 'are far too timid and hesitant, but they
indicate clearly the right line of advance'.[47] In socialist hands, such a
Board must have much greater powers, such as the control of all private loans. Moreover, as the State would lend money to private firms,
it was only reasonable to insist on some form of State control, such as
state representatives on the company board of directors. In this way,
the State would be able to increase purchasing power through an expansion of credit and public works. Moreover, Cole differed not only from
the Labour Keynesians, but also from the *Living Wage* authors, in calling
for the nationalisation of all banks. Public ownership of the Bank of
England could give a socialist government control of the *amount* of
credit, but it was also necessary to control the direction of this credit.
The commercial banks would have to be brought under state ownership
if that was to be done. However, the objective was social justice, not

merely the increase of economic efficiency. The need for public works was because

> it is fatal, in the modern world, to make the possession of purchasing power conditional on the ability to find employment, and to keep those who cannot find it alive in idleness out of the produce of those who can .[48]

Cole was thus very much open to Keynesian economics, but was only prepared to accept the theories critically. In 1933, he edited a collection of Labour Keynesian articles, *What Everybody Wants to Know About Money*, in which he stressed the possibility of escaping from the orthodoxies of the Quantity Theory of Money. Cole now accepted the Keynesian argument that an increased supply of money could only cause inflation under the unusual circumstances of full employment. In a situation of economic depression, an expansionary monetary policy would bring the idle economic resources into play through the multiplier process. Any inflation that occurred would not only be temporary but desirable — 'if reflation starts from slump conditions, in which prices are out of adjustment with the current debt and income structure, it will usually be desirable that prices should be durably raised to some extent'.[49] However, he did not believe that the State could maintain full employment by using Keynesian techniques unless it could control the size, timing and costs of industrial production, as well as the broad distribution of purchasing power.[50]

Cole attemped, then, to make a Hobsonian socialist out of Keynes. He always felt that the credit for the new economics should have gone to Hobson, rather than Keynes, and at the end of his life wrote that 'for me, at any rate, what is commonly known as the Keynesian revolution was much more the Hobsonian revolution in economic thought'.[51] Hobson was more important indeed, because he recognised the importance of class, whereas Keynes was seen by Cole as a mere technician, whose economics could somehow fit either a state capitalist or a socialist economy. In his enthusiastic response to the publication of Keynes' *General Theory* in 1936, Cole argued that Keynes' capitalist concusions were extraneous to his main theories. They were 'but briefly sketched in his closing chapter and . . . not a necessary deduction from his analysis'.[52] The economist in Cole was attracted to Keynes, but his ethical ideal of socialism would not allow him to accept Keynes as a whole.

This reconciliation of Keynes and Hobson was crucial to the fundamental differences on economics between the Labour Right and Left.

Where the Labour Right stressed the necessity of making the economic cake bigger by a policy of state intervention and direct planning, the Left were always to stress the redivision of the cake. The Left were much more aware of social class — it was part of the Labour Marxist legacy — and sought to use state intervention to aid the organised labour movement *against* the capitalists. However, in accepting the analysis of Hobson and Keynes, they ensured the effective burial of the revolutionary insights of Marx's labour theory of value.

Thus, in different ways, Keynesian economics came to be accepted into Labour thinking. The more militant elements of the Labour Left remained hostile for many years,[53] but the bulk of the Labour Party recognised that it was a practical and immediate response to the difficulties of a capitalist economy. It was much clearer than Hobson's economics, because it recognised the role played by investment in developing an economy. Moreover, it involved state intervention in the sphere of production, rather than distribution, and through this the Labour Keynesian from Durbin to Cole saw the necessity of replacing an unplanned market economy with a planned socialist economy. It was through their call for a much more thoroughgoing plan than the Keynesian Liberals had proposed that the Labour Party was able to evolve British socialism into the practical world of administering industry. The acceptance of Keynesian economics was thus crucial in the emergence of corporate socialism.

Planning and Corporate Socialism

In order to escape from its precarious position, capitalism required more than financial planning. The fine-tuning techniques of Keynesian economics, geared to regulating a trade cycle which was causing so much social distress, had to be supplemented by state intervention into the very heart of the productive process. There had to be a major re-structuring of industry in Britain (and the other capitalist powers) to place the nation in a more efficient and competitive position in the world market. This restructuring required not merely an encouragement of new industries, but a political and social regulation of industries which had grown to a size and power much greater than the enter-prises of the *laissez-faire* economy.

The need to regulate the great corporations which corresponded to economic and social reality had a profound effect on political activity. While the State was drawn increasingly into the economy, its monopoly of political life was being undermined. The powerful (if unequal) corporate pressure groups of the economy – the bankers, industrialists, trade union leaders – were gradually drawn into the decision-making process so that the State was on the way to becoming 'first among equals' in its relations with these institutions (a parallel decline in importance of other non-economic pressure groups, from the Churches to the professions, was also taking place). A regulated, or semi-planned, capitalism was emerging, with major consequences for a party which sought major social change on behalf of the labour interest.

Mosley, Labour and Corporatism

While the moves towards corporatist politics were accelerated by Fascist governments in Germany and Italy, and by a liberal Democratic administration in the United States, it was to be the Labour Party which was to take the main initiative in Britain.

Interestingly, it was Oswald Mosley who introduced corporatist ideas into the Labour Party, just as he had introduced Keynesian ideas. Mosley was initially attracted to the guild socialism of the ILP, with its allusions to the regulation of trade by the old medieval corporations. He quickly developed these ideas of extra-parliamentary administration in 1930 to call for a small economic general council which would regulate and plan trade, a proposal which won much left-wing support. After leaving the Labour Party, Mosley was able to develop fully the corporatism implicit in such proposals to call for a corporate state, with the producers as the basis of national life and with the powers of finance guided in the national interest. The state would direct the whole economy through the machinery of a central economic plan. To Mosley, 'the main object of a modern and Fascist movement is to establish the Corporate State. In our belief, it is the greatest constructive conception yet devised by the mind of man'.[54]

However, unlike his former Labour allies, Mosley saw such a planned economy as eliminating class conflict through destroying the freedom of the employers and unions to negotiate their economic contracts. He opposed any section of the nation which was free of state control, and called for the suppression of any vested interest which claimed allegiance to any body but the State. The occupational franchise on which a social Parliament would be based – so similar in form to syndicalist and guild socialist proposals – would not be based on free associations (just as the unions in Nazi Germany and Fascist Italy were so integrated into the State that they ceased to be representative of their members). Mosley argued that, through the machinery of government control,

> existing organizations such as trade unions and employers' feder-
> ations will be woven into the fabric of the Corporate State . . .
> instead of being the general staff of opposing armies, they will be
> joint directors of national enterprise under the general guidance of
> corporative government.[55]

This was very different from the corporatist proposals of the Labour Party, geared as they were to the different conditions of British political and social life. Formed as a party representing the rights of labour in capitalist society, the Labour Party was in the 1930s adapting its ethical brand of British socialism to meet the changing social and political requirements of the unions in a new type of corporate society. The corporatism being evolved by Labour theorists was one based on *free* trade unions – free from state control – which would bargain with similarly free employers' associations in conjunction with a tolerant state. It was a flexible system of 'corporate bias',[56] rather than a corporate state in the rigid sense adopted in Europe.

It was prefigured in the Mord-Turner talks of 1927-8, when TUC leaders met with progressive employers to discuss an agreed solution to the crisis in industrial relations. Ernest Bevin, who took a leading part in their negotiations, saw them as a major pointer to the future.

> For the first time in history, the representatives of organised labour
> have been invited to meet a group of important industrialists to
> discuss the finance and management of industry . . . I look forward
> to the time when the General Council will be coming and laying
> before this great Parliament of its own creation annual reports on
> the discussion of great economic problems . . . Thus and only thus
> will the movement be really intelligently dealing with the great econ-
> omic problems of our times.[57]

The talks failed, but they remain highly significant as a pointer to the more subtle and flexible forms of institutional co-operation between State, industry and unions.

Cole

Just as Labour had incorporated the Keynesian challenge into its frame-work of ideas, so now it incorporated the syndicalist challenge which elsewhere had evolved into either Communist Parties or Fascism. As has been seen, the revolutionary implications of syndicalism had been removed by the guild socialists, especially G.D.H. Cole, who attempted to bring out the corporatist strain of functional representation into Labour thinking. While it had succeeded in being adopted by the ILP, guild socialism had proved both too radical and too irrelevant for the Labour Party of the twenties. However, the idea that social and economic groups outside the formal political sphere of Parliament should have their say in government was now coming to the fore in discussions on the nature of socialist planning. It was none other than G.D.H. Cole, the leading guild socialist theoretician, who took a major part in these discussions. His isolated position after the collapse of the guild movement did not lead him to renounce the ideal of the regulation of industry and trade by workers' guilds, but the ideal became even more distant. The early attempts to stress the necessity of state intervention as a transition to the guild idea were stressed more than ever and the working-class nature of the guilds was gradually reduced in importance. In a series of books beginning with *The Next Ten Years* (1929) Cole proceeded to outline a structure of economic planning in which the different interest groups would have some participation in decision-making. The Keynesian economic techniques proposed by Cole were a necessary supplement to such a structure, as both were expressions of an active economic State.

Cole, more than most British political thinkers, was extremely sensitive to developments in foreign socialist thought, and seized on the *Plan du Travail*, proposed in the early thirties by the Belgian socialist, Henri de Man, as a prototype of a Labour plan. Rejecting left-wing calls for a fully socialised economy, de Man had put forward an anti-crisis plan calling for the immediate establishment of a mixed economy – with the State running finance, monopolist and public service industries, while private enterprise was to run the rest. Cole quickly grasped the significance of the plan,[58] and called on Labour to institute a similar planned economy in which the State controlled the commanding heights of the economy, as it was later to be called. He proposed a series of planning agencies to guide the economy in a socially useful and competitive direction, changing Britain's trading and industrial patterns to produce more for the home market. Since capital was essential as a spur to production, its direction by the government was essential, and Cole called for an Economic General Staff, backed by a National Investment Board, to do this. A National Labour Corps (similar to Roosevelt's Civilian Conservation Corps) would be established as one proposal to clear up unemployment, though Cole argued that this should not be used to undercut union wage rates.

The important change underlying Cole's proposals for a planned economy lay in the major retreat from his earlier ideals. Twenty years earlier, he had marked out freedom for the working class as the major concern of socialism; in the thirties it had become industrial efficiency. He had come to the conclusion that 'the ideal society that matters is not the Utopia of our dreams, but the best sort of society we can hope to help build out of the materials that lie ready to our hands'.[59] It was more a defeatist than a realistic attitude, and it led Cole to see socialism as a pragmatic scheme which would certainly involve nationalisation of a large number of monopolistic and socially necessary industries and enterprises, but hardly the universal public ownership of a Communist economy. It was not the ownership or administration of industries and services, but the control of policy by the State which defined socialism for Cole at this point.

In a major modification of his ideas, Cole now called for industry to be run by experts rather than the workers themselves. The worker as a consumer was only interested in getting the world's produce supplied at the lowest price and quickest time, and as a result he 'will find his best interest in getting industrial administration into the hands of those who are most competent to conduct it'.[60] The administration of industry by experts on powerful public boards and commissions would need to be controlled by an independent department of inspection and audit to prevent bureaucratic rule, but the full-blooded workers' rule called for by Cole in 1913 had been watered down to works councils representing the interests of the workers in regard to wages, conditions and dismissals. It was a poor climbdown from his earlier proposals which challenged the industrial power of the capitalist class. Now, 'the object of this . . . policy, let it be made quite plain, is to bring about a radical redistribution of the productive forces of British industry in the light of a changed and changing economic situation'.[61]

This change from concern with class power to concern with economic efficiency led Cole to advocate a mixed economy, where the continuation of private enterprise was to be left to the ability of the industry or service concerned to serve its part in the economic life of the nation. The State needed to assume a direct role in production to secure both a correct distribution of wealth and balance of employment. While the State sector would be wide-ranging, 'this does not mean that it is necessary to nationalise everything – heaven forbid'. It does mean that the public sector 'of industry must be large enough to set the tone for the rest, leaving private industry to operate within a framework of public enterprise, rather than the other way round'.[62] However, in basing his arguments on efficiency, Cole left himself open to the argument that the achievement of economic prosperity by a regulated capitalism applying Keynesian policies would make a bureaucratic economy of public corporations and enterprises totally unnecessary.

He also ignored the class nature of the State which was to intervene in the economy. In a predominantly private economy, accepted by Cole for the short term, the dynamic of capital accumulation was geared to profit, and any State intervention in such an economy would usually be to restore profitability — which was only another name for efficiency in a capitalist economy. Cole assumed, as he did in his guild socialist days, that the State was fundamentally neutral and beneficial to the labour movement if directed by a Labour majority in Parliament. The fact that a Labour government might be called on to attack working-class living standards if it was to intervene in a regulated capitalist economy was a point left unresolved, for Cole as for the Labour Party in general.

Morrison

It was Herbert Morrison who was to be instrumental in imposing a corporatist view of nationalisation on the Labour Party, as he was later to be responsible for imposing it on the economy. Morrison (1888-1965) was the son of an alcoholic London police constable, and overcame the handicaps of an elementary education and an eye infection to become a minor journalist. After a brief flirtation with the SDF before the Great War, he became prominent in the London Labour Party. He immersed himself in the local problems of transport, health, education and housing; was Minister of Transport in the 1929 Labour government, where he prepared a London Passenger Transport Bill later passed by the National government; and became Labour leader of the London County Council in 1934.

Morrison applied his experience in local government, and as Transport Minister, to bring the debate on nationalisation to a sound business level. Rejecting the utopian platitudes of pre-war British socialism, Morrison concerned himself with the down-to-earth problems of management of the wide range of industries due to be nationalised. Like Cole, Morrison's object was the maximum well-being of the public and the protection of working-class living standards, which he did not see as identical with the destruction of wage-slavery. On the contrary, socialist industry was to Morrison merely a more efficient form of capitalist industry, carried on according to the sound commercial principles of the more responsible private corporations. He scorned any high moral purpose which blurred the realities of the business world, and argued that the ethical ideal of socialism could only be realised through a sensible and orderly administration of public enterprise. To Morrison, 'it is essential that Socialism should be sound public business as well as being healthy in its social morality',[63] since only the competent rule of a dedicated élite could ensure the prosperity of the nation.

Morrison saw the public corporation on the model of the Post Office and the BBC as the best form of administration of industry, combining as it did public ownership, public accountability, and sound business management. It was superior to direct management by the government, since Ministers tended not to be experts and, in any case, should not immerse themselves in the minute detail of commercial enterprise at the expense of keeping a general strategy in sight. It was also superior to the workers' control advocated by syndicalism and guild socialism, since there would be a tendency to concentrate on the interests of the local workforce at the expense of the general interest of the enterprise and the community. The same problem ruled out administration by the technial experts, whose sphere of concern was too narrow for the purpose of the enterprise in serving the community.

To Morrison, the management of the Boards of directors who would run the public corporations should be chosen by Ministers purely on grounds of favouritism or narrow concern with the particular industry, and should have the public rather than any sectional interest in mind. Managers would be offered salaries above the Civil Service level to find the right people — Morrison would have no truck with the older socialist ideas of equality, as put by Marx in *The Civil War in France* — and should be able to make the industry pay its way in the new 'socialist' business world. They should also have the fullest possible autonomy from Ministerial intervention consistent with final governmental responsibility, as an interfering Minister could easily ruin any business project. Only in this way, argued Morrison, could socialised industry prove its competence and superiority over private enterprise.

Morrison's conception of corporate public enterprise — of corporate socialism — was a logical consequence of adopting the syndicalist and guild socialist ideas of functional government to the Fabian ideals of administrative élitism inherent in British socialism. In doing so, the ideas of the freedom of the working class from wage slavery, which distinguished syndicalism and guild socialism as separate ideas, was eliminated. This was not to say that Morrison was oblivious to working-class aspirations to government, but he saw such aspirations in individual rather than class terms. He wanted workers to be appointed to the Public Boards which would run their industry on the basis of ability, not merely because they were workers. Their personal business sense would enable them to meet the other board directors as equals, and not as inferior beings chosen for ideological reasons. As Morrison put it to the 1932 Party Conference,

> We ought, therefore, to say unhesitatingly that real ability − not the technician only, nor the expert − but real business ability, of which the Labour Movement has its share, shall be the test of appointments to Boards of this kind.[65]

The idea that the workers should no longer be a commodity had vanished in the commonsense talk of commerce.

Wooton

The case for a corporate plan with the aim of achieving social equality and full employment was cogently argued by Barbara Wooton (b. 1897). Eventually to become the first woman to enter the House of Lords, she was educated at Cambridge and fought against male prejudice to obtain an academic career after the death of her husband in the Great War. Her influential book, *Plan or No Plan* (1934), attempted to meet the arguments of political economists that a planned economy would destroy the balance between supply and demand which was regulated by price in the market economy. She argued that these economists held an incorrect notion of the selfish motives in a capitalist economy. The result of private ownership was that profit, not price, became the mechanism which governed supply. Moreover, the maldistribution of wealth and the social injustice of unemployment totally distorted demand, so that essential goods were left to rot while people in desperate need of such goods were hungry because they were unable to afford them.

Wooton pointed to the success of the Five-Year plans in the Soviet Union as an example of the superiority of a socialist over a capitalist economy, though she abhorred the lack of political liberty there. In Britain, which enjoyed a much firmer economic base of wealth than Russia, a planned economy would not need any political change. Parliamentary democracy would co-exist with a series of regulatory commissions headed by a Planning Commission, which would determine the general questions of wages and prices, the building of new factories, and the closing of outmoded ones. The corporate nature of such an economy would not destroy political democracy, since the role of Parliament was not to administer industry but to set general guidelines on which the planners would be able to act. Her Fabian notions of administration determined her views of Parliament as 'at best an assembly, not of experts on everything from cost-accounting to maternal mortality . . . but of guardians of common human interest'.[66] In this way, the dangers of over-centralisation would be avoided, as public enterprise would gauge demand and supply much more efficiently than market price.

The experience of nationalised industries, in the Soviet Union and Britain, has demonstrated the incorrect nature of such a view. The destruction of price as a regulator of demand and supply in the USSR has led to gross inefficiency in production and distribution,[67] while in the public enterprises in Britain commercial objectives have generally held first priority to social welfare. The Russian economist, Preobrazhensky, discussed the need for democratic planning to gauge the co-ordination between demand and supply,[68] but he disappeared in the Stalinist purges of the thirties, and the distinction between bureaucratic and democratic planning temporarily disappeared, too. Wooton did not make the distinction – it would have been alien to her corporatist thought – and saw problems of co-ordination as being perfectly soluble in the light of planning by the experts.

This disdain for democratic management in favour of corporate planning led Wooton to endorse the rejection of workers' control by Morrison and the Labour leadership. The need for discipline at work would be ignored under workers' control, as was demonstrated in Russia in the early days of the revolution, and there could be no time for such anarchical propositions. She pointed to Lenin's institution of an appointed management to replace the workers' committees which had initially run much of Russian industry, and concluded that internal management of industry should be in the hands of foremen and managers. The workers would, of course, be free to choose the job they wished, guided by the different pay and prospects offered by alternative occupations, but this did not imply any say in management. The rule of an industrial élite was unaffected by the question of whether business was conducted under a planned or an unplanned economy, according to Wooton. She conceded the possibility of representative works' councils to discuss the effects of management proposals on staff welfare, but they were to be advisory only –

it is not the business of the staff to decide major issues of policy concerning the amount of goods to be produced, or the prices at which they will be sold or the wages payable to those engaged in their manufacture.[69]

Unlike Lenin, who saw appointed management as a necessary transition to a Communist society, Wooton saw it as an end in itself. The socialist vision of a free society was dismissed as just a vision. The fact that democratic planning might be more efficient than corporate planning was not even considered.

Dalton

The similiarity of the corporatist proposals with the institutions of Fascism was recognised by Hugh Dalton. In his editorship of *Unbalanced Budgets* (1934), in which the economics of Fascist Italy and Nazi Germany were studied to assess the possibilities of state planning, Dalton speculated about the economic superiority of such systems over the *laissez-faire* policies of Britain. The suppression of political and trade union liberties was abhorred by Dalton, but this did not blind him to the similarities of institutions like Mussolini's IRI (the industrial development board) with the proposals of the corporate socialists in the Labour Party. As a result, he wondered

whether modern Italy is not moving along a path which will lead, not only to Economic Planning, but to Socialism. This suggestion is repugnant both to most Italian Fascists and to many Socialists . . . Yet it is not to be ruled out as unthinkable, not even as improbable.[70]

In the light of this conception of socialism, Dalton endorsed the Morrisonian ideal of a public corporation as the usual form of management of nationalised industries. Prices and output would be set by a central planning authority, as in the Soviet Union, but competition between public bodies such as gas and electricity services should flourish. He believed that, far from abolishing competition, socialism would be its most perfect realisation. The State would 'institute planned public competition, in place of unplanned private competition, and plan to avoid the waste and misdirection of resources which, under capitalism, are a chronic disease'.[71] This was not merely a major modification of the ethical socialist ideal of a co-operative commonwealth, but a false distinction between capitalism as a system of private ownership and capitalism as a market economy based on competition between different enterprises. A market economy based on a mix of public and private enterprises, or even on public enterprises alone, would be a severely distorted market rather than a planned economy. The conflict between commercial profitability and social welfare which would occur, and the whole question of profit or plan as a regulator, was left in a highly confused state.

Dalton did believe, as a socialist, that the corporate plan should be used to fight against poverty, insecurity, and unemployment. It would be the expression of a welfare state, directed by a Supreme Economic Authority, responsible ultimately to the Cabinet. The task of this Authority would be to co-ordinate the sectional plans put forward by local and industrial authorities into a national investment plan with the immediate aim of conquering unemployment through public works, reduction of the hours of labour, a raising of the school-leaving age, and a lowering of the retirement age. A policy of equal opportunity in industry, the professions and education would be encouraged in the interests of comradeship and morality. In this way, the initiation and ability present in many working-class children would be freed from a caste-divided society to take a major part in social and economic life.

Dalton's corporatism was thus definitely linked to a model of social welfare, as opposed to the Fascist view of corporatism in serving the needs of national superiority. His firm adherence to the traditional political liberties of British society, leading him to reject the paranoid talk of the Labour Left that Fascism was being introduced into Britain, was a reinforcement of the specific difference of corporate socialism from the Fascist form of corporatism practised in Italy.

Corporatism and the Left

The ideas of corporate socialism put forward by Bevin, Morrison, Wooton and Dalton met with vigorous resistance from the Socialist League. Much of the Labour Left's Marxism may have been mere rhetoric, but their recognition of the importance of class conflict alerted them to the élitist notions of the public corporation. The working class was effectively to be excluded from industrial power by new socialist businessmen, a notion inimical to the syndicalist and guild socialist ideas which had become part and parcel of the Left since the war. However, their vocal opposition disguised an underlying agreement with the Labour centre and right about the nature of planning which was to lead to an agreement among all sections of the party on the fundamentals of a socialist state.

Harold Clay, the deputy leader of the Transport Workers Union and a member of the Socialist League, called on the Labour movement to remember the lessons of the syndicalists and guild socialists on the need for workers' control. He criticised those socialists who wished to place the trade unions on the same basis as employers, consumers, and others in industry. If such views were accepted, the Labour Party would 'accept the permanence of the commodity status of labour and deny the possibility of an effective partnership of the workers in socialised industry'.[72] However, Clay accepted the public corporation as a major step towards a socialist society,[73] objecting only to Morrison's exclusion of the unions from representation on the public Boards. This would lead, according to Clay, to an unrepresentative bureaucracy without any check to their power. His opposition helped to defeat the Morrisonian ideal at the 1933 Party Conference, but thereafter the notion of workers' control disappeared from sight, and by 1937 Morrison's ideas were tacitly accepted by the party.

The similarities of the proposals of the corporate socialists to Fascism led to attacks from the Left, who argued that only workers control could prevent the country from drifting in the same direction as Italy. G.R. Mitchison, a prominent Socialist Leaguer, counterposed the socialist planning of nationalisation under workers' control to the corporate state that he saw emerging. He argued that

the Tory Party is being driven, by force of circumstances, from the unregulated and individualist capitalism of Victorian times, via the trusts and employers' associatons of a later period, to a system of producers' corporations on Fascist lines.[74]

However, in identifying corporatism with Fascism the Left failed to recognise the subtleties of 'corporate bias' that was emerging, nor their essential agreement with the assumptions of their Labour opponents

The direct democracy of the working class advocated by the revolutionary syndicalists had been watered down by the Left to representation of the union leadership on the public Boards of nationalised industries. The syndicalist ideal of self government was rejected along with the Morrisonian view of corporations free from political influence. It was not the corporate form of public enterprise that was wrong, but the autonomy and expertise of management. The League called for a National Economic Council composed of trade unions, experts, and representatives from the public Boards of other industries. In this way they sought to make industry 'subject to considerations of public policy and to coordinate all the industries concerned in accordance with a general Plan directed by the working class movement'.[75] It was not corporatism, but its right-wing form, to which the Labour Left objected.

Their sympathy with the bureaucratic planning of the Soviet Union, expressed throughout the decade in calls for a United or Popular Front with the Communists, and their reliance on the trade union movement as expressing the economic interests of the working class, led the Left to accept the idea of centralised planning by a small body of experts,[76] adding only the need for trade union control. As Ben Pimlott has observed,

> Though the Socialist League increasingly adopted the rhetoric of Marxism, its heritage included a body of ideas whose source was closer to Keynes than Marx, and which it shared with politicians of the centre and right. This it never acknowledged, but the links were strong.[77]

It was G.D.H. Cole who served as the intellectual link between the older class-based politics of Labour and the efficiency-orientated idea of corporatism. He was able to supplement Keynes with Hobson to provide a redistributionist aspect to Keynesian economics acceptable to the Labour Left, and he was able to develop the ideas of functional representation of the syndicalists and guild socialists to the notion that employers and unions were political powers in their own right. Cole chaired an interesting series of discussions between leading academics, civil servants, employers and union leaders under the auspices of the Nuffield College Reconstruction Survey in 1941-3 in which each group came to a general agreement on the necessity of state intervention to create a mixed economy of nationalised industries and private corporations based on the fundamental co-operation of capital and labour. A new era of corporate consent was about to open.

An ideology of corporate socialism had evolved by the 1930s, in the sense of corporate bias as defined by Keith Middlemas (and, in a more radical interpretation, by Leo Panitch[78]). Corporatism in Britain was at that time beginning to develop in the vague and non-contractual form which was to be predominant in Britain after 1940. In this way, the employers' and trade union groupings were to be brought into the processes of government consultation on social and economic affairs, in an attempt to curb the tendencies to class conflict in Britain. In the Labour Party in the 1930s, it became accepted that politics could not be restricted to the parliamentary sphere, but must incorporate the great economic corporations of capital and labour into the hitherto sacrosanct realm of the State. For both the Labour Right and Left, behind the political pyrotechnics of the struggles over emergency powers and the Popular Front, an underlying unity had emerged.

The emergence of corporate socialism in the 1930s had been the result of an integration of the twin challenges of Keynesian Liberalism on the Right and revolutionary syndicalism on the Left. The economic thinking of Keynes was accepted as superior to the underconsumptionist economics of Hobson, but in the process it was changed from a call for state regulation of a capitalist economy to a policy for the financial planning of a mixed economy in which the 'public sector' was to be predominant. In the same way, the revolutionary attitude of syndicalism had been eliminated by the guild socialists, who had attempted to make the idea of extra-parliamentary, functional representation palatable to the Labour Party. They failed to do so, but had bequeathed (directly through Cole) the corporatist strain in syndicalism to the new notions of bureaucratic planning which emerged as a necessary supplement to the economics of the Labour Keynesians.

In its final form — nationalised enterprises on the Morrisonian model, planning for welfare, and Keynesian economics — corporate socialism was to reshape British society in the 1940s. The early belief of the Left that they would run into effective opposition from the bourgeoisie turned out to be generally untrue, though they hardly challenged the social relations of capitalist society. On the other hand, their very success in generating economic prosperity was paradoxically to lead to a major crisis for the reforming impulse within the Labour Party.

Notes

1. See, for example, C. Cooke and J. Stephenson, *The Slump: Society and Politics During the Depression* (Jonathan Cape, 1977).

2. See D.H. Aldcroft, *The Inter-War Economy, Britain 1919-39* (Batsford, 1970), p.34.

3. K. Marx, *Grundrisse* (Penguin Books, 1973, trans. M. Nicolaus), p. 651.

4. A. Fenner Brockway, *The Coming Revolution* (London, 1932), p. 13.

5. R.H. Tawney, *The Choice Before the Labour Party* (London, 1932), p. 7.

6. Ibid., p. 9.

7. Cripps to W. Graham, 1 September 1931, quoted C. Cooke, *The Life of Richard Stafford Cripps* (Hodder and Stoughton, 1957), p. 130.

8. S. Cripps, *Can Socialism Come by Constitutional Methods?* (London,

1933), p. 2.

9. S. Cripps, 'More and more the National Government is tending toward the ideology of the Fascist State – the Totalitarian Society which is compelled by force to adopt a united policy for the preservation of private property at all costs', *The Choice for Britain* (London, 1934), p. 4.

10. H. Laski, 'Some Implications of the Crisis' in *Political Quarterly*, vol. II, no. 4, Oct-Dec. 1931, p. 467.

11. H. Laski, *Grammar of Politics* (London, 1941 ed.), p. xii. Commentators see Laski's Marxism as a fashionable veneer rather than a real change. See H. Magill, *English Political Pluralism* (Columbia University, 1941), and Bernard Zylstra, *From Pluralism to Collectivism: The Development of Harold Laski's Political Thought* (Van Gorcum and Company, Netherlands,1968). In fact,such commentators underestimate the radical nature of Laski's theoretical change in the 1930s.

12. H. Laski, *The State in Theory and Practice* (London, 1935), p. 331.

13. H. Laski, *Parliamentary Government in England* (London, 1938), p. 219.

14. Ibid., p. 20.

15. Ibid., p. 37.

16. Ibid., p. 38.

17. Ibid., p. 52.

18. Ibid., though Laski attemptedto be ambiguous on this issue, which was very touchy for a constitutional party like Labour.

19. See H. Laski, 'Lenin and Mussolini' in *Foreign Affairs*, vol. II, no. 1, September 1923; and *Communism* (London, 1927)

20. H. Laski, *The State*, p. 213.

21. H. Laski, *Democracy at the Crossroads* (London, n.d.), p. 24. See also Laski, *Parliamentary Government*, p. 62.

22. H. Laski, *The State*, p. 160.

23. C. Attlee, *The Labour Party in Perspective* (London, 1937), p. 114.

24. Ibid., p. 117.

25. Labour Party *Annual Conference Report* 1935, p. 176.

26. Ibid., p. 156.

27. S. Cripps, *The Struggle for Peace* (London, 1936), pp. 57-8.

28. See, for example, ibid., p. 114.

29. See, for example, G.D.H. Cole, *The People's Front* (London, 1937) and John Stachey, *What Are We to Do?* (London, 1938), Part III.

30. C. Attlee, *The Labour Party in Perspective* (London, 1937), p. 219.

31. See Leon Trotsky, *The Spanish Revolution 1931-39* (Pathfinder Press, New York, 1973); George Orwell, *Homage to Catalonia* (Penguin Books, 1972), especially chapter 5.

32. Labour Party Conference *Annual Report* 1929, p. 227-8.

33. See O. Mosley, *My Life* (Nelson, 1968), p. 178.

34. O. Mosley, *Revolution by Reason* (Birmingham, 1925), p. 12.

35. E.F.M. Durbin, *Purchasing Power and Trade Depression: A Critique of Underconsumptionist Theories'* (London, 1933), p. 107.

36. Ibid., p. 74.

37. E.F.M. Durbin, *Socialist Credit Policy* (London, 1934), p. 30.

38. H. Dalton, *Practical Socialism for Britain* (London, 1935), p. 182.

39. Labour Party Conference *Annual Report* 1932, p. 183.

40. H.Dalton ed., *Unbalanced Budgets* (London, 1934), p. 458.

41.See H. Dalton, *Practical Socialism*, p. 213.

42. Quoted in A. Bullock, *Ernest Bevin* I, p. 430.

43. E. Bevin, *The Britain I Want to See* (London, 1934), p. 7.

44. E. Begin and G.D.H. Cole, *The Crisis* (London, 1931), p. 38.

45. Trade Union Congress *Annual Report* 1930, p. 286.

46. See, for example, G.D.H. Cole, 'Obituary —J.A. Hobson 1858-1940', in *Economic Journal*, June-Sept. 1940.

47. G.D.H. Cole, *The Next Ten Years*, p. 77.

48. Ibid., p. 108.

49. G.D.H. Cole, 'What is Money' in Cole ed., *What Everybody Wants to Know about Money* (London, 1933), p. 62.

50. See, for example, G.D.H. Cole, *Socialist Economics* (Victor Gollancz, 1950), p. 50.

51. G.D.H. Cole, 'J.A.Hobson' in *New Statesman*, 5 July 1958, p. 12.

52. G.D.H. Cole, 'Mr.Keynes Beats the Band' in *New Statesman*, 15 February 1936, p. 222.

53 See the speech by Aneurin Bevan at the 1944 Labour Party Conference.

54. Sir O. Mosley, *The Greater Britain* (London, 1932), p. 26.

55. Ibid., p. 28-9.

56. See K. Middlemas, *Politics in Industrial Society: The Experience of the British System since 1911*, chapter 13 (Andre Deutsch, 1979).

57. TUC Report 1928, p. 451.

58. See, for example, G.D.H. Cole, 'Planning and Socialism', in *New Statesman*, 9 May 1936.

59. G.D.H. Cole, *Next Ten Years*, p. 21.

60. Ibid., p. 154.

61. Ibid., p. 84.

62. G.D.H. Cole, *Socialist Economics*, p. 53.

63. H. Morrison, *Socialisation and Transport* (London, 1933), p. 281.

64. Ibid., p. 178.

65. Labour Party Conference *Annual Report* 1932, p. 212.

66. Barbara Wooton, *Plan or No Plan* (London, 1934), p. 312.

67. See M. Lewin, *Political Undercurrents in Soviet Economic Debates* (Pluto Press, 1975); H.H. Ticktin, 'Towards a Political Economy of the USSR', in *Critique* no. 1 (Spring, 1973).

68. N. Preobrazhensky, *The New Economics*: B. Pearce (Clarendon Press, Oxford, 1965).

69. B. Wooton, *Plan or No Plan*, p. 345.

70. H. Dalton ed. *Unbalanced Budgets*, p. 455.

71. H. Dalton, *Practical Socialism*, p. 99.

72. H. Clay 'Workers Control' in C. Addison ed., *Problems of a Socialist Government* (London, 1933), p. 217.

73. See Labour Party Conference *Annual Report* 1932, p. 215.

74. G.R. Mitchison, 'Corporate State or Socialist Plan', in *Socialist Leaguer*, Nov.-Dec. 1934, quoted in Ben Pimlott, *Labour and the Left in the 1930s* (Cambridge University Press, 1977)

75. G.D.H. Cole and W. Mellor ed. *Workers Control and Self-Government in Industry* (London, 1933), p. 8.

76. See, for example, G.D.H. Cole, *The Essentials of Socialisation* (London, 1932).

77. B. Pimlott, *Labour and the Left*, p. 59.

78. Keith Middlemas, *Politics in Industrial Society;* Leo Panitch 'The Development of Corporatism in Liberal Democracies', in *Comparative Political Studies*, 1977, pp. 61-90.

PART FOUR

THE REVISIONIST CHALLENGE

The entry of Labour into the coalition government in 1940 began a decade of social and economic change for Britain. As a coalition partner of the Conservatives and then, after its 1945 electoral triumph, as a government in its own right, the Labour Party carried the ideas of corporate socialism into practice. In doing so, they took the major steps needed to restructure capital at the same time as their welfare measures sought to ameliorate working-class distress. The decade of the forties thus created the preconditions for a general prosperity never before seen in Britain. The old cycle of boom and slump was replaced by a state-regulated capitalism which appeared to banish forever the scourges of poverty, insecurity and unemployment.

However, the very success of Labour in power created new and unforeseen difficulties for the party. It had always been a coalition of different political interests and ideals grouped around the social power of its trade union base, and the admission of the unions as a formally equal partner with government brought to the fore the tensions between their labourism and their desire to serve the national interest. These tensions were mainly reflected within the unions themselves, especially when the union leaders accepted a policy of wage restraint in the late forties, and were eventually to take institutional shape in the conflict between the union bureaucracies and a new, more lasting shop stewards' movement. In the political party of the unions, such tensions were at first concealed by the size of the administrative tasks facing the Labour Government, but as the middle classes turned back to their Conservative allegiance the debates on whether Labour was to be a national or a class party began to intensify. When Labour was forced into opposition in the 1950s, the Labour Right took the initiative in attempting to force the party to sever its connections with the cloth-cap image of British socialism and present itself as a 'modern', national party.

The call to present Labour as more than a labourist party had been present from the beginning, as seen in Ramsay Macdonald's desire to present the party as the true heir to Liberalism and his attempt to draw the middle-class intelligentsia into its leadership. In one sense, the Revisionists of the fifties were in a direct line of continuity with Macdonaldism, but the new circumstances of affluence and cold war gave them a particular characteristic differentiating them from the old right wing of British socialism. They were marked by the debates of the thirties on Keynes and planning, and felt that Labour had to move on from corporate socialism by reawakening its reforming impulse in the very different conditions of a successful capitalism. The old demand for a socialist society directed by the working class was challenged by a new conception of socialism, a conception which would eventually move into direct conflict with the corporatist nature of Labour's political thought and then lead many out of the party altogether.

9 THE REVISIONIST FORERUNNERS

It seemed more important to carry through major social and economic changes than to theorise about them in the circumstances of the forties. The party created to protect the unions was in power throughout the decade remoulding society in the forms thrashed out in the arguments of the thirties. The debates in the country over the social security demands of the Beveridge Report of 1942, or the Keynesian pledge to full employment embodied in the White Paper on *Employment Policy* of 1944, were merely echoes of the process of policy development which Labour had already evolved. As a result, the Labour electoral landslide of 1945 was the culmination of both a national[1] and party preparation over fifteen years.

The administration of corporate socialism shunted aside any major developments in Labour's political thought. Under Herbert Morrison, the champion of the public enterprise, many of the stable, loss-making industries (coal, gas, electricity, rail and road transport) were taken into public ownership with generous terms of compensation. Trade unionists were appointed to the Boards in a number of cases, but always in the light of the Morrisonian ideal of business ability – they ceased to be trade unionists, and became business executives, on accepting their positions. Under Hugh Dalton at the Treasury, the Bank of England was nationalised painlessly, with the merchant and high-steet banks left in private ownership and subject to overall control by the central Bank. In addition, the State maintained a close scrutiny of the private sector through a series of planning controls and rationing which eventually proved too bureaucratic and cumbersome for a growing capitalist economy. After 1947, Labour economic policy shifted away from the direct intervention of controls to the Keynesian techniques of 'fine-tuning' the economy through fiscal and monetary policy. The government also completed the efforts of the Liberal government of 1905-14 in creating the Welfare State. The establishment of national insurance to cover illness, unemployment and old age was accompanied by the inauguration of a free national health service by Aneurin Bevan, the left-wing Minister of Health who successfully out-manoeuvred the selfish opposition of the British Medical Association.

In foreign affairs, the appointment of Ernest Bevin as Foreign Secretary ensured a tough anti-Communist stance. Bevin's fierce labourism, nurtured in his struggles against employers and Communists in the Transport Workers Union, was transmuted into a close alliance with the Americans against Soviet Russia, Britain's wartime ally. He cast his arguments in trade union terms, denouncing left-wing critics as equivalent to 'scabs' and likening the world struggle against Russia with the Communist attempts to break up 'his' union — as he put it to the Soviet Foreign Minister in 1946, 'You have built the Soviet Union and you have a right to defend it. I have built the Transport Union and if you seek to break it I will fight you'.[2] He was a major figure in the development of the Cold War and in building the anti-Soviet NATO in 1949. Elsewhere, after granting a messy independence to a partitioned India in 1947, the Labour government presided over a vicious war against the Communists in Malaya, as in Greece.

The reform took place on the unstable basis of a capitalist economy, however. The Marxist strand within the Labour Party remained generally quiescent, since they believed that a further major push towards a statified economy would be soon undertaken, but in this they faced major opposition from the Right, around Herbert Morrison. They accepted the need to extend the public sector significantly, but believed that both government and the electorate required time to consolidate the gains already made before any further steps could be taken. As Morrison put it to the 1948 Party Conference,

> The mere transfer from private ownership to public ownership is the beginning of the business, it is not the end. An enormous amount of work needs to be done in adapting, consolidating, and, if need be, reforming and changing the organisation of socialised industries . . . you must expect the new programme to be of a somewhat different character and a somewhat different tempo from the last, for we have to embody in it proposals for the consolidation of existing achievements, proposals for laying still more firmly the economic foundations of society .[3]

Labour's electoral defeat in 1951 made the whole question irrelevant in terms of government, but the first attacks on a free health service by a Labour Chancellor (Gaitskell) in April 1951 were an indication that the Labour dream of a socialist health service was an illusion if it continued to be based on a capitalist economy.[4]

The political debates that took place in the forties remained generally confined to the conceptions and ideas formed over the previous forty years. Morrison's belief that Labour should appeal to the middle classes as a national party, together with the movement away from direct planning controls on private investment to more orthodox Keynesian economic policies, were indications of change on the Right, however. It was the first stirrings of a revisionist challenge to corporate socialism — a challenge whose outlines could already be discerned in the writings of two major Labour theorists, Evan Durbin and Douglas Jay.

Evan Durbin

E.F.M. Durbin (1906-48) was the son of a clergyman who managed, after an elementary education, to win a scholarship to Oxford. Together with Douglas Jay and Hugh Gaitskell, he worked closely in the thirties with Hugh Dalton and the XYZ Club of Labour sympathisers in the City to fight the underconsumptionist ideas of Hobson then prevalent on the Labour Left.[5] His *Politics of Democratic Socialism* (1940) stands out as one of the earliest revisionist presentations of political and social ideas, though his wish to write a companion volume on the economic principles of democratic socialism was cut short, at first by his work as a junior Minister in the Attlee government and then by his untimely death in a bathing accident in Cornwall.

Durbin's reaction to the rise of Fascism and Communism in Europe in the 1930s was not merely an echo of the Labour leadership's rejection of the Popular Front. He extended it to an attack on Labour Marxism, and to propose a much more gradual change which would appeal to the middle classes as well as the trade unions. Where the Left pointed to the class nature of the State and the need to strike at the financial power of the ruling class, Durbin argued that the political democracy of British capitalism was far too valuable to risk any rapid social change. The ruling class and the working class had much more in common in the need to preserve parliamentary democracy than the social philosophies which divided them.

The virulence of Durbin's attack on Marxism was a harbinger of the Cold War atmosphere that would dominate the late forties and fifties, though in his case it was caused by the horrific reports of the Stalinist purges. He saw Marxism as a lack of balance in the human mind, which had led to a stress on the competitive and coercive aspects of human nature. The cruelty released by extremism of any kind was a result of the attribution of the cause of social frustration to human will — whether Nazi identification of the Jews as the incarnation of evil, or the Marxist belief that the capitalist class was the cause of all the ills in the world. The adult powers of imagination and reason were used for aggressive purposes, leading to a peculiar and dangerous fetishism of ideas — 'Men will die like flies for theories and exterminate each other with every instrument of destruction for abstractions.'[6] The fact that men and women could turn to Communism in reaction to capitalist crisis or the rise of Fascism appeared foreign to Durbin's understanding. Instead, he saw only the Communist who thrived on violence in psychological terms — the use of Freudian terms such as 'projection' and 'displacement' were freely sprinkled through the argument. In a manner which tended to betray Durbin's Oxford background, he wrote of the Marxists that

> it is, of course, no argument to call one's intellectual opponent a cad. And yet. . . [they] are conditioned to do so by the necessities of their emotional life and by an overpowering desire to find a scapegoat on which to lay their own aggression. Fanatics, extremists and persecutors of all ages are such as these — men of blood and men of hatred. Their underlying desire for suffering is not hidden by a pair of spectacles or a high-pitched voice.[7]

None of us are perfect, of course, and democratic governments have not been immune to cruelty and torture, but Durbin's emotional revulsion was an indication of the political hatred for Marxism felt by the revisionists.

He saw Marxism as totally alien to the British way of life. The Communist call for proletarian dictatorship as a temporary instrument of working-class rule had frozen into a totalitarian nightmare of rule by one party. Durbin pointed out that even the working class taken on its own requires choice between its parties — in Britain there was the Labour Party, the ILP, and the Communists — and asked why only one should be allowed to represent workers. Just as the Russians had eliminated their opposition, so the Communists in Britain would destroy any dissent from their rule if given the chance. The Communists abused liberty by choosing themselves as the vanguard of the proletariat, and crushed other parties because they recognised that, given the choice, they would be rejected in free elections.

The peaceful changes of government in Britain, where Attlee was not threatened with execution nor Baldwin with imprisonment if either lost an election, stood in stark contrast to the cruelty and oppression of the police state under Nazi and Communist rule. There, the opposition was totally at the mercy of the government, and ruthlessly dealt with in travesties of natural justice. The Communists, like the Nazis, governed by terror and force, not law and consent. If economic injustices had been lessened, the prevalence of political injustice nullified any claims by the Soviet Union to being socialist. (Orwell had a similar hatred of Stalinism, reinforced by his experience fighting with the anarchists in Spain, though his calls to transform England in *The Lion and the Unicorn*, in 1940, distance him from Durbin's|gradualism.)

The other side of Durbin's hostility to Marxism was his conception of parliamentary democracy as a necessary cushion against rapid social change. It was a particular conception of democracy put forward by Durbin, dependent on R.G. Bassett's *The Essentials of Parliamentary Government* (1935). Bassett, whose sympathy with Ramsay Macdonald had led him out of the Labour Party in 1931, believed that consensus and co-operation between the parties was essential for parliamentary democracy to funtion at all, so that ultra-conservatives or politicians who were too radical were a menace to the British system of government. Durbin took up this idea to attack not only Communists but Labour Marxists like Laski and Cripps.

He defined democratic government as a particular *method* of arriving at decisions, rather than a style of life. The freedom of the people to choose a government and the freedom to oppose the government without being persecuted were essential to this method, but there also had to be an implicit understanding between the parties not to persecute the other. 'Mutual toleration is the keystone of the arch and the cornerstone of the building.'[8] If a Conservative government believed that Labour was aiming to break up and destroy the Conservative party, it would naturally move to defend itself. In such circumstances, democracy would become impossible, as no government would willingly surrender power to such an enemy. The solution of profound differences, such as a Marxist believed to exist, would mean social strain which would evenually lead to force, and then the country would be on the slope to terror and civil war.

Since parliamentary democracy as a *method* of resolving class differences thus involved compromise, then the socialist policy of a Labour government should not be so extreme that it would drive the Opposition to illegality and violence. If a Labour Marxist government carried through extreme measures, then Britain could forget about peaceful and democratic change for at least a generation. However, this did not mean that a Labour government should have its policy dictated by the Conservatives. In the real political world, a reforming party's policy should not be so moderate that it would drive the party activists to more extreme parties. These activists, intolerant and partisan as they often appeared to Durbin, were recognised by him as the moving force of the party system on which democracy rested. The balance between progress and national consensus was the narrow path on which any democratic socialist party must tread.

Parliamentary democracy was thus seen by Durbin as both more important than and integral to any social change. It was part and parcel of any socialist achievement — 'in so far as we are democratic we are already, in some degree, socialist, and to betray democracy is to betray socialism.'[9] It was, of course, a highly restrictive and conservative definition of democracy and socialism, but its implication that the Conservatives are more socialist than the Communists because they adhere to parliamentary forms was not accidental. Durbin believed that both Conservatives and Labour, capitalists and workers, belonged to the same nation, bound together by an emotional unity that was far deeper than divisions of social class. Democracy was the only institutional framework within which this emotional unity could be expressed, since it allowed for the mutual toleration of differences.

The Communists, like the Fascists, were outside this emotional unity of the nation, since they denied freedom of speech and opposition — the fruits of the democratic method. As a result, Durbin argued that such anti-democrats had no democratic rights, a much more openly illiberal proposal than most politicians of any party would contemplate. Durbin argued that to allow those who seek the destruction of democracy to gather strength would be a sign of weakness, not freedom

> We should constantly remind ourselves that the enemies of democracy have no moral right to the privileges of democracy; and that a time may come when, to defend ourselves, it will be necessary to suppress their political organisation.[10]

Such an open statement of intent was not only more honest than many politicians, but in terms of the Labour Party was an outright declaration of war on the radical socialists and Labour Marxists who saw democracy as a means to the rapid transformation of society, and who were sympathetic to united work with the Communists.

The Marxist argument that parliament was merely a political facade disguising a bourgeois dictatorship was dismissed by Durbin, who pointed to the major changes in the democratic capitalist economies of Britain and the United States. The existence of political democracy in these countries had meant that the State had been forced to curb the vices of *laissez-faire* capitalism. In a confused but irresistible manner, the common people had gradually pushed the State to regulate capitalism so that *both* labour and property were able to benefit. The growth of the unions to protect the worker against low wages and the arbitrary tyranny of the employer in the factory had been a prelude to political action. State planning to regulate the trade cycle and the use of taxation to protect the individual from the main dangers of economic life — unemployment, illness, old age — were due to a vigorous democracy responsive to popular needs.

Moreover, the changes in capitalism had led to changes in its class character which greatly weakened the Marxist case for a proletarian revolution. The proletariat, far from being impoverished, had obtained small property-holdings for itself in the form of savings — a humble but psychologically important state in society, which had led to a mentality derided by Marxists as 'petit-bourgeois'. The middle classes themselves, far from disappearing as Marx had predicted in *The Communist Manifesto*, had risen enormously in numbers, with the growing army of technicians, 'white collar' workers, and suburban householders. Capitalist property itself had changed, as the growth of the private corporation had led to a dispersion of ownership among a large number of shareholders and a divorce between ownership and control. The upper bourgeoisie was no longer a single class deserving expropriation, but a variety of groups, from a parasitic class of property-owners without any function to the salaried managerial class which administered company affairs on a daily basis.

Durbin believed that Labour should move out from its old trade union base to win over the new middle classes. The Marxist element in the equation of British socialism had become irrelevant and potentially anti-democratic, and needed to be replaced by a more classless outlook. Moreover, the major redistribution of power within the private corporations would enable Labour to turn the new managerial class against the other, useless sections of the upper bourgeoisie. The *rentiers* and property-owners had become useless parasites on the shoulders of the managers, while the company directors who took the strategic business decisions behind closed doors were 'an irresponsible, self-recruiting, nepotic oligarchy.'[11] Their real functions of management had been lost, leaving them on the same useless level as the property-owners. The rejection of Labour Marxism, and the appeal to the new middle and managerial classes, were to be taken up by the revisionists.

Durbin's view of politics as based on psychology was based on false reasoning — he assumed what he sought to prove. He believed that democracy could only survive if the emotional life and character of a nation lent itself to gradual change and toleration. The roots of democracy in his sense of the word were neither rational nor intellectual — 'it is fundamentally a consequence of psychological health and the absence of neurosis.'[12] The British were, of course, the nation Durbin had in mind. He took the characteristics of British political culture (cleansed of blemishes such as Chartist risings, the mass strike wave before and after the Great War, and repression of nationalist resistance to its Empire) and assumed it to be free of neurosis. It was much too insular, leading Durbin to a contemptuous rejection of other national models such as France, and to adopt an over-sentimental view of the Empire.[13]

Just as Durbin accepted the orthodox view of British political culture as a model of mental health a little too glibly, so his identification of Marxism with neurosis and sadism was too self-righteous. It was not merely the fact that he identified Marxism much too easily with Stalinism — its diversity could not be contained in so narrow a frame — but the superficiality of the analysis. The fact that capitalist crisis or war might lead people to Stalinism obviously had a psychological aspect, but this should be ignored in trying to establish whether any political ideology is right or wrong. Many radical psychologists would argue that we are all living in a neurotic society anyway and that nobody is in a position to moralise. In the light of such uncertainty on the scientific status of psychology, Durbin's emphasis on mental health and the lack of it seems on the same level as those dogmatic Marxists who glibly dismiss all twentieth-century ideas not in conformity with their own as petit-bourgeois.

In pointing to the changes in capitalism and the working class, Durbin prefigured much later revisionist writing. However, his belief that the rise of the managerial and middle classes meant that 'we are living in a society whose class composition is shifting steadily against Marx's proletariat'[14] gravely underestimated the ability of Marxism to adapt and evolve to explain new developments in capitalism. His own Keynesian beliefs prevented Durbin from recognising any virtue in the labour theory of value (which was more than ever seen as a bizarre anomaly in economic thought) and to assume that the economy could be painlessly turned away from crisis. In such circumstances, there was no real *need* for radical change, a belief that he would pass on to the revisionists.

Durbin was a major forerunner of revisionist thought in political ideas, but his belief in a centrally planned economy prevented him from breaking out of corporate socialism. He believed that a socialist society – defined as 'fundamentally a demand for social justice. . . for economic freedom and social equality'[15] – was not possible in an economy run on the profit-motive. Any attempt to end social inequality or to extend the social services would lead to higher tax burdens on capitalist companies, leading to a crisis of investment. Only a central planning authority and state direction of capital were compatible with a just society. Thus, 'while the institution of some form of planning is not the object, it is the indispensable preliminary means for the attainment of the new society.'[16] It was to be Douglas Jay who was to point to later revisionist developments away from corporate socialism.

Jay

Douglas Jay (b. 1907), after enjoying the usual education of the upper middle classes of Winchester and Oxford, was closely associated with Durbin and Gaitskell in the XYZ Club. It was his book *The Socialist Case* (1937) which marked him out as a forerunner of revisionist thought.

Like Durbin, Jay was not interested in class power in capitalist society, but in the inequality and injustice that existed as a result of an unfair system of distribution of wealth. This system was the major cause of the poverty that blighted working-class life, preventing the enjoyment of all that is valuable in life. If poverty was an enemy which could be cured, it was necessary to strike at inequality – 'one of the chief reasons why the poor are very poor is that the rich are very rich'.[17] While perfect equality could be ruled out, as the loss of incentives which would result would cause even greater poverty, it was necessary to reduce the wide disparities that did exist.

Jay's own conception of socialism as concerned with equality and security, rather than class power, was a result of his belief that a regulated market economy was a fundamentally sound economy which was accidentally distorted by unequal rewards. He ridiculed Marx's labour theory of value for failing to grasp that the rewards to the different factors of production were all essential and necessary, and used orthodox arguments of neo-classical economics to demonstrate that the reward of interest to stockholders was to induce the capitalist to part with his capital for the length of time needed to pay for the plant and raw materials required for production; rent the reward for persuading the landowner to have his property for one use rather than another; and profit the reward for risk taken by the entrepreneur. To each function a fundamental and necessary economic service corresponded. The price system determined the allocation of the wealth produced by these factors so that, in theory, a balanced equilibrium would result from a just and orderly system.

In practice, Jay pointed out, this elegant system stood in sharp contrast to the unjust and disorderly world of reality, disfigured as it was by gross inequality, extreme poverty and criminal waste. The reason for this, according to Jay, was that the price system 'ignores entirely. . . the absolute difference in consumers' needs. . . between the need for bread of a man who has got enough and the need for bread of a man who has not got enough'.[18] It ignored the reality of social inequality between the classes.

Land, capital and enterprise were certainly essential services, but this did not mean that their rewards were *earned*. Jay argued that the capitalist performed the economic function of capital, but did not really earn the reward of interest. Saving involved a negligible sacrifice, and waiting hardly a sacrifice at all for people who owned an enormous amount of property. The 'abstinence' of the Rothschilds or the Rockefellers was hardly abstinence in any meaningful sense, while their business caution and timidity in investing their capital could lead to a serious crisis in the market economy. In effect, Jay argued that most capitalists enjoyed unearned income, as it arose from waiting rather than working.

To counteract these social inequalities, and the monetary and economic crisis resulting from them, Jay called for state intervention, in particular the nationalisation of the Bank of England. An unregulated price system ensured that the real needs of the poor were sacrificed, while an unregulated monetary system ensured permanent unemployment and insecurity. The regulation of capitalism − the redistribution of wealth by means of a taxation policy which would gradually abolish inheritance, and a managed monetary policy to regulate the trade cycle − was Jay's solution to the flaws he had detected in the market economy.

However, they were *flaws* rather than fundamental defects. Jay saw nothing wrong with the price system as a regulator of demand and supply and, while rejecting the social philosophy of a capitalist society, he saw nothing wrong if state regulation could correct its abuses. The fact that poverty and insecurity exist in capitalism did not validate the radical calls of the Labour Left. To Jay, 'we must emphatically not run to the opposite extreme and assume that the price system is worth-less. . . We have merely shown that there are blemishes in its sacro-sanctity'.[19] All the flaws in the price system were connected to ine-quality of income, and would disappear as that inequality disappeared. Jay, like the neo-classical economists, believed that the market eco-nomy enjoyed a *fundamental* equilibrium, and saw state intervention as restoring the conditions in which that equilibrium could be regained.

In diverting the attention of socialists from questions of class power, Jay pointed to a definition of socialism which had more in common with the New Liberalism at the turn of the century. Unemployment and poverty were no longer seen as caused by a market economy, so that nationalisation ceased to be crucial to the achievement of socia-lism. Jay was challenging the Labour Party's notions of corporate socia-lism when he wrote that

> the tendency of socialists lately to think less of the dispossession of property and more of organisation, 'planning', efficiency and so on, is in many ways unfortunate. What society fundamentally needs is not so much planning as socialism.[20]

The identification of planning with socialism was denied by Jay, who saw socialism as being about the suppression of unearned income, not the abolition of the market economy or the destruction of the social power of the ruling class.

Thus, where the corporate socialists looked to agencies of planning and debated the best form for nationalised industries, Jay attempted to look for safeguards for private enterprise against state intervention. He accepted nationalisation of industries which were natural monopolies like gas or rail transport, but demanded that both small companies *and* large well-established industries which were efficient under private ownership should be free from state control. He argued that nation-alisation was usually wrong, in that it created a monopoly which would extract a monopoly profit from the public and which would fail to re-duce costs. Such a monopoly, whether state or private, was a con-spiracy against the public health — 'To organise such a conspiracy has been almost the first instinct of producers throughout history, from the days of the guild to those of the "Corporative State" '.[21] To safeguard consumers, the price system had to be left intact form state interven-tion, and competition within the public enterprises and between public and private companies should be encouraged to aid efficiency and customer service — for example, Jay argued that a nationalised rail company should compete with private road transport companies. Planning was desirable *only* where inequality and insecurity could be diminished without too great a loss of consumer freedom and without the creation of unnecessary state monopolies in industry.

In his criticism of nationalisation as a creation of an unhealthy monopoly rather than a panacea for the evils of capitalism, Jay rightly pointed to one of the weaknesses of corporate socialism. Planning by the State — whether through public ownership or state direction of capital — could not *in itself* bring social equality or economic security. Indeed, the inevitable creation of a bureaucracy to run the extended economic powers of the state could very well hinder the development of a just society, creating the new inequalities of state patronage and privilege, as was occurring in Stalinist Russia. Jay realised that the co-ordination of demand and supply could not be achieved by centralised planning — it was his main criticism of Durbin — and looked instead to the traditional price system.

However, in divorcing the distribution of wealth from the wage system and locating it in the old Fabian distinction between earned and unearned income, Jay was retreating back to the market economy, regulated though he wished to make it. The consequences of the accept-ance of Keynesian economics by the Labour Party had been grasped most acutely by these forerunners of revisionism. The need for class struggle to defend workers against the ravages of a capitalist society, and the belief that there was a fundamental weakness in the market economy, were denied by political thinkers who saw only the surface reality of capital without probing to the authoritarian and degrading system of wage labour which lay behind it. Jay, in seeking to eliminate the unacceptable face of capitalism while maintaining the essentials of the system, was pointing the way for the revisionist challenge to Labour's corporate socialism.

Socialist Commentary

The administration of the nation in the forties absorbed the critical energies of many on Labour's Right. Jay, Gaitskell and Durbin all worked in the Civil Service during the war and had ministerial duties in the 1945 Labour government. The policies of Labour in power — the public ownership of loss-making industries, the extension of social security, and an anti-Soviet foreign policy — were not such as to arouse rebellion on Labour's Right, while the direct physical controls on industry had been made necessary by the emergencies of war and were gradually lifted.

However, the development of the line of political thought begun by Durbin and Jay was not totally at a standstill. The right-wing Socialist Vanguard Group attempted to criticise the corporatist nature of Labour proposals and to provide ideological backbone for opposition to the Soviet Union through their journal, *Socialist Commentary*. Their criticisms were greatly strengthened by the addition of Dr Rita Hinden to their team. Hinden (1909-71), a close friend of Gaitskell, had been born in South Africa and, after being educated at the London School of Economics, joined the staff of the Fabian Colonial Bureau in 1940. Her background gave her a special interest in colonial affairs which proved influential in the Labour Party as the process of dismantling the British Empire proceeded.

However, the hallmark of the journal was anti-Communism, which extended to an opposition to any domestic policies that smacked of Marxism. *Socialist Commentary* hailed a mixed economy as a third alternative to Russian Communism and American *laissez-faire* capitalism.[22] However, in any conflict between the two systems, it called for Labour to recognise the superiority of capitalism −

Wherever the Russian controlled world expands, democratic socialism and all the values for which it stands are doomed to perish, whilst present-day American capitalism, for all our misgivings about it, at least leaves room for free institutions to flower and survive.[23]

Their anti-Communism suffused the group's attitude to the British colonies. In common with the Labour leadership, they opposed independence for African nations, believing that the principles of social justice and equality would be best granted by a benevolent Britain. At one conference, in April 1946, Rita Hinden clashed with the Ghanaian nationalist, Kwame Nkrumah − 'When Mr. Nkrumah said "we want absolute independence" it left me absolutely cool. Why?. . . British Socialists are not much concerned with ideals like independence and self-government, but with the ideal of social justice'.[24] When she came to accept ultimate independence (after a visit to Nigeria in 1948), she remained convinced that Britain should guard such inexperienced countries from the evils of Communism by the establishment of representative institutions in the colonies *before* independence. These institutions, she declared in an editorial on colonial policy in *Socialist Commentary*, should be centres in the fight against Communist propaganda. The fact that she saw the colonies as remaining outposts of British influence was admitted in the same editorial, where she declared that

> we have not the intention, and we know it, of sacrificing our standard of living for the sake of colonial development; we do not contemplate an evening out of wealth; we know, too, that our development plans are partly inspired by our own needs. We must say this quite frankly.[25]

Her real attitude to representative institutions in the colonies was demonstrated when she persuaded the Labour Party to support the dismissal of Cheddi Jagan's pro-Russian government in British Guiana in 1953, much to the fury of the Labour Left.

The anti-Communism which determined the colonial policy of *Socialist Commentary* expressed itself in demands that Labour should loosen its ties with the unions to become more of a national, and less of a class, party. They argued, in support of Herbert Morrison's desire to establish Labour's appeal among the middle classes, that the achievements of the 1945 Labour government had finally given the working-class movement an equal social status in society. The time to recognise that the demand for social justice had burst beyond the narrow divides of any class or section of the community had come, and *Socialist Commentary* was much more forward than Morrison in identifying the left-wing demand for more nationalisation as the obstacle to this recognition. Echoing Douglas Jay, *Socialist Commentary* called for a movement away from planning to a vision of socialism as concerned with welfare and equality —

> It has repeatedly been argued. . . that nationalisation is not an end, but a means — one means among others — to achieve certain social objectives. No betrayal of principle is involved if, compared with the past, it figures less prominently today, when the key industries are already in the hands of the community.[26]

It was a demand that was to be taken up with increasing frequency in the new boom conditions of the fifties.

Notes

1. See P. Addison, *The Road to 1945* (Quartet 1976).

2. Labour Party *Annual Conference Report*, 1946, p. 167.

3. Ibid., 1948, p. 122.

4. On the non-socialist nature of Labour's record in power, see D.N. Pritt, *The Labour Government 1945-51* (Lawrence and Wishart, 1963); David Coates, *The Labour Party and the Struggle for Socialism* (Cambridge University Press, 1975), chapter 3; David Howell, *British Social Democracy* (Croom Helm, 1976).

5. For the importance of Durbin in Labour's acceptance of Keynesian ideas, see chapter 8.

6. Evan Durbin: *The Politics of Democratic Socialism* (London, 1940), p. 50.

7. Ibid., p. 190.

8. Durbin, *Politics*, p. 241.

9. Ibid., p. 271.

10. Ibid., p. 276.

11. Ibid., p. 126.

12. Ibid., p. 263.

13. See, for example, Evan Durbin, *What Have We To Defend* (London, 1942).

14. Durbin, *Politics*, p. 111.

15. Evan Durbin, *Socialist Credit Policy* (London, 1934), p. 5.

16. Evan Durbin, *Problems of Economic Planning: Papers on Planning and Planning and Economics* (Routledge and Kegan Paul, 1949), p. 45.

17. Douglas Jay, *The Socialist Case* (London, 1937), p. 3.

18. Ibid., p. 111.

19. Ibid.

20. Ibid., p. 237.

21. Ibid., p. 326.

22. See, for example, the editorial in *Socialist Commentary* (October, 1947).

23. *Socialist Commentary* (August, 1950), p. 111.

24. Quoted in Partha Sarathi Gupta, *Imperialism and the British Labour Movement 1914-64* (Macmillan, 1975), p. 326.

25. *Socialist Commentary* (April, 1949), p. 85.

26. *Socialist Commentary* (April, 1950), p. 85.

10 THE REVISIONIST HEYDAY

By the time that Labour's huge parliamentary majority had been all but eliminated in the 1950 election, its programme for transforming British society had been completed. The state had taken a leading role in restructuring capitalism through the policies of nationalisation, fiscal and direct planning and welfare, while the decline of Britain as a world power was partially disguised by the tough foreign policy of Ernest Bevin.

However, Labour had exhausted itself, in ideas as much as energy. It had succeeded only too well in implementing its policies, and was in real danger of becoming a rudderless conservative party. Its ageing leadership drifted, harmed by the retirement of Cripps, the death of Bevin, and the resignation of Bevan and Wilson, until Labour's defeat in the 1951 election. This defeat began a period of thirteen years of uninterrupted government by the Conservatives, who won three successive elections in the decade, each one with a larger majority than the last. The Labour defeats in 1951 and 1955 could be blamed on bad party organisation or on the ferocious divisions between the Left, led by Bevan, and the Right, led by Morrison and Gaitskell. However, the unity of the party under Hugh Gaitskell's leadership after 1955 did not prevent a greater defeat in 1959, leading to speculation on the possibility of Labour's survival.

It was the long economic boom which benefited the Conservatives. After an initial setback, the British economy entered the most sustained period of prosperity in its history, enjoying a boom which raised production figures, incomes and standards of living to heights thought impossible before the war. Unemployment virtually disappeared, and economic growth and political stability began to be considered the norm throughout Europe. Interruptions in economic prosperity, as in 1952 and 1957, were brief and easily overcome by government policy apparently destroying the Marxist belief of the Depression years that capitalism could not survive and grow. It was fondly imagined that a theory and practical policy had been found which would ensure the boundless expansion of the 'mixed' capitalist economy, while the limits of that expansion were concealed by optimism and the very length of the boom.

There were danger signals even in the most halcyon days. The econ omic boom was accompanied by a creeping inflation, but at an average of 3 per cent per year in 1952-65 this was explained as a necessary and minor consequence of full employment. The decline of Britain's share of the world market from 1954 in the face of increasing competition from Japan and West Germany was a genuine cause for concern, but this too was more than offset by the general rise in world trade, which grew at the phenomenal rate of an average 6 per cent per year in the fifties and 7½ per cent in the early sixties. The continuing decline of the manufacturing capacity of British capitalism was concealed by general prosperity in the capitalist world. It was, however, a prosperity which witnessed the further concentration of capital in oligopolies and monopolies — 180 firms employing one third of the British labour force accounted for half the net capital expenditure of Britain in 1963; 74 of these firms, with ten thousand or more workers each, amounted to two-fifths.[1]

The boom led to major changes in working-class expectations with worrying consequences for the Labour Party. Until the late fifties few workers had cars and even fewer had telephones, but the prospect of a continually rising prosperity was always in view. With the sudden access to a range of commodities previously regarded as luxury goods, from washing machines to television sets and cars in the late fifties, the image the working class held of itself began to change. The change was often exaggerated by observers at the time,[2] but there was a real trend for working-class families to cease identifying with the labour movement as closely as had once been the case. However, the real position of the working class as tied to alienating work and long hours did not change. It expressed itself in a new shop stewards' movement and a series of unofficial strikes which were short-lived and usually successful. Their increased bargaining power at a time of full employment gave the unions a renewed sense of industrial power, although this made them intensely unpopular with the middle classes which Labour hoped to win.

New Fabian Essays

The economic prosperity also led to a rising revolt against corporate socialism within the Labour Party by the 'revisionists'. These leading figures in the party took their name from the German Social Democrat, Eduard Bernstein, who attempted to 'revise' Marxism at the turn of the century by expunging its revolutionary conclusions. Just as

Bernstein wanted the Social Democrats to bring their revolutionary theory into line with their reformist practice, so the British revisionists wanted to force Labour to bring its socialist pretensions into line with its acceptance of a 'mixed', mainly private enterprise, economy. They believed that Labour's ideology of corporate socialism had achieved its objective of creating prosperity, leading Labour to lose its reforming impulse, and they hoped to revive the radical traditions of the party by cutting out the shibboleths and Marxist rhetoric which made Labour appear a relic of the past.

It was the publication of *New Fabian Essays* in 1952 which heralded the revisionist onslaught. These were the product of a revival of the Fabian Society by G.D.H. Cole as a research centre and intellectual sounding-board for both Right and Left in the Labour Party. It was a Fabian conference in 1949, chaired by Cole, which decided to produce an updated version of the original *Fabian Essays in Socialism*. The result, in *New Fabian Essays*, was a series of contributions from Bevanites such as Ian Mikardo and Richard Crossman as well as revisionists, but the bulk of the authors had served their intellectual apprenticeship in *Socialist Commentary*.

The revisionists pointed to the need of the Labour Party to find a new and radical direction now that it had achieved its programme. Tony Crosland, in his essay, 'The Transition from Capitalism', pointed out that the prognoses of the Labour Marxists had been dramatically disproved by events. Far from collapsing, capitalism was expanding, bringing with it a rising standard of living for the working class. Crosland argued that Labour must face up to the new realities – 'it is now clear that capitalism is undergoing a metamorphosis into a quite different system, and that this is rendering academic most of the traditional socialist analysis.'[3] A new definition of socialism was required if Labour was not to become the party of the *status quo*.

Public ownership as an instrument of socialist planning was questioned by the revisionist essayists, who pointed out that the equation of socialism with planning was a profound misunderstanding. As Britain was a planned economy, through nationalisation and state direction of the private sector, it followed under the narrow definition of corporate socialism that nothing more needed to be done to change society. In fact, argued the revisionists, a class-ridden and inegalitarian society like Britain was far from socialist in the sense of the traditions of ethical socialism. Roy Jenkins, in his essay 'Equality', argued that public owership should be egalitarian in motive, rather than merely looking to efficiency. It should be 'an essential prerequisite of greater equality of earned incomes and an inevitable concomitant of greater equality in the ownership of property'.[4] Jenkins was pointing to a redefinition of socialism in his call for workers to share in the ownership of property – a form of democratic capitalism, as had been advocated by the Liberals in the twenties – and pointed out that public ownership need not be outright nationalisation as argued by corporate socialists. Instead, Jenkins saw co-operative or part-control by the State as preferable alternatives to the bureaucratic model pressed by Labour since the thirties.[5]

Austen Albu went further in his essay, 'The Organisation of Industry', in his attack on corporate socialism. Nationalisation had not satisfied the need for a democratic sense of responsibility called for by Tawney. Planning for full employment, the redistribution of wealth and the increase in industrial efficiency were being achieved by other means than the traditional model of public ownership. However, the sense of socialism as a sense of democratic participation was still unsatisfied. The model of the public corporation as the model for efficiency needed to be modified, according to Albu, by worker participation if corporate socialism was not to degenerate into a new managerial autocracy, distant and manipulative rather than selfish and brutal. It was, of course, to be participation with management rather than the outright self-management demanded by the more class-conscious syndicalists, whom Albu thought of as primitive.

The *New Fabian Essays* was a tentative document, pointing out the need for a redefinition of socialism while making only cautious sallies in that direction. A common element among revisionists was the need for a classless society, but by this was meant a society without the indignities and inequalities of caste rather than the abolition of the wage-system called for by Marx or the guild socialists. However, its rejection of social revolution did not mean that it was a conservative movement – it was Morrison who represented the conservative tendencies in the Labour Party – or even just a desire to curb bureaucratic excesses. The revisionists were in revolt against corporate socialism, and wished to release the radical energies locked up in the Labour Party by an outmoded class outlook. As Roy Jenkins put it in his book, *Pursuit of Progress* (1953),

The first duty of a party of the left is to be radical in the context of the moment, to offer a prospect of continuing advance, and to preserve the loyalty of those whose optimistic humanism makes them its natural supporters.[6]

The process of elaborating the new definition of socialism took a major step forward with the publication, in 1956, of John Strachey's *Contemporary Capitalism* and Tony Crosland's *The Future of Socialism*.

Strachey

John Strachey (1901-63) was born into a Conservative family – his father was the editor of the *Spectator* – but joined the ILP at Oxford University. He was closely associated with Mosley, leaving the Labour Party with the latter in 1931 to form the New Party. Mosley's increasingly Fascist tendencies soon led Strachey to leave the New Party, and during the thirties he came to be seen as the symbol of the Marxist intelligentsia who closely sympathised with the Communist Party. His books, *The Coming Struggle For Power* (1932) and *The Nature of Capitalist Crisis* (1935), presented the traditional Marxist arguments that capitalism was doomed to collapse and that the ruling class would react with violence.

However, his reading of Keynes modified his earlier views and he became increasingly convinced that state direction of the economy could overcome capitalist crisis. He then played a prominent part in the Labour Party, becoming Minister of Food in the 1945 government, where he was embroiled in a notoriously abortive scheme to grow groundnuts in East Africa. After the 1951 defeat, he contributed a paper to *New Fabian Essays*, where he acknowledged the influence of Keynes and Douglas Jay in winning him away from Marxism. However, it was in *Contemporary Capitalism* (1956) that Strachey most fully presented the revisionist case against the Marxism he had once espoused.

He argued that Marx had, in fact, correctly analysed nineteenth-century capitalism in pointing to the concentration of capital and the increasingly severe cycle of booms and slumps. If left to itself, capitalism would undoubtedly have ended in poverty, class war and social revolution. Marx made his error in his failure to recognise that capitalism was capable of change – 'he under-rated the element of liberty and over-rated the element of necessity in man's condition even within a given social and economic system. His categories were altogether too hard and fast'.[7] In fact, capitalism had been able to change its nature to regulate the trade cycle and to overcome unemployment. The working class, far from becoming 'immiserated' as Marx believed, had increased their stake in society as they grew increasingly affluent.

The social mutation which had occurred in capitalism, according to Strachey, was the ability of the new managerial class to consciously control the economy rather than be controlled by it. The divorce between ownership and management, present through capitalism, had reached a new stage as the joint companies had grown to their present size, leading to a management based on competence and ability to avoid the crisis which had hitherto wrecked hopes of a stable business environment. It was the control of prices which was the key to the situation, according to Strachey. In a competitive economy, prices were outside the control of firms, set by the market conditions of demand and supply; in the economy of large firms and oligopolies of contemporary capitalism, the firms could set their own prices, as they controlled the market.

> Prices, from being objective data which move automatically in accordance with no man's will, became things which may be moved within certain limits, by the conscious decisions of groups of men. Such a change nullifies some of the basic principles of capitalism,[8]

bringing a planned market economy into the realm of possibility. The key function of accumulation had taken on a semi-collective character, while the automatic self-regulating character of the economy was eroded as it came under conscious control.

The present problem of capitalism was not instability, but the question of whether a few oligarchs or the people were to benefit from the economy. If production was left to the capitalists, they would be prevented by the profit motive from investing their capital where the social good required it. However, most businessmen and economists were agreed that the economy could not rest on such a flimsy basis as the selfish decisions of individuals, and that the State itself must become increasingly associated with the economic process.

Strachey called for the new capitalism to be controlled in the interests of the population rather than a few oligarchs. He believed, like Durbin and Jay, that democracy had been the central force in modifying the harsh brutalities of early capitalism, and that democracy was the answer to the present problems of a managed capitalism. Through economic democracy, as expressed in the separation of the managers from the owners, decision-making power had been placed in the much more responsible hands of disinterested managers who would invest to avoid a slump. Through political democracy, state inter-

vention could guide the economy in response to the needs of the electorate – the people. As a result, according to Strachey, the question of
whether capitalism would become more stable or less stable depended
on the democratic pressures brought to bear on a changing system.

The importance of Strachey's book lay in its rejection of the traditional left-wing opposition to capitalism once held by the author.
Such views, Marxist and syndicalist in origin, were still powerful in the
Labour Party, but Strachey insisted that they were based on an old-
fashioned view of a society which had generally vanished. However, it
was still couched in the ideas of the thirties. The questions of economic
stability and efficiency, rather than equality and social justice, pervaded
his writings, which failed to go beyond Keynes. The positive presentation of revisionist socialism was presented by Crosland in a much more
radical break with the concerns of corporate socialism.

Crosland

Tony Crosland (1918-77) had been a tutor at Trinity College,
Oxford, before entering Westminster in 1950. He had written for
Socialist Commentary, the main right-wing Labour periodical, and
contributed a major essay on the new capitalism to *New Fabian Essays*,
but it was *The Future of Socialism* (1956) which established his place as
the main exponent of revisionism in the Labour Party.

Crosland's redefinition of socialist priorities sprang from the belief
that the economic problems which had absorbed the Labour Party's
attention for a generation had been solved. The collapse of capitalism
widely expected by many on the Left in the thirties had not occurred,
as unemployment had been overcome and total output was rising. The
economy of the mid-fifties was behaving in a buoyant and productive
manner, and working-class living standards were on the increase as
national wealth was reaching new heights. The old capitalist enemy had
lost its power to the State, which used fiscal and monetary policies to
aim for full employment, a more equitable distribution of wealth, and
high economic growth. It had become a *welfare* state, interested in
helping business only in so far as this helped the economy on which
the community depended.

Crosland noted, along with Strachey, the managerial revolution
which had transformed the old cut-throat capitalism of self-interested
entrepreneurs into a mixed economy where decisions were no longer in
capitalist hands. However, he did not regard it as being peculiar to

capitalism, as the growth of managerial power could be detected in all industrial societies of a certain size and complexity.

> The new managers (like the capitalists before them) pursue the goals of growth, profits and personal wealth. But such broad statements are true of any industrial system; as true for example, of managers in Kharkov as of managers in Birmingham or Detroit.[9]

There had, of course, been a major change compared with the old capitalists, as the managers had a different relation to property. Where the old capitalists made their business decisions on the basis of maximum profits for the companies they owned, the new managers were merely salaried workers who were more concerned with social status and stability than with the single pursuit of profit. They had much more social responsibility as a result, and took a major interest in welfare schemes and good labour relations.

Crosland admitted that profit still played a major role in the private sector, but he called on socialists to forget their prejudice against the moral overtones of the term and to take a dispassionate look at the real functions of profit in all industrial societies. He argued that

> it is a mistake to think that profit, in the sense of a surplus over cost, has any special or unique connection with capitalism. On the contrary, it must be the rationale of business activity in any society, capitalist or socialist, which is growing and dynamic.[10]

The precondition of economic growth was the ability to take aside part of a firm's output in order to improve the means of production or to invest in expanding areas of the economy. This was true of Russia as much as Britain, regardless of how the extra output is created or who decides where it should be directed. The old socialist argument that it should not be expropriated by the capitalist was outdated by the mixed economy, where democratic institutions could be used to ensure that profit created in the private sector could be used for reinvestment rather than privileged consumption.

Crosland argued that it was the changes that had taken place in the working class which posed the greatest dangers for the Labour Party (a theme which he took up with even greater urgency after the 1959 defeat). It appeared grossly absurd in the conditions of growing affluence to think of the working class as wage-slaves, or of the unions as the powerless representatives of the underprivileged. In fact, the conditions of full employment had given the unions a new and much greater power. It was a seller's market for labour power, in which the employer was in a poor negotiating position if his labourforce was not to be lost to a competitor offering higher wages. It could be argued that profit was still squeezed out of the workers, but this was indirectly determined by government management of the economy rather than the greed of the employer. The workers were no better off in this respect in the nationalised industries (or in the collectivist economies of Eastern Europe) and affluence made a nonsense of any grievance that might otherwise be felt.

However, while prosperity and social security were softening the hostility between the classes, and the militant language of class war was passing out of use, the Labour Party remained trapped in the past. The traditionalist conservatism of the labour movement and the dogged persistence of class antagonisms among a minority of British workers were responsible for a poor image for Labour with the voters. Labour owed its whole existence and historic growth to the trade union movement yet, ironically, this unique identification was a clear political liability, for the simple reasons that the old industrial working class was both shrinking in size and growing in material comfort. Crosland pointed out the

> clear political implications here for the Labour Party, which would be ill-advised to continue making a largely proletarian class appeal when a majority of the population is gradually attaining a middle-class standard of life, and distinct symptoms even of a middle-class psychology.[11]

In the face of these changed conditions — a buoyant economy which could no longer be meaningfully described as 'capitalist', and a gradual disappearance of class antagonisms — Crosland called for a restatement of socialism if Labour was to be a credible government in the second half of the century. The old objectives of socialism had been either achieved — as with full employment and social welfare — or had become irrelevant — as with the need to abolish private property or to increase the power of the proletariat. The old shibboleths were increasingly absurd in the new age, and the traditions which dominated Labour's language and thinking had to be left behind. 'Keir Hardie cannot provide, any more than can the Gracchi, the right focus with which to capture the reality of the mid-20th Century world'.[12] Sweep-

ing away the conservative stagnation which threatened to clog up
Labour's channels of radical energy, Crosland sought a new socialist
philosophy for an affluent age.

   In doing so, he concentrated his criticisms on the belief of the
corporate socialists that public ownership and planning were fundamental to socialism. This belief was based on a confusion between
means and ends. Nationalisation was merely a means to achieving the
goals of socialism, not one of the goals. In justification of this, he
pointed to the post-war experience of public ownership, which had
belied all the hopes held by Labour in the thirties. It did not lead to an
extension of planning, as the public corporations were as independent
of government control as the private companies. The state was able to
exercise control over the whole economy, but this depended on the
willingness of the government to use fiscal and monetary controls
rather than ownership.

   Moreover, Crosland argued that the creation of state monopolies
had led to restrictions on individual liberty, encouraged sloth and
prevented individual initiative. An unresponsive bureaucracy, remote
from the workforce and generally deaf to consumer interests had hardly
led the country nearer to a socialist society. In this situation, competition should be seen in a more favourable light by socialists, who should
cease planning any further extension of public ownership, at least in
the traditional form of the public corporation covering a whole
industry. The basic utilities had been already placed under state
control, while the remaining large industries − cars, chemicals, aircraft,
shipping, and others − were neither private monopolies nor inefficient.
Any further programme of public ownership should be strictly
governed by fixed criteria that economic improvement could take place
by no other means, and that competition would be encouraged by, for
example, part-state ownership. Whatever the form of future state intervention, Crosland was clear that the old confusion that nationalisation was necessarily connected with socialism should be jettisoned.

> State ownership of all industrial capital is not now a condition of
> creating a socialist society . . . What is unjust in our present arrange-
> ments is the distribution of private wealth; and that can as well be
> cured in a pluralist as in a wholly state-owned economy, with much
> better results for social contentment and the fragmentation of
> power.[13]

Just as nationalisation was generally rejected by Crosland, so the faith of the corporate socialists in planning was called into question. He accepted, of course, the Keynesian prescriptions for state intervention to regulate the trade cycle and to create full employment, but the direct physical controls advocated by Labour in the thirties should be rejected. According to Crosland, such planning was detrimental to any expansionist economic strategy. It denied the consumer a free choice of goods, was highly unpopular, and needed a cumbersome and insensitive bureaucracy to administer the industries concerned. He agreed that certain industries did require direct state intervention to help them in certain circumstances – for example, they might need an exceptionally large amount of capital, or to be directed to a region of high unemployment – but, generally, planning in the form envisaged by the corporate socialists was no longer viable.

Having pushed aside the dogmas of nationalisation and direct state planning which had confused people about the real nature of contemporary socialism, Crosland pointed to the positive values which still needed to be attained. These concerned, above all, the questions of welfare and equality. On the first, Crosland pointed out that the aim of the welfare services was not social equality, but the relief of social distress and hardship. There was still an enormous amount of suffering, despite the welfare state, due to genuine parental ignorance in regard to the care of their children; and to the disintegration of the family unit as a result of increased occupational mobility and the development of new housing estates, which had led to neglect of the old and the unmarried. Above all, there were the special cases at the fringes of society – the mentally ill, neglected children, the blind, and the chronically sick. As economic prosperity rose, socialists should ensure that society concentrated on increasing the amount of its resources towards these special cases.

Indeed, as the impoverished nature of the welfare services became more apparent, Crosland later saw the major task facing socialists as closing the appalling gap between private affluence and public squalor, as it had been put by the American economist, J.K. Galbraith.[14] In 1962, in *The Conservative Enemy*, Crosland pointed to the outdated and bleak hospitals; overcrowded classes in schools; the shortage of university places; the uncivilised mental hospitals; and the oppressive ugliness of the industrial towns as examples of public squalor. The worst area was housing, where overcrowded slums and decaying substandard houses spelled out misery and a lack of hope for the future, particularly for the newly married. This was particularly vulgar given the general rise in prosperity – 'we are now rich enough for the uncivilised state of the social sector, so deadening to happiness and vitality, to stand out as unendurable'.[15]

The reason for this stark contract between private wealth and public poverty could not be traced to the profit motive of capitalism according to Crosland. The private sector did not determine the amount of government expenditure on health or education. This was determined by the *political* decisions of the government in power on the amount of taxation and the direction of public spending. It was, then, natural that a Conservative government committed to the philosophy of private affluence and selfishness should spend as little as possible on welfare services. It should be equally natural that a Labour government should be morally obliged to increase the proportion of the national income due to the social services. It was, according to Crosland, a distinguishing mark of socialist values to relieve social distress and hardship on the grounds of compassion and human concern, not on grounds of equality. Indeed,

> the relief of this distress and the elimination of this squalor is the main object of social expenditure, and a socialist is identified as one who wishes to gve this an exceptional priority over other claims on resources.[16]

The other pillar of socialism concerned social equality, identified by Crosland as the aspiration towards a classless society. In view of his understanding of post-war capitalism, Crosland quite naturally rejected the Marxist view of class — the relationship between capital and labour — as much too narrow. Ownership had become irrelevant, and social classes had grown more complicated with the growth of a managerial and white-collar class. To Crosland, caste and class were mixed together, as he pointed to the multitude of factors — income, occupation, job hierarchies, lifestyle, accent and perception — which went to create a division between 'superior' and 'inferior' people. Taking class in this wider sense, he saw a rigidly defined class structure as pervading national life —

> Class, in the sense of class consciousness and the existence of clearly defined classes, is an exceptionally marked phenomenon in British life. The hierarchies of education, occupational prestige, and style of life all show pronounced breaks; and these breaks broadly coincide.[17]

This class system had to be challenged by the socialists despite the absence of class violence. It created frustration, resentment and envy, leading to the collective manifestations of discontent seen in strikes and to the suspicious antagonism between management and workers in British industry. This antagonism could not be traced to poverty, falling wages or unemployment, which did not exist in Britain at that time. It had a social, rather than an economic, cause. Moreover, there was an understandable element of merit in this feeling of resentment, as working-class parents were just as anxious as middle-class parents that their children should not miss out on the opportunities available at a time of rising prosperity, and were prepared to use their bargaining power to the full to ensure that this would not happen.

Inequality was, moreover, both wasteful and inefficient. The tight restrictions on social mobility between the classes meant that genuine social communication within the country was lacking. People born into the working class with a genuine capacity for leadership or with a real talent to contribute towards society were, unless they were lucky enough to win a scholarship, condemned to a life of frustrated ability. On the other side of the coin, people born into a ruling élite which had become hereditary and self-perpetuating became the leaders of society though they might be totally unsuited to the task.

Above these practical arguments against the British class system, Crosland also pointed to the question of social justice. He admitted that this involved a moral judgement, which was not subject to proof or disproof, but it was a moral judgement which distinguished social-ism from the selfish philosophy of the Conservatives. To socialists, people had social *rights*, such as equality of opportunity and equal dignity. Moreover, the ability of people to inherit enormous wealth to flaunt in the face of their fellow citizens was seen as morally abom-inable.

Nevertheless, Crosland qualified his argument by pointing to the educational system to prove that equality of opportunity, as advocated by the Tories in the fifties and sixties, was not enough. The creation of a meritocracy, an élite based on merit rather than birth, would merely change the personnel of a class-divided society, not alleviate class inequalities. If the public and grammar schools were opened to all purely on grounds of merit, the gulf between the superior education and style of Eton and that of a secondary modern school would still engender frustration and resentment among those left behind. Indeed, the one comfort that working-class children had, that they would *really* have succeeded if the system was not weighted against them, would be removed. Crosland concluded that 'if the inequality of rewards is excessively great, the creation of equal opportunities may give rise to too intense a competition, with a real danger of increased frustration and discontent.[18] To overcome this, he called for a non-segregated comprehensive school system; the gradual abolition of the eleven-plus examination; a greater opening of university education; and ensuring that public schools enrol a wide cross-section of the community.

Finally, Crosland pointed to the changing arena of political conflict as material standards of living rose and economic problems faded from the popular consciousness. They were the problems of leisure and privacy which did not directly concern socialism. However, socialists should take a special interest in the intolerable moral restrictions on abortion, divorce, homosexuality and censorship. There was a need for more liberty and jollity which would eventually, he believed, prove more important than the need for higher exports. In the new and happier age that was arriving, Crosland called for the demand for liberty to be championed above all by socialists, 'in whose blood there should always run a trace of the anarchist and the libertarian, and not too much of the prig and the prude'.[19]

Crosland's analysis of the changes in capitalist society were criticised by the New Left on the grounds that the 'new' managerial class were still capitalists because they owned large numbers of shares in their firms, and that consequently they were still guided by the profit motive. The attribute of 'welfare' capitalism noted by Crosland, such as the concern with good labour relations and welfare schemes, had been present in the twenties, pioneered by Henry Ford in the interests of squeezing more productivity out of his workforce. However, such criticisms were not really relevant to Crosland's analysis, as he believed that state direction of the economy would force private enterprise to behave in a socially responsible manner. It was this indirect control of private enterprise which was the essential difference with the old cut-throat capitalism of the days of *laissez-faire*, according to Crosland, and as such the whole question of ownership was succeeded by one of political *will*. The decision on whether welfare and education or private affluence should take priority was dependent on the political complexion of the government.

However, Crosland's dismissal of nationalisation and direct planning as only one means to achieve socialism, and an inadequate one at that, had the effect of dismissing the question of the power of capital. In one sense, Crosland could correctly point out that the paranoid predictions of the Labour Marxists that capitalism would thwart socialist policies had been proved wrong by the success of the 1945 Labour government, but that government had never really challenged the basis of capitalist power. Moreover, the ability of capital to pay for welfare *and* to achieve economic growth at the same time was assumed by Crosland without investigation. The Marxist analysis of the laws governing capitalism seemed to be discredited by events, of course, and all the empirical evidence in 1956 suggested that capitalism had overcome its tendency towards crisis, but Crosland's failure to investigate the conditions of prosperity further seems, in retrospect, as short-sighted as it was understandable. Welfare and equality were treated as though they had nothing to do with the power relations which underlay the 'mixed' economy, and the consequences for socialism of the possible failure of Keynesian economic policies were ignored.

This seemed perfectly justifiable in the full employment conditions of the fifties, and the publication of *The Future of Socialism* was soon followed by the ideological capture of the Labour Party by the revisionists. Crosland himself helped to write *Industry and Society* (accepted by the 1957 Conference as official Labour policy) which called for public ownership of individual firms rather than whole industries, and stressed the preference for state purchase of shares in those firms rather than outright nationalisation.

However, it should not be thought that this heralded a more conservative party. In rejecting nationalisation and direct planning, the revisionists hoped to release the radical energies of the Labour Party to direct it on progressive social policies. Crosland's book inspired a number of radical criticisms of contemporary capitalism which were much more forward-looking than many of the old corporate socialists.

Titmuss and the Radicals

This was demonstrated clearly with the publication of *Conviction* (1958), a series of essays edited by the journalist Norman MacKenzie. They were expressions of faith in the moral values of socialism against the acquisitive nature of private affluence. MacKenzie (b. 1921), in his essay 'After the Stalemate State', called for a return to the socialist creed of William Morris and the ethical socialists in protest at a society which 'is in many ways more moral, more humane, than any society we have known, and yet it has made too many of us morally indifferent'.[20] Brian Abel-Smith (b. 1927), in his essay, 'Whose Welfare State?', was critical of the mean-minded hypocrisy of the middle classes who carped at the welfare services while actually taking advantage of them more than the working class and the needy. Like Crosland and Galbraith, he pointed to the stark contrast between the poor quality of education and health on the one side, and the palatial prestige offices, new factories, and superstores of private enterprise. Together with Peter Townsend (b. 1928), Abel-Smith undertook much valuable work in uncovering the poverty and suffering which lay hidden behind the protective façade of the 'welfare' state.

It was Richard Titmuss, however, who exercised a major influence on Labour's social policy. Titmuss (1907-73) worked in an insurance office for fifteen years from the age of 18. He used his time and experience to write on poverty, ill-health and family planning. His *Problems of Social Policy* (1950), part of the official History of the Second World War, established his reputation and he was appointed Professor of the new Department of Social Administration at the London School of Economics, despite his total lack of any university experience.

In a series of books and essays beginning with *Essays on the Welfare State* (1958), Titmuss drew attention to the major social problems in Britain which had been concealed by myth and ignorance. The built-in tendency of capitalism to cause unemployment and injustice may have been cured by Keynesian economics, but the social problems of the working class and the forgotten people at the margins of society were put forward as the new concerns for socialists. In doing so, Titmuss took a much more class-conscious view of society than Crosland (though he acknowledged the importance of Crosland's own analysis for a new socialist thinking.[21]) Thus, he used an empirical study of wealth and income to disprove the general belief that the rich and poor were becoming more equal, which was based on selective statistics by intellectually narrow-minded sociologists. The growth of tax advisers and pension consultants meant that cash in hand was less important than trusts, overdrafts and other forms of wealth for the middle class. Moreover, by confining their studies to individuals, the major changes in the family life and status of women in wealthier classes went unexamined.[22] He concluded that, far from becoming a more integrated society, income inequalities had been growing in Britain since 1949.

The disguised improvement of middle-class living standards at the expense of the working class in the provision of welfare was pointed out by Titmuss in his influential essay, 'The Social Division of Welfare', which had a major effect on Labour's social policy (changing it from concern for a floor of benefits and services to an extension of middle class benefits to the working class[23]). He pointed out the mythical nature of right-wing complaints that working class scroungers were impoverishing the middle classes. In fact, a close look at the social administration of welfare revealed that it was the middle classes who were the main beneficiaries through fiscal and occupational benefits exempting them from the full weight of taxation. To Titmuss, such benefits tended 'to divide loyalties, to nourish privilege, and to narrow the social conscience.'[24]

It was the continuing pattern of class rigidities and snobberies that concerned Titmuss in his studies of the welfare state. The social services had been created at the beginning of the century in accordance with middle-class expectations of how working class people were supposed to behave, so that the social problems of family and environmental life were treated as cases of individual failure. Real insight into the problems of poverty and insecurity were lacking, as outside observation by the 'better' classes could never be the same as genuine acquaintance with working-class reality. Many of the institutions formed at the times of the Poor Law survived into the modern welfare state with few modifications in structure, bringing fundamental problems of *ethical values* to the service. Thus, as the emphasis shifted to a higher quality in education and health, there was a clash with the élitest values of the old administrative structures, which were too inflexible and conservative for a democratic age. The resolution of the conflict would depend on how 'needs' were to be defined, and that in itself depended on *who* defined them.

In this respect, Titmuss was particularly worried about the bureaucratic nature of the social services. The growth of specialisation and professionalism had given the groups with an exclusive knowledge the *power* to decide the fate of others, and the influence and prestige of these groups was rising with the growth of scientific and technical knowledge. 'As the social services become more complex, more specialised and subject to a finer division of labour they become less intelligible to the lay councillor or public representative'.[25] The changing role of the family, the social emancipation of women, and a longer life span all required new and, above all, *intelligible* changes to the social service, yet this new professional élite were as distant from ordinary people as they ever were.

The consequences of this for democracy were spelled out by Titmuss in a Fabian tract, '*The Irresponsible Society*' (1960), which became a full-scale attack on the corporatist nature of society which was in many ways akin to that of the New Left. Using the example of private insurance companies which catered for the wealthier classes, Titmuss pointed to the amount of power 'concentrated in relatively few hands, working at the apex of a handful of giant bureaucracies, technically supported by a group of professional experts, and accountable, in practice, to no-one.'[26] He argued that the moral values of society were being warped by these directors, managers and professionally trained advisers who made the decisions which shaped society. They saw the technical administration of the economy, industry and services without being aware of the social use to which rising prosperity must be directed, and they imposed policies without democratic discussion or consideration for moral consequences. This élitist rule had combined with the success of Keynesian economics to strengthen conservative governments committed to inequality and privilege, while distorted statistics and a decline in the quality of Royal Commissions had created a myth that social protection extended to all under the auspices of the benevolent welfare state. In such circumstances, it was necessary for the Labour Party to rediscover its ideology, and to set an example of moral leadership and social responsibility. It should attack the centralisation of decision-making in social administration which had led, paradoxically, to less spending for welfare and to accelerating inequality in society.

It was a radical attack on corporate socialism, similar to that of Crosland, on the grounds that centralised élites in the social sector were a menace to the values of socialism. Titmuss wrote, 'to me, the "Welfare State" has no meaning unless it is positively and constructively concerned with redistributive justice and social participation'.[27] It was a sense of community rather than an order of command from a faceless few, or an undignified hierarchy of snobbery and hypocrisy. It was this sense which fed his belief that social policy was concerned with altruisms and the reclaiming of the lost and forgotten into a warm-hearted fellowship. It was fitting that his last book, *The Gift Relationship* (1970), should be concerned with social welfare as a gift to strangers, thereby denying that they were strangers. It was a study of the recent decline of the voluntary gift of blood in the United States, and the consequent rise in the commercial value of blood. Titmuss saw this as a horrifying sign that the primal bonds which knit society together were breaking up, and pleaded for social policy to be concerned with 'the unquantifiable and unmethodical aspects of man . . . [and to] promote an individual's sense of identity, participation, and community'.[28]

Titmuss demonstrated the radical nature of the call by the revisionists to forget about the outmoded ideas of nationalisation, and to

[handwritten margin note: LOSE IT'S CLOTH CAP IMAGE]

concentrate instead on promoting a classless society concerned with welfare for all its inhabitants. He was more aware than Crosland of the dangers to democracy posed by the new managerial class, but did not really present any viable structural alternative to their rule. He over-estimated the role played by political and moral will in changing social values and attitudes, and underestimated the social and economic reali-ties of class society. Like the revisionists, Titmuss was confident that the economic success of Keynesian policies would be uninterrupted, yet it was to be the re-emergence of economic crisis which would lead to major attacks on the inadequate social services by Labour as well as Conservative governments.

[handwritten margin note: V. IMP]

Gaitskell

It was the success of Hugh Gaitskell which ensured the triumph of revisionism in the Labour Party in the fifties, just as it was his character which drew a limit to that success. Gaitskell (1906-63) had come from an upper middle-class background — his father was an official in the Indian Civil Service — and received the conventional education at Winchester and Oxford. He joined the Labour Party at the time of the General Strike, and was a lecturer for the Workers Educational Associa-tion at Nottingham. His direct experience of the bloody repression of the Socialist rising in Vienna in 1934 instilled a sense of caution into his politics, and this was reinforced by his close friendship with Evan Durbin, whose untimely death in 1948 seemed to have shaken Gaitskell particularly badly. After entering Parliament in 1945, Gaitskell's career advanced rapidly, and he succeeded Cripps as Chancellor of the Exchequer in 1950. He soon succeeded Morrison as the standard-bearer of the Labour Right in the bitter struggles of the early fifties, and his election as Labour Leader after Attlee's retirement in December 1955 was a major victory for revisionism.

[handwritten margin note: V. IMP]

Where Attlee was a great conciliator of the different factions within the party, Gaitskell believed that clarity and decisive leadership were necessary if Labour was to lose its clothcap image and become a credible political force. He was not aware of the fact that he was leader of a party and not a faction, but his belief in his own ideas and the fear that Labour would be badly harmed if those ideas were not carried through ensured a stormy period for the Labour Party. As one of his colleagues recalled,

Integrity, absolute integrity, that was the essential quality of Hugh Gaitskell's character. When he considered it was his duty to say or do something, nothing could stop him. The sharp edge of intellectual integrity would cut through all barriers .[29]

He had early set his sights on nationalisation, putting forward the argument that nationalisation was only one of many means to achieve a socialist society in a Fabian tract, *Socialism and Nationalisation* (1956), where he pointed to the frustrations of bureaucracy and remote management brought to the fore by the experience of state monopolies. Indeed, in 1959, he went so far as to call for the deletion of Clause IV – which called for 'the common ownership of the means of production, distribution, and exchange'– from the party constitution. He argued that, while the state must preserve the right to intervene to end monopoly and inefficiency in the private sector, the Labour Party must recognise in theory as it recognised in practice that nationalisation was not the first principle and aim of socialism.

We have long ago come to accept, we know very well, . . . a mixed economy, in which case, if this is our view – as I believe it to be at 90 per cent of the Labour Party – had we better not say so instead of going out of our way to court misrepresentation.[30]

This attack on the shibboleth of nationalisation was an attempt to release the radical impetus within the Labour party, for Gaitskell as for other revisionists. He wanted Labour to stand for a view of socialism on public morality against the acquisitive values of traditional capitalism. This became clear soon after Gaitskell became Labour leader, when the Egyptian nationalist leader, Colonel Nasser, nationalised the Suez Canal without compensations, leading to an abortive Anglo-French military expedition in November 1956. Initially, Gaitskell stood firmly behind the government, echoing its comparison of Nasser with the Fascist dictators of the thirties, but as the government defied United Nations resolutions by taking military action he led the party into opposition. He believed that the armed intervention not merely damaged the whole notion of collective security but took world attention away from the simultaneous Russian invasion of Hungary. As he argued in the Commons,

Do not Hon. Member appreciate that, at this time above all, when the news of Russian intervention in Hungary, is coming through, it is an immense tragedy that the moral strength of this country, and of the United Nations, because of our action, is so gravely damaged?[32]

✳ The combination of moral aptitude and anti-Communism expressed Gaitskell's approach to policy issues.

The moral aptitude certainly came to the fore on the question of race, which was becoming increasingly important as immigrants from the old Empire began to arrive in Britain, which was at that time desperately in need of labour. The white community, especially those working-class areas of the cities where immigrants congregated, did not take kindly to this intrusion by people over whom they once felt they had ruled. A race riot in Notting Hill in 1958, which was accompanied by a minor revival of Fascist activity, led to racist calls for controls on immigration as a threat to the nation. These calls found a response among Labour as well as Conservative MPs, and the Labour leadership were quick to affirm their opposition to *all* immigration controls on Commonwealth subjects.[32] Gaitskell's radicalism was allowed full play on this issue, particularly when the Conservative Government caved in to backbench pressure by introducing a Commonwealth Immigration Bill in the autumn of 1961.

In what he regarded as one of his most important Commons speeches, Gaitskell attacked 'this miserable, shameful, shabby Bill' as 'a plain anti-Commonwealth measure in theory and . . . a plain anti-colour measure in practice'.[33] He accused the Tories of wanting to forget about the former Empire of which they had been so proud, yet in doing so they were striking at the central principle of non-discrimination against race on which the Commonwealth was based. He attacked the myths that immigrants were 'scroungers' on the social services, had a high birth rate, were diseased or criminal, using government evidence to contradict the falsehood, and pointing to the natural anomalies of a newly arrived group to explain other allegations. He pointed out that those who called for immigration controls as the only way to prevent racial friction were admitting a shameful failure to fight racism wherever it existed in Britain. The acceptance of such defeatist arguments would place Britain on the level of the US Southern States, and the government should have the courage to fight racism rather than to appease it. Gaitskell's arguments were based on a belief that racism weakened the moral strength of Britain, and he recognised that immigration controls were necessarily racist, despite all the economic and social arguments cobbled up by the control lobby.

ANTI - COMMON MARKET

His moral approach was firmly anchored in the nation-state, however. He was profoundly concerned about the impact of racist measures on Britain's image in the Commonwealth. He appealed to the government to remember that the West Indies, from which a large proportion of immigrants arrived, 'are still our Colonies. We are responsible for them, and they think of themselves, as anybody who has been there knows, as British people. Oh, yes, they do. It is rather moving'.[34] It was this same nationalism which led him to break with many other revisionists by opposing entry into the European Common Market. The economic arguments for entry did not appear too pressing in the early sixties, so that Gaitskell could base his decision on the grounds of opposition to political union with the other European countries. As he told the 1962 Conference,

> We must be clear about this; it does mean, if this is the idea, the end of Britain as an independent European state. I make no apology for repeating it. It means the end of a thousand years of history.[35]

This combination of morality and nationalism could be radical when applied to questions of the welfare state and domestic racism, but in terms of foreign affairs it became a conservative defence of Britain's alliance system. Gaitskell particularly believed that the important issues which divided the parties on home policy should be held in check by a fundamental consensus on the basic questions of national defence and parliamentary democracy. He followed his friend, Evan Durbin, in arguing that 'a certain basis of consent, a willingness to compromise, to accept the rules of the game is absolutely essential'.[36] This sense, combined with his deeply felt anti-Communism, led him to place his leadership on the line in opposition to the Campaign for Nuclear Disarmament, which called for Britain to set a moral example to the world by renouncing nuclear weapons unilaterally. The 1960 Party Conference endorsed this demand, despite a challenge by Gaitskell that he would 'fight and fight and fight again' to save the Labour party from such extremism.

His arguments against unilateralism were based on the *realpolitik* of power in the world, not the moral righteousness with which he approached most other questions. The retention of nuclear weapons gave Britain an independent voice in the world, while unilateralism would severely weaken NATO against the threat of Communism. It was because Gaitskell, like other revisionists stretching back to Durbin, believed that Russian Communism was an aggressive and immoral force which recognised only brute force that he defended the frightening concept of the 'balance of terror', the belief that Russia would not use nuclear weapons if faced with an annihilating nuclear response. As he put it to the delegates,

> I do not believe that Mr. Khruschev has any intention of deliberately starting an aggressive war in present circumstances . . . but I do believe that if you give them the opportunity of advancing the cause they believe in without cost or serious risk to themselves, they will not reject the opportunity. I ask you, bearing in mind all these things, and reflecting on the events of recent years — what they did in Hungary . . . to say that it would not be wise for us to take the risk.[37]

It was a coherent argument, but it was based on the Cold War paranoia against Russia which has always set a limit to the radicalism of the revisionists. The weakness of their opponents' case, which will be studied in a later chapter, could not disguise the basic agreement of the revisionists with all the conservative circles in Europe and the United States who were convinced that the Communist threat to the national identity was a far greater evil than any of the problems of poverty and inequality within that identity.

Healey

This was brought out particularly clearly by Denis Healey (b.1917) who, after a youthful membership of the Communist party in the thirties, became one of the clearest and toughest followers of the foreign policy of Ernest Bevin. As Secretary of the party's International Department after the war, Healey was in a good position after his election to Westminster in 1952 to rise to become Labour's Defence spokesman. His views on foreign policy as *realpolitik*, and his attacks on the neutralism becoming popular in the Labour Left, were expounded in his contribution to *New Fabian Essays* and in pamphlets such as *Neutralism* (1955).

Healey argued that foreign policy could not be governed by traditional socialist ideas of welfare. The element of power in politics became the crucial factor in the international arena which tended to override the traditional moral approach of simple co-operation and brotherhood preached by Labour between the wars. International politics was determined by brute force, or usually the threat of force. This did not mean that Healey totally rejected morality in foreign policy; merely that he pointed to its limitations. He argued that 'Power is not, of course, the only reality in world affairs. But it is a pervasive reality which has its own laws and fixes the limits within which moral criteria can operate'.[38] The ability of modern nuclear weapons to wreak a devastating havoc on the world made the moral case for international co-operation greater. but this moral case had to be tempered by realism if it was not to end in the very war it sought to avoid.

On this basis, Healey rejected the Left's attempts at neutralism as utopian and gullible. A neutralist foreign policy was suitable to anyone who refused all political commitments as inconsistent with a fine spiritual life, but it was unacceptable to anyone who had a sense of responsibility. In the real world of power, Britain must recognise the necessity to ally with the United States against Russia. He took up Durbin's argument that Russia was not socialist because it was not democratic, and compared the totalitarian Communism with the democratic United States, where state intervention since the New Deal had promoted social progress and made capitalism more acceptable. Moreover, when it came to accusations of imperialism, Healey felt that the Russian denial of independence to its own subject nationalities compared most unfavourably with the peaceful ending of the British Empire and the reluctance of the United States to take up many political responsibilities. He certainly had a point on Russian oppression, but his ability to overlook US intervention in countries from Guatamala to Iran in the early fifties, as well as Britain's ability to resist by military force any nationalist resistance which appeared dangerous to British interests whether in Guiana or Malaya, is breathtaking. Nevertheless, given his basic premises, Healey concluded that 'only the most absolute pessimist about political action as such can remain morally neutral in a struggle where the totalitarian state is opposed by a state with less pretentious claims'.[39]

Healey was quite clear on the result of any conflict between the needs of defence and those of welfare, as were other revisionists. It was Gaitskell who, as Chancellor, imposed health service charges in 1951 to help pay for an increase in arms expenditure caused by the Korean War. It was this increase which had led to the resignation of Bevan and Wilson from the Government. Healey rejected Bevanism as confusing wish with reality. The Left made no attempt to assess the nature and extent of any military danger which must decide the nation's level of rearmament. Against their wish to concentrate on welfare, Healey argued that 'all the will in the world is worthless if we have another war. False teeth and spectacles are small comfort to a corpse'.[40] It may be a brutal way of putting it, but it was undoubtedly true. The point was how to avoid a nation of corpses, and Healey's prescription of the Western Alliance did not strike everybody as the best way. The fact that socially progressive policies may have to take a back seat to defence against Communism indicated the conflicts within the revisionist call for social reform, though few would be as blunt as Healey in pointing them out.

Revisionism and Labourism

The political ideas which had gained ascendancy in the Labour party in its first fifty years had all generally fitted into the framework of labourist ideology. Some political tendencies enjoyed a tenuous relationship with labourism, such as the Labour Marxism of Tom Munn and James Maxton, or the evolutionary socialism of Macdonald, but generally the realities of the political and social power of trade unionism ensured the subordination of any elements in their thinking which lay outside labourism. When those elements could not be subordinated, as with Macdonald's belief in 1931 that Labour's class interests should be sacrificed to the 'national' interest, the result was either the marginalisation of the groups which held to them or to their secession.

The revisionists gained ascendancy in the Labour party in the 1950s as a result of trade union support — Gaitskell was fervently supported by Arthur Deakin of the Transport Workers, Will Lawther of the Miners, and Tom Williamson of the General and Municipal Workers — but their relationship to labourism was less congenial than any other political tendency in the preceding half century. Ramsay Macdonald had wanted Labour to be both a national and a class party, and in doing so had fallen foul of the party he had helped to create, but he had always seen the working class as socially outcast from the nation. He had, indeed, joined the ILP in 1894 precisely because of the anti-working class prejudices of the Liberals, and saw the Labour party as the means by which the trade union movement would find its rightful place in the nation. The revisionists shared with Macdonald the belief that Labour must become a national party, but went much further than he did in seeking to divest Labour of its class image.

This was clearly expressed by Crosland, who argued that the changes in the standard of living and in the very composition of the working class must force Labour to face a new electoral reality. He summed up his view of Labour's dilemma in pointing to the historic link between the party and the labour movement.

> The Labour Party owes its whole existence and historic growth to the working class; one cannot think of the one without the other. Yet today, ironically, this *unique* identification is a clear political liability, for the simple reason that the working class is shrinking in size.[41]

Unless a steady decline was to be its fate, the Labour Party must become a broadly based national party. It was an extension of the message of Ramsay Macdonald, but in the prosperous conditions of the fifties it took the ideological and political initiative.

However, it was a message which struck at the heart of labourism. The fundamental belief that the working class must organise itself separately from the employing class was pushed aside as irrelevant by the revisionists, who called for an end to the class antagonisms present in British industry. Where Macdonald saw Labour as *both* a national and a class party, the revisionists wanted Labour to be *merely* a national party. They believed that the capitalist system which had led to the unions to form their own political party was dead, and that the task of any progressive lay in radical social and cultural policies to help the poor and the forgotten at the margins of the existing system. That system itself had to be administered, not changed, and its administration required a rejection of the old talk of class in favour of a role of partnership in industry and the services.

This attack on labourism was the real issue which lay behind the controversy over nationalisation and Clause IV after the 1959 election defeat. Immediately after the defeat, Douglas Jay wrote an article for the periodical *Forward*, calling for Labour to sever its links with the unions and to accept the mixed economy as permanent. As Gaitskell's biographer has pointed out, 'Jay's bugbear was the Party's working class image, and he brought up nationalisation only as an afterthought'.[42] Gaitskell himself rejected such overtly anti-labourist talk as politically suicidal — Labour needed the unions for finance and support — and, at the special party conference after the 1959 defeat, said,

> I have always looked upon the Trade Union Congress and the Labour Party as part of the same great Labour movement, and our close integration as one of our greatest strengths. I see no reason to

change my mind.[43]

However, his call to drop Clause IV from the Constitution was couched in terms of its unattractiveness to an electorate which was ceasing to identify itself as working class. It was a symbolic move which was sought by Gaitskell, just as the main opposition came from trade unionists worried at the implications for the class nature and purposes of the Labour Party. Gaitskell succeeded in getting Labour to accept the mixed economy as one of its basic aims, but trade union opposition thwarted his attempt to drop Clause IV from the Constitution.

The anti-labourism implicit in revisionist thinking could co-exist, if sometimes a little uneasily, with the political realities of the Labour Party as long as the economy was booming and the union leaders relatively free from the pressure of their members. In the prosperous conditions of the fifties, the unions could combine free collective bargaining and regular consultation with relatively friendly Conservative governments. They were growing stronger in numbers, and, apart from a few left-wingers, the union leaders were less willing to appear partisan than they had been for decades (a trend exemplified by George Woodcock, the TUC General Secretary, who was anxious to distance the union movement from identification with any one particular party). In such circumstances, the revisionists seemed to be much more in tune with events than a dogmatic Left which appeared not to notice that capitalism had changed, or with the ideological stagnation of the corporate socialists.

In fact, the revisionist success could only be temporary, as it was predicated on the solution of the old problem of boom and slump which had bedevilled the economy before the war. The post-war boom disguised the fundamental conflict between the labourism of the trade unions and the revisionism of the party leadership. If the boom had been as indefinite as the revisionists then believed, the radical and progressive nature of their ideas would have been allowed to blossom. As it was, the gradual ending of the long post-war boom spelled out a limit to their radicalism, and brought into the open their antagonistic relationship to the labourism of the unions. It was significant that, in a new introduction to his *The Future of Socialism*, written in 1964, Crosland should note,

Were I completely revising the book, I should substantially alter only one major argument, that relating to economic growth. Here I was too optimistic — not about the *capabilities* of the Western-type mixed economy. . . but about the performance of the Anglo-Saxon economies in particular.[44]

The performance of these economies were to have dire results for Crosland's revisionism.

Notes

1. See Michael Kidron, *Western Capitalism Since the War* (Penguin Books, 1970 ed.), p. 267.
2. See, for example, F. Zweig, J.H. Goldthorpe *et al. The Affluent Worker*, 3 volumes. (Cambridge University Press, 1968)
3. C.A.R. Crosland, 'The Transition from Capitalism' in *New Fabian Essays* (Turnstile Press, London, 1952), p. 35.
4. Roy Jenkins, 'Equality' in *New Fabian Essays*, p. 83.
5. See Roy Jenkins, *Pursuit of Progress* (Heinemann, 1953), p. 104-05.
6. Ibid., p. 161.
7. John Strachey, *Contemporary Capitalism* (Victor Gollancz, 1956), p. 95.
8. Ibid., p. 27.
9. C.A.R. Crosland, *The Conservative Enemy* (Jonathan Cape, 1962), p. 91-2.
10. C.A.R. Crosland, *The Future of Socialism* (Jonathan Cape, 1956), p. 35.
11. Ibid., p. 286.
12. Ibid., p. 96.
13. Ibid., p. 496-7.
14. See, for example, J.K.Galbraith, *The Affluent Society* (1958), (Penguin Books, 1962).
15. C.A.R. Crosland, *The Conservative Enemy*, p. 12.
16. C.A.R. Crosland, *The Future of Socialism*, p. 113.
17. Ibid., p. 185-6.
18. Ibid., p. 235.
19. Ibid., p. 522.
20. N. MacKenzie, 'After the Stalemate State', in N. MacKenzie ed., *Conviction* (Macgibbon and Kee, 1958).
21. See, for example, his Preface to *Essays on the Welfare State* (Allen and Unwin, 1958).
22. See R.M. Titmuss, *Income Distribution and Social Change* (Allen and Unwin, 1962).
23. See the Introduction by Brian Abel-Smith to the 1976 edition of Titmuss' *Essays on the Welfare State* for this.
24. R.M. Titmuss, *Essays on the Welfare State*, p. 52.
25. Ibid., p. 27.
26. R.M. Titmuss, *The Irresponsible Society* (Fabian Tract 323, 1960), p. 17.
27. R.M. Titmuss, 'Goals of the Welfare State' in Perry Anderson ed., *Towards Socialism* (Fontana, 1965), p. 365.
28. R.M. Titmuss, *The Gift Relationship: From Human Blood to Social Policy* (Allen and Unwin, 1970), p. 224.
29. James Griffiths, quoted in Philip Williams' *Hugh Gaitskell: A Political Biography* (Jonathan Cape, 1979), p. 547.
30. Labour Party *Annual Conference Report* 1959, p. 112.
31. Hansard *Parliamentary Debates 1955-6*, volume 558, col. 1861.

32. For the different Labour attitudes to race and immigration in this period, see P. Foot, *Immigration and Race in British Politics* (Penguin Books, 1965).

33. *Hansard, Parliamentary Debates 1961-2*, volume 649, col. 803, 799.

34. Ibid., col. 800.

35. Labour Party *Annual Conference Report* 1962, p. 159.

36. H. Gaitskell, *In Defence of Politics* (Birkbeck College, 1954), p. 8.

37. Labour Party *Annual Conference Report* 1960, p. 199.

38. Denis Healey, 'Power Politics and the Labour Party' in *New Fabian Essays*, p. 166.

39. Denis Healey, *Neutralism* (Ampersand Ltd, London, 1955).

40. Denis Healey, John Freeman, *Rearmament – How Far?'* (Fabian Tract 288, 1951), p. 25.

41. C.A.R. Crosland, *The Conservative Enemy*, p. 150-1.

42. P.M. Williams, *Hugh Gaitskell*, p. 539.

43. Labour Party *Annual Conference Report* 1959, p. 109.

44. C.A.R. Crosland, Preface to 1964 edition of *The Future of Socialism*, p. XI.

11 REVISIONISM IN CRISIS

The Call For Dynamism

It was the beginning of the sixties which witnessed the dawning realisation that the comparatively sluggish growth rate of the British economy, manifesting itself in low investment and a worsening balance of payments, was making an increase in state intervention necessary. The belief that Britain had a stagnant economy because of its stagnant social institutions led to a renewed questioning, often cheaply satirical of British society and politics. It also led the government to seek entry into the European Common Market; to intervene in wage bargaining by means of a 'pay-pause' in 1961-2; and to establish the National Economic Development Council (NEDC) in which the tripartite relations between the State, the employers and the unions were institutionalised.

In this situation, the crisis in revisionist thought came to the surface. The promise of higher social spending and greater social equality had always been dependent on a high economic growth rate, and the stagnant growth in the British economy in the early sixties presented itself as the most pressing problem facing any radical who sought change within the mixed economy. The deep schism which emerged within the revisionist camp over the Common Market was the most dramatic demonstration of its crisis. Where Roy Jenkins called for entry as the best means of overcoming the weakness of the British economy and as an excellent chance to find a new role in world affairs, Douglas Jay and Hugh Gaitskell opposed the government on the grounds that Britain could solve its economic problems outside Europe.[1] The French veto on British membership in January 1963 ended the debate abruptly, but it would return.

The increasing sense that measures needed to be taken to overcome economic stagnation presented a major chance for the corporate Socialists. The revisionist belief in further State intervention in the economy, as opposed to social affairs, seemed increasingly irrelevant as the traditional fiscal techniques of Keynesian economics were unable to push the economy forward. As a result, the accession of Harold Wilson to the Labour leadership after Gaitskell's sudden death in January 1963, presented the opportunity to reunite the Labour party by integrating revisionist ideas with the old corporate socialist calls for direct planning. The divisions which had torn Labour apart for a decade were healed by a technocratic appeal which sought to obliterate ideological debate by posing a pragmatic solution to Britain's problems.

Harold Wilson (b. 1916) was a perfect representative of this trend. Ambitious and shrewd, he moved from an academic career at Oxford to Westminster in 1945 and, at thirty-one, became the youngest Cabinet Minister in the government as President of the Board of Trade. He presided over the 'bonfire of controls' in 1948 which heralded a move of the government away from the concerns with direct state planning to indirect guidance through Keynesian techniques. His resignation from the Cabinet in April 1951 and his subsequent association with the Bevanites gave him an appeal to the Left, while his willingness to desert Bevan for Gaitskell in 1955 established both his refusal to be closely linked with any faction and a reputation for duplicity. He was, in fact, concerned above all other matters with electoral victory and saw party unity as a key to that victory. He was never really a revisionist because he distrusted the divisive nature of ideas, seeing Gaitskell's conflicts with the Left on Clause IV and defence as being dangerous and fundamentally irrelevant. The same results could be obtained without a divisive public debate. In a revealing discussion with John Junor, then editor of the *Sunday Express*, Wilson pointed to the success of Harold Macmillan in reuniting the Conservatives after their Suez débâcle, saying,

> The man's a genius. He's holding up the banner of Suez for the party to follow, and he's leading the party away from Suez. That's what I'd like to do with the Labour Party over nationalisation.[2]

It was this contempt for ideas and public discussion which makes it difficult to weigh Wilson's contribution to Labour's political thought. He was too responsive to party and popular moods while in Opposition to have many fixed political ideas, while his concern with administration in government gives his record in office a sense of endurance rather than innovation. However, in the early sixties he caught the national and party mood in his appeals to a technocratic, classless society as the dynamic solution to Britain's problems. Like the revisionists, he identified the social privileges of the Establishment as the barrier to socialism, but he no longer identified socialism in terms of equality and welfare. The Establishment was a *cause* of Britain's stagnation, and a barrier to the basic dynamism in the British economy waiting to be unleashed. To Wilson, 'we are living in the jet age but we are governed by an Edwardian establishment mentality'.[3] The old boy network of connections through birth and wealth were clogging up the vital arteries of Britain's economic system. The commanding heights of the economy had been taken over by the State, but the old aristocracy still remained in control. As a result, the scientific revolution had passed Britain by, leading to stagnation — 'in science and industry we are content to remain a nation of Gentlemen in a world of players'.[4]

Wilson's solution lay in the new meritocratic class of socialists and professionals who would bring purpose to Britain's stagnating economy and society. Only they could competently apply the latest statistical and analytical techniques to the problem of economic expansion. It was the very class against which Titmuss had warned in his *The Irresponsible Society*, condemning them as élitist administrators with neither morality nor compassion, but to Wilson they were the harbingers of a new age of technology and scientific planning. The difference of this vision of socialism with that of the revisionists was concealed by a general agreement that the British economy needed to escape from stagnation. This was why Wilson could unite the Labour Party when he wrote,

> Socialism, as I understand it, means applying a sense of purpose to our national life: economic purpose, social purpose, moral purpose. Purpose means technical skill — be it the skill of a manager, a designer, a craftsman, a nuclear physicist, or a doctor, a nurse, a social worker.[5]

He was making it clear that the social radicalism of the revisionists could only be satisfied if the economy could recover its dynamism.

It was the old ideas of corporate socialism on which Wilson relied to do this, and it was to Thomas Balogh that he turned for the application of these ideas to the Britain of the sixties. Balogh (1905-85) was a Hungarian who had taught at Balliol College, Oxford, since 1939. He had served as an adviser to various governments and to the United Nations, and was to serve as Economic Adviser to Wilson's Cabinet from 1964 to 1968. Long before, in *The Economics of Full Employment* (1944), Balogh had endorsed the corporate socialist interpretation of Keynes, accepting that a market economy would lead to instability and unemployment if left to itself. By the early sixties, he had come to identify Britain's economic stagnation as due to 'a deep-rooted failure to acquire technical and scientific dynamism',[6] which had led to an uncompetitive situation in world markets and a fall in investment. The insufficient growth rate in the economy that resulted undermined social investment in schools, hospitals and housing, and led trade unions to demand higher wages to prevent a fall in their members' living standards. The wage inflation that was caused led to a further decline in investment, and so the circle of decline continued.

In seeking a solution to stop this process, Balogh admitted that wartime planning had failed because of its rudimentary, crude and negative nature. Moreover, it had been thrust on a reluctant bureaucracy by the needs of war. However, the Conservative rejection of planning had also failed through a tragic waste of Britain's resources in private consumption. This was hardly surprising, since a non-planned economy was one where businessmen and financiers were simply unaware of the implications of their investment decisions for their own prosperity. The real solution lay in neither of these alternatives, but in a fully planned economy, with industrial modernisation being given a priority by a more powerful NEDC. It was not the *principles* of corporate socialism which had been wrong, but its inadequate *application*. The Development Councils set up to plan individual industries under the post-war Labour government should be revived, but this time they should be free of business domination. Moreover, it must be an economy which was centrally planned, not a compartmentalised series of competing plans – 'a mechanism is necessary which would elaborate, and implement, a set of coherently chosen targets enforcing social priorities in a plan which takes into account the effects of the totality of investment projects'.[7] The technical management of such an economy need require no fundamental changes in private ownership – though Balogh wrote 'I doubt whether the moral or psychological handicaps could be overcome without extending public ownership'[8] – but it *did* need a conscious co-ordination of the process of decision-making.

Balogh was nothing if not consistent, and his call for a planned economy necessarily involved a planning of *incomes*. He did not go so far as to advocate direct state interference in free collective bargaining, based as it was on the invaluable knowledge of employers and unions, but 'what is needed is to add to this sectional knowledge, a due regard for the requirements of the general economic position'.[9] An Arbitration Board, for example, could decide a dispute between employers and unions where both sides agreed to apply. He acknowledged the natural hostility of the Labour Party's trade union base to an incomes policy, but the requirements of a planned economy overrode all sectional considerations. Moreover, he believed that the economic success of planning would in itself win the co-operation of the unions, and argued that the sacrifice will not be in vain, that the restraint on wages *on which the restoration of British industry depends* would in the due — and not too distant — future yield positive results in increased living standards. [10]

It was in the light of this strategy that the 1963 Labour conference unanimously passed a resolution calling on the party to develop an incomes policy in association with the trade unions, and that the Labour government elected in October 1964 prepared a National Plan to bring about a 25 per cent increase in output in five years. Neither Balogh nor the Labour Party asked themselves what would happen to wages and the unions if the hoped for growth did not take place.

In fact, the Labour Government of 1964-70 failed in its economic objective, and thence in every other. The strategy of planning was a miserable débâcle with George Brown's National Plan stillborn. The balance of payments crisis dominated government policy from beginning to end, forcing it into a series of stringency measures which fell on its own working-class constituency. The failure of a statutory incomes policy in the summer of 1966 was followed by the failure of the chauvinist policy of maintaining the value of sterling, signalled by the devaluation of the pound in December 1967. The growing opposition of the unions to government policy led to tremendous strain within the Labour movement, rising to a head with the government's attempt to curb the unions by legislation in 1969. The failure of the government even to produce a Bill as a result of the opposition in the parliamentary party and the unions marked the final failure of Labour's economic policy, underlined by the rise in unemployment to over half a million after 1967, and by a series of strikes in 1969-70 which destroyed the effects of income policy. The attainment of a surplus in the balance of payments in 1969-70 was due more to the restraint on working-class demand rather than any drastic restructuring of British industry. [11]

If the government was a failure of corporate socialism, it was also a failure for revisionism. The hopes of liberal reform were kept alive by the tenure of Roy Jenkins at the Home Office in 1965-7, when a series of social reforms on censorship, abortion and homosexuality were pushed through the Commons with Jenkins' active support. However, James Callaghan, Jenkins' successor as Home Secretary, was generally seen as a disgrace by revisionists. [12] He capitulated, for example, to racist demands to restrict the entry of Kenyan Asians in 1968. John

Mackintosh expressed revisionist feelings when he told the Commons,

> I do not know who has put the wind up the Home Office and destroyed the reputation of the Labour Party for non-racialism by suggesting that we could not absorb 26,000 people this year into a humane and reasonable society. I will certainly not listen to any more speeches from either Front Bench advocating multi-racialism in other countries. I feel humiliated to have to stand here and make this speech.[13]

Revisionist frustration was particularly marked by the failure in social policy. While there were innovations in a progressive direction — official support for comprehensive education, and the introduction of a system of wage-related social security contributions and benefits, for example — the savage cutbacks in social expenditure and the increase in unemployment more than balanced them. The growth in spending on health, education and social security merely kept pace with the increased demand for and cost of basic services. The distribution of wealth and social privilege was left untouched, while poverty may well have worsened.[14] However, a number of revisionists were in leading positions in the government — Jenkins was the Chancellor who reimposed charges for health prescriptions — and it had always been assumed that reforms depended on a healthy economy.

At the 1968 Labour Party Conference, Roy Jenkins told delegates that the revisionist hopes of social reform had to mark time on economic success —

> until we get that success, we cannot achieve our other goals except by mortgaging the future. For success here is the key to a higher and more secure level of unemployment . . . It is the key to a steady and satisfactory rate of growth, and with such a . . . rate of growth, but not without it, new horizons in social policy would open up.[15]

The government record was a failure of revisionism as much as it was of corporate socialism.

Reappraisal

The failure of the 1964-70 Labour government led to a bottled mood of doubt among the revisionists. Harold Wilson himself could point to the machinations of speculators and subversives as the cause of his government's failure,[16] but many revisionists felt a much less superficial reappraisal was needed, a belief which was intensified by the growing strength of the Labour Left after the 1970 defeat.

Tony Crosland attempted to come to terms with the failure of the Labour government in a Fabian Tract, *A Social Democratic Britain* (1971), and in *Socialism Now* (1974). He argued that there was no need to redefine socialism as concerned with equality and welfare, but the *means* needed to achieve socialism had to be reappraised in the light of the government's disappointing failure to modify class differences. Britain in the early seventies was as class-divided as ever, with poverty and homelessness increasing. In spite of trade union strength, the working class was still inferior in terms of income, status, fringe benefits and job security. The growing wave of strikes stood as a stark reminder that Crosland had been premature in once dismissing class divisions as outmoded — 'the labour issue continues to dominate our society, and class relations in industry are characterised by a mutual distrust amounting often to open warfare'.[17] Above all, the economy was continuing to deteriorate, bringing into doubt even the wisdom of state spending, so crucial to revisionist thought.

However, Crosland was unwilling to reject his original belief that capitalism was no longer an enemy for socialists. While capitalist industries had certainly increased in size, he did not detect any increase in capitalist *power*. On the contrary, the strength of the unions and the sharper competition from abroad had made the private sector more precarious than ever. He was not worried about the growth of the multi-national corporations either, as the real income of British workers had been increased by their investment, which should be encouraged by any Labour government. He did recognise their potential dangers — to the balance of payments, or to the revenue as a result of evasion — but argued that these dangers could be met by government action on a national and international level. Nationalisation was still seen as a weapon of the last resort, since the ability of governments to legislate, tax, police or embargo large companies could be just as effective. In view of this, and in view of the general failure of nationalisation to achieve equality, Crosland wrote, 'I see no reason to alter the revisionist thesis that government can generally impose its will (provided it has one) on the private corporation'.[18]

In the face of this, Crosland pressed once again the revisionist cure that the broad objectives of any Labour government must be to help the poor and deprived, and to promote greater social and economic equality. He was also forced against the fact that high economic growth was necessary to attain this, albeit with a strict social control over the environment to prevent pollution and the destruction of rural beauty. The problem was the failure of the Labour government to attain the increasingly elusive goal of higher production levels.

This was ascribed by Crosland to its deflationary policies, caused by its original obsession with maintaining the parity of sterling. There were, of course, deeper reasons for the general decline in the vitality of the British economy during the century, ranging from the faulty structure of British industry to the public-school system, but he believed that this decline could be halted by government will. Crosland held that a Labour government should choose its priorities and stick to them, refusing to be blown off course. If a problem arose with the balance of payments, it should choose a policy of flexible exchange rates rather than a cut in social welfare. If the problem was inflation, then the government should choose an incomes policy, on the basis of agreement with the trade unions, rather than let low-paid and poorly organised workers get left behind in a wages free-for-all. If the Government could do this, then radical policies to reduce poverty and redistribute wealth could be successfully undertaken. Crosland could then conclude from the failure of the sixties that

> a move to the left is needed, not in the traditional sense of a move towards old fashioned Clause IV Marxism but in the sense of a sharper delineation of fundamental objectives, a greater clarity about egalitarian priorities, and a stronger determination to achieve them.[19]

This was a theme taken up by Roy Jenkins in *What Matters Now* (1972), a series of speeches largely written by David and Judith Marquand. Jenkins (b. 1920) had a dry urbanity and upper-class lifestyle which disguised his working-class origins and which earned him much unpopularity with the increasingly powerful Left. For the Left his liberal tenure at the Home Office had been more than compensated for by the deflationary measures he had taken as Chancellor of the Exchequer in the late sixties, and by his enthusiastic support for the Common Market.

In the aftermath of the 1970 defeat, Jenkins followed Crosland in returning to revisionist fundamentals. He called on the next Labour government to make the elimination of poverty as a social problem to be its central aim. To Jenkins, poverty and inequality remained the principle barriers to the freedom of human choice sought by the democratic Left. The impoverished tenant of a sub-standard flat with only a pittance left after the rent and costs of keeping alive had been paid was a standing insult to a humane society, and to talk of the freedom to choose his or her own way of life was a cruel joke for such a person. Jenkins held that a *voluntary* incomes policy agreed between Labour and the unions, combined with the old Labour demand for a national minimum wage, would be enough to produce a more just and free society. Of course, such a policy could be held to infringe *economic* freedom, but Jenkins held that this was no bad thing.

> Ironically, many Conservative MPs who so strongly proclaim the virtues of individual freedom in the economic field, where it can do great harm to others, have bitterly resisted the growth of greater legal tolerance in the field of personal conduct, where individual behaviour rarely interferes with the rights of others.[20]

Both Jenkins and Crosland failed to probe adequately the reasons for Labour's failure. The increasing inability of the State effectively to combat economic crisis by use of Keynesian policies was ignored by them, and they called for a greater use of such policies to eradicate poverty and inequality. The fact that Keynes had written at a time of high unemployment and low prices, whereas the seventies was a decade of rising unemployment and *rising* prices, did not lead them to revise their original ideas. Instead, they held that inflation could be kept in check by an incomes policy. Apart from the fact that an incomes policy faced enormous difficulties in its operation and produced inequities of its own, it was a solution to the wrong problem. The wage is merely a price — the price for labour power — and to believe that rising prices are caused by rising prices is to fall into tautology. The demand for higher wages was itself caused by the rise in prices. The revisionists had failed to grasp the root cause of inflation which lay in increased state expenditure and credit to meet the rising demands of a threatened capitalist economy.

Jenkins himself faced increasing political isolation in the Labour party, largely as a result of his enthusiasm for the Common Market. His support, consistent for over a decade, was based on the belief that Britain could only shake off the stagnation which had settled over her and regain a sense of purpose in economic activity and in world affairs by joining with her natural European allies. This belief was out of touch with the mood of the Labour party of the early seventies, and

Jenkins resigned as Deputy Leader in April 1972 in protest at the Party's decision to hold a referendum on whether Britain should withdraw from the Market. It was evidence of a decline in revisionist influence in the party, and the advance of a new Left which was succeeding in winning Labour to a policy of increased public ownership and hostility to the Common Market.

It was in protest against the rise of the Left that the call to go beyond revisionism was raised. John Gyford and Stephen Haseler, in an influential Fabian pamphlet, *Social Democracy: Beyond Revisionism* (1971), called on the old Gaitskellite wing of the party to adopt a new and more populist strategy which would come to terms with the new desires for participation. They called themselves Social Democrats to differentiate themselves from the old revisionists, and emphasised that inequality in power and status should be reduced by a more local, grass-roots approach. This call was taken up by Dick Taverne who resigned from parliament in protest at left-wing activity and was elected as a Democratic Labour MP in the Lincoln by-election in March 1973. In his book, *The Future of Labour* (1974), he called on Labour to break its links with the big unions and cultivate community politics and small business. He wrote that 'when in doubt, we should favour the small. Indeed, our guiding principle should be "small is beautiful", that variety provides for independence, and that independence provides for greater security and freedom.'[21] It was an appealing message, in touch with much middle-class sentiment, but it was combined with the call for the followers of Jenkins to form a new party. To Taverne, Labour had become too left-wing and union-dominated to be capable of reform.

The Labour Government of 1974-9 was another disappointment for revisionists. Its initial sensitivity to the Left and the more militant unions was replaced from the summer of 1975 by yet another lurch to conservative economic policies as inflation rose to 25 per cent and unemployment to over a million. There were hints of a new type of politics — as seen in the abortive proposals for devolution to Wales and Scotland, or the pointer to a centrist government from the pact made by Labour with the Liberals in 1977-8 — but generally the failure of the government only reinforced the glaring need for a break with the revisionist politics of a bygone era. This was above all underlined by the ultimate failure of the 'Social Contract', the voluntary incomes policy agreed between Labour and the unions. The inability of the union leaders to control the militancy of the rank and file in the 'winter of discontent' in 1978-9 sealed Labour's fate and brought to power a

Conservative government of the militant Right. The electoral liability of the Labour Party's link with the trade unions was evident to many revisionists by this time.

It was during the lifetime of this government that the most able of the revisionists, John Mackintosh, began the radical reappraisal that was needed. Mackintosh (1929-78) had been born in India and educated at Edinburgh and Oxford. He wrote *The British Cabinet* (1962), a major study of the institution, and enjoyed an academic career in Nigeria and Edinburgh before his election to Westminster in 1966. His fierce independence earned him no love from the Labour leadership, and he never obtained a ministerial post. The failures of Labour in power convinced him that the revisionist politics of the fifties to which he held were outdated and irrelevant, and he was working on a restatement of revisionist socialism when he died.

By the late seventies, Mackintosh had come to the conclusion that revisionism was inadequate because it had no economic understanding of or prescription for the mixed economy. The revisionists had merely assumed that their programme could be implemented once theTories, seen as the cause of economic stagnation, were removed. Mackintosh now admitted,

> I had not thought about or appreciated how far the views of what is now called the social democratic section which was then dominant in the Labour Party depended on the kind of growth we had claimed was possible once the Tories were out of office.[22]

There had been no adequate theory of how the mixed economy should work and, despite the different twists and turns of every government since the early sixties, a long-term economic revival still evaded the country. The Wilsonian explanation that this was due to a series of accidents which blew governments off course seemed much too superficial, failing to explain the sheer persistence of government failure, or the ability of other countries like Japan and West Germany to escape such 'accidents'. To Mackintosh, there had to be a search for much deeper causes if Labour's failure was to be understood and remedied.

The adversarial politics of Conservative and Labour were partly to blame, but Mackintosh eventually rejected this cause, too, as insufficient. Hopes had been raised for partisan purposes, but this was understandable given the length of the post-war boom. There had been drastic policy changes – on trade union legislation, incomes policy, administrative reform of health and local government – which had a disruptive effect on industry, but this was a result of the stagnation of the economy rather than its cause. The party system had been around a long time, and there was no reason why it should permit industrialisation to take place at one point and then cause its decline at another. In fact, the parliamentary system had been very responsive to the needs of industry, moving to stem an apparently irreversible decline.

Mackintosh traced the defects to the very growth of corporatism which Labour had done so much to bring about, leading as it did to a feeling of impotence and indifference in the electorate and its parliament. He argued that the extension of the vote to a new working-class electorate with major social needs had upset the old Westminster model of checks and balances between the executive (constitutional monarch, Cabinet) and legislature (the parties, the Commons). Power had shifted from Westminster to the Cabinet, imposing a tight discipline on the party system and increasing executive control over the legislative process. While the outward features of government and Parliament remained the same, the reality was very different as the ability of the Commons to force policy changes on governments and significantly amend legislation had generally disappeared.

The adoption of a referendum to decide complex policy issues such as membership of the Common Market merely underlined the trend towards a plebiscitary democracy, where the government could bypass Parliament to appeal directly to the electorate in a form which could be easily loaded in the official favour.

This had been paralleled by the rise of corporate pressure groups, mainly the Confederation of British Industries (CBI) and the TUC, which had come to exercise the power once held by the Commons. These groups had been able to claim the first loyalty of their members, as witnessed by the successful defiance of the Industrial Relations law by dockers in July 1972, and as a result had denied the legitimacy of Parliament.

> The denial of legitimacy is a clear consequence of two concepts. First, that passage by the House of Commons is not of itself an adequate indication of the consent of the community, and second, that prior consultation with recognised groups has become an essential part of the legitimising process.[23]

This growth of corporatism had led the Commons to become a mere registry for the wishes of the pressure groups, who had grown so powerful that they had become able to disregard the will of governments successfully. The House of Commons was excluded from the essential information needed to judge decisions properly, while the Cabinet and the pressure groups consulted one another on the major issues of the day in an atmosphere of secrecy and reticence.

Revisionism has itself contributed to this devaluation of parliamentary democracy, according to Mackintosh. Crosland's libertarian rejection of nationalisation had not gone far enough, and he had been unable to break adequately from the statist approach of the corporate socialists and the Fabians in his demands for welfare and equality. He did not realise that mere changes in social and economic institutions by the State could not in themselves change the social attitudes of the people. As a result the whole social, political and industrial atmosphere in Britain had contributed to a feeling of impotence against the vested interests of big business and organised labour which really ran the country, and of contempt against a parliament which only pretended to rule. The dangers for democracy were all too clear to Mackintosh, who wrote, 'It is, I fear, basically unhealthy for a country to depend on a political system which is not backed by positive conviction and understanding, and whose original principles have become corrupted and confused'.[24]

In this context, the task of the social democrats in the Labour Party was clear. The importance of parliamentary democracy and the independence of the individual Member of Parliament must be reaffirmed against the power of the Cabinet, while the devolution of political responsibility to the regions and the locality must revive the feeling of participation and citizenhood essential if the whole nation was to revive its faith in democracy. This would inevitably mean a fight against the corporate interests which ran the country, including the trade unions on which the Labour Party depended. However, Mackintosh did not let party considerations prevent his

> primary emphasis on putting the mass of the community before the interests of those with a monopoly-hold on economic power, be they financiers, multi-national corporations, or unions controlling key sectors of the labour force.[25]

Mackintosh was an exceptionally able thinker who was experienced in both the theory and practice of politics, and his elaboration of a new social democratic doctrine was still in a process of transition at his death. He was able to pinpoint the weakness of revisionism as its lack of an economic theory which could stimulate growth, but was himself unable to dig deeper than the political manifestations of corporatism and the decline of Parliament which had accompanied the mixed economy. The *economic* causes of an economic decline — lying in the process of production itself — were ignored as Mackintosh attempted to combat the feeling of impotence and indifference which had settled over once-mighty institutions like Parliament. The fact that this mood may have been created by economic decline as much as corporatism was not really investigated, but the solutions of devolution and a revival of the independence of Parliament would fall into the same trap as that of Crosland — the belief that institutional changes would lead to a change of attitudes. The fact that power over an ailing economy would be held by Westminster and regional assemblies **would** not be necessarily more inspiring than the exercise of power by the Cabinet or the corporate pressure groups.

Moreover, Mackintosh made the mistake of treating organised labour as an evil similar to organised capital. The unions had definitely grown in numbers and were regularly consulted by government on the important industrial issues of the day, but this does not necessarily imply that they were equal in power and status to the leaders of industry in an economy desperate for investment by those leaders. It was true that the unions had denied the legitimacy of Parliament by defying the Industrial Relations legislation in 1972, but they had done so in 1834 when workers were deported for attempting to form a union. When a law is aimed at a section of the community, there should be no surprise when that law is defied. In overlooking this, Mackintosh and his supporters overlooked the limits to the legitimacy of parliamentary legislation marked out by the founders of liberal political thought such as John Locke.

In his attacks on the corporate power of organised labour, Mackintosh was developing the anti-labourism implicit in revisionist thinking to a new and more dangerous stage. The social democrat wing of the Labour party, as it was by now called, was reaching a point where the revisionists could find no home in the Labour party.

The Social Democrat Break With Labour

The failure of the 'social contract' in a series of strikes in the 'winter of discontent' in 1978-9 sealed Labour's electoral fate. It also appeared to be a final proof that the party's unique relationship with the unions was not capable of delivering the incomes policy felt to be essential by the social democrats. The power of the Left, growing throughout the decade, was making the existence of the old revisionist wing increasingly uncomfortable, and the displacement of sitting moderate MPs by their local parties was threatening to make it intolerable. The conditions for a major schism were present, and it was Roy Jenkins who set the final process into motion.

Jenkins had been increasingly alienated from the party during the seventies, and his failure to win the Labour leadership after Wilson's retirement in March 1976 may have finally convinced him that he had reached the end of the road in British politics. He withdrew from Westminster to take up the Presidency of the European Commission — the archetype of the 'Eurocrat' so hated by the Labour Left. He had not, however, finished with British politics, and the final failure of the Labour government, paving the way for the divisive and tough regime of Mrs Thatcher, made him aware of the possibility of a new party, committed to the concerns once praised by Evan Durbin. The strength of the Left in the Labour Party, and the rise of the New Right in the Conservatives, indicated to him that an important political vacuum had grown in the centre which would hold the support of the majority of the electorate.

It was at the Dimbleby Lecture in November 1979 that Jenkins put forward his new views. His acceptance of the present contours of the mixed economy, with a rejection of any further public ownership, was new but less startling than his call for a major change in the political system. The present system, based on a fixed party system, was a century old, yet during that century the society on which it rested had been transformed. Britain had seen its world power and status gradually disappear, while the strict social divisions which had characterised a class society had become weaker than ever before. The disparity between the stable political system and the changed society was emphasised by Jenkins, who argued that the stability had become a sign of ossification.

> Traditionally this British stability was considered a major national asset. Now the question is whether the stability has not turned into political rigidity, whether the old skin is not drawn too tight for effective national performance.[26]

Jenkins traced the decisive changes to Suez, which had marked the end of Britain as a world power, and the formation of the Common Market without British membership. The result had been an isolated Britain which failed to enjoy European economic growth and prosperity and suffered instead an inexorable decline into one of the poorest countries in Europe. By the time the country finally joined the Common Market, it was too late to take part in Europe's thriving boom, which had finally exhausted itself. The political system had failed to halt Britain's economic decline, despite their wildly enthusiastic promise by the major parties that they held the key to prosperity. The result was a decline in the prestige of the House of Commons and a growing desire for a third party by an increasing number of the electorate.

The answer to these problems given by Jenkins was for an end to the ideological politics which was coming to characterise the party system. Mackintosh had, of course, defended the party system believing that adversarial politics was a result rather than a cause of the crisis, but to Jenkins it was a major threat to the consensus celebrated by Durbin and Gaitskell, a consensus which had presided over the long post-war boom. Such intense political partisanship only harmed the economy, as controversial legislation was repealed and then passed again, while conflict on the shop floor between workers and employers was only encouraged by the sight of the two parties bitterly attacking one another. Jenkins did not present any proof of this point — the fact that employers and workers might have different economic interests was not really investigated — but he did believe that a change in political attitudes towards a sense of harmony and conciliation would have a major effect for the better on industrial relations. It was, then, a call for a politics of the *centre* made by Jenkins —

> The vocation of politicians ought to be to represent, to channel, to lead the aspirations of the electorate. These aspirations, not on every issue, but in essential directions, pull far more towards the centre than towards the extremes.[27]

To attain this 'politics of the centre', Jenkins called for institutional reforms, particularly in the electoral system. The greatest alienation from the two parties was not able to be politically expressed through the present system of 'first past the post', which grossly distorted the wishes of the electorate. The fact that the Liberals could take only 2 per cent of the seats at Westminster from more than 18 per cent of the vote in October 1974 was merely the latest proof of the inequities of the system. The old argument that the current electoral system ensured stable and coherent government had been manifestly disproved in the last two decades, argued Jenkins, while he pointed to the old Labour

Party as a combination of liberal social democrats and responsible trade unionists to demonstrate that coalition politics could be a healthy phenomenon. However, he held that 'the great disadvantage of our present electoral system is that it freezes the pattern of politics, and holds together the incompatible because everyone assumes that if a party splits it will be electorally slaughtered'.[28]

It was an ominous warning that the arguments about electoral reform were basically an attempt to ensure the survival of a social democratic break from the Labour Party, which Jenkins now attacked for its domination by the unions. The Labour Party had once called for electoral reform, too, only to forget the inequities of the system once it enjoyed the fruits. Jenkins appeared to have remembered that the 'first past the post' system was unfair only when it became necessary to unfreeze the system.

Moreover, his call for a 'politics of the centre' was a mark of the crisis into which revisionism had fallen. In the hands of Crosland, the rejection of nationalisation had gone hand in hand with a desire to unleash the radical impulse within the Labour Party. There was a desire to attack the citadels of wealth and privilege, and to transform capitalist and materialist values into the socialist values of compassion and welfare for the poor and the outcast of society. The failure to achieve economic growth had ruined this radical impulse, which had now degenerated to a politics of moderation and gradual reform.

Many social democrats rejected the moderate centrism of Jenkins and, during 1980-1, as the need and preparations for a new party took shape, attempted to revive the original radicalism of the revisionists in a form more suitable to the eighties. In doing so, they looked to the decentralist ideas, towards which Taverne and Mackintosh had first pointed, in an attempt to link up with a socialist tradition in the Labour Party running back to Cole and Tawney. The political atmosphere among the middle class was certainly ripe for such politics, prepared by the local concerns of Liberal populists, ecologists, and even ideas of direct 'participatory' democracy which had become popular in sections of the radical Left.

Shirley Williams (b. 1930) proved herself adept at taking up the new ideas. The daughter of Vera Brittain, she had been active in the Labour Party throughout her life, serving as General Secretary of the Fabian Society before entering Parliament in 1964. A charismatic personality, she was a member of Labour's National Executive Committee throughout the seventies, and served in the Labour government of 1974-9 as Prices Secretary and then as Education Secretary. Her defeat at Hertford and Stevenage in the 1979 election freed her for the necessary re-thinking to write *Politics is for People* (1981) and gradually to be pushed out of the Labour Party by the constitutional victories of the Left in 1980-1.

The revisionist critique of corporate socialism elaborated by Cros-land was taken to its logical conclusion of the rejection of state socialism by Williams, who was forced as a result to trace her ideas to other tradi-tions in the socialist movement. In seeking to sharply differentiate the social democratic tradition from the Labour Marxists and those on the Left who flirted with Marxist ideas, she looked to the traditions of democratic tolerance found in Owen and Tawney. The goals of equality and the abolition of poverty may have been common to social democrats and Marxists, but these goals could not bridge the gulf separating the two strands of socialist thinking. Marxism was, according to Williams, basically hostile to political democracy because of its rejection of the mixed economy, and led inevitably to the bureaucratic privileges and vicious repression of dissent seen in the Soviet Union. She drew the dis-tinction with social democracy clearly in her argument that 'a pluralist democracy complements a pluralist economy; a monolithic political system complements monolithic economic ownership and control'.[29]

With this permanent acceptance of a mixed economy, Williams pro-ceeded to attempt to incorporate the new decentralist ideas which had arisen in the previous decade, particularly in the ecological movement. Unlike the political extremists, whose forefathers she traced back to Stalin and Hitler, these ecological romantics were concerned with the quality of life, more important to them than any economic system or talk of class oppression. They saw industrialism, not capitalism, as their main enemy, and recognised the need for 'a sense of belonging, of being cared for, of being wanted, of being part of a network of relationships with people and also with objects'.[30] It was a need which led to a resentment against the impersonal nature of the State and technology which threatened the fragile ecology on which we all depend. It was a need which led to the demand for the preservation of the small com-munity from the encroachment of the ugly cities, and demanded the right of ordinary people to run their own affairs. It was a movement that she felt the political parties must learn from, and which would respond to the old libertarian traditions of social democracy. After all, 'Owen and Tawney are to political thought what Vaughan Williams was to music; pastoral, gentle and humane'.[31]

This was not only very quaint, but also amounted to a restatement of the politics of consensus — the belief that the social harmony of the community was far too important to risk any change which might destroy that harmony. Williams had always seen liberal democracy as dependent on the agreement of all parties that the rules of the game were far more important than actual victory in the game. Such an agreed framework of political activity was 'indispensable in any society whose inhabitants and whose major parties believe the continuation of that free society itself to be an even greater good than the changes they seek to bring about in it'.[32] When a positive feeling of participation was high in the community, the tendencies to disruption would be weak; when it was low, those tendencies would be strong.

It was, then, in the interests of democratic consensus that she called for decentralisation and community politics to escape from the bureaucratic regulation and restrictions of corporatism. Industrial democracy, in which workers would be more involved in their industry in partnership with capital, was the answer to the strife which had bedevilled British industry. In creating a better-informed workforce, it would be a far more effective agency to restrain wage demands than a statutory incomes policy, which would be too rigid to last long. The measures to be taken if workers still insisted on higher wages were not really investigated, however, though any hope that workers would cease to defend their living standards purely by having their representatives involved with management was in danger of being a pipedream without them.

The formula of local democracy was seen as a panacea for the problems of British society, though Williams reluctantly maintained that public schools should be abolished on the grounds that the restrictions on freedom of choice were outweighed by the profound harm of segregated education to society. The need to increase spending on social services advocated by Crosland had now been reduced in importance to the problem of making the existing welfare services less bureaucratic and remote, throwing the administration of schools, hospitals and housing open to the community. The problems of staffing could easily be met by imaginative thinking — for example, voluntary service could be encouraged as unemployment and early retirement provided a pool of people 'willing to participate in working for it for nothing'.[33] The consequences of this for the labour force in posing the danger of lower wages, was not raised, however.

The radical nature of the break with revisionism was brought out in her call for a modest and self-sustaining economic growth to be led by the small firm. The revisionists had always regarded the large corporations as a progressive step compared with the cut-throat competition

which had characterised the small capitalists, and regarded the economies of scale enjoyed by large firms as crucial to the high rates of
economic growth needed to pay for social reform. However, Williams
rejected such large firms as a cause of rigidities in the working of the
economy. 'The history of natural selection tells us that size is irrelevant
to survival. What matters is functional efficiency. The dinosaur proved
to be an evolutionary dead end; the fish and the bird survived and
flourished'.[34] The obsession with size shown by post-war governments
had contributed towards the impersonal élitism which has denied
people a sense of responsibility, and led towards the general crisis in
which Britain found herself. Williams argued that in their grants of
financial aid and their primary concern, the government should cease
concerning itself with state monopolies or big business, and look
instead to the small firm. This exaltation of the petty capitalist, long
dear to the hearts of the middle classes, ignored the needs of many
small businessmen, faced with a harsh economic climate and stiff competition, to reduce costs by the very unromantic methods of the sweat-
shop and appallingly low wages. The fact that Williams was looking to
the small firm as an engine of economic growth demonstrated how far
social democrats were moving from both labourism and the old revisionists.

This call for a new, decentralist socialism tied to modest economic
growth was echoed by David Owen (b. 1938). Owen had been educated
at St Thomas' Hospital, where he was a research doctor until his
election to Westminster in 1966. He had risen rapidly to become, on
Crosland's death in February 1977, the youngest Foreign Secretary
since Anthony Eden. After the defeat of the Labour government, Owen
rapidly established himself as one of the leading social democrats in the
party and, in *Face the Future* (1981), attempted to link the new ideas
to older traditions in the labour movement.

He argued that Labour was facing the eighties with the old formulae
of 1945, with their calls for more centralisation and state control. In
fact, these very formulae had turned into the very problems which
needed to be confronted. It was the undemocratic nature of corporatism, where decisions were taken by unrepresentative pressure groups
like the CBI and the TUC, which had succeeded capitalism as the real
enemy of socialists. These corporate pressure groups were insensitive to
individual cases, and their very size discouraged the initiative and innovation so needed by Britain. The smaller business firms, like the homeless and workers not in unions, found themselves excluded from the
political and economic decisions which concerned them. To Owen

'Britain cannot be revived unless corporatism is rejected and democracy allowed to flourish in its place'.[35]

However, the Labour Party was identifying itself more closely with the centralised politics of corporatism. Owen traced this to the pursuit of equality at the expense of freedom. This pursuit of equality was certainly worthwhile, as there was much evidence that inequality and poverty were closely linked, but the problem of how to overcome inequality was becoming particularly difficult at a time of low economic growth when all social classes held on to their existing wealth. He did accept the need to continue egalitarian measures, but his advocacy of tax reform and the raising of social benefits hardly amounted to a major assault on the bastions of social privilege. As he did not see the problem of equality merely in terms of the distribution of wealth, this was not necessarily surprising.

In fact, according to Owen, 'what is needed is a socialist philosophy outside the restrictive confines of much of the present polarised political debate, which asserts the radical democratic libertarian tradition of decentralised socialism'.[36] It was a tradition with an honourable lineage, stretching back to G.D.H. Cole and to William Morris, concerned with freedom from the tyranny of the State rather than the Fabian anxieties about poverty and inefficiency. Moreover, Owen linked this concern with a growing movement on the European Left which took up the rights of workers in the workplace, demanding that they be treated as human beings rather than mere cogs in a factory. This was the motive behind the demand for *autogestion* (workers control) put forward by Michel Rocard, a leader of the moderate wing in the French Socialist Party. This old demand, abstracted from the anti-capitalist terms in which it was once couched, was now taken up as an alternative to the old panacea of state intervention.

It was this hostility to the State which Owen took up as he attempted to change the revisionist concerns for poverty and equality to a new concern for freedom. He accepted state intervention in the marginal sense of providing finance for new capital-intensive industries such as computers and the micro-chip, but generally the corporate state stood in the way of the development of a participatory democracy and wider ownership by the community. As a result, he called for more open government and an end to the secrecy traditionally shrouding the processes by which decisions were taken in Britain. The evasion of Parliament by corporate organisations such as the CBI and the TUC, which had succeeded in curbing democracy by arrogating decision-making to themselves, would be ended by an increase in the parliamentary powers of scrutiny and the authority of the backbench MP. To Owen, as to Mackintosh,

> Parliament cannot cease to be the forum for the representation of a wide variety of views and must never accept being the endorser of decisions curbing the individual rights of citizens that are taken by departments or Ministers without specific Paliamentary authority.[37]

Members of Parliament must rediscover and reassert their rights as the traditional practitioners of government.

In common with Shirley Williams, Owen took the revolt against corporate socialism to a new phase of positive encouragement of private enterprise. Attacking the Labour Left as centralists who were unable to reconcile themselves to the freedom and initiative of the private sector, he called for a much more resolute and clear-headed approach to the mixed economy. The corporate socialists had never considered the market sector of the economy to be worthy of any other study than that of curbing its size, while the revisionists were more concerned with equality and welfare than the economy on which any policies had to rest.

In accepting the existing frontiers of the mixed economy as permanent, Owen believed that he could point to the failure of its working. This failure was due to an inversion of values, as private corporations willingly looked to the State for financial aid to compensate for their lack of enterprise, while the public corporations acted as though they were commercial companies in search of a profit rather than services to help industry and the community. The social democrats, in advocating a mixed economy, should be prepared to accept the full consequences of a market sector, which should be free from the detailed restrictions of central government control, to find a full scope for private initiative and thereby make its full contribution to the economy. Private firms had become commercially irresponsible, refusing to confront militant unions or dismiss workers who had become unnecessary. They looked to fiscal benefits from the State, rather than normal commercial critiera, as the basis for the siting of new firms. A *realistic* commitment to the mixed economy would involve a recognition that the private sector must not be emasculated by the public sector. It involved a questioning of 'the extent to which inducing a sense of social responsibility in the private sector is compatible with the economic dynamic that should come from the private entrepreneur'.[38]

If Owen and the social democrats wished to break away from both revisionism and corporate socialism in its hostility to the State, they remained committed to the restrictions on incomes sought by the Wilsonian technocrats. Freedom for the small business enterprise did not extend to collective bargaining as the social democrats reaffirmed the need for an incomes policy. Owen argued that 'full employment, reasonable price stability and free collective bargaining are mutually incompatible',[39] and called for an incomes policy which would avoid the rigidity which had led to the collapse of previous attempts in the past two decades. To the social democrats, it was not the principle of State restrictions on incomes which had failed, but the will and the intelligence to carry that principle through to the end. This belief was shared by many others on the Labour Right, but the social democrats felt much more independent of trade union interests in elaborating their policy.

The most consistent of their theorists on this question was Professor James E. Meade (b. 1907). An academic Keynesian who had taught at Oxford and Cambridge, Professor Meade had won the Nobel Prize for Economics in 1977, mainly for the four-volume *Principles of Political Economy*. He believed that a curb by the State on the monopolistic powers of the unions was essential if inflation was to be controlled and an equilibrium of full employment achieved. However, he regarded neither statutory restrictions nor mass unemployment as acceptable solutions to the problem. The freedom of unions to bargain was seen as sacrosanct by Professor Meade, who wrote that 'the real question is not whether trade union bargaining should exist, but to what measures of social control it should be subjected'.[40] Nevertheless, *some* form of incomes policy was felt by Meade to be essential if the Keynesian policy of economic expansion was not to be choked off by wage-push inflation.

He called for an increase in impartial arbitration between the two sides of industry in order to set an upper limit on decentralised bargaining between employers and workers, which would otherwise continue unhampered by outside intervention. It would be preferable for both labour and capital to agree to such arbitration, but in the absence of such agreement Professor Meade called for various penalties on strikers such as a loss of redundancy payments during a strike, or the payment of social benefits to strikers' families by a trade union.[41] Where an employer granted excessive wage rises, there should be a special tax on the workers' gains to ensure that they remained within the norm.[42]

In the final analysis, it was mass unemployment – which climbed to three million by 1981 – which was to act as the force which restricted the unions' power to bargain with the employers. As in the thirties, a large reserve army of labour served as an excellent weapon with which to frighten a suddenly insecure workforce. The social democrats were, of course, opposed to such a policy, but they were unable to demonstrate how their advocacy of an incomes policy would have any other effect than cutting working-class living standards. The abeyance of wage militancy in the mid-seventies did not curb inflation, as increased wages were not a cause of inflation. As has been argued, the wage is merely a price − the price for labour power − and to argue that rising prices are caused by rising prices is to fall into a tautology. When workers struck for higher wages, it was an attempt to maintain living standards in the face of inflation. It was a result, not a cause.

Just as social democrats called for a continuation of the attempts at income controls, so they saw themselves as continuing the traditions of revisionist foreign policy. Where the Left was becoming committed to calls for a withdrawal from the Common Market and a unilateral renunciation of nuclear weapons, the social democrats remained passionate defenders of the Western Alliance and a more positive approach to Europe. Owen himself, an ex-Foreign Secretary, rejected the pacifist tendencies of a renewed CND as a council of despair in the face of the Soviet military build-up. The CND's call for Britain to take a moral lead in the world by a policy of disarmament was seen as a policy which was absolutely unrealistic, given the ruthless Soviet contempt for weakness and their refusal to heed moral considerations when their power was threatened, as seen in their occupation of Czechoslovakia and Afghanistan.

The social democrats called themselves internationalists to distance themselves from the insularity of the Left. This was a little unfair, however, as their internationalism was defined in highly conservative terms of support for NATO and the Common Market. In this sense, the old imperialists before the Great War could be seen as internationalists because they supported the *Entente* with France and Tsarist Russia. In fact, they shared with others on the Labour Right the *realpolitik* approach to foreign affairs put forward by Bevin and Healey. The difference between social democrats and the rest of the Labour Right − the bulk of which, around Denis Healey and Roy Hattersley, remained committed to traditional revisionism − lay in domestic, not foreign, policy.

The upshot of these differences was a final break with the Labour Party. A Social Democratic Alliance had been founded in 1975, but its McCarthy-type accusations against the Left limited its effectiveness, and it was finally proscribed for preparing to stand candidates against official Labour candidates. However, the inexorable advance of the Left in the constituencies, threatening to unseat moderate MPs, led the Right to organise more seriously — in the Manifesto Group of MPs and the Campaign for Labour Victory in the constituencies, both formed in 1977. The return of Roy Jenkins to the political fray, together with a series of Labour conferences in 1980-1 which made far-reaching constitutional changes to the party and severely weakened the Right, finally led to the decision to quit. In March 1981 the Social Democrat Party (SDP) was launched by Jenkins, Williams, Owen and William Rogers in a flurry of media publicity. In alliance with the Liberals, they were to pose a major electoral threat to Labour.

Social Democracy and Revisionism

Social Democracy grew out of the revisionist movement of the fifties in terms of ideology and even personnel. Shirley Williams, William Rogers and Dick Taverne were prominent figures in the Campaign for Democratic Socialism, a Gaitskellite group launched to fight unilateralism in the early sixties, while Roy Jenkins had been prominent in the revisionist cause since the *New Fabian Essays*. However, the claims of the Social Democrats to be a radical party of renewal disguised the fact that their ideas were a fundamentally conservative restriction of the early revisionist ideas.

The commitment of the revisionists to welfare and equality had been an attempt to rescue the Labour Party's radical impulse from what they regarded as the dead hand of semi-Marxist ideas. The commitment had always been dependent on high economic growth and general prosperity — in the belief that capitalism had basically solved its major problems — but the long period of almost uninterrupted boom in the fifties had seemed to be manifest proof that a new technique had been found which could guarantee precisely the growth rates required.

However, the history of Britain since the beginning of the sixties has been one of consistent failure to achieve economic growth. It has not been a failure which could be ascribed to any one party, as both Labour and Conservative governments have shared in the failure. It has not been a failure of political or social institutions — as Mackintosh argued, the parliamentary system has always been particularly sensitive to the needs of industry, while the corporatist nature of politics since the forties thrived during the post-war boom. The causes of economic decline must be located in the economy. There has been a failure of Keynesian economics – the old techniques have ceased to work for more than a limited period, as the new conditions of 'stagflation' and then 'slumpflation' made a mockery of the economic experts who had believed that capitalism had found a means of overcoming its problems. Keynes had called for an expansionary policy to overcome mass unemployment and falling prices, but such a policy was grossly inappropriate at a time when prices were constantly in danger of rising to alarming levels. Capitalism had found itself unable any longer to offset crises, and the revisionists were powerless to solve or even understand them.

The Social Democrats were the heirs of this failure of Keynesian economics. Unable to find new prescriptions for economic prosperity, they called for the community to adapt to an era of much lower economic growth than the revisionists had once expected. They were not *against* growth, which they recognised as essential to any social progress, but they accepted the need for *lower* growth. As a result, the radicalism of the revisionists, who wanted to attack the bastions of social privilege and caste snobbery, was muted. The old concerns with welfare and equality were shifted away from the foreground of Social Democratic thought to be replaced by new concerns with decentralisaation and ecology. The old demands for equality were replaced by new demands for freedom, and the old belief in economic growth led by large and socially responsible corporations had been replaced by the new belief that 'small is beautiful'.

However, it was Tony Crosland himself who had pointed out the upper- and middle-class bias of these demands. As he wrote about the new ecologists in the early seventies,

> They are highly selective in their concern, being militant mainly about threats to rural peace and wildlife and well-loved beauty spots; they are little concerned with the far more desperate problem of the urban environment in which 80% of our citizens live .[43]

The working class has lived in ecologically unhealthy and crowded conditions since its birth, but the new concerns for ecology have arisen only as the middle class have been threatened with the pollution and urban crowding that they have always expected others to accept peacefully. The new-found belief in lower economic growth and ecology is a mark of the Social Democratic appeal to a comfortable middle-class constituency which has rarely demonstrated any concern for the problems and aspirations of the labour movement.

It is in their calls for freedom that the conservative nature of the Social Democrats is revealed most starkly. In harking back to the decentralist traditions of G.D.H. Cole and William Morris, they were throwing a veil over the class nature of those traditions. Both Cole and Morris were aware that freedom could not be divorced from the social conditions in which people acted towards one another. In a society where the majority of the population were forced to sell their labour power to others in order to live, it was a travesty of ideas to talk of individual freedom without talking of *social* freedom. This was why Cole, in his activist days as a guild socialist, called for a militant pursuit of the class war by the labour movement. It was not because he believed class war to be a commendable state of affairs, but because class struggle was a *normal* condition of a capitalist society. If labour refused to fight this struggle, they woud be defeated by capital and *social* freedom would be pushed aside as a viable alternative. William Morris saw Parliament as a representative institution of the enemy of the working class, and warned that the propertied classes would kill to preserve their privileges. Both Morris and the young Cole were passionate believers in a pluralist and libertarian socialism, but it was hardly the same sort of socialism as that of the Social Democrats.

In contrast, the Social Democratic calls for freedom have been expressed in the conservative calls for more small business firms and voluntary social work. To David Owen, who became the SDP leader after the 1983 election, the market sector has become *too* socially responsible in its attitudes to dismissals and wage bargaining, and has prevented the mixed economy from working as a result. His response that the market should be freed from the fetters of state control is an indication of the conservative retreat from the revisionist values of social equality and welfare. It was an almost inevitable result of the divorce of freedom from its social context of a class-divided society. As Harold Laski once put it,

> Less government only means more liberty in a society about the foundations of which men are agreed and in which adequate economic security is general; in a society where there is grave divergence of view about these foundations, and where there is the economic insecurity exemplified by mass unemployment, it means liberty only for those who control the sources of economic power.[44]

Notes

1. See Roy Jenkins and Douglas Jay, *The Common Market Debate*, Fabian Tract 341, 1962.

2. Quoted in Paul Foot, *The Politics of Harold Wilson* (Penguin Books, 1968), p. 127.

3. Harold Wilson, *The New Britain: Labour's Plan* (Penguin Books, 1964), p. 9.

4. Labour Party *Annual Conference Report* 1963, p. 140.

5. Harold Wilson, *Purpose in Politics: Selected Speeches* (Weidenfeld and Nicholson, 1964), p. ix.

6. Thomas Balogh, 'The Drift Towards Planning', in Perry Anderson ed., *Towards Socialism* (Fontana, 1967), p. 76.

7. Ibid., p. 64-5.

8. Thomas Balogh, *Unequal Partners, Volume I: The Theoretical Framework* (Basil Blackwell, Oxford, 1963), p. xi-xii.

9. Thomas Balogh, *Planning for Progress*, Fabian Tract 346, 1963, p. 15.

10. Ibid., p. 5.

11. For estimations of the failure of the Government, see W. Beckerman ed., *Labour's Economic Record 1964-70* (Duckworth, London, 1972); D. Howell, *British Social Democracy* (Croom Helm, London, 1976), chapter 9; D. Coates, *The Labour Party and the Struggle for Socialism* (Cambridge University Press, 1973), chapter 5.

12. For the horror felt by Jenkins for Callaghan's illiberalism at the Home Office, see John Campbell, *Roy Jenkins: A Biography* (Weidenfeld and Nicholson, 1983), p. 127.

13. Hansard, Parliamentary Debates 1967-8, vol. 759, col. 1591.

14. On this point, see the conflicting claims in P. Townsend and N.Bosanquet, *Labour and Inequality* (Fabian Society, 1972).

15. Labour Party *Annual Conference Report* 1968, p. 138.

16. See Harold Wilson, *The Labour Government 1964-70: A Personal Record* (Weidenfeld and Nicholson, 1971), especially pp. 34-8, 236.

17. Tony Crosland, *Socialism Now and Other Essays* (Jonathan Cape, 1974), p. 24.

18. Ibid., p. 34.

19. Ibid., p. 44.

20. Roy Jenkins, *What Matters Now* (Fontana, 1972), p. 14.

21. Dick Taverne, *The Future of Labour* (Jonathan Cape, 1974), p. 147.

22. John Mackintosh, 'Britain's Malaise: Political or Economic?', May 1978, in David Marquand ed., *John P. Mackintosh on Parliament and Social Democracy* (Longman, 1982), p. 203.

23. John Mackintosh, 'Taming the Barons', December 1974, in Marquand, p. 115.

24. John Mackintosh, 'Anybody Still for Democracy?', November 1972, in Marquand, p. 112.

25. John Mackintosh, 'Socialism or Social Democracy?' Oct.-Dec. 1972, in Marquand, p. 167.

26. Roy Jenkins, 'Home Thoughts from Abroad: The 1979 Dimbleby Lecture', in Wayland Kennett ed., *The Rebirth of Britain* (Weidenfeld and Nicholson, 1982), p. 14.

27. Ibid., p. 21.

28. Ibid., p. 23.

29. Shirley Williams, *Politics is for People* (Allen Lane, 1981), p. 33-4.

30. Ibid., p. 45.

31. Ibid., p. 23.

32. Shirley Williams, *Freedom and Order in a Liberal Society* (Liverpool University, 1973), p. 6.

33. Shirley Williams, *Politics is for People*, p. 150-1.

34. Ibid., p. 118.

35. David Owen, *Face the Future* (Jonathan Cape, 1981), p. 55.

36. Ibid., p. 5.

37. Ibid., p. 295.

38. Ibid., p. 44.

39. Ibid., p. 147.

40. J.E. Meade, *Principles of Political Economy Volume 3: The Controlled Economy* (George Allen and Unwin, 1971), p. 374.

41. See J.E. Meade, *The Intelligent Radical's Guide to Economic Policy: The Mixed Economy* (George Allen and Unwin, 1975).

42. See J.E. Meade, 'The Restoration of Full Employment', in Kennett ed., *The Rebirth of Britain*, p. 184-5.

43. Tony Crosland, *Socialism Now*, p. 78.

44. Harold Laski, *Reflections on the Revolution of Our Time* (G. Allen and Unwin, 1943), p. 12.

PART FIVE

THE CHALLENGE OF THE LEFT

The reaction against corporate socialism on the Right of the Labour Party was not at first echoed on the party's Left. Indeed, the Bevanite Left of the 1950s remained in many ways trapped in the role of guardian of an ideology which was no longer inspiring and looked increasingly like a conservative support of the *status quo*. At a time of increasing prosperity, the Bevanites remained committed to a cloth cap image of the manual working class symbolised by their leader, the ex-miner Aneurin Bevan. At a time of Cold War, they advocated a foreign policy which smacked to many of neutralism. At a time when it was becoming clear that nationalisation was not bringing in the New Jerusalem, they remained committed to an extension of public ownership on the same corporatist lines.

It was in reaction to this that the New Left began to gather strength after the twin shocks of Suez and Hungary in 1956. Disillusioned with Stalinism and uninspired by Bevanism, they heralded an intellectual renaissance for the Left in Britain in their stress on the need for a democratic culture and a more radical conception of politics than that held by the Labour Party. They appeared to be part of a popular radical movement as tens of thouands mobilised around the issues of unilateral nuclear disarmament and then the Vietnam war, and the failures of the 1964-70 Labour government led many on the New Left into a romantic revolutionism which rejected the Labour Party with contempt.

However, the impact of New Left thinking on the Labour Left, especially through groups such as the Institute of Workers Control, was to lead to a break with corporate socialism. Gradually at first, under Michael Foot in the late 1960s, and then more radically under Tony Benn in the 1970s, the Labour Left was revitalised by an absorption of New Left ideas on radical democracy which was eventually to lead them to their greatest victories within the party. Their greatest success came at the 1981 special conference when the independence of the parliamentary party from the party in the country – an independence which Gaitskell and Wilson had used to thwart previous conference victories by the Left — was finally curbed.

The break with corporate socialism had its limits, however. The increasing failure of the mixed economy — a failure which led to a victory of the Thatcher, pro-market wing inside the Conservative party — did not lead to a break with Keynesian economics among the Labour Left. The need for reappraisal was recognised, but the Left's commitment to the expansion of demand in the economy remained unshaken. The failure of the Labour government of 1974-79 to implement the expansionist proposals of its manifesto was seen as a failure of will, while the economic constraints of a simultaneous rise in inflation and unemployment — conditions which Keynesian economics was not equipped to face — were underestimated. The Marxist wing of the Left saw the alternative economic strategy as a transitional programme to a socialised economy (as the ILP Marxists of the 1920s approached *Socialism in Our Time*), but the bulk of the Left remained wedded to an expansion of public ownership *within* a mixed economy.

12 THE BEVANITE LEFT

The entry of Labour into the coalition goverment in 1940 shattered the major assumptions built up by the Labour Left in the previous decade. The Left had never really disagreed with the leadership on the nature of corporate socialism (with the exception of industrial democracy), but had argued that Labour should not underestimate the resistance of the ruling class to any government trying to put corporate socialism into practice. They had called for an uncompromising resistance to the National government and the preparation of emergency measures, in the likelihood that capitalists would take every advantage of delay.

Suddenly, the emergency of war had ranged Labour on the side of the ruling class so deeply distrusted by the Left, while the new coalition government was forced by military disaster to organise the nation on lines very similar to those elaborated by the party in the thirties. The very ruling class which was supposed to be drifting towards Fascism had now militarised the whole nation, capital and labour, in a struggle to the death with Fascism. The ruling class which was supposed to be contemplating the destruction of the labour movement had welcomed Labour as equal partners in the coalition and, as the war progressed, was drawing up reconstruction plans of its own which would involve major benefits in health, education and employment for the working class.

Harold Laski, because of the clarity of his semi-Marxist analysis, was most aware that reality was making that analysis redundant. In his *Reflections on the Revolution of Our Time* (1943) he was forced to come to grips with the fact that the ruling class was not playing the pro-Fascist role which he had initially envisaged for them. He held that it was the fact of war which had transformed the situation, awaking the dormant nationalism of Britain's rulers as they realised that German victory meant economic ruin as well as national enslavement for them. To Laski,

> In the summer and autumn of 1940 there was something that is not difficult to describe as a regeneration of British democracy. The character of the struggle was defined in terms which made the identities between citizens a hundred times more vital than the differences which had divided them.[1]

Laski had not totally given up his previous distrust of the ruling class, however. While capitalists and workers were united against the Fascist threat, their inherent conflicts of interest had not been resolved. Capitalism and democracy were ultimately inconsistent, as had been demonstrated in the thirties when Hitler had been financed by German monopolists as the strongest opponent of the workers' movement. It was true that Fascism had developed into a despotism which was nearly as harmful to capital as it was to labour, but Laski argued that fear could drive the British ruling class to turn to Fascist solutions when the end of the war had removed their need to rely on working-class support. If reason could prevail then there would be no cause for concern, but Laski was apprehensive at the possibility that fear for their privileges would still lead Britain's rulers to contemplate the suspension of parliamentary democracy.

It was this suspicion of Conservative promises of social reform after the war that led Aneurin Bevan to launch major verbal attacks on the Labour leaders whenever they appeared to subordinate the interests of the working class to those of coalition unity. In *Why Not Trust the Tories?* (1944), Bevan pointed to the betrayal of Lloyd George's pledge of 'a home fit for heroes' after 1918, and warned workers that they were about to be duped once more. He held that, because the Conservatives existed to protect the property and privileges of the rich,

> honest politics and Tory politics are contradictions in terms. Lying is a necessary part of a Tory's political equipment, for it is essential for him to conceal his real intentions from the people. This is partly the reason for his success in keeping power.[2]

Bevan's belief that the ruling class had not changed its spots, and was preparing to resist a socialist government by fair means or foul, impelled him to furiously attack the Labour leaders whenever they contemplated a continuation of the coalition after the war.

In fact, the 1945 Labour government finally laid to rest the fears of the Labour Left. The natural leaders of the Left, Cripps and Bevan, were taken into the Cabinet, the former to impose a policy of austerity on the working class as Chancellor of the Exchequer, while the latter won the hearts of the Left by instituting a free national health service. A programme of nationalisation, planning and welfare was put into practice with a minimum of overt resistance on the part of the capitalists. The point was rubbed in by Hugh Dalton, who wrote,

Once, in some Left Book Club circles, I had listened to the tedious theory that the capitalists would resist, if necessary by force, a Socialist Government which tried to nationalise the Bank of England . . . Impatiently, I had replied: 'Make me Chancellor of the Exchequer and give me a good Labour majority in Parliament, and I will undertake to nationalise the Bank of England over a dinner party'. And now no dinner party had been necessary; only tea for two .[3]

Keep Left

With a Labour government actually carrying through its measures of corporate socialism, the Left after 1945 was a much tamer echo of the ILP Left which had harried Ramsay Macdonald. It was usually unorganised and, apart from foreign affairs, found itself in fundamental agreement with the Government. The main organised opposition on the left coalesced around a critical amendment to the Address by 53 MPs in November 1946. A number of these produced *Keep Left*, a manifesto written mainly by three left-wing MPs, Michael Foot, Richard Crossman, and Ian Mikardo, in April 1947. This was an early formulation of what came to be called Bevanite policy.

In domestic affairs, this *Keep Left* group acknowledged the achievements of the government, calling only for a much greater sense of urgency in the socialist measures already begun. To these left-wing backbenchers, 'present difficulties are not the result of socialist planning; they are the result of not enough boldness and urgency, and too much tenderness for vested interests. You can't make socialist omelettes without breaking capitalist eggs'.[4] What was needed included an effective incomes policy in the form of differential real wages, in which taxation would favour the incomes of workers essential to the export drive. Such a policy would, of course, be linked to a national profits policy in which taxation would be lighter on those firms seen as essential to the national interest. In addition, the group proposed a negative direction of labour, by which they meant the prevention of inessential firms from increasing their workforce without a licence. In general terms, their domestic proposals amounted to a much tighter control over capital and labour by the State rather than the all-out assault on the citadels of capitalism called for by the Socialist League thirteen years earlier.

It was in their attitude to foreign policy that the Keep Left group emerged as both distinct and portentous. They denounced the anti-Soviet policy of collective security being pursued by Ernest Bevin as a counsel of despair, assuming an unbridgeable gulf between the Soviet Union and the West which was in danger of becoming a self-fulfilling prophecy. They argued that while Russia was a totalitarian police state, it could not be seen in the same light as the expansionist Fascist powers, as the Russians had no economic motives for aggression such as the relief of unemployment. Moreover, the anti-Soviet policy pursued by Britain and the United States was merely fanning Soviet suspicion of Western motives. The *Keep Left* authors called on the government to remember that Communist Russia had suffered enormously as a result of Western invasions in the Wars of Intervention which followed the Bolshevik Revolution, and in the recent war. The current state of Cold War could only deepen the suspicions harboured by the Soviet leaders and prepare the way for a new world war.

As an alternative, the *Keep Left* group called for a third way, distinct from both Soviet Communism and American capitalism. This would be a socialist foreign policy which would establish a moral leadership for Britain in the new world of power politics, a leadership which would soothe antagonisms and ensure that the world would not have to endure another and more terrible war.

> The task of British Socialism must be, wherever possible, to save the smaller nations from this futile ideological warfare and to heal the breach between the USA and the USSR. But we cannot do this if we ourselves have taken sides either in a Communist bloc or in an anti Bolshevik axis.[5]

Instead of turning to either of the great powers, the *Keep Left* authors argued that Britain should look to Europe instead (though, ironically, they were to be the most virulent opponents of the Common Market at a future date). They called for an Anglo-French alliance to be used as a basis for a European security pact powerful enough to be independent of Soviet-American rivalries. In this way, Britain would again be a distinctive voice in the world.

In looking at the moral lead which could be given in world affairs, the *Keep Left* group showed themselves more aware of the military aspects of imperialism than its economic roots. For example, they argued that 'the oil of the Middle East is a legitimate British interest. But a large British army in the Middle East does not in the long run make our oil supplies any safer or ward off the Communist menace'.[6]

Consequently, they called for the withdrawal of British troops as their presence stirred major feelings of resentment which could prove fertile ground for Communism. The sincerity of Britain's socialist intentions demonstrated by such a withdrawal was seen as the best defence of Britain's oil reserves — rather than a recognition that the oil did not actually belong to Britain.

This belief of the Left in a more humane Empire was even more manifest in the case of Africa, where the *Keep Left* authors called for more schemes of capital investment by the colonial power rather than political independence for the colonies. To the post-war Labour Left,

> We have the opportunity in Africa to make good the ravages of a hundred years of Western imperiaism and exploitation. By developing the vast resources of manpower and material and by raising the standard of living, we shall do a great deal more to confront Communism than we shall achieve by an attempt to hold the Empire by force.[7]

It seemed to be the military consequences of imperialism, rather than imperialism itself, which was at fault.

The success of Labour in the forties had thus taken its toll of the Left's distinctive analysis. The class basis of its ideas in the thirties had in the main disappeared from view, as the calls for emergency measures to quickly strangle ruling class power were succeeded by demands for tighter state controls and direction on capital and labour, while the demand for a Popular Front with the Communists was replaced by pleas for a moral combat against Communism.

Morever, the distinctive demands for workers control were diluted or dropped in these years. The *Keep Left* authors saw the issue in terms of increased efficiency rather than class power, arguing that 'industrial democracy is not so much a matter of machinery as of attitude',[8] and seeing an extension of joint consultation committees between capital and labour as an excellent supplement to the higher levels of discussions between the TUC and the employers. Harold Laski recognised the problem of bureaucratic management in the public sector as a major source of inefficiency. He wrote, 'It is disturbing that we have not yet found the proper forms through which to associate the trade unions with the management of a nationalised industry in a way that makes their relation democratically effective'.[9] However, he rejected workers management in terms of efficiency, arguing as an alternative the education and training of workers in citizenship and skills. Stafford Cripps, one-time doyen of the Left, said in one speech in October, 1946,

> From my experience there is not as yet a very large body of workers
> in Britain capable of taking over large enterprises ... until there has
> been more experience of the managerial side of industry, I think it
> would be almost impossible to have worker-controlled industry in
> Britain, even if it were on the whole desirable.[10]

Finally, the liquidation of non-Stalinist parties in Eastern Europe in
1947-8 led to a retreat on the only distinctive ideas remaining on the
Left — the moral third way. The Left's main weekly, *Tribune*, founded
to support the United Front, now supported the ban on Communists
holding positions in the Transport Workers Union. The formation of
the anti-Soviet military alliance NATO in 1949, led to a split in the
Keep Left group. While Ian Mikardo continued to argue for a neutralist
policy, Michael Foot now accepted that the democratic way of life made
a British alliance with the United States inevitable. To Foot,

> the choice was not the result of some similar plot or some betrayal of
> Socialism contrived by Ernest Bevin. It was the inexorable conse-
> quence of the combined Soviet challenge to the British Common-
> wealth, American capitalism and democratic Socialism.[11]

The publication of *Keeping Left* in January 1950 was a mark of this
shift in left-wing thinking.

In his posthumous book, *The Dilemma of Our Times* (1952), Harold
Laski was left to bemoan the disappearance of any radical alternative
to the Soviet-American conflict, and facilely blamed the whole post-war
tension on Churchill's anti-Communist intransigence.

It was the resignation of Aneurin Bevan from the Government in
April 1951 that broke the torpor which had settled over radical thinking in the party.

Bevan

Aneurin Bevan (1897-1960) was born into a South Wales miners'
family, and his ideas bore the imprint of his working-class background
throughout his life. He became a miner at 14, and was steeled in the
militant class conflict of the years before and after the Great War. He
imbibed the syndicalist doctrine of James Connolly and Noah Abblett,

combining them with membership of the Labour Party, and learned an abiding hatred of the capitalists through his experience of the ruthlessness of the mine-owners. The defeat of the 1926 General Strike convinced him that trade unionism as such had no chance of success. The absurdity of the notion that political victory could be attained simply by making industry idle was obvious at a time of mass unemployment, when most workers were idle anyway.

Instead, Bevan turned his attention to Westminster as the seat of real power. His election to Parliament in May 1929 opened a tumultuous career in which he was a thorn in the side of the Labour leadership as much as he was against the Conservatives. He was a born rebel, signing the Mosley manifesto, supporting the Popular Front, and attacking the Labour leaders in the coalition government during the war. However, he remembered the fate of political isolation reserved for the ILP or the Communists, and refused to break his links with the Labour Party no matter what the provocation. He was expelled from the party in January 1939 for his open support of Cripps and the Popular Front, but he rejoined before the year was out (unlike Cripps, who maintained a steadfast independence from Labour for six years after his expulsion). His 'loyal dissidence' and his ability led to his appointment as Minister of Health in 1945, and he cleverly manoeuvred the British Medical Association into accepting a free National Health Service. When that service was cut in order to meet the rising cost of armaments, he resigned in protest from the government together with Harold Wilson and John Freeman. In doing so, he revived the Left as a major source of fractious discontent against the leaders, stamping on it his style and ideas.

Those ideas were basically a restatement of Labour Marxism, but presented in a manner appealing to the emotions of labourism. Bevan's own working-class background made him the epitome of the proletarian base and purpose of the Party, and his attacks on Hugh Gaitskell as a 'dessicated calculating machine' and on the Conservatives as 'vermin' were designed to point out the middle-class nature of the opposition to Bevanism. Against these intellectuals, isolated by background and social life from the interests and feelings of the labour movement, Bevan wished to recapture the socialist strain in the working class from which he had sprung. He believed that

It is among the solid artisan classes that you will find the the most tolerance and the least bellicosity. Their attitude corresponds most closely with democratic socialism. Their lives are rounded by the consciousness of acquired skills and by the rhythm of daily labour.[12]

It was, perhaps, a romantic view akin to Tolstoy's belief in the nobility of labour, but its appeal was undoubted and was authenticated by Bevan's own experience.

This emotional labourism underlay Bevan's restatement of Labour Marxism. He argued that the two major social forces in British politics were private property and poverty, and that the mediating factor in their struggle was democracy. Private property, the foundation of the competitive society, had been the force which had transformed society into a modern industrial economy, but it had failed to provide either security or moral values for the individual. Its credo was too grossly materialistic and its social climate too much based on the fear of failure for it to produce anything but misery and poverty. The size of the bank balance was its highest value, while its momentum broke up families and perverted the natural sense of compassion and comradeship in people.

Poverty – the awareness of unnecessary deprivation – stood opposed to property. It was this awareness which led to a growing discontent with private wealth and the class which had monopolised that wealth. To fight that class and defend itself the working class, who were aware of poverty, had created the Labour Party and looked to it for a transformation of society in its own interests. It was their only real alternative, as the individual strivings of personal ambition characteristic of the middle class were absurd to those who worked in the steel mills, foundries and mines. The question of how to rise in the social hierarchy was certainly present, but 'the texture of our lives shaped the question into a class and not into an individual form'.[13] The social conflict between property and poverty was thus, for Bevan, the compelling question facing British politics.

Parliament was the arena in which that conflict was being fought, as Bevan held that democracy was the third force which mediated between the other two. Parliament had, of course, existed long before democracy, functioning as an assembly where the ruling class had resolved their differences without resort to armed force. It was only in 1928, the year before Bevan's own election to Westminster, that democracy had really arrived in the form of a universal franchise for men and women. With the weapon of the ballot-box, Bevan held that the working class had stepped onto the public stage of history. However, they had chosen to give their democratic backing to the propertied class; the Churchills and the Cecils continued to rule the country as they had done before democracy because 'the people have not clothed the bones of political democracy with the flesh of economic power'.[14] As a result, Parliament was a passive assembly which acted as the servant of social privilege and private property.

This was a major danger to democracy, as the failure to meet public grievances would discredit Parliament itself. Acting as the apologist for the miseries inflicted by capitalism, Parliament had responsibility but no power; monopolising the disposal of the economic surplus and thereby disfranchising the people from the outset on the use of that surplus, property exercised power while free from all responsibility. In such circumstances,

> democratic parliaments under private property, under capitalism, are the professional public mourners for private economic crimes. So long as parliaments divest themselves of economic power, then democratic institutions are bound to be always the whipping-boys for private enterprise.[15]

It was Parliament itself which would suffer from the selfish pursuit of private profit at the expense of the social good by the tiny class which controlled the commanding heights of the economy.

Against this threat, Bevan called on Labour to turn Parliament — 'a sword pointed at the heart of property-power'[16] — into an active assembly fighting the class struggle on the part of the labour movement. Wealth used parliamentary democracy to persuade poverty to use its political freedom to maintain the rule of wealth; the task of Labour was to use the same weapon to expose the social privilege and selfish immorality of wealth to the attack of the people. Bevan called on his party to fight against the sense of parliamentary tradition which in countless ways impressed upon Members the customs and procedures of those who had ruled Britain for hundreds of years. They must remember that Labour's ancestors had tended sheep or ploughed the land, shut out from the colourful pageantry and glory of English history, enduring poverty and short lives uncomforted by recognition or leisure. The time had now come when the common people would make their voice heard, and the time must not be wasted. 'The issue therefore in a capitalist democracy resolves itself into this; either poverty will use democracy to win the struggle against property, or property, in fear of poverty, will destroy democracy'.[17]

Bevan's hostility to capitalists, couched though it was in Marxist terms, did not lead him to the perspective of a Communist society. He accepted the mixed economy as a permanent feature of British society, rejecting Communism as a utopian dream whose unrealistic nature should be rejected as incompatible with any constitutional political party seeking power. Thus, he argued that

> the victory of socialism need not be universal to be decisive. I have no patience with those socialists, so called, who in practice would socialise nothing, whilst in theory they threaten the whole of private poeprty. They are purists and therefore barren. It is neither prudent, nor does it accord with our conception of the future, that all forms of private property should live under perpetual threat.[18]

This belief in the mixed economy was in perfect accord with the main traditions of the Labour Party's political thought. It was one of the characteristics which excluded a full-blooded Marxism from ever being accepted, and its belief was one of the unifying factors between Right and Left in the party.

The revisionists were indeed to seize such statements to demonstrate that the whole party agreed in its heart of hearts on the need to reject wholesale nationalisation measures, but in doing so they overlooked a fundamental difference separating Bevan from them. Bevan was interested in *power* for the labour movement, and always saw power as the main instrument which could secure welfare and equality. He supported private ownership in a mixed economy, but was always aware that the planned sector must be the dominant sector. At the 1959 Conference, Bevan distanced himself from the revisionists in arguing that

> if we managed to get a majority in Great Britain by the clever exploitation of contemporary psychology, and we did not get the commanding heights of the economy in our power, then we did not get the priorities right. The argument is about power and only about power, because only by the possession of power can you get the priorities correct.[19]

Where the revisionists believed that the old arguments about capitalism were outdated, Bevan held that the domination of the economy by capitalists or by the State was still the crucial element determining all other socialist aims.

He thus firmly upheld the difference between corporate socialism and the Keynesian challenge to state ownership. In the debate on the

1944 Employment White Paper, Bevan had rejected the Keynesian neutrality towards public ownership expressed in the coalition government's proposals. In holding that full employment could be achieved in either a market or a planned economy, Bevan held that Keynesian economics was denying a fundamental principle of the corporate socialism evolved by Labour —

> This party did not come into existence demanding socialism, demanding the state ownership of property, simply because there was some special merit in it. This party believes in the public ownership of industry because we think that only in that way can society be intelligently and progressively organised. If private enterprise can deliver all these goods, there will not be any argument for socialism and no reason for it.[20]

In rejecting the Keynesian challenge to nationalisation, he was at one with Labour Keynesians as different as Durbin and Cole. Bevan did hold, with Keynes, that ineffective demand was the key to overcoming the economic crisis[21] (he had been one of the signatories of the Mosley Manifesto as early as 1930), but he was much closer to Hobson in his belief that this was due to the privileges of the capitalists and the underconsumption of the working class. The nationalisation of industry was thus infinitely superior as a method of control than the indirect fiscal policies advocated by Keynes. Public ownership reduced the dangers of evasion by private vested interest, and made industry available as an instrument of direct planning of production and consumption. Bevan's roots in syndicalism and labourism thus led him to a different analysis than the revisionists. Where Crosland and Gaitskell saw the inefficiency of the market economy as characteristic of a by-gone capitalism, Bevan saw the social power of private property as the persistent danger of a capitalism which was very much alive.

However, he remained trapped in the confines of corporate socialism. He was not really interested in the demands for direct management by the producers which had been at the centre of syndicalist thinking, and which had found a faint echo in the Socialist League in the thirties. As far as Bevan was concerned, the total weakness of Labour in power had not lain in its strategy, but in the lack of *will* by which that strategy was ineffectively applied. He objected to the corporate boards which ran the nationalised industries on the grounds that they should be fully accountable to Parliament, not to the direct democracy of the working class. He did not see industrial democracy in terms of workers becoming managers, but in terms of a spirit of co-operation between workers and managers. In his view,

> the advance from State ownership to full Socialism is in direct proportion to the extent the workers in the nationalised industry are made aware of a changed relationship between themselves and the management. The persistence of a sense of dualism in a publicly owned industry is evidence of an immature industrial democracy.[22]

Even the old worries of the Left on the constitutional measures necessary to overcome capitalist prosperity found no echo in Bevan's political ideas in the fifties.

He was above all a parliamentary socialist, stressing the importance of Parliament as an agent of social change with all the intensity of a man whose old syndicalist faith in the unions had been shattered by the defeats of the twenties. He was certainly aware of the continuing importance of the unions (as demonstrated by Mark Jenkins)[23] but they were seen in terms of voting power at conferences rather than industrial muscle which would sustain a socialist government against unconstitutional measures. It was Parliament, not the unions, which had become the most formidable weapon of the class struggle for Bevan. It was the ultimate repository of political power, as he once argued in the Commons —

> When I got older I said to myself: 'The place to get to is the Council. That's where the power is'. So I worked very hard and . . . I got on the Council. I discovered when I got there that the power *had* been there, but it had just gone. So I made some enquiries, being an earnest student of social affairs, and I learned that the power had slipped down to the County Council. That was where it was and where it had gone to. So I worked very hard again and I got there and it had gone from there too.[24]

Power always seemed to elude Bevan, near enough to see but never near enough to grasp. When he finally became a Cabinet Minister he proved unable to bring the free welfare state into being for any length of time. Its basis was chipped away almost from its birth, and the health service was always to be one of the first victims of any recession in the capitalist economy from which it was ultimately financed.

For Aneurin Bevan in particular, as his biographer, Michael Foot, has pointed out, 'the belief that a nation's foreign policy must be shaped by domestic necessities, that the two could never be disentangled, was an axiom of politics'.[25] This was true of the thirties when his hostility to the pro-capitalist policies of the government was linked to his support of a popular front against Fascism throughout Europe. It was also true of the fifties, when his concerns for world peace and social progress at home were two sides of the same coin. The difference lay in the degree of his fear of the domestic and foreign threats to the working class. In the thirties, the threats were direct and aggressive; in the fifties they seemed more elusive and difficult to combat effectively. It was no longer the Fascists, with their pledge to crush all traces of Marxism and the workers' movement, but the Soviet Union, professing Marxism and the cause of the liberation of the working class, who stood as the main enemy of the nation. It was the United States, democratic home of capitalism and in the grip of a reactionary 'Red Scare', which presented itself as Britain's ally.

Bevan resolved the dilemma by taking up the demands of the old *Keep Left* group that Britain take a third road which would heal the difference between the major powers by demonstrating the superiority of non-aggressive social reform. To Bevan,

we have allowed the Russian threat to divert us from the one policy that might help to pacify the world. The answer to social upheaval is social amelioration, not bombing planes and guns; yet we are making the latter on such a scale that we have no resources left for the provision of the industrial equipment which the underdeveloped areas of the world must have.[26]

Communism fed on the poverty and discontent of these areas, yet the West was choosing the short-sighted course of a military policy which would lead to more poverty and discontent. The military response to Communism was both superficial and ultimately self-defeating, according to Bevan. The only effective reply to the Soviet Union was a social and economic policy of development and equality, and for this there had to be a re-examination of social attitudes.

With this analysis, Bevan hailed the development of 'non-alignment' championed by Jawaharlal Nehru of India, Josip Tito of Yugoslavia, and Achmed Soekarno of Indonesia. In the third world, societies which had been dormant for centuries were awakening to national independence and an awareness of a new role in the world. This was as true of Communist powers like China (which Bevan acutely perceived as a national power independent of Soviet control) as it was of non-Communist nations. Bevan argued that the West could not take these powers for granted as natural allies. Their history of exploitation and cruelty suffered at the hands of Western imperialism made them naturally wary of Western overtures and more prone to sympathy for the anti-colonial record of Soviet Russia. If the West posed as a militarist force in the world, it would turn nationalism in a Soviet direction. Instead, Bevan called on the West to accommodate the new nations in a general pattern of world co-operation. The proportion spent on arms in Western budgets should be reduced to be replaced by aid in a new plan for world economic development.

Bevan's attitude to armaments has often been misunderstood. His old opposition to giving arms to a bourgeois government in the thirties had been considerably modified by the fifties, though his mistrust of the Tories' intelligence and sincerity was still strong. He maintained that the Soviet military threat must be countered by military force from the West if fear was not to rule world affairs – 'no-one who is not a pacifist or a partisan of the Kremlin woud argue that military strength is not needed'.[27] It was not effective national defence against Communism which was wrong, according to Bevan, but the paranoid fear of Russia which had led to the building of vast war machines far out of proportion to the threat posed. It was not Western rearmament (caused by the Korean War) which was opposed by Bevan, but the *level* of rearmament, threatening as it did social reforms such as a free health service. He made this crystal clear in his 1951 resignation speech,[28] and he underlined it a year later when he wrote,

Against the background of mounting tension, it is idle to talk of general disarmament. People are not, and never have been, prepared to throw their guns away while they feel unsafe . . . This applies as much to atom bombs as to more primitive types.[29]

It should have come as no surprise, then, when he rounded on the advocates of unilateral nuclear disarmament – the bulk of them his ex-supporters – at the 1957 party conference. It was perfectly consistent with his view of politics as *power* rather than a seminar on moral philosophy or a Quaker sermon. Bevan had been consistently opposed to militarism, but he had recognised the reality of nuclear weapons as a new phase of military destructive power which could not be reversed by morality. In this sense, he held the unilateralists to be guilty of an emotional spasm, born of moral self-righteousness and fear, and called for genuine disarmament negotiations. The alternative was to send a British Foreign Secretary, whoever he may be, naked into the conference chamber. Able to preach sermons, of course; he could preach good sermons. But action of that sort is not necessarily the way in which you take the menace of the Bomb from the world.[30]

Such sentiments were not an opportunistic betrayal, nor were they a result of his sympathy for Stalinism;[31] they were a logical consequence of his basic political ideas on pacifism and defence.

In another sense, however, it is one more example of his softened militancy compared with the thirties. At that time, Bevan and the rest of the Left had been aware of the imperialist antagonisms between the major powers, and attempted to draw attention to the class nature of the State which was determining foreign policy. By the fifties, this awareness had virtually disappeared, at least on Bevan's part. He opposed the militarist language and postures of the Cold War, but the belief that Britain and the United States were imperialist powers directed in the interests of their ruling class was now absent, regarded as belonging to a view of the world held by partisans of the Kremlin. In its place, a British Foreign Secretary was conceived as capable of *negotiating* peace between West and East as though the antagonisms dividing them were irrational rather than fundamental. Bevan's old *class* outlook, formed and tempered in his syndicalist days, had become softened by the fifties to one based on reconciliation.

The Crisis of Bevanism

There was something peculiarly inappropriate about Aneurin Bevan's ideas on the struggle between poverty and wealth in the boom conditions of the fifties. The existence of class divisions remained fundamental to British society, but the impression given by Bevan was one of a society frozen in the political and social attitudes of twenty years before. The revisionists seemed to have the edge in theoretical terms as well as in terms of political power during the decade. His Labour Marxism belonged to an earlier age than that of washing machines, televisions and rising living standards.

Moreover, the power of Bevan's own personality appeared to dominate the rest of the Left. The political development of the Bevanites was measured more by personal loyalty to Bevan himself rather than political ideas as seen in the cries of treachery which greeted the reconciliation of Harold Wilson and Richard Crossman to the Labour leadership in 1954-5. There remained a conflicting set of political tendencies on the Left — pacifists and 'fellow-travellers' vied with neutralists in the '57 varieties' of MPs who followed Bevan in the early fifties — and, on the issue of German rearmament, the Bevanite revolt brought out an anti-German xenophobia which was not always welcome. However, Bevan himself was the epitome of the Labour Left and, when he was finally reconciled to Gaitskell's leadership in 1957, the coherence and strength of the Left appeared to be shattered.

Bevan himself had not changed his views on disarmament or public ownership, but the conciliatory tone adopted represented a softening of what seemed essential in Bevanism — its style of revolt. Where Gaitskell highlighted political differences in his assault on Clause IV in 1959, Bevan swallowed his personal anger to argue that nothing fundamental divided the party. He himself made clear his continued Labour Marxist convictions in his only published comment on the issue, when he wrote,

> the controversy is between those who want the mainspring of economic power transferred to the community and those who believe that private enterprise should still remain supreme but that its worst characteristics should be modified by liberal ideas of justice and equality.[32]

The socialist ideas remained the same as those of Keir Hardie, but they were more like the echoes of a man who is reluctant to surrender his youth. He had once said that if private enterprise could provide security there would be no need for public ownership, yet that was precisely what private enterprise appeared to be doing, at least in Britain. Bevan, whose economics was derived from Hobson rather than Marx, was unable to present any convincing analysis of why the disruption involved in social change should be undergone.

Richard Crossman was one of those Bevanites who was aware of the need to develop a new analysis more suited to conditions of prosperity. Crossman (1907-74), after the almost obligatory education at Winchester and Oxford, had been a tutor in political philosophy at Oxford. He was active in the Oxford Labour Party in the late thirties at a time when that party supported a Popular Front candidate in a by-election and, after a period as a Director of Psychological Warfare, had been elected to Parliament in 1945. There he quickly established a reputation as an intellectual who listened to the dictates of his own reasoning process at a level which was too abstract for the more sordid mechanics of the real political world.

As one of the authors of *Keep Left*, Crossman was a natural ally of Bevan on the latter's resignation. Much of his writings in the early fifties was a reflection of the Bevanite Left, but already he was aware of the sterility of merely repeating the old nostrums of Labour Marxism as though nothing had changed since the days of Keir Hardie. In his contribution to *New Fabian Essays* (1952), Crossman had agreed with the revisionists on the need for the Labour Party to regain its sense of direction after its post-war success. The achievement of its programme had placed Labour in danger of becoming the conservative party of the *status quo*, concealing from it the corporatist dangers of the new society. Unlike the revisionists, however, Crossman's critique of corporate socialism concentrated on social and political power. He argued that

the planned economy and the centralisation of power are no longer socialist objectives . . . The main task of socialism today is to prevent the concentration of power in the hands of *either* industrial management *or* the state bureaucracy – in brief to distribute responsibility and so to enlarge freedom of choice.[33]

This belief separated Crossman from the centralist ideas of Bevan and many others on the Left. Crossman was the intellectual in politics, extremely sensitive to the currents of thought which were beginning to emerge on the New Left and determined that Labour should not be frightened by the series of electoral defeats during the fifties into jettisoning its old commitments to public ownership. When Gaitskell sought to eliminate Clause IV after the 1959 defeat, the whole of the Left recognised the importance of the debate for the basic orientation and philosophy of the party. Frank Cousins, the left-wing leader of the Transport Workers Union, argued at the 1959 Conference that 'we have all accepted in the past that, whilst we can have nationalisation without socialism, we cannot have socialism without nationalisation',[34] while Barbara Castle attempted to remind delegates that the old enemy of private enterprise in which 'economic might has become social right and the Devil has taken the communal interest'[35] remained as immoral as ever. However, Crossman went much further in attempting to rethink the old corporatist arguments for public ownership.

He called on the Left to recognise that the old Marxist nostrums were no longer appropriate at a time when Keynesian economic techniques had made unemployment and economic crisis nightmares of a past never to return. However, while Keynes had made the economic case for socialism redundant, the political and moral case had grown stronger than ever. It was Marxism, not the socialism of the Labour party, which had been discredited by economic prosperity. For Crossman,

> Labour's real dynamic has always been a moral protest against social injustice, not an intellectual demonstration that capitalism is bound to collapse; a challenge to capitalist privilege, not a proof that these privileges must inevitably be replaced by a classless society.[36]

In the light of this moral ideal, Crossman was able to argue that while the basic economic problems of capitalism had been solved, a new political problem of an irresponsible oligarchy protected by government had arisen. The vulgarity and wastefulness of capitalism remained as strong as they had ever been, as J.K. Galbraith demonstrated in *The Affluent Society* (1959), but it had been supplemented by the growth of corporatism. In both the private corporations and the nationalised industries, a managerial oligarchy had arisen which was a direct threat to freedom and democracy. This was particularly damaging in the nationalised industries, where remote centralised Boards outside the sphere of parliamentary investigation or control operated to the detriment of efficiency and the interests of the producers and consumers. These Boards, created according to the Morrisonian ideals of corporate socialism, had become a major bureaucratic burden on the industries of the public sector, discrediting public ownership and socialism itself. The answer to these problems was not, however, the revisionist demand to drop public ownership itself. Nationalisation remained for Crossman the only means by which freedom could be enlarged against the selfish abuses of free competition. Instead, he called on Labour to admit the mistakes of corporate socialism and call for decentralising the power now held by their oligarchies.

Public ownership must be subjected to the control of Parliament and to the workers themselves if it was to remain socialist in motive and operation. Labour must

> seek to make economic power responsive both to the community as a whole (the consumer) and to the worker in any particular industry (the producer). Plans for nationalisation which do not satisfy the aspirations to workers' control are the technocrats' perversion of

our socialist ideal.[37]

In taking up the call for a libertarian socialism based on industrial democracy rather than jettisoning its socialist principles for short-term electoral considerations, Crossman believed that the Labour Party would hold true to its radical traditions, establishing itself as a fighting opposition rather than a mere alternative government.[38]

Crossman himself was in many ways a political dilettante flitting from idea to idea without ever really considering the full practical consequences or committing himself fully to fighting for them. His anti-technocratic ideas were dropped when Wilson became leader as quickly as he continually changed his mind on unilateral disarmament. However, in distancing himself from the rest of the Bevanite Left in an ideological attack on the corporatist nature of public ownership he both heralded and reflected a new movement of ideas, originating outside the sterility of the established parliamentary Left, which was to have a major impact on the Labour Party's political thought.

Notes

1. Harold Laski, *Reflections on the Revolution of Our Time* (George Allen and Unwin, 1943) p. 143.
2. Aneurin Bevan, *Why Not Trust the Tories?* (Victor Gollancz, 1944), p. 25.
3. Hugh Dalton, *The Fateful Years* (Muller, 1957), p. 481.
4. *Keep Left* (New Statesman Pamphlet, 1947), p. 15.
5. Ibid., p. 35.
6. Ibid., p. 43.
7. Ibid., p. 44.
8. Ibid., p. 24. See also Ian Mikardo, 'The Problem of Nationalisation', in *Current Affairs* No. 60 (7 August 1948); and Ian Mikardo, Consultation or Joint Management, 1949.
9. Harold Laski, *Trade Unions in the New Society* (George Allen and Unwin, 1950), p. 156.
10. Quoted in Ken Coates and Anthony Topham, *Industrial Democracy in Great Britain: A Book of Readings and Witnesses for Workers' Control* (Macgibbon and Kee, 1968).
11. Michael Foot, *Tribune*, 20 May 1949. See also Ian Mikardo in the same issue for a counter-argument.
12. Aneurin Bevan, *In Place of Fear* (Heinemann, 1952), p. 169.
13. Ibid., p. 1.
14. Aneurin Bevan, *Why Not Trust the Tories*, p. 83.
15. Aneurin Bevan, *Socialist Values in a Changing Civilisation* (Fabian Tract 282, 1951), p. 7.
16. Aneurin Bevan, *In Place of Fear*, p. 5.
17. Ibid., p. 3.
18. Ibid., p. 118.
19. Labour Party *Annual Conference Report* 1959, p. 153.

20. *Hansard, Parliamentary Debates 1943-4*, vol. 401, col. 527.

21. See, for example, Aneurin Bevan, *Why Not Trust the Tories?*, p. 61.

22. Aneurin Bevan, *In Place of Fear*, p. 103.

23. See Mark Jenkins, *Bevanism: Labour's High Tide* (Spokesman Books, 1979).

24. *Hansard, Parliamentary Debates 1943-4*, vol. 395, col. 1617.

25. Michael Foot, *Aneurin Bevan Volume I 1897-1945*, p. 197.

26. Aneurin Bevan, *In Place of Fear*, p. 135.

27. Aneurin Bevan, Harold Wilson, John Freeman, 'Foreword' to *One Way Only* (Tribune Pamphlet, 1951), p. 9.

28. See *Hansard, Paliamentary Debates 1950-1*, vol. 487, col. 37.

29. Aneurin Bevan, *In Place of Fear*, p. 143.

30. Labour Party *Annual Conference Report* 1957, p. 181.

31. For the betrayal thesis, see Leslie Hunter, *The Road to Brighton Pier* (Arthur Barker, London, 1959); for the argument that Bevan was too partial to Stalinism, see Mark Jenkins, *Bevanism*, p. 248; Michael Foot's *Aneurin Bevan Volume 2 1945-60*: (Granada edition, 1975), p. 425-6 points out Bevan's consistency.

32. Quoted in Michael Foot, *Aneurin Bevan Volume 2*, p. 647.

33. Richard Crossman, 'Towards a Philosophy of Soialism', in *New Fabian Essays*, p. 27.

34. Labour Party *Annual Conference Report* 1959, p. 131.

35. Ibid., p. 85.

36. Richard Crossman, 'Planning for Freedom', in Richard Crossman, *Planning for Freedom* (Hamish Hamilton, 1965), p. 62-3.

37. Ibid., p. 73.

38. See Richard Crossman 'The Affluent Society' (1959), in his *Planning for Freedom*, where he develops the argument that 'the prime function of the Labour Party, as of the Liberal Party before it, is to provide an ideology for nonconformist critics of the Establishment' (p. 91), even at the cost of semi-permanent opposition.

13 THE CHALLENGE OF THE NEW LEFT

As the Bevanites attempted to defend the ideas of the thirties against the revisionist onslaught, a new movement was emerging, well to the Left of the Labour Party. The rumblings of revolt in Eastern Europe had finally erupted in Hungary in 1956, leading to a major crisis in the British Communist Party as intellectuals and workers suddenly broke from Stalinist orthodoxy.

Since the demise of syndicalism, the Communist Party had virtually monopolised political activity on Labour's Left. After early attempts at independence from Soviet control in the twenties, the Communists had been frozen in the grip of Stalinism, concerned with the defence of the Soviet Union, the workers' homeland, rather than with the furtherance of international revolution. In so far as they represented a country in which the working class had seized power, the Communists could always depend on an emotional reservoir of sympathy and support on the Labour Left. This was particularly the case when Russia was seen as the main bulwark against Fascism, as in the days of the Popular Front, or when the gigantic Soviet war effort against Hitler presented a spectacle of heroism and sacrifice. Moreover, the party was a home for frustrated Marxist intellectuals and for workers who felt the need for a more radical break with capitalism than that made by the Labour Left.

In 1956, the changes in the Soviet bloc following the death of Stalin shook British Marxism out of the torpor which had allowed Bevanism and Stalinism to be the only viable alternatives for the left. The denunciation of Stalin's crimes by the Soviet leader, Khruschev, at the Twentieth Congress of the Soviet Communist Party led to a major crisis of conscience throughout Western Communism. The culmination of East European reform movements in the Hungarian Revolution in November, 1956 — when workers set up independent workers' councils[1] and were crushed by Soviet tanks — led to a major exodus of intellectuals and workers from the ranks of British Communism. The Soviet Union was no longer the lodestar of revolution and many, such as Les Cannon and Frank Chapple, rejected Marxism altogether.

However, the British military attack on Suez in November 1956 seemed to many others proof that imperialism had not changed its spots. The evident degeneration of the Soviet Union did not make capitalism any better as a social system, nor did it invalidate the insights of Marxism into class power or the superiority of socialism. The Labour Left did not offer an attractive alternative for these Marxists, particularly as Bevan himself was absorbed into the Labour leadership. They looked for a different cause, more relevant to the new age of Cold War and growing consumer affluence than the alternatives then on offer. Many turned to the Trotskyists, finding in *The Revolution Betrayed* a powerful Marxist explanation of the degeneration of the Soviet State. They helped to form the Socialist Labour League in 1959,[2] but after a promising beginning found themselves in a new trap of orthodox formulae bearing little relation to the real world.

One group, around John Saville and E.P. Thompson, found a different solution. As Marxist intellectuals, they sought to establish a New Left, separate from both Bevanism and Stalinism, seeking to give a political expression to the new cultural and social trends emerging in an affluent Britain. They founded the *New Reasoner* after leaving the Communist party in 1957, and worked closely with other intellectuals on the *Universities and Left Review*. These papers combined in 1960 as the *New Left Review*, under an editorial board including E.P. Thompson, Stuart Hall, and Raymond Williams.

It was E.P. Thompson (b. 1924) who expressed their ideals most clearly when he called for a libertarian socialism in tune with the traditions of Engish working-class radicalism, romantic yet pragmatic in its collective attitudes and actions. As an ex-Stalinist, Thompson was aware that Marxism had been cut off from this tradition by becoming 'Russified', leaving the field wide open to liberal social democracy. The result had been frustration, disillusionment and apathy on the Left, which could offer no alternative to the division of Europe into two sterile ideologies, Stalinist and 'Natopolitan', which were actually Eastern and Western perversions of both Marxism and freedom. The horrors of Stalinism had created a cultural default among the Western intelligentsia, who had generally surrendered their radical inheritance in a tired acceptance of the *status quo*. The anger of the middle-aged and disenchanted intellectual Establishment was reserved only for their own disillusionment with the Communism of their youth.

Thompson, with his New Left comrades, looked to the socialist humanism which had emerged among Marxist dissidents in Eastern Europe after Stalin's death. This form of 'Marxism with a human face' (as it was later to be called) seemed to the New Left to be a liberation of thinking from the sterile dogmas imposed on them by the Communist Party. The stress on alienation found in the writings of the 'young' Marx was revived by these 'socialist humanists' (who tended to discount as less important the insights of the 'old' Marx into the economic dynamics of a capitalist society). It presented the possibility of a rekindling of moral and intellectual passion in the labour movement in Britain, steering it away from the narrow bread-and-butter questions which had so stunted working-class initiative. Thompson was particularly keen that dissidents in both East and West should rediscover the common ideals and principles which had been buried by the Third International. He wrote that 'this does not constitute a conversion of sections of the Western labour movement to Communist orthodoxy, nor of disillusioned Communists to liberal social democracy. It represents, rather, a rejection of both orthodoxies'.[3] The New Left sought the best elements in both traditions in an attempt to understand and criticise a contemporary, affluent capitalism which was defying the old Marxist theories.

Their criticisms of affluence belonged firmly to the cultural ferment of the 'Angry Young Men' in Britain in the fifties. John Osborne's play, *Look Back in Anger* (1956), and John Braine's novel, *Room at the Top* (1957), began a cultural assault on the vulgar materialism and narrow obsession with success which seemed to dominate British society. It was a moralistic critique of capitalism which was developed by the politically 'angry young men' of the New Left in *Out of Apathy* (1960). They expressed a disgust at its vulgar commercialism rather than a warning of its economic weakness. They pointed to the contrast of its bright advertising and attractive packaging with the reality of a neglected and meagrely financed system of education and health care. The desolate landscape of cultural creativity was compared with the perverted scale of values which made material wealth and commodities symbols of success. The apparent solution of its economic problems, far from making capitalism a desirable system, had exposed the ugly and selfish nature of the market economy, making a return of the labour movement to the old ideals of a co-operative commonwealth more necessary than ever.

It was the democratic strain which Thompson saw in English radicalism which was used as the yardstick by which the New Left measured contemporary capitalism. They saw a society with democratic forms of government, but not a democratic way of life. As a consumer, the citizen was the hero of modern capitalism, free to buy and equal to all other citizens in front of the bargaining counter. However, it was an illusory freedom and a sham equality. The genuine needs of any citizen for security of employment, adequate health care, or a worthwhile education were denied, while artificial needs based on material affluence and competitive success were created and inculcated by advertisers in order to sell their goods. The consumer was subjected to a debased form of persuasion and manipulated by an authority outside any real democratic control. It was this capitalist power structure which lay behind the contrast between private affluence and public squalor noted by Galbraith and Crosland. As Stuart Hall noted, they were not incidental problems – 'they are central to the system itself; they are *structural* faults and weaknesses which have survived the managerial and corporate "revolution" in capitalism, and come out of the other side, unresolved'.[4]

The result of this undemocratic system was a general apathy which paralysed any possibility of change. Social grievances had been transformed into apparently personal problems, while private ambitions of career success and social superiority had replaced the social aspirations for a new society. The democratic processes themselves had been drawn into the maintenance of the *status quo*, making a mockery of Chartist and radical beliefs that universal suffrage would ensure popular control of government. Instead, the great corporations which controlled capitalism had entwined themselves with government to rule the country in their own interests, while fewer and fewer people felt it worthwhile to express their needs through an increasingly bureaucratic political system.

To Thompson, a 'Natopolitan' culture of quietism and social atrophy had smothered the old impulses of a labour movement which had once longed for higher goals than consumer satisfaction. Instead, the Keynesian techniques which had solved the economic problems of capitalism had also removed the social motor of dissatisfaction which had driven the radical movement. A bipartisan acceptance of demand management – known as 'Butskellism' after Butler and Gaitskell, two Chancellors of the Exchequer who epitomised consensus politics – had replaced the socialist challenge of William Morris and the pioneers of the labour movement. To Thompson,

> economists are forever 'priming pumps', politicians 'meeting consequences', trade union leaders keeping up with the cost of living index. The most challenging issue is reduced to a nice choice of expediences. At the heart of a disintegrating imperial system, with weapons of annihilation poised over the earth, the Natopolitan walks carefully down well-known streets, putting his faith in his securities in the bank.[5]

Thompson's own desire to point to a radical alternative led him to write the historical classic, *The Making of the English Working Class* (1963), in which the popular democratic movements of the past were masterfully portrayed to demonstrate the hidden potential of the present.

Culture and Politics

The importance of culture for the New Left was a natural reaction to the Stalinist orthodoxies which had straitjacketed many of them before 1956. Indeed, the first issue of *New Left Review* editorialised about the influence of cinema, television and teenage music in society. The old left-wing concerns about unemployment and the unplanned anarchy of the capitalist production process may have become redundant with Keynes, but the cultural desert of modern capitalism, containing within it a subterranean youth culture which was potentilly subversive of existing social values, had replaced economics as the concern of the New Left. As the first *New Left Review* put it, the new cultural concerns of the young 'are directly relevant to the imaginative resistances of people who have to live with capitalism . . . The task of socialism is to meet people where they *are*, where they are touched, bitten, moved, frustrated, nauseated'.[6]

It was Raymond Williams (b. 1921) who was the main exponent of cultural politics for the New Left. He had risen to academic work in Literature at Oxford and Cambridge from a Welsh working-class background, and had been an editor of the journal *Politics and Letters* just after the war. His books, *Culture and Society* (1958) and *The Long Revolution* (1961), had a major influence (along with Richard Hoggart's *The Uses of Literacy*) in awakening an interest in the cultural domination of the British working class by their rulers.

In doing so, Williams veered away from the old Marxist distinction between economic structure and cultural superstructure, rejecting its consequent absurdities such as the definition of modern poetry as capitalist poetry made by the Marxist, Christopher Caudwell. Raymond Williams accepted the importance of economic and social organisation in shaping and transforming social experience, a factor which had to be taken into account in moral and intellectual life. However, the arbitrary and artificial *reduction* of all culture to economics or social organisation was indefensible, and would lead to the cultural totalitarianism which had descended on the Soviet Union under both Lenin and, particularly, Stalin. Indeed, Williams held that the final importance of the economy (a qualification made by Engels to the old model of historical materialism) was impossible to measure or judge, and called on radicals to look at society and culture *as a whole*. He held that

> a Marxist theory of culture will recognise diversity and complexity, will take account of continuity within change, will allow for chance . . . but, with these reservations, will take the facts of the economic structure and the consequent social relations as the guiding string on which a culture is to be understood.[7]

This would be a far more fruitful approach than the forcing of cultural and intellectual life into a rigid socio-economic grid.

In concentrating on culture, Williams sought to expose its nature as a force of domination. The communication of the ruling class with the educated bourgeois was fundamentally different than their communication with 'the masses', which they regarded as gullible and herdlike. This contempt for ordinary people, found in the style and content of advertisers and journalists, was a keynote of popular culture as it was developing in an age of the mass media. As Williams put it,

> If our purpose is art, education, the giving of information or opinion, our interpretation will be in terms of the ratonal and interested being. If, on the other hand, our purpose is manipulation — the persuasion of a large number of people to act, feel, think, know, in certain ways — the convenient formula will be that of the masses.[8]

The institutions of education and communication were created *for*, and not *by*, working people, with the intention of moulding public opinion in the ideas of the dominant social images — the eternal nature of the social hierarchy, the organised market, the natural distinction between an expert élite and an ignorant mass. In this way, dignity was stripped from the working class, who absorbed the inferior status accorded to them by a dominative culture.

The reaction of the despised 'masses' to this dominative culture was, to Williams, highly dangerous for democracy. The only means for working-class people of asserting dignity often seemed to be the strike or the riot, but Williams saw the inertia and apathy which had shrouded the British working class since the defeat of the General Strike as an equally dangerous reacton. There was something profoundly degrading about the way British people calmly submitted to the manipulation of their rulers, making a mockery of democratic processes of government by refusing to take an active part in them. They accepted their place in a profoundly undemocratic culture by a withdrawal of interest and a sceptical disbelief in the information given them. It was a mood which was disastrous for British society, where a degree of common interest and mutual effort was necessary.

The answer, however, did not lie in exhortation, but in the destruction of the dominative nature of culture. Williams argued that communication should be seen in democratic terms, an offering to equals rather than a proclamation from above. An élitist class culture which stressed the hierarchy of individual success and esteem must be replaced by a democratic culture in which the working class were accorded the dignity and respect which they deserved. It was Williams' own experience of his father, a Welsh signalman with quiet pride in his family, leisure interests and work, which suffused his democratic solutions to the insensitive and insulting society around him. In looking at modern tragedy, Williams pointed to

> the life of a man driven back to silence, in an unregarded working life. In his ordinary and private death, I saw a terrifying loss of connection between men, and even between father and son: a loss of connection which was, however, a particular social and historical fact: a measurable distance between his desire and his endurance, and between both the purposes and meanings which the general life offered him. I have known this tragedy more widely since[9]

– in the conditions and habits of millions of working-class people whose lives mean nothing to their rulers. If they were recognised as genuine equals in a democratic society, the great creative fertility in the needs of men and women would be truly released.

The New Left, CND and Labour

With its belief in the need for an alternative radicalism to that of Labour and the Communists, and with its call for a democratic cultural politics, the New Left was a movement of intellectuals with no immediate consequences for practical politics. However, it was intimately connected with a popular, middle-class movement[10] which rose in the late fifties to protect against the frozen divisions and thermonuclear terror of the Cold War.

The Campaign for Nuclear Disarmament (CND) was formed in February 1958 by a diverse collection of radicals, Bevanites, and Christians to call for Britain to set a moral lead in the world community by unilaterally renouncing its nuclear weapons. As a logical consequence of the politics of *Keep Left*, it naturally attracted the old Left, and Michael Foot, one of the authors of *Keep Left*, was indeed one of its founding members. However, in its mobilisation of thousands of young people in demonstrations and marches, it fitted perfectly with the New Left call for an end to apathy by a mass democratic movement. New Left clubs were set up throughout the country, putting forward the distinct views of the New Left on the need to break from the orthodox politics of the Eastern and Western Establishments. While CND was certainly active in the established Left, as seen by its temporary success in winning the Labour Party to unilateralism in 1960, its emphasis on extra-parliamentary agitation separated it from previous radical movements since the war. The militancy of the Committee of 100, set up in 1961, with its tactics of non-violent direct action, was much more in tune with New Left thinking than the less spectacular pressure-group activities of CND.

The New Left eagerly took up CND as a sign of the radical change in politics for which they had been looking. Stuart Hall (b. 1932) called for a policy of *active* neutrality in which Britain would be able to lead Europe away from the two armed blocs of NATO and the Warsaw Pact. In *Breakthrough* (1958) he argued that the militarist Cold War rhetoric of the NATO powers was preventing democratisation in Eastern Europe, solidifying the hold on power of Stalinist bureaucracies who could always defuse any threat to their rule by pointing to the Western threat. Moreover, the Western Alliance had helped to keep reactionary regimes in power throughout the 'free world' from Portugal to Latin America simply because they were anti-Communist. This reactionary role into which the West had let itself be trapped had forced many progressive movements of national liberation into the Communist camp.

Hall drew out the unilateralist implications of this analysis by arguing that a break from the alliance system was necessary in order to save the world from war. The existence of two armed camps led inexorably to an accelerating arms race which would one day bring about the war it was meant to prevent. The theory of the balance of terror, whereby the very nature of nuclear weapons would deter any government from launching an attack, was sound in logic but terrifying in reality. At some point the bluff would be called, and the world would be plunged into the horrors of thermo-nuclear destruction.

Hall argued that Britain was in an excellent position to break the alliance systems of East and West. Her position as both a strategic pivot of NATO, and as a possessor of the H-bomb, gave Britain a major opportunity of forcing the leading powers to the disarmament table by renouncing nuclear weapons and becoming a leader of the non-aligned Third World. He did *not* call on Britain to leave NATO, though he later changed his mind on the grounds that

> if it is wrong for Britain to manufacture, store and test her own weapons, then it is surely wrong for her to be an active partner in a military alliance which is based on the use of nuclear weapons.[11]

He did not specify, however, the exact manner in which a renunciation of nuclear weapons would have the practical effect of forcing politicians to any disarmament table or, if they finally got there, to an ending of the antagonisms which lay behind the arms race. The importance of moral persuasion was stressed by Hall, who wrote that 'what we need most of all is not military shields but moral imagination; for we are in one of these peculiar situations in which moral and political considerations are one'.[12] The New Left, like CND, appear often to overestimate the role of morality in politics, as though statesmen who in the past have been able to kill millions in the world wars have suddenly become different because they possess more powerful weapons.

The later demands of both CND and the New Left to break from NATO had major implications for their relationship to the Labour Party. It was a Labour government which had established NATO, and Labour as a party was fully committed to the Western Alliance against Soviet Communism, though Gaitskell and Healey had been putting forward plans for a demilitarised central Europe as a first step in *multilateral* disarmament. The CND were themselves highly ambiguous about their relationship to Labour. As a pressure group, they wanted to remain free from identification with any one political party, but they could hardly hope for the Conservatives to embrace the unilateralist cause. Canon Collins, one of the CND leaders, has written that 'the balance of those in the spearhead of CND was not political as such . . . certainly the bulk of the Executive . . . were left of Toryism – but it was (based) on moral principles uncompromisingly'.[13] This dissociation between morality and party politics could not be held as a practical proposition, however, and Ian Mikardo only expressed political reality in writing that 'the *only* political force capable of effecting such a change was the Labour Party . . . It was the only arena in which the Campaign could ride'.[14] In 1960, the Labour Party actually adopted unilateralism as its policy, but the refusal of Gaitskell to accept unilateralism made the political nature of the party crystal clear. There was no way in which the party could control its leader, who was generally free to ignore conference as long as he enjoyed the support of the parliamentary party. Indeed, the Labour revisionists fought successfully through the Campaign for Democratic Socialism to have the unilateralist policy reversed at the 1961 party conference.

The New Left had as ambiguous an attitude to the Labour Party as the CND. On the one hand, Labour under Gaitskell was hopelessly compromised with the Establishment, obsessed with electoral victory to the exclusion of any democratic challenge to the existing order. Hugh Gaitskell's call in 1959 for Labour to shed its working-class image in order to fit in with the new way of life portrayed by television and the glossy magazine only confirmed the tendency of the New Left to reject Labour as an adequate instrument of social change. Stuart Hall expressed the general feeling of his comrades in his protest:

> Has the Labour movement come through the fire and brimstone of the last fifty years to lie down and die before the glossy magazines? Has Labour no sense of the capacities, the potential of a society — more various, more skilled, more literate, less cramped and confined, less beaten down and frustrated? [15]

Its failure to comprehend the cultural nature of capitalist rule had absorbed Labour into the very social order which it should attack, leaving it as indifferent or even hostile to any challenge to that order.

However, the New Left could not afford to distance itself totally from a party which still commanded the electoral support of the working class. The Labour Party, like the trade unions and the co-operative movement, was seen as a creative achievement of working people, founded to establish new social patterns of co-operation and equality. In spite of the pressures on these organisations to adapt themselves to a subordinate role in a competitive and unequal society, they still remained as expressions of potential hope and aspiration for their class. As Raymond Williams put it,

> the choice as it presents itself [for Labour] is between qualified acceptance in a subordinate capacity or the renewal of an apparently hopeless challenge. The practical benefits of the former have to be

balanced against the profound loss of inspiration in the loss of the latter.[16]

The possibility that Labour could still be an effective instrument of socialism determined the degree to which the New Left distanced itself from the party. After the unilateralist victory at the 1960 Labour conference, the *New Left Review* argued that CND must recognise both the importance of fighting within the labour *movement*, which was much wider than any party machine, and of fighting within the Labour Party itself.

Scarborough both generalised and politicised the issue of nuclear weapons, and either the members of the CND who are in touch at *any* point with the organised political life of the Labour movement put the case for unilateralism there, or it will go by default.[17]

The New Left committed itself to a fight on two fronts, within and outside the Labour Party, through resolutions *and* demonstrations, in order to win the unilateralist case. It was an ambiguity which was to continue after the defeat of unilateralism at the 1961 party conference.

It was Ralph Miliband who constructed the most powerful New Left arguments on the Labour Party. In a series of articles culminating in his book, *Parliamentary Socialism* (1961), he argued that Labour's commitment to parliamentary democracy disqualified the party from ever becoming a socialist party. Turning Labour's claim to be a non-ideological party against them, Miliband argued that

of political parties claiming socialism to be their aim, the Labour Party has aways been one of the most dogmatic — not about socialism but about the parliamentary system. Empirical and flexible about all else, its leaders have always made devotion to that system their fixed point of reference and the conditioning factor of their political behaviour.[18]

It was a commitment which prevented Labour from ever mobilising its working class support in extra-parliamentary agitation to supplement any parliamentary attack on capitalism, as was seen in the isolation and destruction of the Labour Left in the thirties when the constitutional position of the monarchy and parliament *was* called into question. As a result, any Labour government was doomed to be the working-class manager of capitalism, as in 1945-51, or would be actually forced out of office, as in 1931. Without the countervailing balance of working-class agitation, Labour was condemned to absorption into the existing system.

To Miliband, Labour had become a necessary part of the capitalist system. Its policy of state intervention was perfectly in accord with the needs of capital for a corporate society in which labour would participate in the search for greater profits. Its very nature as a *labour*, rather than a socialist, party made the Labour Party an ideal instrument for this. 'Social democracy, for most of its existence, has been primarily engaged in political brokerage between labour and the established order. This is a function which is of crucial importance to modern capitalism.[19] The trade unions were unable to carry out this function, as their role was restricted to the sphere of collective bargaining. Only the political party of the unions, offering the promise of a socialist future if the working class was prepared to endure the present, would be able to fulfil this part.

Miliband did leave open the possibility that Labour might change by adopting a more class-conscious, socialist outlook which would survive initial electoral defeat by providing a genuine opposition which would enlist the devotion and support of its members, and which would eventually win *real* power for social change. He had not made a *fundamental* attack on Labour as a party, as he recognised that its conservative past did not preclude any radical change on its part. He was merely criticising its acceptance of corporate capitalism as an eternal, natural order. He wanted Labour to recognise that in such a society the working class could never be more than a subordinate partner, without any power to make decisions and subject to movements of capital which would dramatically affect its freedom of manoeuvre. Labour's failure to challenge this system had led it, and would lead it, to attack its own working-class base in the interests of capital. However, while Miliband recognised Labour's weakness, he was not able to prove the weakness to be a fundamental and permanent condition. In Miliband's analysis, the potential for change would always be present as long as Labour was tied to the working class, and his later pessimism proved to be highly superficial.

The Change in the New Left

In terms of ideas, the New Left had a distinct contribution to British socialism, but as a political movement its fortunes were intimately bound up with CND. When the unilateralist cause collapsed, the New Left collapsed with it. The huge Aldermaston march at Easter 1963 was a spectacular but final manifestation of CND support. As the whole of the Left rallied around a rejuvenated Labour Party led by Harold Wilson in the hope that unity would end more than a decade of Tory government, the unilateralists were forced to place their hopes in an abortive Labour commitment to renounce the Polaris missile. The political incoherence in CND's ranks – ranging from radicals and Christian pacifists to anarchists and Trotskyists – had always made its strength more apparent than real, while the *détente* between Russia and the United States following the Cuban missiles crisis of 1962 removed the international tension on which it had risen.[20]

It may have been a coincidence that the original editors of *New Left Review* – E.P. Thompson, Stuart Hall, Raymond Williams – were ousted as CND was losing its impetus, in 1962, but the decline of CND marked the end of their *collective* contribution to British socialist thought. After the twelfth issue, their eclectic, libertarian approach was replaced by the less Anglicised, more rigorous Marxism of a new editorial board led by Perry Anderson. There was, apparently, much acrimony involved, as was demonstrated by a furious attack on the new editors by Thompson. In an article in the 1965 *Socialist Register*, Thompson defended the original radical democratic notions of the first editors by pointing out that they were in touch with the English tradition of humane and libertarian socialism. Anderson's conviction that the New Left should be concerned with the debates in Western Marxism on the correct relation between structure and superstructure or the best tactics on a revolutionary seizure of power had resulted in a narrow-minded dogmatism which had done great harm to the movement. Thompson characterised Anderson as 'a veritable Dr. Beeching of the socialist intelligentsia. All the uneconomic branchlines and socio-cultural sidings of the New Left which were, in any case, carrying less and less traffic, were abruptly closed down'.[21] It was a sectarian form of Marxism which looked at classes as categories rather than human beings, and which considered power while ignoring morality.

Thompson had reason to feel angry. As the impetus of the original New Left declined apart from the *Socialist Register*, edited by Miliband and Saville, there remained little trace of any further collective action. The *May Day Manifesto*, issued in 1967 by Thompson, Hall and Williams as a protest against the betrayal of the Wilson government, was a final glimmer. Its call for more radical policies to be followed at home and abroad was merely one manifestation of the growing left-wing dissatisfaction with Labour. Thereafter, the original New Left engaged in their individual contributions to socialist academia — Williams in literature, Thompson in history, and Hall in the sociology of culture — until a much later rise of CND put Thompson on the political map once more.

The New Left had developed considerably since 1962, developing well beyond the boundaries of the *New Left Review*. The attacks on working-class living standards by the Wilson government, particularly after the 1966 wage freeze, disaffected a growing section of the Left from the Labour Party. The success of revolutionary struggles in the Third World, particularly in Cuba, combined with the ugly excesses of the American war in Vietnam to create an extra-parliamentary Left throughout Europe (mainly among students, though it momentarily appeared that workers in France had become infected with revolutionary fervour in May 1968). The disgust of this Left with the consensus politics of social democracy — the 'Great Coalition' in West Germany, the cautious and discredited Stalinism of the French Communists, the overt reformism of the Italian Communists, and the conservative pro-Americanism of the British Labour government — helped to fuel the discontent of young people who looked to Trotsky and Rosa Luxemburg as the idols of a romantic vision of revolution.

In Great Britain, the *intellectual* expression of much of this ferment was channelled into the *New Left Review*. The abstruse and florid theories of Lukacs, Althusser, and the Frankfurt Marxists were important in the history of the Marxist intellectual tradition, but in the conditions of Britain they remained mainly the mark of a well-educated person rather than a positive contribution to the ideas of the Labour movement. The technical neologisms and academic style characterised the *Review* as an offshoot of a European tradition which was unable to take root in British conditions, sacrificing clarity of language to theoretical rigour. Their attacks on the conservative nature of British culture[22] may have been to the point, but merely underlined their isolation from the working class.

However, there was an important continuity in several respects with the original New Left which was to have great importance for the Labour Party. The original editors had stressed the politics of culture at the expense of the revolutionary political and economic conclusions of the mature Marx, and the new editors did the same, albeit in a more subtle and sophisticated form. Where Thompson looked to Morris and Milton as a balance to Marx, the new editors looked to the Italian Marxist, Antonio Gramsci. Gramsci (1891-1937) had died in one of

Mussolini's prisons, but his romantically named *Prison Notebooks* had already had a great impact on the politics of the Italian Communists. Through the channel of the New Left, his ideas were to have an equal impact on most of the British Left. They were a wide-ranging attempt to revise the Marxism of his own day, and different aspects of his writings have been dissected in diverse left-wing journals, particularly by the Eurocommunists of *Marxism Today*, but it was his notion of hegemony — a term used in different senses by Gramsci, but generally meaning the ethical and cultural control of civil society — which was to be crucial for the New Left.

Perry Anderson took up Gramsci's idea of ruling-class hegemony as a more relevant Marxist analysis of Western democracy than that given by Lenin. From his article 'Origins of the Present Crisis' (1964), when he called on the Labour Party to become a hegemonic party of the working class, to his 'The Antinomies of Antonio Gramsci' (1977), Anderson stressed the differences, highlighted by Gramsci, between political rule in Eastern and Western Europe. Where the State had had shallow roots in the East, leading it to be easily overthrown, its roots were much deeper in the West. The military might of the government had no need to be used because of the general acceptance of capitalist cultural values and political ideas. The achievement of democracy had been a major advance for the cultural hegemony of the ruling class in the nations of the West — 'their highly advanced economies and their complex, dense, tessellated histories have created a social and cultural world entirely their own.'[23]

To attempt to fight this world by concentrating on political and legislative action alone, as social democracy attempted to do, was to fail to grasp that the hegemony of the ruling class in civil society was a major brake on gradual *political* change. The need for cultural criticism by a radical intelligentsia was greater than ever in order to combat this hegemony, so that a process of gradual persuasion must replace the traditional legislative gradualism of social democracy. This process of persuasion would take the form of working through civil society — the schools, the family, the media — as well as the directly political institutions of Parliament. Anderson initially saw the Labour Party as a potentially hegemonic force which would be able to attack the cultural hegemony of the ruling class. It should present a total alternative to the existing social order, so that

its arc of action must embrace not only the bare institutions of the State, but the whole complex landscape of civil society as well. This is the most fundamental of all the tracts of a hegemonic party, the one which divides it most absolutely from social democracy.[24]

Anderson was to change his mind on his hope that the Labour Party might fulfil such a role, but the fact that such a role needed to be filled remained constant. It was a direct heritage of the original New Left, expressed though it was in the fashionable language of Western Marxism.

Feminism, the New Left and the Labour Party

The recognition of the needs for a cultural criticism of civil society made the New Left a natural home for the first manifestations of socialist feminism. Feminism has yet to make a major impact on the Labour Party's political thought, but the increasing presence of feminists in the party[25] seems to make this event only a matter of time.

The social rights of women had been a perennial issue in the Labour movement since the days when Isabella Ford had called for an alliance between the suffragettes and the Labour Party. However, there had been little development of political thought, so that the arguments about family allowances and birth control took place within the confines of acceptance of the traditional family. Similarly, regular attempts to organise working women in trade unions seems to have aroused little thinking on the relationship between women and the labour movement outside the traditional framework of labourism. The women's section of Labour's National Executive Committee was elected by the whole conference (i.e. the unions), in contrast with the constituency section; women MPs and, even more, women Ministers were a rarity.

Shirley Williams summed up traditional Labour thinking on women's emancipation in 1980 when she accepted that women could not enter politics because of the demands made on them by the raising of a family, as well as their general lack of confidence. The reason for this lack of confidence was not investigated because Mrs Williams felt that the main political achievement of women had been already attained in the success of the suffragettes. The *social* oppression of women was covered up by their *political* emancipation. To Williams,

the woman's vote has reshaped the geography of politics much more fundamentally than the election of a handful of women to Parliament. MPs of both sexes now spend a great deal of time discussing welfare questions, health, care of the elderly, maternity services, education, abortion and so on.[26]

Victory of the suffragettes had been vital for this, and no other major campaign for emancipation seemed to have been contemplated.

This was not good enough for the radicals of the New Left. They were much more open to intellectual influences from abroad, and the writings of Simone de Beauvoir (*The Second Sex*, 1948) and Betty Friedan (*The Feminine Mystique*, 1963) shaped their thinking in a very different mould. They were aided by the major social disruption in the traditional family in the long period of the post-war boom, as the number of working women increased dramatically and the limited development of contraception and abortion rights led to a slackening of a restrictive sexual morality. The general conditions for a rebirth of feminism were being prepared, and the New Left were among the first to point the way.

It was Juliet Mitchell (b.1940) who acted as the intellectual catalyst for the women's movement. In a seminal article in the *New Left Review*, 'Women: the Longest Revolution' (1966), she pointed out that the emancipation of woman, once regarded as a major socialist project, had become marginal and neglected. The reason for this lay in the original Marxist analysis which had related women's oppression to capitalism and had assumed that it would be automatically overcome by the advance of socialism. It had been a formal analysis which had not investigated the specific manner in which women were deprived of their social and economic rights by men, and had lapsed as concentration shifted exclusively to class questions. Now, as then, 'the liberation of women remains a normative ideal, an adjunct to socialist theory, not structurally integrated into it'.[27] Mitchell sought to restore the question to its rightful place.

In doing so, she began an important debate which owes much of its contours to its origins in the New Left. The rejection by modern feminists of the 'economism' of the traditional Left — by which is meant its concentration on economics as the source of all other human activity — is an echo of Gramsci and Althusser; their emphasis on cultural forms of oppression has its roots in the original writers of the New Left who sought to break from the philistinism of their old Stalinist politics; and the new emphasis on Freudian psychology, as seen in Juliet Mitchell's influential *Psychoanalysis and Feminism* (1974), can be traced to the libertarian Frankfurt Marxism of Adorno and Marcuse as much as French structuralists like Lacan. However, the women's movement has become a highly influential movement of its own accord, seeking to define Marxism in its own image[28] or even to separate itself from the 'male' left altogether.[29]

Despite the increasing tendency of feminists to join the Labour Party, it must be said that feminism remains external to the Labour Party's political thought. The trade union movement, the base of the party, has occasionally shown tendencies to accept some of the feminist demands that it change its language (for example, substituting 'chairperson' for 'chairman'), but its primary interest in organising women necessarily lies in the oppression of working women by individual (male *and* female) employers, not in their oppression by men. The problems of male oppression lies outside the general wage-relationship, and it is difficult to see how the Labour Party could take them up as anything more than subsidiary to their main task of defending the labour movement within capitalist society, especially given the almost exclusively middle-class composition of the women's movement.

Middle-Class Radicalism

The New Left has come under sustained attack for its over-intellectualised language and its failure to connect itself to any political movement.[30]   In a sense, such criticisms are unfair, as the New Left consciously sought to clarify and modernise radical and Marxist theory by distancing itself from practical politics. Its experience of the theoretical straitjacket imposed by Stalinism, which prostituted theory to serve as a mere justification for its every twist and turn, has given it ample justification for such an approach, despite its obvious limitations. The sectarian approach to theory expressed by many of the revolutionary groups to which much of the New Left temporarily turned in the late sixties only confirmed the need for a certain independence in theoretical work.

However, it was the *theory* of the New Left which remained stamped by its middle-class milieu. In a study of the CND, Frank Parkin has written sympathetically of middle-class radicalism, which he differentiates from the more selfish goals of the old working-class radicalism. Parkin wrote that middle-class radicals

are more typically concerned with issues of a moral or humanitarian nature — as, for example, Anti-Apartheid, the campaign against capital punishment. . . CND, and so on. These goals are intrinsically different from those pursued by working class movements in that they offer no particular benefits to those who support them. . . The main pay-off for such activity is in the emotional satisfaction derived from expressing personal values in action .[31]

This is not quite accurate, as working-class movements *have* had 'altruistic' goals of a better society as part and parcel of their own material aims. However, middle-class movements have tended to separate humanitarian and moral aims from the general context of a society divided by social class, while middle-class intellectuals have often had the tendency to be obsessed with fashionable trends.

The New Left have been aware of a society divided by class — theoretically, at the very least — but they have often seemed more open to intellectual fashion for its own sake. The constant flirtation with a semi-Marxist language has often disguised a fundamental rejection of basic Marxist categories. The labour theory of value which lies at the heart of Marx's revolutionary critique of society has generally been replaced by the more fashionable 'neo-Ricardian' theory of value, while Marx's analysis of capitalist crisis as a result of the falling rate of profit has been at least modified.[32] This is partly the consequence of the replacement of Lenin by Gramsci as the ideological mentor of the Left, so that the concern with cultural and political questions has often been *to the exclusion* of the socio-economic dynamics of accumulation which have driven capitalism forward. The absence of a theory of crisis in the original New Left has been as influential as its stress on culture and radical sociology.

Nevertheless, within these limits, the New Left did present a powerful ideological challenge to the variant of corporate socialism which had come to be held by the traditional Labour Left. The demand that men and women should take control of the decisions which govern their lives by a struggle against the Establishment was to be applied to the workers' movement with major consequences for the Labour Party.

Notes

1. See Andy Anderson, *Hungary 56* (Solidarity, 1964).

2. See Duncan Hallas, 'Building the Leadership', in *International Socialism* No. 40., (Oct.-Nov. 1969).

3. E.P. Thompson, 'The New Left', in *New Reasoner* No. 9 (Summer, 1959), p. 7.

4. Stuart Hall, 'The Supply of Demand', in E.P. Thompson ed., *Out of Apathy* (Stevens and Sons, 1960), p. 63.

5. E.P. Thompson, 'Outside the Whole' in Thompson ed., *Out of Apathy*, p. 181.

6. Editorial in *New Left Review* No. 1 (Jan.-Feb. 1960), p. 1.

7. Raymond Williams, *Culture and Society 1780-1950* (Chatto and Windus, 1958), p. 269.

8. Ibid., p. 303.

9. Raymond Williams, *Modern Tragedy* (Chatto and Windus, 1966), p. 13.

10. See Frank Parkin, *Middle Class Radicalism: The Social Bases of the British Campaign for Nuclear Disarmament* (Manchester University Press, 1968).

11. Stuart Hall, *NATO and the Alliance* (London CND, 1961), p. 4.

12. Stuart Hall, *Breakthrough* (Combined Universities CND, 1958), p. 22.

13. Quoted in Richard Taylor and Colin Pritchard, *The Protest Makers: The British Nuclear Disarmament Movement of 1958-65, Twenty Years On* (Pergamon Press, 1980), p. 53.

14. Quoted in ibid., p. 59.

15. Stuart Hall, 'The Supply of Demand', in Thompson ed., *Out of Apathy*, p. 95-6.

16. Raymond Williams, *The Long Revolution* (Chatto and Windus, 1961) p. 303.

17. 'Scarborough and Beyond', editorial in *New Left Review* No. 6 (Nov-Dec. 1960), p. 6.

18. Ralph Miliband, *Parliamentary Socialism* (Merlin Press, 2nd ed., 1972), p. 13.

19. Ralph Miliband, 'The Politics of Contemporary Capitalism' in *New Reasoner* No. 5 (Summer, 1938), p. 46.

20. For contrasting reasons for the failure of CND, see Peggy Duff, *Left, Left, Left: A Personal Account of Six Protest Campaigns 1945-65* (Alison and Busby, 1971), who argues that there was insufficient political clarity (p. 200), and Taylor and Pritchard, *The Protest Makers*, who argue that there was too much politics for a *moral* campaign (p. 13).

21. E.P. Thompson 'Peculiarities of the English', in Ralph Miliband and John Saville ed., *Socialist Register 1965* (Merlin Press, 1966).

22. See Perry Anderson, 'Components of the National Culture', in *New Left Review* No. 50 (July-Aug., 1968).

23. Perry Anderson, 'Problems of Scialist Strategy', in P. Anderson ed., *Towards Socialism*, p. 230.

24. Ibid., p. 244.

25. See, for example, the debates at the Labour Party *Annual Conference*, 1982.

26. Shirley Williams, *Women in Politics* (Bedford College, University of London, 1980), p. 7.

27. Juliet Mitchell, 'Women: The Longest Revolution' in *New Left Review* No. 40 (Nov-Dec. 1966), p. 15.

28. The most important of these attempts is Michele Barrett, *Women's Oppression Today* (Verso, 1980), See also Sheila Rowbotham, Lynne Segal, Hilary Wainwright, *Beyond the Fragments: Feminism and the Making of Socialism* (Merlin Press, 1979).

29. See, for example, some of the esssays in Lydia Sargent ed., *Women and Revolution: A Discussion of the Unhappy Marriage of Marxism and Feminism* (Pluto Press, 1981).

30. See, for example, Peter Sedgwick, 'The Two New Lefts', in *International Socialism* No. 17 (Summer, 1964). Also Ian Birchall, 'The Autonomy of Theory: A Short History of *New Left Review*' in *International Socialism* No. 10 (Second

Series, Winter, 1980-81).

31. F. Parkin, *Middle Class Radicalism*, p. 41.

32. Witness the reception given to Ian Steedman, *Marx After Sraffa* (New Left Books, 1977), a rejection of the basic categories of Marx's *Capital*.

14 THE BENNITE LEFT

The ideas of the New Left were absorbed into the Labour Party as the long post-war boom was coming to an end. The Keynesian policies of state intervention in a mixed economy which had been introduced in the forties were ceasing to be adequate as a means of overcoming economic crisis, and the financial basis of the welfare state itself began to appear increasingly shaky. As unemployment and inflation began to grow together, contrary to all the established theories of the mixed economy,[1] the State began increasingly to intervene in society in a coercive manner.

It was the effect of the slowly growing economic crisis on the hopes and policies of the Wilson Labour government of 1964-70 which opened the way for a rethinking of strategy by the Labour Left. The government's initial hopes for an extension of corporate socialism through a National Plan proved stillborn, and thereafter it found itself increasingly locked into a series of measures aimed against the labour movement itself. The attempt to restrict working-class living standards through successive incomes policies and the failure of the Government's strategy of maintenance of the value of sterling after the devaluation crisis of 1967 was followed by the first cutbacks in the welfare state itself, the most prized gain of the Labour movement. By the time the government unsuccessfully attempted to bring collective bargaining under state control through its abortive White Paper, *In Place of Strife*, in 1969, the whole Labour movement was beginning to mobilise in its own defence.

In these circumstances the political ideas of the Bevanite Left began to seem increasingly dated to many socialists, who did not accept the hostile attitude to the Labour party cultivated by the New Left in the late sixties. Michael Foot (b. 1913), one of the authors of *Keep Left* (1947) and the natural heir of Nye Bevan as the leader of the Labour Left, was certainly open to the strategy of CND (which he helped to found), and was implacably opposed to the Labour government's attacks on working-class living standards. However, his political thought remained trapped in the past. In an interview with the *New Left Review* in 1968, Foot argued that there was no reason to change the strategy of state ownership, welfare, and Keynesian economics which had guided the Labour party since the thirties. Indeed, he accepted the economic analysis of contemporary capitalism put forward by the revisionists —

> I think Strachey's account of what has occurred in modern capita-
> lism is correct. Keynesian economics plus democratic pressures have,
> in fact, greatly improved the standard of life for the majority of
> people. Strachey did not provide a satisfactory programme for the
> future, but I think that his account of what has happened to modern
> capitalism is much more accurate than what I suppose might be re-
> garded as an orthodox Marxist account.[2]

It was not the original policies of corporate socialism which were at
fault, but the will of the government to pursue those policies which had
led to the retreats and compromises of the late sixties, according to
Foot. The Labour Party's pledges of increased state intervention in the
economy had collapsed in the face of opposition from international
bankers. These bankers had taken control of Britain's economic
destiny, and Foot saw the planning policies of the labour movement as
the only means of regaining national independence. As Labour's failure
was a failure of will, rather than policy, Foot saw no need to re-
examine Labour's political and economic ideas. Instead, he merely
called for a *return* to the original strategy. As he wrote in *Tribune*,

> it is not true that the only choice left to the country in its economic
> affairs is between the orthodox Treasury doctrine with trimmings. . .
> or the atavistically-deflationary jungle-law onslaught on the unions
> which Messrs. Heath and Powell have now persuaded Messrs.
> Macleod and Maudling to approve. There is the Third Policy, the
> expansionist-plus-state interventionist policy on which Labour was
> elected. . . which offers the best hope of saving the Labour Govern-
> ment from its failures and timidities.[3]

Instead of attempting to conciliate the bankers, the old enemies of
labour, the Government should return to the principles of the Attlee
government. The brilliant pamphleteering style concealed an atrophied
political approach which convinced many on the New Left that the
future no longer lay with the Labour Party.[4]

The IWC

However, the ideas of participation and direct democracy current in the

New Left were already being incorporated into the Labour Party by many who refused to wander into what they believed to be a self-righteous political wilderness. Under the auspices of one Labour journal, *Voice of the Unions,* the Institute for Workers Control (IWC) was set up in 1964 by a group of academics and socialist journalists. By the late sixties, the IWC was beginning to arouse a major interest in the trade union and labour movement, and the election of a prominent member, Hugh Scanlon, as head of the Engineers in 1967 was a major fillip to its campaign. When Jack Jones, another advocate of workers' control, became head of the giant Transport Workers' Union in 1969, it was becoming obvious to all that a new Left was moving to the ascendent in the Labour Party, very different from the Bevanites in its rejection of corporate socialism.

It was Ken Coates, together with his comrade, Tony Topham, who emerged as the principal inspiration behind the IWC. Through books and pamphlets, he tirelessly argued the case against the Morrisonian model of the public corporation accepted by the Labour Party since the thirties. The traditional programme of public ownership adopted by Labour had to be revised in the light of the experience of nationalisation since the war. The state sector of the economy had become a form of businessmen's syndicalism, serving the private sector in a strictly subordinate role. The management of the nationalised industries had become a bureaucratic oligarchy, seeing the workforce only as subjects of manipulation. The hopes held by the labour movement that nationalisation would be a panacea for economic ills and an embodiment of the New Jerusalem had turned into a bitter disillusionment among the working class, endangering the hope and determination which had kept the socialist ideal alive.

In reaction to the corporatist form of nationalisation, Coates and the IWC sought to recapture the traditions of syndicalism and guild socialism, which had asserted that the producers themselves should run their industry. Coates pointed out that wage-slavery was still the predominant social relationship in Britain, a fact which all the glossy advertising and claims to affluence made by consumer capitalism could not conceal. Most people still had nothing to sell in the market except their labour power, and were totally dependent on the whims and decisions of their employers. The workers were not free to fix their own rhythm of work or rest-breaks, were subject to deafening noise, and frequently suffered physical mutilation as a result of their poor work-conditions. Throughout industry, men and women expended their labour power on an increase in the power, prestige and wealth of others.

To Coates, the struggle for workers' control was a struggle to over-come the power of one person over another. As the first step in over-coming the alienation of the workers from their product highlighted by the young Marx in the Paris Manuscripts, the control of industry by the direct producers would be a major step towards the full dignity of free-dom in the economic sphere. Coates argued that

> workers' control brings back into the working class. . . all that tremendous weight of self-esteem, of self-recognition, of self-respect, which has been stripped away by years of bureaucratic intrigues and manoeuvres in political institutions. A man who wants workers' control is a man who's aware of his fundamental humanity. . . men who are convinced that they're not merely 'hands', that they're not merely 'cogs', but that they have human dignities and rights.[5]

It was a direct call to the libertarian tradition of socialism, which stressed the attainment of freedom rather than the alleviation of poverty as its aim.

However, workers' control was not the same as workers' manage-ment of industry. Coates and the IWC pointed out that control meant constraint on the power of employers to act against the interests of the worker. If such control was put into effect, the educational effects on the workforce as they realised the superfluous and unnecessary role of the capitalists would lead to the demand for an end to capitalism and a full role in the management of their enterprise. The demand for a 'social audit', an analysis of the social costs and benefits of local and national economic policy which would involve opening the books of capitalist firms, was the means by which this process of educating workers in the need for socialism was to be achieved. Apart from the educational role of workers' control, it had the added advantage of avoiding the corporatist solution of participation in management.

Workers' participation was rejected by the IWC on the grounds that it was merely an aid to the capitalist search for higher profits. The adoption of such a policy would merely lead to the absorption of the unions into a role hostile to the workforce they were supposed to re-present, and a sophisticated means of self-exploitation by the workers. It was a corporatist, not a socialist, solution to the problems of industrial relation, in that it left intact the present real distribution of wealth. Ernie Roberts, an Engineering Union official who later became a Labour MP, argued that the aim of workers' control must be the immediate issue of protection of workers' rights, particularly with regard to job security and working conditions. Any participation with private management would merely be an exercise in class collaboration. To Roberts,

> the reason for the existence of the Labour Movement is to bring about a redistribution of. . . wealth in the interests of those who create it. When we think of planning our economy, this again depends upon real ownership and control of the economy.[6]

Without this control, workers' participation would be an anti-working class measure.

It was no accident that the IWC, which harked back to the days of syndicalism and the first shop stewards' movement, should have risen to prominence at this particular time. The conditions of prosperity and labour shortage in the fifties and early sixties had led to the consolidation of rank and file organisation around a new shop stewards' movement. As the union bureaucracies became ever more 'integrated' into the corporatist institutions of the State,[7] so the immediate demands of union members expressed themselves in a series of short and often successful unofficial strikes led by these shop stewards. It was the type of grass-roots democracy which was seen as a symbol of hope by the New Left[8] and an indication of disruptive anarchy by governments and many union leaders. The IWC rested their hopes for workers' control on the dynamics of this new shop stewards' movement, and were amply rewarded with the election of Hugh Scanlon, an avowed defender of rank and file organisation, to the presidency of the Engineering Union.

Scanlon (b.1913) represented the attack on corporate socialism within the trade unions. He believed that

> the leadership of the trade union movement is now almost a part of the establishment — more important still, is a recognised part of the establishment. That wasn't as apparent in the thirties and during the war. It's more a phenomenon of full employment and employers utilising the trade union leadership rather than the heavy stick of unemployment.[9]

He saw the shop stewards' movement as the crucial element which would reunite the trade union leadership with the militant rank and file, ending the days of corporate consensus in which the unions had forgotten their fundamental task of defending the working class against the capitalists.

Scanlon identified the cause of workers' control with the shop stewards' movement. In a sense, as he pointed out, the workshop bargaining already taking place constituted a certain control over managerial functions, though it fell far short of the effective voice in management which was needed. Moreover, worker control itself would find itself constantly frustrated without an extension of the state sector of the economy. As long as industry remained privately owned, workers would find themselves faced with a brick wall of evasion and secrecy because of the capitalist need to make a profit at the expense of his workforce. It was in the public sector where a real movement could take place, as it was only through nationalisation that planning for need could be effective. Workers' participation in the management of publicly owned firms — in the form of representatives elected by the workshop or the department with the powers of appointment, promotion and dismissal — would avoid the corporatist form imposed by Morrison.

Barratt Brown

The corporatist nature of capitalism and Labour's role in managing the economy against the interests of the working class came under a closely argued attack by Michael Barratt Brown, a councillor of the IWC and a particular influence behind the Tribune group's alternative economic analysis in the late sixties. Barratt Brown located the failure of the 1964-70 government in its pursit of corporate solutions in a society characterised by class conflict. He took over the Ricardian conception of profit as determined by the wages of the workers, so that if the minimum subsistence level which constitued the basis of wages was raised, it would

jack up the whole pyramid of earnings at the expense of profits . . . So long as there are pressures upon private companies to maximise profits if they are to survive and grow in the economic system we have, just so long will there be equally strong pressures to keep real wage increases under control.[10]

In returning to challenge corporate capitalism, the Labour government had found itself obeying the dictates of the capitalists to increase profitability by driving down wages. It was the inevitable consequence of managing an economy with an in-built, structural hostility to Labour, and electoral unpopularity was the government's reward for sacrificing the interests of its supporters.

In *From Labourism to Socialism* (1972), Barratt Brown sought to analyse the new changes which had taken place in capitalism since the war. He pointed to the new industrial revolution by which technological innovation in every branch of the economy was threatening eventual mass unemployment unless the State intervened with a strategy for maintaining full employment. The fact that such predictions had been made since before the time of the Luddites and had proved false was not really investigated by Barratt Brown, who was more interested in the social forms in which this new industrial revolution was taking place.

He argued that the control of Britain's economic destiny was being taken over by the development of the new, giant transnational companies which had been established on a world scale in the concentration and centralisation of capital. As a result, 'the rivalry today is not so much between capitalist *states*, in which finance capital is integrated with the state machine, as between transnational *companies*'.[11] These companies no longer relied on a home base, but were able to operate through plants established throughout the world. Their size and strength were a major threat to national sovereignty, dictating the whole economic structure and strategy of development of Third World countries. They were also able to undermine the political and economic structures of developed countries like Britain through their effect on the balance of payments, the national taxation system and the scale of investment needed to regulate the economy. To accept the corporate system by which these transnational companies exercised their power would be to acquiesce in the surrender of national sovereignty to small groups of people interested only in profit.

In such circumstances, Barratt Brown argued for an end to the consensus of 'Butskellism'. It had been a fated consensus from the start, based as it was on a compact between two irreconcilable classes of capital and labour, and had amounted only to an agreement by labour that the system of private ownership should operate with its acquiescence. In the circumstances where the ability of the State to manage the British economy was under increasing danger from the transnational companies, it was only a radical socialist platform which could regain the initiative for the Labour Party. The revisionist politics of Crosland had proved useless in its analysis, as capitalism retained all its old anarchical and anti-social tendencies. Barratt Brown sought a return to the fundamental analysis of socialism –

> Socialism is not primarily about equality, as Crosland insisted, nor even about liberty, important as reforms in these directions may be; it is about the eradication of class, about social control and production for use, instead of profit, for socially formulated needs in place of privately managed markets.[12]

Unless the Labour Party agreed to end the politics and economics of consensus, it would find all its hard-fought gains eaten away as the private capitalists increasingly called for an end to public expenditure on welfare and full employment.

It was in the grass-roots democracy of the working class and in the growing demand for workers' control that Barratt Brown saw the hope for change. In the work-in at the Upper Clyde Shipbuilders (UCS), he saw a growing trend by which 'working class organisations can and will increasingly establish checks and controls over capitalist economic power'.[13] On this basis, a radical Labour government would be able to use its potential power *against* the transnational companies. It would be able to rally national sentiment against such undemocratic groupings as the Common Market, symptomatic as it was of the power of international capitalism. It would be able to impose Keynesian policies of demand management, backed by the strength of the organised working class, on a world scale by cornering the markets of the Third World. The adoption of a policy of direct physical controls on prices, capital flows and imports was an alternative method of curbing the economic crisis in Britain.

It was a nationalist, as much as a class, policy which was being proposed by Barratt Brown. Just as his analysis of class conflict was Ricardian rather than Marxist, so his grasp of the role played by the working class was only superficially similar to Marxism. It was a *national* alliance led by the working class to regain British sovereignty which he envisaged, and not that of class conflict *within* the nation-state. He justified this by referring to the changes within the old ruling class brought about by the transnational corporations. The old national capitalist had been replaced as the enemy by the international financier, just as the usurer replaced the hardworking manager for the Fabians in the late nineteenth century. Barratt Brown argued that 'the division emerging in the ruling class in the 1970s is between the giants of industry and finance with international connections and the pygmies in the national market'.[14] In exploiting these divisions, Labour, as the party of the working class, would be able to rally the nation behind its banners.

Left on the Offensive

Through the IWC, the ideas of democratic control and an end to corporate socialism were being demonstrated as relevant to the Labour Party in the changed circumstances of the late twentieth century. Where the New Left were agnostic or hostile to the party, believing it from the late sixties to be incapable of change, these representatives of New Left politics inside the Labour Party argued that decades of work must not be thrown away in an emotional wave of 'ultra-leftism'. Ken Coates, himself expelled from the Labour Party in 1965 for his opposition to government policy on Vietnam, fought successfully for reinstatement and called on the new revolutionaries to rejoin the 'natural' party of the working class.

In an article in the 1973 *Socialist Register*, Coates poured scorn on the talk of 'hegemonic' aspirations which ignored the practical need of workers to defend their own interests. When the Left deserted the Labour Party they were deserting the working class, leaving them to the ideological and political lead of the Right in exactly the same way as the SDF secession from the LRC in 1901 had left the field clear for the Fabians. He pointed to the fate of the ILP, which had collapsed as a political force after it left the Labour Party in 1932, as a chilling lesson for those who wished to found a new socialist party. Against the New Left, Coates argued that the right-wing bureaucracies which ran the Labour movement were not impregnable, nor its leaders irreplaceable. The old, corporatist trade union leaders, could be and, indeed, had been replaced, as seen in the victories of Scanlon and Jones. He wrote that

> whatever else British socialists may be doing, whatever experiments they feel meet to conduct, either in community action or trade union agitation, the one thing they should *not* do is to turn their backs on the official Labour Movement . . . It would be time enough to talk about defeat if the battle were over, assuming our victories left us time, but it is quite, quite wrong to concern ourselves with it now, as the battle lines are just beginning to form.[15]

It was a powerful appeal which appeared to be borne out as a wave of militant strikes and demonstrations against the policies of the Heath Government of 1970-74 carried the Labour Party to the Left. The demands of the IWC for a 'social audit' were placed at the centre of political debate when workers occupied the yards of the Upper Clyde

Shipbuilders (UCS) in 1971 to begin a work-in, demonstrating to all that workers could run an industry without the capitalist usurers. The ability of a parliamentary government to rule against determined working-class opposition was itself called into question after the successful miners' strike of January-February 1972, followed by the government's capitulation in the face of a threatened general strike in July 1972 over the arrest of five pickets under the new Industrial Relations Act. This period of working class militancy reached its height when the Heath government was forced to call an election in February 1974 when faced with a new miners' strike.

The leader of the Yorkshire Miners (and later of the national union), Arthur Scargill, emerged as the symbol of the renewal in syndicalist politics, trusting more in the trade union movement than in any political party. He told one interviewer that

> it appeared to me that, irrespective of what I did politically in the . . . Labour Party or the Communist party or any other political organisation, the *real power* — and I say that in the best possible sense — the real power lay either with the working class or the ruling classes. Now the working classes were obviously identified with the trade union movement and not directly identified with the Labour Party which in my opinion had, and indeed still has, lost complete contact with the basic problems of the movement and the rank and file.[16]

However, even Scargill was aware of the need for *political* action by a political party, and worked in the Labour Party as it moved to the Left after its defeat in 1970.

As the party of the trade union movement, Labour could not escape the ferment in the union rank and file in the early seventies. The passage of the Industrial Relations Act in 1971 and Britain's entry into the Common Market in 1973 served as a focus for the Left to urge their rejection of corporatism on the Labour leadership. One of the emerging leaders of the Labour Left, Eric Heffer, urged Labour to return to its working-class origins. In *The Class Struggle in Parliament* (1973) Heffer pointed to the trade union base of the Labour party as the reason why there could be no other party of the working class. If Labour remained true to the first principles of defending that class, then its radical potential could not be lost.

These principles, enunciated in the ideas of Britain socialism at the turn of the century, were embodied in *Labour's Programme, 1973,* adopted at that year's party conference. Calling for an extension of public ownership and a measure of industrial democracy, that *Programme* stated Labour's main aim was 'to bring about a fundamental and irreversible shift in the balance of power and wealth in favour of working people and their families'.[17] The Labour leadership was well aware of the need to avoid a repetition of the disastrous split with the unions of 1964-70, and a Social Contract with the TUC was arranged, whereby Labour agreed to push for radical economic measures such as a wealth tax in return for trade union co-operation. The extent of the Left's advance was seen in the composition of the Labour government formed by Wilson in March 1974, with Michael Foot as Employment Secretary and Tony Benn as Industry Secretary.

Holland

It was Stuart Holland who proved to be one of the principle sources of theoretical inspiration behind the 1973 Programme. Holland (b. 1940) had worked as an economic assistant to the Cabinet Office and then to the Prime Minister in 1966-8, and his studies of the Italian models of public enterprise fed his work on the various sub-committees set up by the Labour NEC to work on its radical programme. It was in defence of this programme that he wrote *The Socialist Challenge* (1975), and his ideological prominence on the Left ensured his election to Westminster in 1979.

Holland developed the analysis already begun by Barratt Brown by pointing to the erosion of the Keynesian foundations of modern Labour economic thinking. The old Keynesian nostrums were suited to an age that was quickly disappearing, as capitalism moved to a new phase of development. The Labour Keynesians had distinguished between the micro-economic capitalist firms and the macro-economic policy of the government, which was able to regulate those firms through demand management. However, the development of the multinational economy had created an intermediate or meso-economic sphere between the two traditional sectors of the economy. To Holland, 'the new giant companies have created a new mode of production, distribution and exchange in the heartland of the British economy',[18] undermining the traditional control exercised by the State. Through their sheer size, they were able to enjoy a near monopolistic power, so that the competition so beloved of Tory ideology had degenerated into a competitive struggle between these multinational trusts over the takeover of smaller firms. They enjoyed abnormal profits which they were able to use to their own advantage against smaller firms, and their ability to transfer debt and payments allowed them to declare lower profits (for tax purposes) than those actually made.

As a result, these large multinationals had advanced to the centre of the economy, pushing the small firms to the periphery. In doing so, they had pushed the *British* government and *British* firms into a subordinate position. The government was becoming less and less able to control their meso-economic power, and was actually increasing this power — through public subsidy. Thus, the attempt of government to encourage regional investment and technical efficiency through its fiscal policy ended up by merely giving money to multinationals who would set up branches in deprived areas, often without creating much employment as they were mainly capital-intensive projects. The result was merely to worsen the regional problem of unequal distribution of resources in the economy.

The development of this meso-economic power was totally undermining the Crosland thesis that capitalism had developed into a democratic economy through the managerial revolution and the ability of a larger number of people to buy shares. In fact, argued Holland, personal shareholders were increasingly becoming a capitalist anachronism as the institutional shareholders — the pension and investment trusts — increased their share of ownership of the large firms. Personal shareholding did, of course, continue to exist, but it was becoming a mere cover to disguise the extent to which Britain's economic destiny was controlled by the multinationals. Their power made a mockery of the claims of the revisionists in regard to the managerial revolution. To Holland, 'the rise of managerial capitalism has not diluted the power of capitalism as a mode of production, but has increased the power of managers in the dominant mesoeconomic sector'.[19]

The growth of the multinational company had a major impact on the international strength of the British economy. Since the war, the *inter*national system of trade and payment had been replaced by a *multi*national system in which trade was conducted between the *same* firms in different countries, intensifying the threat to national economic sovereignty. The normal incentives and constraints of the price system had been suspended by the multinationals because they were their own main market. Their global strength only served to reinforce their economic power in the British market, a power by which the effectiveness of traditional Keynesian policies had been totally undermined. For example, monetary policy had been nullified by the access of the multinationals to finance outside Britain, while fiscal policy was totally distorted by the need to offer tax concessions to attract and retain these giants in the home market.

To counteract this power, Holland argued that the Labour party must realise that the present mix of the economy between the private and the public sectors had outlived its use. It was not the public sector which had failed. The State had merely concentrated its power in the social services and the infrastructure of the economy, a crucial but unprofitable sector of the economy which had been taken over to help the private sector. However, 'while such a public sector base is a *necessary* condition for the success of the remaining sectors, it is not a *sufficient* condition'.[20] The public sector was a passive, growth-dependent sector which in itself was not capable of overturning a deficit in the trade balance or of promoting a more equitable regional sector.

It was the active growth-initiating sector of the economy, the private sector, which had really failed, according to Holland. It had failed to maintain a rate of growth high enough to maintain an adequate provision of social services; it had failed to sustain a level of investment sufficient to guarantee price stability and full employment; it had failed to reduce the regional imbalance of wealth and jobs in the country; and it had failed to export sufficient goods to maintain Britain's strength in a competitive world. Through this failure the main source of revenue for the public sector, wich inevitably derived from taxation of the wealth generated by the private sphere, had dried up, producing a fiscal crisis of increasing proportions. The private sector had thus become a deadweight on the British people.

It was in the context of a meso-economic private sector which was failing the public that Holland sought a socialist remedy of state intervention through planning and public ownership. The modern state had not fully realised the changes which had taken place in international capitalism, undermining traditional Keynesian solutions by undermining the national sovereignty on which those solutions were based. It was this failure of understanding which had led to the failure of the Labour government's National Plan, according to Holland. As a capitalist plan it had aimed to alleviate rather than abolish poverty, and had sought to maintain intact the class structure which was the principal cause of inequality. Summing up Labour's failure in 1964-70, Holland argued that, 'having failed to grasp that social redistribution depended on socialist transformation, it was forced to cut back on the very social expenditure supposed to alleviate injustice and inequality.'[21]

This was matched by a failure to learn the lessons of indicative planning in France after the war. As a result of the purges after the German occupation, France had enjoyed a timid Civil Service and a much greater control over private enterprise than that held by the Wilson government in Britain. In Labour's experience, the power of the Civil Service and the private sector over the interpretation of any policy had strangled national capitalist planning in its adolescence. The growing trend to monopoly and multinational domination had made nonsense of any plan which failed to challenge that domination.

Any government which seriously wished to counter the trend to meso-economic power must, according to Holland, harness the market power of leading manufacturing companies to its own purpose by an extension of state intervention. This intervention would take the two main forms of public ownership and a state agency which would directly guide private investment into socially useful sectors of the economy through planning agreements. The traditional socialist response of public ownership was necessary, of course, as a spearheading function which would give the government and the unions a leverage over the meso-economic sectors which had been hitherto unaccountable. It would enable a government to be more aware of the real structures of cost and price by providing comparative information in such subjects and by identifying areas in which the meso-economic sector would be able to transfer funds and profits. It would also place the government in a position to counter the blackmail employed by some of the multi-nationals on a hitherto passive public sector.

However, it was with the idea of a state planning agency that Holland hoped to show the new possibilities open to a more just economy. He looked to the Italian example of IRI (the Industrial Reconstruction Institute) set up by Mussolini and used by subsequent Italian governments to develop the economy. This had, of course, already been tried through the IRC (the Industrial Reorganisation Corporation) set up as a part of the National Plan in 1966, but the IRC had been too small to have much effect on the British economy. A revamped IRC in the form of a National Enterprise Board would, however, have a major effect in stimulating the private sector through an active policy of state intervention and direction. To Holland, 'a British IRI type state holding company . . . could place an instrument of unprecedented flexibility and effectiveness at the disposition of the government'.[22] Its own entrepreneurship in a multitude of sectors in the key manufacturing sectors which promoted economic growth would make a socialist plan a reality.

Holland was aware of traditional socialist objections that this was merely a new mix of the economy rather than an end to the private sector, but he rejected them as purist. The existing state *could* be used on behalf of the working class if that class was willing to learn from the new modes of state intervention used abroad to benefit the capitalist class. Holland argued that

> to ignore the techniques of state capitalism because they *are* state capitalist is not only to allow the devil some of the best tunes, but also to risk siren seduction of some sections of the working class, who would readily change job insecurity for job security, whatever the prevailing mode of production.[23]

This did, of course, assume that a British version of IRI in a 'mixed economy' would provide job security. It was not public ownership as much as increased state intervention which was required, according to Holland (though this did not rule out a later extension of the public sector).

He was, however, very much aware of the dangers of a renewed national corporation — IRI was, after all, founded as a key element of the corporate state in Italy — but he saw industrial democracy as the means by which this could be avoided. Through giving workers a *majority* control over decision-making at the plant level, a major step to a non-corporatist socialism would be taken. Thus,

> the question of social control is crucial . . . Without a socialisation of control, with new forms of industrial and economic democracy, and new negotiation of changed ends for the use of resources, the institutions of state ownership and planning would tend to mean corporatism or state capitalism rather than a transition to socialist planning and socialised development.[24]

In workers' control lay the escape from corporatism, but it was a long way from the direct democracy of the producer put forward in the syndicalist and guild socialist traditions.

Moreover, it was an industrial democracy restricted to the context of the nation-state. Holland's analysis was geared to the survival of the *British* economy in a competitive world market. As with Barratt Brown, the *British* capitalist was not the villain as much as the multinational companies, floating around the world economy without any concern for national sovereignty. Holland therefore saw a Labour government as *leading* the *nation* by redirecting the *outward* flow of investment back into the British economy where it should be contributing to raising British industrial capacity.[25] Indeed, Labour's 'hopes of acting on behalf of the nation *as a whole* have been undermined by the erosion of national economic sovereignty by the new mesoeconomic power'[26] (my italics). The working class was seen by Holland as acting against the enemies of *the nation*, not against any class enemies it might itself have. The Marxist language used by Holland was, as with so many of the New Left both inside and outside the Labour party, superficial in its resemblance to Marx's own analysis.

Godley and Cripps

Holland's analysis was not universally accepted by the Labour Left,[27] but its presuppositions of a corporatist economy dominated by supra-national companies, together with his prescriptions of a recapture by the state of national control, proved highly influential. The twin policies of Keynesian economics and corporatist management adopted by the corporate socialists were identified as defective for any socialist strategy, but the theorists of the Labour Left sought to remedy the defects by a process of updating the original model rather than rejecting it altogether.

Thus Wynne Godley and Francis Cripps, two leading members of the Cambridge Economic Policy Group and intellectual mentors of the new Tribune Left, accepted the *inadequacy* of Keynesian economics in the circumstances of the slumpflation of the seventies (mainly because Keynes did not take money adequately into account), but this did not lead them to reject the Keynesian analysis. Instead, they worked 'to re-establish the quintessentially Keynesian principle of effective demand as the determinant of real output and employment'.[28] It was the absence of external controls over investment and imports which had negated the demand management policies used so successfully after the war. Fiscal policy was no longer sufficient to maintain a level of full employment and price stability in the face of a deteriorating performance of the country in international trade.

To offset this situation, Godley and Cripps called for import controls as a means of regaining control of the national economy. A policy of demand expansion and reflation could then take place without the increased expenditure being diverted to imports. This policy would both save British jobs and, if used against relatively successful countries with preferential treatment for non-industrialised countries, would lead to an expansion of world demand which would eventually benefit all nations. The dangers of setting off a protectionist war would be avoided if import controls were used correctly and discriminately, as the relatively successful economies like West Germany and the United States would recognise the benefits of expanded trade for them from the increasing prosperity of the rest of the world.[29]

Godley and Cripps were able to maintain their faith in Keynesian economists only by transferring the causes of economic crisis to an unspecified source *outside* the nation-state in which demand management policies were supposed to work. Moreover, their hope that a trade war could be avoided was based on the belief that inflation could end the international crisis, and that other governments would idly sit by while it happened. However, the breakdown of the international system of regulated trade in the seventies has increased the tendencies towards a trade war irrespective of different governments' economic policies, as pressure from domestic industries and unions to protect investment and jobs has intensified. The readiness of the United States to impose restrictions on steel imports from Europe is an indication that American economic policy is becoming governed by the fear of imports as much as the economic thinking of the Labour Left. As all other capitalist countries seem to characterise their failures by reference to everybody else as well, the real cause of economic crisis is probably concealed.

Hodgson

The corporatist, undemocratic nature of British society was the main object of attack for the Labour Left in the seventies. However, where the New Left were highly suspicious of Labour as a parliamentary party hostile to extra-parliamentary activity, the new Labour Left saw no reason why parliamentary *and* extra-parliamentary activity could not go together hand in hand. The assertion by Ralph Miliband that Labour was too immersed in parliamentary practice to support action by the labour *movement* was disproved in practice as Tony Benn marched arm in arm with the UCS workers, and as the IWC reminded Labour that it had a tradition other than the Morrisonian and Fabian stress on the expert. The criticisms of the Labour Party by the New Left were nullified as Miliband's call for a broader strategy of action was integrated into Labour thinking.

The most cogent presentation of the new labour thinking was made by Geoff Hodgson, in his *Socialism and Parliamentary Democracy* (1979). Hodgson (b. 1946), an economist who had been closely involved in Trotskyist politics before joining the Labour Party, rejected insurrectionary politics as an infantile adventure, but he also rejected any simple reliance on parliamentary democracy. Parliament, on its own, could have little power to effect social change against the social customs and forces which had acted as a brake on such change throughout British history. Without the mass participation of workers through their struggles for better working conditions and control over the autocratic rights of the manager, any Labour Cabinet would be isolated in the face of the awesome power of capital. With the strength of an organised and active working class behind them, a Labour government with all the legitimacy of parliamentary power behind it would be able to wrest social and economic power from the capitalists.

Hodgson even envisaged the advocacy of soviets, the workers' councils which had served as the basis for the ideas of direct democracy put forward by Lenin in *State and Revolution*. However, the resemblance with Leninism was merely superficial, as Hodgson envisaged such soviets as instruments of local economic government which were to be strictly subordinate to Parliament. Unlike Lenin (and Marx), Hodgson did not see Parliament as a legitimatist façade for a bourgeois dictatorship, and saw no reason why it should be smashed rather than modified. The notion of a proletarian dictatorship, in which the middle classes who refused to accept working-class rule would be disfranchised, was explicitly rejected by him. It was absolutely alien to the constitutionalist politics of Labour, so that Hodgson's conception of the soviets did not differ at all from Cole's conception of the workers' guild. To Hodgson,

Parliament would act as a counter-balance, an expression of the general interest in counterposition to the particular will of the soviet. It would be the main arena for bringing together the various aspirations of the workers, for the forging of a common hegemonic policy.[30]

The revolutionary language concealed a mode of thought very much in Labour's political traditions.[31]

Benn

The hopes and aspirations of the Labour Left were savagely frustrated by the performance of the 1974-9 Labour government. Its radical potential was never fulfilled, and Wilson took advantage of the Left's defeat in the EEC referendum in June 1975 to shift Tony Benn from the sensitive Industry post to that of Energy. The economic crisis, culminating in the run on sterling in December 1976, led to a policy of subservience to the dictates of the International Monetary Fund, to wage restraint and to cuts in public expenditure. The Social Contract became a tactical measure to retain formal union support for the government, and was finally destroyed by the discontent of the union rank and file in the winter of discontent in 1978-9. The return of a government of the radical Right in May 1979 threw Labour into disarray as the Social Democratic wing of the party prepared to move out on its own. It was Stuart Holland who pointed out the ominous fact that

> the edge of Thatcher's axe was not only ground in the Treasury under a Labour administration, but fell and fell again in successive Labour budgets. The monetarism blue in tooth and claw which we now see . . . was adopted against Party opinion by Labour ministers in the Treasury and Cabinet.[32]

In the face of this disappointment, the demands of the Left for democracy to be extended to the party as well as industry grew in intensity. Already, in 1972, three Labour MPs, Frank Allaun, Ian Mikardo and Jim Sillars, had demanded the election of the party leader by the party as a whole in a Tribune pamphlet, *Labour – Party or Puppet?* Ken Coates had made a powerful plea for reform in his *Democracy in the Labour Party* (1977), where he compared the narrow circle of MPs who elected the Labour leader with the more democratic forms of election adopted by socialist and Labour parties elsewhere. Coates specifically linked his call for the democratisation of the party with his own campaign for workers' control, as he pointed out that

> it becomes distinctly illogical for Labour activists to canvass vigorously for the widening of the industrial franchise, and yet to leave unquestioned all the rituals which have crystallised in the interaction between their own Party bureaucracy and the least desirable conventions of constitutional practice.[33]

The calls for increased democracy in the party and in society focused on the personality and politics of Tony Benn. Born in 1925 into a radical family, his father had been a Minister in Ramsay Macdonald's second Labour government, and had become Viscount Stansgate. Benn himself achieved notoriety when he succeeded to the title and fought a long constitutional battle to renounce it. His eventual victory established his radical democratic credentials, but there was little else to mark him out as particularly left wing, and he became closely identified with the Wilsonian technocrats as Minister of Technology in 1966. However, as he himself said,

> it was then that my political position changed, because the more I saw of this process [i.e. State coaxing of the private sector] the more I became convinced (a) that it would not work, (b) that it was corporatist, and (c) that it was anti-trade union and undemocratic.[34]

He gradually moved to a much more militant position in the Labour party, taking up the calls for workers' control, radical redistribution of wealth, and nuclear disarmament. By the time of the 1979 election defeat, his standing as a Cabinet Minister with eleven years' experience gave him an authority which established him as the successor to Bevan as leader of the Labour Left. In his *Arguments for Socialism* (1979) and *Arguments for Democracy* (1981), he gave an authortative exposition of the ideas of the new, 'Bennite' Left in the Party.

He certainly rejected the Marxism of which he was often accused, basing himself instead on radical Christian doctrine. Like the ethical socialists, he placed himself in the long tradition of English radicalism, which had expressed itself in the language of religion in its call for the establishment of a human brotherhood based on equality and liberty. In reducing all emotions and moralities to the level of economic forces, Marxism was held by Benn to be unacceptable. His libertarian sense of tolerance certainly led him to acknowledge the debt owed by the Labour Party to Marx's teachings, and he accepted a legitimate place in the party for Marxists. However, he himself looked to Christian morality as the touchstone of his political motivation, describing himself as

> a Christian whose political commitment owes much more to the teachings of Jesus — without the mysteries within which they are presented — than to the writings of Marx, whose analysis seems to

lack an understanding of the deeper needs of humanity.[35]

As a radical Christian, Benn pointed to the decline of democracy in Britain as capitalism took on an increasingly corporatist form. The powers which controlled the lives of the British people were becoming more concentrated, international, secretive, and unaccountable, so that parliamentary democracy itself was becoming a dangerous façade behind which decisions were taken by an unrepresentative group who were thinking only of their own interests. Its deliberations concealed an impotence in the face of a systematic transfer of power in Britain to the Common Market, the multinationals, the IMF, and the Pentagon.

The Establishment, according to Benn, had covered up this transfer of power by means of its control of the media – part of its 'cultural hegemony', in the language of the New Left. The media, which had a tremendous power over public opinion, was owned by a few large firms which used it to defend capitalist interests and policies. Overwhelming pro-Conservative, it had split the Labour party by a sustained and long campaign to separate the Labour leaders from what the press described as the 'extremists' of the constituencies. It had constantly attacked the trade union movement, both openly and in more subtle forms, as opposed to 'the national interest' and had conducted a skilful campaign to spread fear of the Soviet Union in order to maintain the US military presence. The media had become a major threat to the working of British democracy, and they were virtually free from any accountability to the public.

In many ways, Benn's arguments were a continuation of the Labour Marxist analysis of the British Constitution by Harold Laski. He pointed to the dangers of the royal prerogative which could be used to unseat a constitutionally elected Prime Minister (as had happened to Gough Whitlam in Astralia in 1975); the delaying powers of the House of Lords; and the power of the media to mobilise popular opinion. Like Laski, he recognised the dangers of an unwritten Constitution created by the 'Establishment'. He pointed out that

> unlike countries where the overthrow of elected governments by a non-elected military elite has to take place in open defiance of the constitutional safeguards enjoyed by the people, and is thus seen to be illegal, the British Constitution reserves all its ultimate safeguards for the non-elected elite. The democratic rights of the people can, in a crisis, be adjudicated to be illegal, thus legitimising the military in extinguishing them.[36]

His own experience as a Cabinet Minister had convinced him that sensitive information was kept a secret from the Cabinet itself.

However, Benn introduced the startling idea that Britain had now become a colony which faced a national liberation struggle to free itself from the United States, the IMF, and the unpatriotic Establishment. He admitted the paradox of the idea, as Britain had until recently been the centre of a great Empire. However, as the colonies had won their freedom from the rule of the British imperial Establishment, Britain was the last colony to be ruled by that Establishment, buttressed as it was by the new colonisers of the Pentagon and the EEC. The sovereign right of any nation to make war or peace had itself been ceded in law to the United States, Benn believed, and in practice there was no limitation on the use of US nuclear weapons based in Britain. When British laws conflicted with the laws of the Common Market, the latter took precedence. In theory and in practice, Britain had become a colony of the international forces of capitalism. In declaring that she faced a struggle of national liberation, Benn was merely giving startling form to the ideas already elaborated since the late sixties that Britain was no longer in control of her own destiny.

Like Laski, Benn did not reject the institutions of parliamentary democracy on which the Labour Party had been nurtured. He saw a constitutional Parliament with real power as a crucial element in the logjam of democracy which had arisen. The forces of capital and labour were mediated by the ballot-box, which gave to the poor who have no financial resources to buy with their votes the hospitals and schools that they need. The balance of forces between capital and labour was a very unequal one though, since capital controlled the media through its wealth and was able to persuade the electorate that Labour was responsible for the weakness of the economy. In this sense, the Labour government should realise that, 'until there is a new constitutional settlement between capital and labour and the electorate, what will happen is that capital when it's strong will be deadlocked by labour and that the economy will fail'.[37] It was this new constitutional settlement, in which Labour had the part it deserved in running the country, which could alone recreate the consensus which would unleash the British economy from the vice in which it was caught.

However, these radical democratic and labourist ideas should not be confused with the type of socialism which sought the end of capitalism. Benn rejected full-blooded nationalisation, as he did the policy of no compensation put forward by Marxists, in favour of the mixed economy. He sought to modify the behaviour of capitalism rather than to destroy it root and branch. He talked of a new constitutional settlement between capital and labour, and a continuing role for private investment, as did Holland and the Labour Keynesians.

It is in this light that Benn's proposals for workers' control should be seen. On the one hand, it was located in the New Left rejection of corporate socialism, as elaborated by Morrison and enacted by the postwar Labour government. As Benn argued,

> We have waited too long for the transformation of the public corporation. . . We should be talking about the transfer of power within industry, and we should not accept existing forms of nationalisation as a form for the future. We have had enough experience now to know that nationalisation plus Lord Robens does not add up to socialism.[38]

As Industry Secretary, he encouraged the development of worker co-operatives on the model of the UCS work-in, and supported 'alternative' plans like that drawn up by the Lucas Aerospace shop stewards, who called on their employers to plan production on the basis of social need rather than profit. He also wrote of the need to make consumer representation more effective and an increased integration of the planning mechanisms of nationalised industries to prevent unnecessary conflicts between them. Above all, he saw industrial democracy as a means of breaking down the secrecy in which decisions concerning the lives of millions were taken. It was essential if the existing public sector was not to develop into a corporatist nightmare.

It was a radical democratic demand, which sought to modify the relationship between capital and labour by establishing their partnership on a more genuine and equal footing. To Benn,

> Investors there will always be, but there is no valid reason why the investors' money should give them first claim to control, before those who invest their lives. Political democracy wrested the control of Parliament from those who owned the lands and the factories. Industrial democracy is a logical and necessary development of it.[39]

In his call for labour to control the capitalists in their own interest, Benn fell into the long labourist tradition which sought a better and more equal relationship with the capitalists, subjecting them to the democratic control of the unions. It was a better deal for labour in its relationship with capital, not the abolition of that relationship which he sought.

Thus, in spite of his analysis of the Constitution in Britain being designed against the working class, Benn and the Labour Left refused to jettison constitutional methods (just as Laski refused to fully accept the Leninist theory of the State in the thirties). Democracy in Britain was only partial, and needed to be completed by major constitutional reform. Benn thus pressed for a whole series of measures, including a Freedom of Information Act which would confirm statutory right of access to all public papers (with the exception of a clearly defined category of papers relating to defence and personal matters); a constitutional Civil Service, accountable and open to public inspection; abolition of the House of Lords; and a constitutional premiership under the control of the House of Commons. It was to be a completion of the work begun by English radicals in the late eighteenth and early nineteenth centuries. The Labour Party, as a democratic party born in the mass movement of the organised trade unions, was regarded by Benn as excellently placed to carry through these reforms, uniting the nation in a democratic Britain as it did so.

It was this conception of a national alliance, led by the Labour movement against the forces of foreign capital, which was a major characteristic of the 'Bennite' Left. It was not an aggressive chauvinism – as demonstrated by Benn's stand against the Falklands War of April-June 1982 – and it enabled the Bennite Left to free themselves from the Cold War rhetoric of anti-Sovietism which began to rise from the late seventies. Benn himself refused to go as far as advocating withdrawal from NATO, admitting that 'I'm an old collective security man because of my age, and I remember the pre-war years, and the idea that if nations are attacked they should defend one another is a sound principle'.[40] He did call for Britain to become a non-nuclear member of NATO, however, expressing the vague hope that NATO and the Warsaw Pact would be able to dismantle themselves through mutual trust and a recognition of the dangers that confronted the world otherwise. The fact that other motives than distrust might exist behind the two power blocs was not really investigated.

Nevertheless, the national alliance called for by Benn and the Labour Left fell into the long democratic traditions of the Labour Party's political thought. The assumption that the social forces which divided the nation should be healed as they are less important than the forces which united the nation fell into an established pattern of thought which had maintained the unity of the Labour Party in the Great War, and which had prevented the emergence of any Marxist politics outside the confines of that party.

The adequacy of 'Bennite' politics as a challenge to corporate socialism must be questioned. The two basic components of corporate socialism as it had developed by the thirties were the Keynesian economic strategy of state guidance of the economy and the corporate form of public enterprises, run by experts free from daily interference by the State. It would be on this basis that the social services would grow into a true welfare state.

However, the Keynesian analysis was not rejected by the 'Bennite' Left as much as modified. The Labour Left had always held to the underconsumptionist analysis of lack of effective demand put forward by Hobson, and this had been merely reinforced by Keynes. The demand that wealth should be redistributed within the Keynesian framework was, indeed, a restatement of the Hobsonian ideas expressed by the ILP in *The Living Wage* in 1926. It was not too surprising, then, that the Left should not wish to jettison Keynes altogether. Even Geoff Hodgson, one of the more radical economists of the Labour Left, wrote that 'there is no reason. . . to abandon Keynesian policies; it is simply necessary to *supplement* them with radical intervention in the industrial sphere'.[41]

However, Keynesian policies had manifestly failed as a means of offsetting crisis and regulating a capitalist economy. It had been formed in the *specific* conditions of the thirties, at a time of high unemployment and falling prices, so that increased state expenditure ran little risk of the crippling inflation that bedevils today's mixed economies. The Left's call for a reflationary policy to expand demand has, therefore, been based on a supplement to Keynes, which tries to explain crisis as caused by *foreign* forces. The belief that foreign goods cause the crisis, and need to be controlled, may well make sense in looking at the world economy through national eyes, but from the viewpoint of capital as a whole it is a fallacy. Virtually every country regards the others as the cause of the crisis, and as a result there has been an increased tendency to protectionism and trade wars. In this context, the Left's hope that import controls could avoid a trade war appear increasingly forlorn. In retaining the essence of Keynesian policies, transferring the cause of the failure of Keynesianism out of sight by relegating it to other countries, the 'Bennite' Left remain trapped in the confines of the corporate socialism they sought to break.

There was a similar failure to break from the other tenet of corporate socialism by advocacy of workers' control. The demands of the IWC tended to fall into the same traps as their syndicalist forefathers. In their underestimation of the political power of the State, and their overestimation of the social power of the worker at the factory, they failed to challenge the power of capitalist society effectively. It was the factory, rather than the state, which they hoped to influence, with the result that their own hopes of the educational value of the worker co-operative were dashed by the hostile attitude of the government once Tony Benn had been shunted out of the Industry post. The co-ops were finally destroyed by the harsh logic of the market, which they had never really challenged.

Indeed, the demand for workers' control had always been tied to the dynamics of the shop stewards' movement. Just as the post-war depression of 1920-1 had destroyed the impetus behind the first shop stewards' movement, so the increasing Depression of the seventies crippled the power of the second.[42] The fate of Hugh Scanlon, whose militancy declined along with the power of the shop stewards and who eventually went to the House of Lords, is an indication of the movement's failure. The demand for industrial democracy seems to have wavered as the efficacy of workshop bargaining has declined, and the problems of mass unemployment have overridden many other industrial issues.

Most crucially, in its emphasis on a change in the relations between labour and capital so that the former was given more power, it failed to pose the abolition of the system of wage-labour. It fell into the same trade union politics which had predominated in the British labour movement since the days of Hodgskin, in that its hostility to *capitalists* left the social power of *capital* intact. The destruction of the power of capital advocated by Marx was shelved or cancelled altogether in favour of control of capitalist enterprises, in the hope that employers would not conceal vital information from their workforce. The call for a new constitutional settlement between capital and labour made by Tony Benn was a logical result of this failure to make a fundmental challenge to the nature of capital. Without this challenge, however, the Bennite demands for a constitutional premiership and a constitutional civil service might well run into the evasions and frustrations by rulers so brilliantly analysed by Robert Michels[43] when he formulated his iron law of oligarchy. The hope that accountability through devices like immediate recall and referendum might modify this law seems forlorn if there are direct material and social interests at stake. Without the destruction of those interests, the 'Bennite' Left may well find themselves attacking the shadow rather than the substance of power.

The consequence of this failure to break from corporate socialism adequately has been the failure to resolve the dilemma of the Labour Party analysed by Aneurin Bevan in 1931 — whether Labour was to represent the nation or the working class. The new Labour Left had hoped to resolve the dilemma by demonstrating that Britain had become a colony of the multinationals and the IMF. However, the basis of their analysis of the strength of the multinationals in the British economy is questionable statistically,[44] while figures on how far the nature of domestic production is undercut by foreign competition are neither available nor easily computed.

However, the undoubted presence of foreign competition and multinational companies does not detract from the role played by *British* capitalists both in their relation to British workers and in relation to their own investment in the rest of the world. Benn's description of Britain as a colony which must fight a national liberation struggle does not fit with the level of capital exports to Africa and Latin America, nor with its imperial role in Malaya and Aden since the last war. The role of the British army in Northern Ireland since 1969, and the refusal of the British working class to oppose that role, indicate a very different part played by Britain in the post-war world to that of a colony.

The 'Bennite' Left, and Benn in particular, have opposed much of the aggressive nationalism which came to the fore in the 1982 Falklands War on the basis of a humanitarian radicalism which had much in common with the UDC and the ILP in the First World War. Their nationalism is liberal and humane, but the consequences in a world drifting towards protectionism and trade war remain the same. Foreign goods are the cause of the crisis, and foreign goods must be kept out of the country through import controls. It is exactly the same argument with which the Left supports non-racist immigration laws — it is foreign workers who threaten British goods and foreign workers must therefore be kept out through immigration controls.

Behind the 'Bennite' Left is the assumption that the class divisions in British society are less important than the forces which unite the nation against foreign capital. It is not a xenophobic assumption, but the Left should not be surprised if the British labour movement sees foreign workers as well as foreign capitalists as their enemies. The same situation occurred, as has been seen, in August 1914, when socialists and workers of countries throughout Europe similarly lined up behind their rulers against the rulers and workers of other countries.

Notes

1. For a critique of the workings of the mixed economy, see Paul Mattick *Marx and Keynes; the Limits of the Mixed Economy* (Merlin, 1971).

2. Michael Foot, 'Credo of the Labour Left', in *New Left Review* No. 49, May-June 1968, p. 25.

3. Michael Foot, 'Can We Save the Government', in *Tribune*, 29 March 1968, p. 12.

4. See, for example, the savage attacks on the Labour Left in P. Foot, *The Politics of Harold Wilson* (Penguin, 1968).

5. Report of Plenary Session of the Workers' Control Conference 1968, in K. Coates and W. Williams, *How and Why Industry Must be Democratised* (IWC, 1969), p. 25.

6. Ernie Roberts, 'Workers Control and the Trade Unions', in K. Coates ed., *Can The Workers Run Industry?* (Sphere, 1968), p. 97.

7. For this process, see K. Middlemas, *Politics in Industrial Society* (Andre Deutsch, 1979).

8. See, for example, Colin Barker, 'The British Labour Movement: Aspects of Current Experience', in *International Socialism* No. 28, Spring 1967.

9. Hugh Scanlon, 'Interview' in *New Left Review* No. 46, Nov.-Dec. 1967, p. 4.

10. Michael Barratt Brown, 'Limits of the Welfare State', in K. Coates ed., *Can The Workers Run Industry*, p. 31. See A. Glyn and B. Sutcliffe, *British Capitalism, Workers and the Profit Squeeze* (Penguin, 1972) for a development of this Ricardian argument.

11. Michael Barratt Brown, *From Labourism to Socialism: The Political Economy of Labour in the 1970s* (Spokesman, 1972), p. 224.

12. Ibid., p. 12.

13. Ibid., p. 71.

14. Ibid., p. 62.

15. K. Coates, 'Socialists and the Labour Party', in *Socialist Register*, 1973, p. 177.

16. Arthur Scargill, 'The New Unionism' in *New Left Review* No. 92, July-August 1975, p. 4

17. Labour Party, *Programme for Britain, 1973*, p. 7.

18. Stuart Holland, *The Socialist Challenge* (Quartet, 1975), p. 51.

19. Ibid., p. 70.

20. Ibid., p. 146.

21. Ibid., p. 34.

22. Stuart Holland, 'Adoption and Adaptation of the IRI Formula', in Stuart Holland ed., *The State as Entrepreneur – New Dimensions for Public Enterprise* (Weidenfeld and Nicholson 1972), p. 251.

23. Holland, *Socialist Challenge*, p. 154.

24. Stuart Holland, 'Introduction', in Stuart Holland ed., *Beyond Capitalist Planning* (Basil Blackwell, 1978), p. 3.

25. See Holland, *Socialist Challenge*, p. 77.

26. Ibid., p. 155.

27. See, for example, Geoff Hodgson, *Labour at the Crossroads: The Political and Economic Challenge of Labour in the 1980s* (Martin Robertson, 1981), who points out that transfers of capital are due to the lack of profitability rather than the nationality of any particular owner of capital.

28. Wynne Godley and Francis Cripps, *Macroeconomics* (Oxford University Press, 1983), p. 305.

29. For the classic 'Tribunite' case for import controls, see W. Godley and

F. Cripps, 'Control of Imports as a means to full employment and the expansion of world trade: the UK case', in *Cambridge Journal of Economics*, vol. 2, no. 3, Sept. 1978. The authors see deflation and devaluation as the only alternatives to import controls.

30. Geoff Hodgson, *Socialism and Parliamentary Democracy* (Spokesman, 199), p. 78.

31. Interestingly enough, this was linked with Hodgson's rejection of the Marxist theory of crisis in 'The Theory of the Falling Rate of Profit in *New Left Review* No. 84, March-April 1974.

32. Stuart Holland, 'Capital, Labour and the State', in K. Coates ed., *What Went Wrong?* (Spokesman, 1979), p. 208-9.

33. Ken Coates, *Democracy in the Labour Party* (Spokesman, 1977), p. 15.

34. Tony Benn, *Parliament, People and Power* (Verso, 1982), p. 10.

35. Tony Benn, *Arguments for Democracy* (Jonathan Cape, 1981), p. 130. See particularly his lecture to the Marx Memorial Library printed in *Marxism Today*, May 1982.

36. Tony Benn, *Arguments for Democracy*, p. 9.

37. Interview with author, in *Capital and Class* No. 17, Summer, 1982, p. 27.

38. Tony Benn, *Arguments for Socialism* (Penguin Books, 1980), p. 60.

39. Ibid., p. 43.

40. Interview with author in Ibid, p. 26. He has recently advocated withdrawal from NATO *–see Marxism Today*. January, 1986, p. 14.

41. Geoff Hodgson, *Labour at the Crossroads* (Martin Robertson, 1981), p. 210.

42. See, for example, Christine Edwards, 'The Activities and Power of Workplace Representatives on the Railways: a Comparative Study'. Social Science Research Council research paper, 1982; Christine Edwards, 'Power and decision-making in the workplace: a study in the coalmining industry', in *Industrial Relations Journal*, Spring 1983.

43. See R. Michels, *Political Parties: A Sociological Study of the Oligarchical Tendencies of Modern Democracy* (London, 1915).

44. See the discussion in Jim Tomlinson, *The Unequal Struggle: British Socialism and the Capitalist Enterprise* (Methuen, 1982), chapter 6.

15 CONCLUSION – LABOUR IN THE EIGHTIES

The victory of the Bennite Left at the special party conference in January 1981 appeared to be decisive. A fundamental change to the party constitution had shifted the balance of power away from the parliamentary party, subjecting it to more control by activists in the constituencies, and had established the predominance of the unions in the party as a whole by giving them two-fifths of the vote in an electoral college to elect the party leader (the rest of the vote being divided equally between the constituencies and the MPs). At the same time, the Bennites had succeeded in winning party support for unilateral nuclear disarmament, withdrawal from the Common Market, and a radical programme of economic planning.

However, the conference was the high-water mark of the Bennites. Their victory in the Labour Party was not the same as a victory in the country as a whole. Despite a massive rise in unemployment under a tough government of the militant Right, the Labour Party collapsed as a viable alternative to Thatcherism. It was badly disrupted in the spring of 1981 with the secession of the SDP, and became identified with extremism after a virulent press campaign against Tony Benn. The indecisive leadership of Michael Foot, who failed to unite the party's warring factions, and the long drawn-out controversy over Trotskyist infiltration merely heightened the contrast with a decisive (and, after the Falklands conflict, militarily victorious) government.

The result, in the election of June 1983, was a major shock for the Labour Party. Its vote slumped to only 28.3 per cent (against 26.1 per cent for the Alliance of Liberals and SDP), and it was placed in the apparently impossible electoral position of needing a bigger swing to gain power at the next election than that obtained in the halcyon days of 1945. As, for the first time in decades, Labour failed to capture a majority of the trade union vote, the Left finally realised that its own radicalism was not shared by the majority of the working class. It was a badly frightened party which elected the youthful Neil Kinnock as its leader in October 1983, and a party which would go to great lengths to avoid the discussion of ideas which seemed to symbolise the divisiveness which had brought Labour to the brink of a political catastrophe worse than that of 1931.

However, the period since the election is witnessing an evolution, rather than an end, to the Labour Party's political thought. In one sense, there has been a reinforcement of trends which have been developing over the past decade. The rejection of corporate socialism has been accepted by the bulk of the party, which is becoming committed in its opposition to the centralised state, while left-wing policies on defence have been reaffirmed. The traditional revisionist wing of the party has been left to cope with the changes, and is successfully putting its own stamp on the party's economic policies through the new deputy leader, Roy Hattersley. Moreover, the Left of the party has been badly split and demoralised after the defeat of the long and violent miners' strike of 1984-85. A 'realigned' Left has rejected the politics of direct action in the interests of unity, leaving their former comrades isolated.

While the 'hard' Left of the party seeks to recapture the lost voters by basing their appeal on the left wing of the working class, the leadership has pinned its hopes on an adaptation of the party's programme to the aspirations of the right wing of that class. They have sought to modify party policy in order to present Labour as a national, rather than a class, party.

This moderate approach is symbolised by Neil Kinnock (b. 1942), catapulted into the leadership years ahead of expectations, as a result of the election débâcle. An active supporter of CND since his student days at Cardiff, Kinnock talked in the language of the radical, post-Bevan Left. In a pamphlet, *Why Vote Labour?* (1979), written with Nick Butler and Toby Harris, he described democracy as the touchstone of the Labour Party's socialism, and refused to identify democracy with the narrow political sphere of parliamentary representation. It was a more far-reaching concept, applying to home and the workplace, and was seen in the libertarian light of decentralisation of power. Above all, democracy meant taking control of the economy from the hands of the multinationals in order to use to the full the human and natural resources of the country. Kinnock argued that

> for democratic socialists political democracy and economic emancipation are inseparable and interdependent. Political power is dependent upon economic ownership, and economic ownership must be subject to the will of democracy. These must be the lessons of the nineteen eighties.[1]

This assertion of left-wing orthodoxy has now been channelled into a moderation of the style and substance of Labour's post-1979 policies.

This has become evident, for example, in a modification of Labour's commitment to withdraw from the Common Market. In calling for a new deal for Europe, Kinnock has sought to call for a genuine European Community rather than the food price-fixing system which it has become. It is a call couched in the radical language of democratically planned trade and industrial expansion by means of neo-Keynesian economic policies, however, and it envisages a Europe free of nuclear arms and acting as the moral force for peace once called for by the *Keep Left* group of MPs in the 1940s. There is a *modification*, rather than a rejection, of left-wing policies in Kinnock's call for a European version of the 1944 Bretton Woods conference which 'should take initiatives to harness multinational finance capital. It should aim to achieve the conditions for modern full employment policies in Europe and positive policies for the rest of the world.'[2]

Unilateralism has been accepted as party policy (confirmed at the 1984 conference) with the old guard around Callaghan and Healey resigned to being in a minority. However, it is now placed in the context of a strong conventional defence within NATO, a natural result of the Left's concentration on the evils of *nuclear* weapons.

Kinnock is no political thinker, but this should be neither surprising nor worrying in a party which has only rarely been led by people with an awareness of the importance of political theory. With the exceptions of Macdonald and Gaitskell, it has been the task of Labour leaders to unify a disparate coalition of groups with the object of electoral victory. This is not in itself disastrous, *provided* that the leader is able to give expression to a clear strategy for furthering the objectives of the labour movement in a capitalist society. Clement Attlee was hardly on an intellectual par with Durbin or Cole, but his political ability to harness the party's strategies for planning a capitalist economy into a viable programme of government was the measure of his success.

Kinnock's success or failure will ultimately depend on the understanding of Labour's theorists and strategists of how to further the aims of the labour movement and its allies. If they have the same grasp of the needs of a capitalist economy as their predecessors of the 1930s, then a future Labour government would be able to avoid the failures of the previous two decades. If they are unable to measure up to the task, then Labour's long-term electoral decline is unlikely to be halted.

The auspices for *government* as opposed to short-term electoral fortunes, do not seem bright. The international environment of the 1930s had everywhere seen the triumph of planning as confidence in the market waned. Stalin's Five Year plans, Hitler's Four Year plans, and

Roosevelt's New Deal buttressed the confidence of Labour's theorists that a planned economy was the only way forward to halt Britain's economic malaise. In the new context of the 1980s, the visible failure of corporatism has led to a revival of faith in the free market. It is not merely the New Right which has advocated economic liberalisation and hostility to nationalisation, but the Left has noted the visible ineffic-iency of the Soviet economy, the failure of Mitterand's expansionist strategy in France and the vigorous 'market socialism' of David Lange's government in New Zealand. The advocates of capitalism seem for the moment at least to have created a new context for political argument, condemning the Left to an intellectual disarray and lack of confidence which they find both strange and difficult.

It is in this context of electoral decline and ideological uncertainty that Kinnock has sought to project a particular version of British socialism both to unify the party and to present it as a 'consensus' alternative to the divisive policies of the Thatcher government. The same vague nostrums and moral platitudes which once allowed Mac-donald to captivate the Labour conferences of the 1920s have been repeated in a decentralist form. For example, he defines the general object of the party as

> to produce in plenty and distribute in justice. Producing in plenty must clearly mean maximising the efficient use of resources by planning and co-ordinating and investing capital resources and human effort. The short-sighted, speculative market system . . . never will produce the plenty necessary to meet human need.[3]

However, on being pressed on this point, Kinnock admitted the need for a mixed economy, as opposed to Thatcher's commitment to the private sector. He called for the encouragement of small employers and co-operatives, arguing that 'to pose stark alternatives of the public economy and the market economy is a supreme folly'.[4]

This rhetorical style has been seen as covering up a political vacuum by some critics,[5] but this is to misunderstand the real nature of Kinnock's project. He recognises that without electoral victory the Labour Party will be condemned to becoming a mere debating chamber, to be eventually eliminated by more relevant forces. As he put it to the 1985 party conference, 'There are some who would say that I am too preoccupied with winning. There are some who would say that in the course of seeking that objective, I am prepared to com-promise values. I say to them: there is no need to compromise values, no need to surrender socialism, no need to abandon principles; but there is the implacable need to win . . . There is not a collision between principle and power: for us as democratic socialists the two must go together.'[6] The rhetorical stress on socialist values and the attacks on the 'hard' Left of the party are an attempt to prevent the party from sinking into a principled sterility rather than a cover for an absence of ideas.

Kinnock seeks to project a radical alternative to Thatcherism by means of a return to socialist values. In a lecture to the Fabian Society in October 1985, Kinnock sought to stress the importance of the values of liberty and equality to democratic socialists in order to convince a sceptical British electorate that Labour is the party which can prevent further unemployment, and that there is a need to educate that electorate 'in the truth that the great majority of people . . . have a direct vested interest in standards of care and opportunity which can only be provided with sufficient quantity and quality by collective, democratically administered services'.[7]

This concentration on socialist values can be traced to the arguments of the political scientist, Bernard Crick, who argued in his *Socialist Values and Time* (1984) that 'when ordinary people have said that they no longer know what socialism stands for, it is unlikely that they are thinking either of details of policy in manifestos or striving for "the correct theoretical perspective"'.[8] Crick argues against both Marxists and the technocratic pragmatists that it is values which bind a society together, and that socialists must reassert the traditional values of liberty, equality and fraternity (within which he nervously includes sisterhood), if they are to recapture their political appeal. To convince people that social reform is both possible and desirable, it would be a hopeless task to indulge in 'the refining and reiteration of abstract and sometimes incomprehensible socialist theories, but rather by reawakening traditions and . . . by argument appealing to existing common beliefs and common interest'.[9]

The reassertion of socialist values is not, then, a cover for a political vacuum, but is part and parcel of a strategy to win a crucial ideological battle against the acquisitive values of a pure market economy which cares nothing for the social failures of poverty and indignity. It is seen as an attempt to win Britain back to the national unity and welfare values of the Attlee consensus.

A more fundamental criticism of Kinnock must surely focus on the *adequacy* of this strategy in combatting unemployment and industrial decline. There seems to have been a marked retreat from the need to confront the social and political power of the capitalist class to an acceptance of the state as a libertarian instrument which will promote equality of opportunity and local initiative. Corporatism is certainly rejected (at least in theory), as is seen in Kinnock's view of the state as 'an *enabling* state which is at the disposal of the people, instead of being dominant over the people . . . a servant state'[10]; but the socialist concern with class power and the immediate defence of the labour movement against the violence of the *actual* state is either evaded or denied.

The shift in presentation, and *partial* shift in policy, is influenced mainly by the realisation that Labour must recapture political viability with an electorate which is in many ways conservative. However, there is also a theoretical influence at work, in the arguments of the Communist Party historian, Eric Hobsbawm (b. 1917). The author of several studies of the labour movement, such as *Labouring Men* (1964), Hobsbawm was one of the first to begin questioning the working class foundations of the Labour Party. He had held that a fundamental social change was taking place in the labour movement's composition which would be ignored by the Left at its own peril.

This was put most succinctly in Hobsbawm's 1978 lecture to the Marx Memorial Library in London, subsequently printed as *The Forward March of Labour Halted?* (1981), and was elaborated in his controversial article, 'Labour's Lost Millions', in the *Marxism Today* journal in October 1983. He pointed to the major changes which had taken place in British capitalism in the past century, with the increasing mechanisation and technological advances enabling the working class to enjoy a major rise in living standards, especially since 1939. These living standards were now mainly affected by the political power of the Labour movement rather than the laws of capital, and this political power of labour had led to the rise of a huge public sector which co-existed with the new monopoly capitalism of the multinationals.

These changes in capitalism had been accompanied by new changes in the working class itself. More women were employed in the workforce than ever before, with the number of married women employed rising from a fifth in 1951 to a half by the end of the 1970s. There was also an increased immigrant section which had grown up, with no history of natural identification with the organised labour movement. At the same time, the traditional working class had become less homogeneous as manual occupations had declined, and a new white-collar working class was rising. Class consciousness had declined at the same time, as wage struggles had become directed at other workers, in their role as the consuming public, rather than the employers. There was a growing sectionalism in the working class, whose militancy was economistic in the narrowest sense of the term. The decline in working-class politics could be measured by the decline in the Labour vote and the membership crisis of the Labour Party, as it was by the failure of the trade union movement to make any significant advances in membership.

As a remedy, Hobsbawm called on the labour movement to look to the record of the Italian Communist Party, which had retained and built upon its working-class support as a result of its ability to become a *popular* party rather than a party exclusively associated with the traditional working class. Unlike the Italian Communists, the British Labour Party was able to win independent electoral power, but only if it was able to become a broad movement appealing to the mass of the population. To Hobsbawm,

> the future of Labour and the advance to socialism depends on mobilising people who remember the date of the Beatles' break-up and not the date of the Saltley pickets; of people who have never read *Tribune* and who do not give a damn about the deputy leadership of the Labour Party.[11]

A party which merely catered to the small minority of left-wing activists was a party doomed to electoral isolation and eventual disappearance.

In building a broad movement, Hobsbawm pointed out that principle had no need to be sacrificed to opportunism. As an example, he pointed to the broad appeal of CND, which had revived after 1980 to organise mass demonstrations with a wide appeal to the middle classes as well as the traditional labour movement. What was needed was a presentation of radical policies in a manner which would recapture the millions of voters who refused to vote Labour and, as a result, allowed the victory of a radical and reactionary government of the Right. 'If labour cannot get back the sort of community represented by Stevenage, or Harlow, or Swindon, or Slough, we can forget about the British or any other realistic road to socialism.'[12] To win these people back, Hobsbawm was calling for a modern version of the 1930s Popular Front of the middle and working class. The Popular Front tactic had formed Hobsbawm's own politics in the 1930s, and had generally served as the basis of the Communist Party's attempts to affiliate to the Labour

Party since that time.

However, the necessity of recapturing the votes of the 'upwardly mobile' working class, more interested in buying their own homes than in class solidarity, *does* involve a modification at the very least of Labour radicalism. Unilateralism must be presented in terms of strengthening conventional defence, rather than in the naively moralistic tones of *Keep Left* neutralism, if it is to appeal to working-class aspirants to Surbiton. A concern for the poor and homeless must not be allowed to become associated with any major defiance of law and order if vital votes may be lost in the process. The fatal dilemma of a radical party seeking the 'middle ground' of a conservative electorate in order to win office cannot be avoided, as has been recognised by the astute managers of the Labour Party in the aftermath of electoral defeat.

This has been expressed most clearly by Paul Whiteley in his analysis of *The Labour Party in Crisis* (1983). He argues that middle-class activists, idealist in their politics and articulate in their language, have been driving the working-class members, concerned as they are with more material interests and inarticulate in their language, out of the party. Whiteley expresses the politics of the new leadership in arguing that the party should reject the 'maximalist' proposals of the Bennite Left in favour of a more realistic programme of moderate reflation, incomes policy and gradual social reform. He argues that 'this does not mean a wholesale revision of party policy, but it does mean abandoning extravagant commitments which cannot be credibly met'.[13] As an example, he points to the Labour commitment to bring unemployment down to a million in the short term or to phase out nuclear defence in a short period. There is nothing wrong with such policies, but they must be seen as long-term commitments rather than immediate promises which cannot be fulfilled. Only in this way can electoral realignment be avoided, and the lost voters be brought back into the Labour camp.

Hobsbawm and Whiteley are right to point out that socialism cannot be achieved overnight, and to stress the obstacles and problems that lie in the way of convincing a conservative working class of the need for socialism. It is particularly necessary to stress the need for political, rather than merely trade union, action if any major advance is to take place. The failure of the 1926 General Strike, and the transitory success of more recent strike movements, all indicate that the working-class movement must take up issues – such as Northern Ireland and immigration controls – which are far wider than their own living standards.

However, it is the actual achievement of a socialist society by the new Labour leadership which must be in grave doubt. Their acceptance of a mixed economy is combined with neo-Keynesian policies to plan capitalism by expanding public spending. The failure of such policies in the seventies is generally explained away in the same way as the Bennite Left explained it away — as due to international competition — while its future success is still based on the hope that a protectionist trade policy will not worsen the crisis or intensify a growing trade war. In particular, an increasing number of the new Labour politicians from Paul Whiteley to Geoff Hodgson are arguing for a policy to control wages in order to prevent the hoped-for economic recovery from being choked off by wage militancy. This may work if the unions fail to recover from the union legislation and unemployment of the Thatcher government, but if the working class fight to protect their living standards a future Labour government would find itself once more reliving the agonies and failures of the Wilson/Callaghan years.

The change in the composition of the working class pointed to by Hobsbawm has certainly taken place (though this does not mean that the traditional industrial working class has lost its importance), and no socialist movement could succeed without attracting the support of people who do not at the moment see socialism as particularly relevant to their lives. However, Hobsbawm seems to be calling on the labour movement to adapt to the political values of the non-socialist sections of the population. His attacks on public sector workers who harm the community, together with his calls for a movement based on 'the people' rather than the working class, prevent Hobsbawm (or the new Labour leadership) from seeing the need to risk a temporary unpopularity by advocating a class politics which are at the moment out of fashion. Instead of an attempt to rally and organise the dispirited left-wing sections of the working class, there is an appeal to those non-socialist sections who hunger after an illusory individual security from the frightening world outside.

A major consequence of the shift away from the Left is the acceptance of the distinction between middle-class idealists concerned about freedom and working-class materialists concerned only about satisfying their own stomachs. This distinction — initially made by Frank Parkin in his study of the middle-class radicals in CND and raised again by Paul Whiteley — is both insulting and false. The working-class movements of the past were committed both to satisfying their own material needs *and* to the creation of a better society. The middle classes themselves have not exactly been unaware of their own material interests, nor have their calls for reform usually been associated with any major self-sacrifice.

The different sections of the party have continued their old strategies in the new context of Kinnock's leadership. The traditional revisionists, now led by Hattersley, have resurrected their opposition to traditional nationalisation in a manner strikingly similar to the Gaitskellite proposals of *Industry and Society* (1957). Hattersley (b. 1932) has made a series of important speeches in which he has sought to put forward a new definition of a socialist economy as well as a feasible economic policy. He is one of those traditional revisionists whose basic tribal loyalties lie with the Labour Party. In his autobiography, *A Yorkshire Boyhood*, he recounts the warmth and humour of a close working-class environment, and points out that most Labour supporters did not regard themselves as socialists. He describes himself as 'a revisionist in the sense that Crosland defined revisionism in *The Future of Socialism* . . . I am a classical revisionist in that I believe socialism is about the nature of society, not about ownership and not about industrial organisation.[14]

However, the traditional revisionist aims were originally formulated in the halcyon days of full employment when it was possible to believe that equality and freedom could be achieved by the high economic growth of a regulated market economy. In the context of the present economy, racked by high unemployment and a declining industrial base, that belief becomes more questionable.

Hattersley himself hopes to achieve economic growth by avoiding the mistake of rushing too fast, as Mitterand did in 1981-82. He seeks to avoid inflation by a *gradual* expansion of the economy, to be achieved by a policy of prudent government borrowing combined with an incomes policy and encouragement of local enterprise boards. As he put it, 'I won't make the mistake the French made in the first two years and, to be perfectly frank, the mistake the Labour government made in the first two years here. The one mistake that I can be guaranteed to avoid is to try to do so much in the first two years that we slide back in years three, four and five. Mitterand made the mistake Wilson made, spending money the country didn't have . . . We look for and intend to create a gradual growth, in which the growth is equitably distributed'.[15] Labour's hopes of combatting unemployment and industrial decline will thus be restrained by the potential of Britain's capitalist economy for growth.

However, the history of the last twenty-five years has been one of failure to achieve that growth. The attempt of every government — Conservative or Labour, 'Butskellite' or 'Thatcherite' — has failed to revive a declining capitalist economy, and has failed to generate the wealth on which equality and social justice could be based. Given Britain's record of more or less gradual economic decline, it is highly likely that any policy of expansion would soon reach its limits, facing a Labour Chancellor with intractable problems of unemployment and trade union demands for increased living standards.

To Hattersley, nationalisation would be replaced by the sale of shares to workers in the enterprise. In this way he claims to 'abandon the idea of a mixed economy in which the public and private sectors are wholly distinct from each other'.[16] The new 'socially sound' enterprises are seen as an extension of economic democracy which can 'offer working men and women an increasing ability to influence the decisions which influence their daily lives'.[17] The firm where shares are owned by the workers themselves is an example of a redistribution of power, he argues, because the shares carry a degree of control.

However, they are to operate in the context of the market. Social ownership in this new sense is to be extended into industry 'with the insistence that each new enterprise must operate with competitive efficiency'.[18] They will be able to be as successful as the old private firms because, as the firm is owned by the workforce, workers will toil as hard as small employers to ensure their company's success.

While rejecting the market socialism put forward by Peter Jay and Geoff Hodgson, Hattersley is a firm believer in the beneficial workings of the market economy, *provided* that it is guided and regulated by the state. Following the revisionist tradition established by Douglas Jay, he believes that 'market forces are a fact of life in a free society. Unless you tell people what they want, what they are going to buy, and what prices they are going to pay, market forces are going to determine these things. Market forces are not only related to efficiency, but to choice and freedom.'[19] The only alternative to a market economy would be the inefficient and authoritarian system of Stalinist Russia.

Such a contrast has become very popular in the new conservative politics of the eighties, and has found strong theoretical expression in Alec Nove's *The Economics of Feasible Socialism* (1983). Nove has long been a student of the Soviet Union, and has convincingly demonstrated that the inefficiency of authoritarian socialism there lies in the absence of an effective price mechanism to bring the forces of supply and demand together. The rejection of the market has led to an absurdly inefficient system of centralised bureaucracy which takes the basic economic decisions on behalf of millions of consumers, fixing prices unrealistically from above. To Nove, 'the existing price system renders necessary the existence of the central apparatus',[20] and must be replaced by a market mechanism which combines planning with autonomous enterprises owned by the workers.

This hardly entails democracy in the sense traditionally envisaged by libertarian socialists such as the syndicalists and Cole, however. Workers in the new enterprises envisaged by Hattersley and Nove will have as little real control over their lives as the small shopkeeper, forced to work all hours by the harsh logic of the market. Such profit-sharing schemes, espoused by the Liberals for half a century, are a far cry from the workers' control demanded by those socialists who saw it as an expression of class power over capital and its market. These socialists saw workers' control as a preparation for a socialised economy where the market would not be replaced by the command economy of Soviet Russia, but by an economy in which supply and demand would be brought together by democratic planning from below.

Realignment on the Left

However, in an important assertion of the fundamental unity of the Labour Party, sections of the Labour Left have begun to move away from their neo-Marxist rhetoric of the late seventies to accept the need for local enterprise and incomes policy as advocated by Hattersley and Kinnock. Hitherto united on the need to change the party constitution, the Left had begun to divide in the wake of the 1981 reforms, but the 1983 election defeat and, in particular, the catastrophic defeat of the 1984-85 miners' strike have accelerated the process.

This realignment, which has been fought out much more fiercely in a parallel argument inside the tiny Communist Party, is neither clear-cut nor particularly coherent. Many, such as the GLC leader Ken Livingstone, remain in many ways on the 'hard' Left, while there remains a general agreement on various policy issues. As Frances Morrell, a leading 're-aligner', has put it, 'Most of our objectives are exactly the same. We are still essentially a liberationist force which wants to democratise and open up the major institutions of the state . . . But time hasn't stood still, remedies we believed in ten or fifteen years ago won't work today.'[21]

Nevertheless, an (often acrimonious) realignment is taking place. In an important article on 'Bennism without Benn' in *New Socialist*, Patrick Seyd made a strong attack on the 'hard' Left, and on Tony Benn in particular, for dividing a party in the face of its enemies. Policy prescriptions are not really presented, but emphasis on party unity around Kinnock and the rejection of electorally embarrassing direct action was indicative of a new attitude to politics. In particular, the leadership of the miners' strike by Arthur Scargill has been vigorously criticised by this realigned Left as an example of Stalinist 'vanguard-ism' and reliance on the decreasing ranks of the industrial working class.

Indeed, it is not so much particular policies that divide the Left as much as their attitude to the importance of the working class. Where the 'realigned' Left accept Hobsbawm's thesis and look to an American-style politics of a 'rainbow coalition' of new social forces in local government, the 'hard' Left still accepts the need to defend the working class movement against the unemployment and political attacks launched by the state, even if it means questioning the legitimacy of that state.[22]

Thus, in a critical reply to Hobsbawm, the Labour Marxist, Eric Heffer, defended the traditional stress on the class struggle, arguing that 'It is not true to say the working class has overall diminished. It is a different working class'.[23] Tony Benn himself vigorously criticised the new trends, arguing that 'all this analysis of a fundamental change which means that everything is different is designed to demoralise and defeat'.[24] Benn's own defeat in the 1983 election served to emphasise the increasing isolation of the 'hard' Left in the Labour Party, while his return to Parliament in a by-election fought in a Labour unity campaign in March 1984 underlined the electoral popularity of the new leadership.

The outbreak of the long miners' strike immediately after Benn's by-election victory gave a new confidence to this section of the Left. Arthur Scargill's condemnation of the violence of the State against the striking miners, and his whole-hearted commitment to his class, under-lined the belief of the Left that only a determined and militant lead could reverse the profound social changes taking place under the Thatcher government. Only by risking a short-term unpopularity through industrial action could the long-term reward of electoral office be obtained. As Benn stressed at the 1984 conference, in implicit criticism of the embarrassed Labour leadership, 'If you fudge, you fail; if you fight, you win'.[25] This uncompromising, but in electoral terms risky, commitment to class politics has always derived its appeal from the fact that Labour can only suffer in the long term if it refuses to take sides in the class conflict inherent in capitalism.

However, this section of the Left has been badly hurt by the defeat of the miners. They have been left open to the accusation that 'liberal concerns about ballots and mass picketing and intimidation of working miners were shrugged off, though these issues lost the miners much public support'.[26] It would not be in place here to discuss such issues, though it must be said that attacks on strike-breakers and a reliance on trade union loyalty have long been manifestations of working-class conflict internationally. The fact is that the strike's defeat was fundamentally a result of the fact that the miners were fighting a class war in a country where class-consciousness was not particularly high.

Nevertheless their defeat has opened the way for the realigned Left to argue that 'the miners' strike is not the vindication of class politics but its death throes'.[27] Indeed, many of the new arguments emerging on the realigned Left seem to accept Hobsbawm's basic analysis that class is no longer so important in British politics. The popularity of Andre Gorz's *Farewell to the Working Class* (translated in 1982) is a mark of the new radicalism which is emerging. Gorz saw the working class as a mirror-image of capitalism, which sought only to make production more efficient, rather than redefining the meaning of work in order to stress leisure. This traditional working class had become a privileged minority in relation to the new 'post-industrial neo-proletariat' of educated radicals who felt no identification with their jobs. This new group, with no class identity, would be able to play a much more radical role than the old socialist movement. Groups such as the ecology and women's movement were the new hope of the Left, in that they stressed moral values rather than merely production.

This was particularly true of the women's movement. Gorz noted the growth of feminist ideas which saw male aggression as the enemy, rather than the old-fashioned notions of class. Challenging the 'productivist' ideology of the traditional working class, feminism asserted non-economic values and autonomous activities of different social groups. Thus,

> post-industrial Socialism . . . will be female or will not exist at all. This implies a cultural revolution which will eliminate the principle of performance, the ethic of competition, accumulation and the rat-race . . . replacing them with the supremacy of the values of reciprocity, tenderness, spontaneity, and love of life in all its forms.[28]

It was a movement of women to liberate men as well as other women.

This restatement of Edward Carpenter's socialism certainly struck a chord at a time when the labour movement was quiescent compared with the radical activities of CND, while the feminist exclusiveness of the women who surrounded the US missile base at Greenham Common seemed to many an indication of the new sources and directions of radical action. A middle-class radicalism which saw male hierarchies and insensitivity to the environment, rather than capital, as the main enemy appeared to be coming into its own.

The new radicals in the Labour Party did not reject the organised labour movement, but they appeared to see the working class as one group among many fighting for a new type of democracy. Peter Hain (b. 1950), a South African-born radical who led the Young Liberals until joining the Labour Party in 1977, stressed the libertarian rejection of corporatism and the centralised state in his book, *The Democratic Alternative* (1983). He argued against the state socialism with which the Labour Party had become associated, and called on the party to 'embrace a radical new approach, involving decentralisation of power and resources through state policies designed to mesh in with a wider grass roots strategy for socialist mobilisation'.[29]

This was, of course, very similar to the arguments which emerged around Shirley Williams and David Owen, but Hain rejected the consensus approach of the SDP in favour of a confrontationist style of direct action. In doing so, he called for the Labour Party to turn away from its obsession with the hackneyed system of parliamentary and town hall bureaucracy to get in touch once more with the ordinary people. Labour needed to rebuild its shattered political base by looking out to the extra-parliamentary movements of tenants groups, squatters, CND and the women's movement. A campaigning, populist party would maintain its radicalism in government, because:

> the more pressure on Labour governments from the grass roots, the stronger will be the popular support for changes it wishes to implement. The best prospect for socialist transformation lies in such a dual strategy of working inside and outside the system.[30]

The strategy adopted by the Young Liberals in the 1960s — community politics — was seen by Hain as the path by which the Labour Party could be renovated.

However, Hain's concern with industrial democracy and a non-aligned foreign policy should not obscure his modest conception of socialism. He rejected centralisation and corporatism rather than capitalism, and his positive proposals were for a radical democracy rather than a socialist democracy under working-class control. With regard to finance, for example, his rejection of trade union participation with big business was tied to an advocacy of the small financial concerns. He called for 'legislation which prevented any investment fund from being too big — perhaps £100 million would be the limit',[31] so that local autonomy and socialist intervention in investment decisions could be encouraged. It was bureaucracy and remote power, not capital, which was the target of Hain's radical politics.

Many of Hain's ideas had been formulated in the context of the Labour Co-Ordinating Committee (LCC), one of a number of left-wing groups which emerged in the party after the 1979 election defeat. The LCC agreed with Hobsbawm in his analysis of the working class, but argued that Britain was still a class society which demanded a radical, campaigning party. They rejected both the Marxist Left, who ignored electoral realities, and the new populist approach of Hobsbawm. In a pamphlet on reconstructing the party's fortunes, John Denham argued that

> it will be no good just following a purely electoralist strategy or concentrating simply on mass, mobilising politics irrespective of public support. Our aims must be a Party that can gain sufficient votes to be elected as a government and where those votes reflect an understanding and determination to move Britain in a socialist direction.[32]

In doing so, the LCC concentrated their policies on opposition to the centralised state. They argued for a renewed commitment to local democracy and libertarian politics. The radical elements of the 'new' working class — particularly ethnic minorities, the women's movement, and the peace and environment movements — need to be won to a renewed trade union movement in a new, mass politics, parliamentary and agitational. However, in common with the bulk of the Labour Left, the LCC no longer regarded public ownership as crucial. State intervention was seen as a threat to local initiative,[33] while the debates about a mixed economy were seen as irrelevant.

This libertarian defence of decentralised power was reflected in the arguments for a new politics based on 'a broad class alliance which can resume the post-war advance towards a more democratic, egalitarian but also pluralist society'.[34] Michael Rustin has called for an acceptance that a fully socialist society is beyond our immediate grasp, and a rejection of the politics of class war in favour of a cautious advance towards social reform for *all* the different social groups. He argues that socialists must be pluralist, recognising 'the diversity of interests and life-styles which political programmes must reconcile'.[35] Thus, regional diversity should be encouraged, the autonomy of different social move-ments acknowledged, and social differences celebrated as a virtue of a good society. The radical language fails to conceal a retreat from the radicalism of the seventies. Rustin does not seem to recognise the fact that class interests may be irreconcilably opposed, and fails to investi-gate why an incomes policy has been invariably used against the interests of the labour movement. Apart from the bizarre proposal for the repartition of Ireland to which his version of pluralism leads, the upshot of his political theory leads him to support proportional repre-sentation because 'it would make possible a de facto truce between the Labour Party and the SDP-Liberal Alliance, in place of the present war to the death',[36] and to accept that socialism can be relegated to the distant future rather than fought for as an immediate necessity.

However, his advocacy of the planning of the economy through developing socially necessary projects is generally accepted by most sections of the Labour Left. Dating back to the alternative plan of the Lucas Aerospace Shop Stewards Combine in the late seventies, this resurrection of the old strategy of replacing competition by co-opera-tion has been adapted to the new demands for local socialism.[37] This has been put forward most succinctly in the *London Industrial Strategy* (1985) of the Greater London Council. In calling for 'a new type of strategic planning from an alternative standpoint',[38] they call for a change of direction in economic strategy to involve both union and community initiatives in the creation of employment on a sectoral basis. As a prime example of such popular planning, the *Strategy* points to the Greater London Enterprise Board (GLEB), set up in 1983 to plan the local market economy on the basis of social need.

The failure of the *Strategy* to mention wider economic realities than the (relatively small) creation of local employment has enabled the GLEB enthusiasts to ignore the whole question of class politics and thereby to draw the support of all sections of the party. The peripheral nature of its proposals does not, however, confront the reasons or remedies for the central problem of general economic decline.

Nevertheless, its libertarian defence of local initiative has been echoed by those feminists who have been increasingly vociferous in the Labour Party since the election. These Labour feminists are part of the women's movement, calling for positive discrimination in favour of female parliamentary candidates and the election of the women's section of the NEC by women only (rather than the whole conference). Hilary Wainwright, a co-author of the influential *Beyond the Frag-ments* (1979), may have refused to join Sheila Rowbotham in joining the Labour Party, but she has been in full agreement in looking to the grassroots democracy of local government as an illustration of resistance to authoritarianism. These women point to the Greater London Council and Sheffield City Council as examples of resistance of the local state against the interference of the centralised state, and call for a radical democracy in Britain. They see their task as:

> to challenge and change the hierarchical and undemocratic assumptions of existing social provisions . . . It is not just a question of making bureaucrats and experts more approachable and accountable to those they serve, it is enabling users and workers in state services to gain the confidence and creativity to run things differently — to run things themselves.[39]

In this way, the oppression of women by the male patriarchy is tied to the oppression of workers and consumers by employers and bureaucrats.

However, it seems very superficial to assume that there is not a fundamental difference between the exploitation of the working class by those who employ them and the oppression of other social groups. The oppression of women, for example, has been persistent through many societies, but the exploitation of the working class is specific to one type of society — capitalism. It is an exploitation which Marx demonstrated would automatically release a dynamic of capital accumulation and capitalist crisis which confronts the working class with the choice of destroying capital or of accepting an accelerating barbarism. It is also an exploitation which has created the material prosperity which allows women to see the real possibility of their own liberation from domestic labour and the role of capitalist social relations in preventing that emancipation.

This is not to deny the importance and contribution of the women's movement, which has jolted the Left into the long-forgotten recognition that over half the population has been in subordination to the other half, sometimes by physical violence but more often by more subtle forms of persuasion and manipulation. They have reminded the Left that women are oppressed as *women*, not merely as workers, and that women must organise themselves to ensure that a socialist society is run for *all* people.

However, many feminists have seen the working class as just another element in the struggle against authority, or have even denied any role to male workers in the struggle against their oppression.[40] The tone of the women's movement often seems to outsiders to be determined by those radical feminists who see men, rather than capitalism, as the main opponent. This may be understandable given the reactionary attitudes and family position of many male workers, but runs the danger of dividing people who should really be allies. The recent activity of working-class women in the mining communities, who see the employers and the State rather than their husbands as the enemy, may herald a modification of previous attitudes, and certainly indicates the potentialities of women taking part in a *class* struggle.

Women as women (though not as wage workers) are too isolated in the family to form a group which could be in a strategic position to deliver a death blow to the power of capital. It is still the case that the working class − racist and sexist though parts of it may be − is the only social force which is really capable of leading the struggle for human emancipation. When the working class see women and ethnic minorities as their allies, rather than their inferiors, that struggle will take on a more threatening form to the British Establishment than it has so far faced.

Any history of the ideas of a political party is bound to be partial. Ideas often appear to be merely a distant echo of the din of political battles fought out in the manoeuvres for electoral power or in the industrial conflicts which occasionally loom large in the popular sight. It is in these battles that the decisions are made, for good or ill.

However, these decisions are determined to a large extent by preconceived notions and ideas which feed strategy and tactics in the realm of political action. The world of ideas is an arena in which different conceptions of our society and different visions of an alternative are proposed and fought over. They point to underlying social and political trends which a party needs to understand, and their contours indicate the limits of political action within which they are bound.

This is particularly true of the Labour Party. The different arguments that have taken place within its boundaries − from those between Labour Marxists and Fabians to those between Social Democrats and Bennites − indicate the wide differences of political opinion which have vied for supremacy in the party, and Labour's evolution in the past eighty years demonstrates its flexibility as a political organisation.

Within the confines of this organisation, there has always been a powerful movement (usually on the Right) which has never been fully committed to the working-class cause. They do not see the division between the working class and their employers as fundamental, and from the early Fabians and Hobson to the revisionists and social democrats they have looked to the Labour Party as the only party able to carry through the necessary social reforms. Their relationship to labourism has tended to be tactical, and their loyalty to the labour movement contingent. This does not by any means mark them out as reactionaries – indeed they were often more committed to social reform than those solid trade unionists who have acted as the sheet anchor of the party. However, it does indicate the absence of a *class* approach to society, and a tendency to adopt an *organic* approach. The existence of social conflict between the classes has been regarded as unnecessary, and the unity of interest between the 'industrious' classes has been emphasised.

In contrast, the Left has been much more committed to the organised labour movement. They have accepted the existence of class conflict and have (generally) supported the working class in that conflict. From the Labour Marxists and guild socialists to the New Left, they have shared a common hostility to the authoritarian state and the market economy, and a common commitment to the redistribution of wealth from the excessively rich to the working class. Their belief that the existing state would be the instrument by which this redistribution would take place indicates their acceptance of the constitutional limitations on political activity. After all, they belong to a party nurtured and dependent on a British Constitution which was never made by the forces of labour and is not geared to the triumph of the lower classes in society. When that Constitution is threatened by internal or external threats Labour rallies around the national flag, and the Left is usually forced to rally with Labour.

The different trends within the Labour Party does not mean that it is an empty shell into which any vaguely left-wing cause or belief can be inserted without difficulty. It is a 'broad church', but it is not an incoherent organisation. Its financial and organisational dependence on the trade union movement has meant that Labour is (ultimately) the political expression of that movement. As Neil Kinnock has said,

> there are so many shared objectives . . . The alliance between ourselves and the trade unions as part of the means of representing the aspirations and attitudes of the people of Britain is a source of great advantage to us.[41]

This is a *power* relationship, but it is a power relationship which can be expressed in the *ideas* of labourism.

There is nothing special about labourism in itself — as Marx demonstrated, it is in many ways an incoherent ideology, riddled with inconsistencies — but it is important as a reflection of the practice of a constitutional trade union movement. These ideas are the result of the acceptance by the trade union movement of the practice of collective bargaining within capitalism. They call for more wages rather than the end of the wage system; for a redistribution of wealth rather than an end to the exploitative production of wealth. The various factions of Right and Left which have fought within the party have been forced to adapt — with ease or difficulty — to the power relationship of party and unions, and therefore to the labourism which was once an ideology and has now become an assumption.

This does mean that the Labour Party has its ideological limits which excludes those unable to accept trade union dominance and those Marxists unable to accept the feasibility of a constitutional road to socialism. The delineations which mark the Labour Party off from Right and Left are much sharper, and the barriers to its flexibility much higher, than is often assumed. These delineations and barriers are created by the labourist assumptions which underlie the Labour Party, constantly preventing it from breaking with the organised trade union movement. They also prevent the party from moving beyond the maldistribution of wealth to the rejection of capitalism as a political and social system of power. They prevent the party from developing a rejection of the existing State and the constitutional rules of action which that state has laid down. The general rejection of the revolutionary conclusions of the Marxist labour theory of value in favour of a Fabian theory of rent, a Hobsonian theory of distribution or a neo-Keynesian theory of planned capitalism is a natural consequence of the limits of the party's politics.

The Labour Party, rightly or wrongly, has become the only party to represent the organised working class in Britain. The divisions between social democracy and Communism which have split the European workers' movement have not occurred in Britain, and it is small wonder in the light of this fact that the bulk of the Left have been reluctant to break from the party. On the one side, successive failures of labour governments to act on behalf of the working class have demonstrated its unsuitability, and the intolerable position of a party with a working-class base trying to administer a capitalist economy. On the other side, the fate of parties such as the SDF, the Communists, the ILP or the many splintered Trotskyist groups to emerge from a political desert, have served only to underline Keir Hardie's belief that the fate of socialism lies in the labourist alliance.

There has thus been a constant dilemma for the socialist movement – a dilemma recognised by socialists from Hardie to Hobsbawm. If socialists strike out on their own, they suffer from the fate of the SDF or the ILP – political isolation. If they remain tied to the Labour Party, they become associated with the failure of Labour governments to satisfy working-class aspirations. It is a dilemma which has haunted British socialists for a century, and their failure to resolve it has led to demoralisation and defeat for socialist politics in Britain. As Hobsbawm has written, 'it is a historical fact that, since 1917, the Left. . . and support for the Labour Party have tended to grow and fall *together*, and not at each other's expense'.[42] This has certainly been true of the past, but if it remains true of the future then the Left has indeed much cause for worry. Should a Labour government once more fail to operate a planned capitalism in the interests of the working class, and should it once again attack working-class living standards as a result of the 'economic situation', the constitutionalist Left could well hang on its dilemma.

This is not necessarily reason for despair, nor does it prove that socialism is becoming an outdated project. As long as we live in a society characterised by wage labour, the need for unions to protect workers against their employers remains. The social and economic dynamics of such a system will remain to force the necessity of a different social order on all those who do not benefit from the existing one. The left wing of the working class may be forced to recognise that it is a minority, and that the belief in social care and democratic rule is not inevitably held by the majority of British workers. This means that the difficult struggle to win the majority to a socialist perspective has yet to be won, which should not be surprising given its labourist traditions and values. If the left is to move away from this labourist tradition towards a clear policy of total opposition towards capital, they must recognise that corners cannot be cut in the long struggle ahead. However, as the 1984 miners' strike has demonstrated, they are as capable of self-sacrifice, courage and determination as their ancestors. As long as people are willing to fight the social struggles inherent in capitalist society there is hope that a socialist order will be eventually achieved.

Notes

1. Neil Kinnock, Toby Butler, and Nick Harris, *Why Vote Labour?* (NCLC, 1979), p. 19. See also the statement of principles by Neil Kinnock in *The Times*, 18 July 1983.

2. Neil Kinnock, 'A New Deal for Europe', in *New Socialist*, March/April 1984, p. 9. See also *Financial Times*, 2 February 1984, for the Shadow Cabinet request to Labour's Home Policy Committee to reconsider the issue of party opposition to council house sales as an example of this shift after the election defeat. Labour's opposition was eventually dropped.

3. Interview with Eric Hobsbawm, *Marxism Today*, October 1984, p. 9.

4. Ibid., p. 10.

5. See, for example, Anthony Barnett, 'Whistling in the Wind', in *New Socialist*, January 1986.

6. Neil Kinnock, 'It can be done, it must be done', Speech to Labour Party Conference, Bournemouth 1985 (Labour Party, n.d.), pp. 11, 13.

7. Neil Kinnock, *The Future of Socialism* (Fabian Tract 509, 1986), p. 2.

8. Bernard Crick, *Socialist Values and Time* (Fabian Tract 495, 1984), p. 12.

9. Ibid., pp. 8-9.

10. Neil Kinnock, 1985 Conference Speech, p. 4.

11. Eric Hobsbawm, *The Forward March of Labour Halted?* (Verso, 1981), p. 181.

12. Eric Hobsbawm, 'Labour's Lost Millions', in *Marxism Today*, October 1983, p. 10.

13. Paul Whiteley, *The Labour Party in Crisis* (Methuen, 1983), p. 217.

14. Interview with author, 4 September 1985.

15. Ibid.

16. Roy Hattersley, 'The Extension of Social Ownership', Speech to Socialist Economic Review Conference, 23 September 1984.

17. Roy Hattersley, 'Economic Democracy', Speech to the Crosland Society, Trinity College, Oxford, 7 June 1985.

18. Roy Hattersley, 'Social Ownership' speech.

19. Interview with author, September 1985.

20. Alec Nove, *The Economics of Feasible Socialism* (Allen and Unwin, 1983), p. 101.

21. Quoted in Patrick Seyd, 'Bennism without Benn', in *New Socialist*, May 1985, p. 46.

22. The 1984 Labour Party Conference passed one motion demanding that the police should play no part in future industrial disputes on the ground that they were not neutral, leading Leslie Curtis of the Police Federation to declare that the police may not obey a future Labour government.

23. Eric Heffer, *Marxism Today*, October 1983.

24. Tony Benn, *City Limits*, 20 January 1984.

25. See *Financial Times*, 1 October 1984.

26. Mike Rustin, *For a Pluralist Socialism* (Verso, 1985), p. 23.

27. Michael Ignatieff, 'Strangers and Comrades', in *New Statesman*, 1984.

28. Andre Gorz, *Farewell to the Working Class* (Pluto, 1982), p. 85.

29. Peter Hain, *The Democratic Alternative: A Socialist Response to Britain's Crisis* (Penguin, 1983), p. 54.

30. Ibid., p. 164.

31. Ibid., pp. 66-7.

32. John Denham, *Reconstruction: How the Labour Party – and the Left – can Win* (LCC, 1984), p. 12.

33. Ibid., pp. 19-20.

360 *Conclusion*

34. Michael Rustin, *For a Pluralist Socialism*, p. 24.

35. Ibid., p. 35.

36. Ibid., pp. 139-40.

37. See M. Boddy and C. Fudge eds., *Local Socialism* (Macmillan, 1984). Also see Robin Murray, 'New Directions in Municipal Socialism' in Ben Pimlott ed., *Fabian Essays in Socialist Thought* (Heinemann, 1984).

38. Greater London Council, *London Industrial Strategy* (GLC, 1985), p. 39.

39. Doreen Massey, Lynn Segal, Hilary Wainwright, 'Stop the Great Male Moving Right Show', in *New Socialist*, January/February 1984.

40. See Bea Campbell, *The Road to Wigan Pier Revisited* (Virago, 1984), for an example of emotional hostility to male workers.

41. Neil Kinnock, speaking in *British Socialism Redefined*, presented by David Watt, Radio 3, 25 February 1984 (transcript).

42. Eric Hobsbawm, 'Labour: Rump or Rebirth?', in *Marxism Today*, March 1984, p. 11.

CHRONOLOGY

(Relating the principal writings to major events)

1791-2	– Tom Paine, *The Rights of Man*.
1813-14	– Robert Owen, *A New View of Society*.
1825	– Thomas Hodgskin, *Labour Defended Against the Claims of Capital*. Coincides with the beginning of the modern trade union movement.
1834	– Defeat of the Grand National Consolidated Trades Union.
1848	– Karl Marx, *Communist Manifesto*. Defeat of Chartism, followed by a period of moderate trade unionism.
1862	– John Ruskin, *Unto this Last*.
1867	– Karl Marx, *Capital* Volume I.
1881	– (Social) Democratic Federation; H.M. Hyndman, *England for All*.
1882	– Edward Carpenter, *Towards Democracy*.
1884	– Fabian Society; William Morris' Socialist League.
1888	– Scottish Labour Party.
1889	– Dock strike heralds the New Unionism; *Fabian Essays in Socialism*.
1890	– J.B. Glasier and K. St John Conway, *The Religion of Socialism*.
1893	– Independent Labour Party (ILP).
1894	– Robert Blatchford, *Merrie England*.
1899-1902	– Boer War.
1900	– Labour Representation Committee (LRC); *Fabianism and Empire*.
1903	– Gladstone-Macdonald Pact; Socialist Labour Party; Philip Snowden, *The Christ That Is To Be*.
1905	– J. Ramsay Macdonald, *Socialism and Society*.
1906	– 29 Labour MPs elected; LRC becomes Labour Party.
1907	– J. Keir Hardie, *From Serfdom to Socialism*.
1910	– Industrial Syndicalist Education League (ISEL).
1911	– J. Ramsay Macdonald Labour leader; Mass strike wave erupts, involving among others miners, dockers, railway-

men.

1912	– *The Miner's Next Step.*
1913	– G.D.H. Cole, *The World of Labour*; ISEL splits.
1914	– Labour supports World War I; ILP opposes; Macdonald resigns as Labour leader.
1915	– Labour under Arthur Henderson enters coalition; Clyde Workers' Committee; National Guilds League (NGL).
1917	– Leeds Convention. G.D.H. Cole, *Self-Government in Industry*.
1918	– New Labour Party constitution; Labour gains 3 million votes in the election, but only 57 MPs.
1919	– Post-war unrest, including strikes and riots.
1920	– Communist Party of Great Britain
1921	– Black Friday sees the defeat of the miners; G.D.H. Cole, *Guild Socialism Restated*; R.H. Tawney, *The Acquisitive Society*.
1922	– Failure of Builders Guild ends Guild Socialism, just as ILP adopts Guild ideas in its constitution; Labour, with 142 MPs, becomes official Opposition, under Macdonald.
1924	– First Labour government, under Macdonald.
1925	– Harold Laski, *A Grammar of Politics*. Oswald Mosley, *Revolution by Reason*.
1926	– General Strike; *The Living Wage*.
1928	– Cook-Maxton manifesto denounces 'Mondism', or class collaboration; The Liberal Yellow Book, *We Can Conquer Unemployment*.
1929	– Second Labour Government, under Macdonald. G.D.H. Cole, *The Next Ten Years*.
1930	– Mosley Memorandum.
1931	– Collapse of Labour government; Macdonald forms National Government, and is expelled from the Labour Party, along with Snowden; Only 46 Labour MPs returned in election; R.H. Tawney, *Equality*.
1932	– ILP disaffiliates; Socialist League formed.
1933	– Evan Durbin, *Purchasing Power and Trade Depressions*.
1935	– Brighton Conference supports sanctions; Attlee leader; Hugh Dalton, *Practical Socialism for Britain*; Harold Laski, *The State in Theory and Practice*.
1937	– Socialist League disaffiliated; Douglas Jay, *The Socialist Case*.
1938	– Harold Laski, *Parliamentary Government in England*.

1939 — Cripps and Bevan (temporarily) expelled for their support of a Popular Front.

1940 — Labour enters Churchill coalition; Evan Durbin, *The Politics of Democratic Socialism.*

1943 — Harold Laski, *Reflections on the Revolution of Our Time.*

1945 — Attlee forms first majority Labour government, after landslide election victory, and sets about a programme of state intervention in industry and welfare.

1947 — *Keep Left.*

1951 — Bevan resigns over attacks on the health service; Labour election defeat begins a 13-year period of opposition.

1952 — A. Bevan, *In Place of Fear; New Fabian Essays.*

1955 — Gaitskell leader.

1956 — Suez; Hungary; C.A.R. Crosland, *The Future of Socialism;*
John Strachey, *Contemporary Capitalism.*

1957 — Bevan attacks unilateralism at Brighton Conference.

1958 — Campaign for Nuclear Disarmament.

1959 — Clause IV controversy after third Labour election defeat;
Richard Crossman, 'The Affluent Society'.

1960 — CND victory at Scarborough Conference (reversed a year later);
New Left Review. R. Titmuss, 'The Irresponsible Society'.

1963 — Wilson leader; R. Titmuss, *Essays on the Welfare State.*

1964 — Labour government under Wilson. Institute of Workers' Control.

1966 — Wages Freeze; Juliet Mitchell, 'The Longest Revolution'.

1967 — Devaluation, and cuts in welfare.

1969 — Troops sent to Northern Ireland; *In Place of Strife.*

1970 — Labour defeated at election; Conservative government under Heath.

1971 — Industrial Relations Act (virtually nullified by industrial action on the docks and railways the following year).

1972 — Roy Jenkins resigns as deputy leader; A Crosland, *Socialism Now;* R. Jenkins, *What Matters Now*; M. Barratt Brown, *Labourism to Socialism*; J. Mackintosh, 'Socialism or Social Democracy'.

1974　— Miners' strike leads to election, and a Labour government under Wilson.

1975　— EEC referendum defeat for Labour Left; S. Holland, *The Socialist Challenge*.

1976　— Callaghan Prime Minister; Sterling crisis.

1979　— Conservative government under Thatcher; R. Jenkins, Dimbleby Lecture; Tony Benn, *Arguments for Socialism*.

1980　— Foot leader.

1981　— Constitutional changes in Labour Party; Social Democratic Party formed; Shirley Williams, *Politics is for People*; David Owen, *Face the Future*; Tony Benn, *Arguments for Democracy*; Eric Hobsbawm, *The Forward March of Labour Halted*.

1982　— Falklands War.

1983　— Catastrophic Labour election defeat; Kinnock leader; Peter Hain, *The Radical Alternative*.
　　　Alec Nove, *The Economics of Feasible Socialism*

1984　— Miners' strike.
　　　Bernard Crick, *Socialist Values and Time*

INDEX

D/I 6444.